The Modern Scottish Novel

For Gregor and Carys

THE
MODERN SCOTTISH
NOVEL:

NARRATIVE AND
THE NATIONAL IMAGINATION

Cairns Craig

Edinburgh University Press

© Cairns Craig
Edinburgh University Press, 1999
22 George Square, Edinburgh

Typeset in Ehrhardt by the author
and printed and bound in Great Britain
by the University Press, Cambridge

A CIP record for this book is available from the British Library

ISBN 0 7486 0893 1

CONTENTS

ACKNOWLEDGEMENTS

Readers who have read my collection of essays, *Out of History*, published by Polygon in 1996, will recognise some of the main lines of my argument. Sections of this book were written before that one and some passages have translated themselves from one to the other, as have passages and ideas from my essays on Alasdair Gray ('Going Down to Hell is Easy', in Robert Crawford and Thom Nairn (eds), *The Arts of Alasdair Gray*, Edinburgh University Press, 1991), on Muriel Spark ('Doubtful Imaginings: the Sceptical Art of Muriel Spark', *Etudes Ecossaises*, 2), on Iain Crichton Smith ('The Necessity of Accident', in Colin Nicholson (ed.), *Iain Crichton Smith: Critical Essays*, Edinburgh University Press, 1992), and on James Kelman (in Gavin Wallace and Randall Stevenson (eds), *The Scottish Novel since the Seventies*, Edinburgh University Press, 1993). Chapter 1, 'Fearful Selves' is a very different version of an article with the same title published in *Cencrastus*, No. 4, 1980–81.

In relation to this book, my thanks in particular must go to all those who have been involved in the Canongate Classics series, particularly Roderick Watson, J. B. Pick, Tom Crawford, Stephanie Woolf-Murray, Jamie Byng, Hugh Andrew and Dorothy McMillan, without Canongate Classics many of the books I have written about would not be generally available.

My thinking on the Scottish novel has been helped by a number of excellent postgraduate students at Edinburgh University and I would like to thank all of them for their stimulus to the interpretations I offer in this book — especially Glenda Norquay, Ian Cameron, Alan Freeman, Bob Irvine, Martin Phillip, Gavin Miller, Laurence Nicol and Alex Thompson. My thanks, too, to my colleagues at the University of Edinburgh who have worked to increase our understanding of Scottish Literature – R. D. S. Jack, Ian Campbell, Colin Nicholson, Randall Stevenson, Penny Fielding and Aileen Christianson – and to the staff of the National Library of Scotland and of Edinburgh University Library. My gratitude, as usual, to Edinburgh University Press and, in particular, to Jackie Jones, for their patience and support.

My thanks especially to Linda Rickis for the inspiration and help to get this book to completion and for suffering through the time it has taken. My deepest debt, however, is to the dedicatees of this book, Gregor and Carys Craig – I hope the Scotland they inherit is worthy of them.

INTRODUCTION

NOVEL, NATION, TRADITION

The development of the novel is profoundly linked to the development of the modern nation. As Timothy Brennan has noted, it can hardly be accidental that 'the rise of European nationalism coincides especially with one form of literature – the novel'.[1] In the era of developing capitalism and global imperialism, the nation states which emerged as the standard political formations of the world required a populace committed not to an individual social superior, nor to a religion potentially encompassing all humanity, but to a particular territory and to a purposive history. As Benedict Anderson has argued,[2] it was through the newspaper and the novel that the people of the new national states came to see themselves *as* communities, as the carriers of a national identity and as participants in a national history. The rage for national origins, inspired largely by MacPherson's *Ossian*,[3] might send peoples in search of the epic poems that were the foundation of their national existence, but it was through the great historical novels of the nineteenth century that the accidental boundaries of the nation were formed into those symbolic systems which would provide readers with a sense of the fundamental unity and purpose of their social world. There is a profound similarity between the modern nation, with its implication of all the people of a territory bound together into a single historical process, and the technique of the major nineteenth-century novels, whose emplotment enmeshes their multiplicity of characters into a single, overarching narrative trajectory. The unfolding of the complex plots of those nineteenth-century novels provided a model of how the divergent groupings that found themselves to be part of a single nation could discover in the underlying necessity that bound them together a higher purpose, turning the accidental outcomes of ancient wars and power struggles into the organic unities of a national destiny.

In the work of the historical novelists of the nineteenth century what was being created was a national imagination: an imagining of the nation as both the fundamental context of individual life and as the real subject of history. In the novel, the nation – that enveloping reality which, since it included everyone within the territorial boundaries of the nation as well as all of the narratives of the past of those people and that place, could never be seen or touched[4] – was made imaginatively present to the mass public which was one of its principal constituents, and through the novel that public could grasp itself not as an anonymous accumulation of isolated individuals but as the temporary manifestation of the eternal being of the nation. It is upon such national imagining that the political and economic agency of the nation state depended. However much nations have an imagined existence, they exist only to the extent that they are agents in the world;[5] in order to act, however, the individuals of which they are composed and through which that agency is exerted have to know – have to imaginatively identify with – the ends towards which that agency is directed. In the competitive struggles between nations which modernity unleashed, people would act and would sacrifice themselves for the *national* good in ways that they would never act or sacrifice themselves for purely personal ends, because the narrative of the nation and the narrative of their own existence are imaginatively intertwined. A national imagination is the means by which individuals relate the personal shape of their lives, both retrospective and prospective, to the larger trajectory of the life of the community from which they draw their significance. It is the means by which that trajectory of personal and communal history is made the carrier of unique values, values which are the justification of the national community that maintains them. This is why nationalism is never simply 'my country right or wrong' – a nationalism is always a value system, and the death of the nation would be the death of those values. The imagination is the medium through which the nation's past is valued, and through which the nation's values are collected, recollected and projected into the future in the acts of governments and by the actions of those bodies, both individual and collective, of which the nation is composed.

The fundamental role of narrative in the formation of national identity has come increasingly to be recognised in 'nation theory': indeed, it is now often argued that nations are nothing more than narratives and that it is through the narrative arts that national identities are established, maintained and elaborated. Analysts of the nation have often in the past regarded the nation as either a leftover from an earlier stage of human history that has little to do with the real requirements of the modern world, or as the means by which the economic power of a particular class is maintained and defended: more recent commentators on the nature of the nation have, however, tended to focus, as Anthony Smith does, on the nation's 'imaginative' qualities:

> the 'core' of ethnicity, as it has been transmitted in the historical record and as it shapes individual experience, resides in this quartet of 'myths, memories, values and symbols' and in the characteristic forms or styles and genres of certain historical configurations of populations . . . In other words, the special qualities and durability of *ethnie* are to be found, neither in their ecological locations, nor their class configurations, nor yet their military and political relationships, important as all these are for day-to-day experiences and medium-term chances of survival of specific ethnic communities. Rather one has to look at the nature (forms and content) of their myths and symbols, their historical memories and central values, which we can summarize as the 'myth-symbol' complex . . .[6]

If it is in epic poetry and poetic drama that nations summon up the founding origins of their *ethnie*, it is in the day-to-day world of the novel that they show how those founding origins survive, by resistance and adaptation, to allow the national community to continue to know itself and to recognise its own identity despite the transformations of history. Thus modern *ethnie*,

> are nothing if not historical communities built up on shared memories. A sense of common history unites successive generations, each with its set of experiences which are added to the common stock, and it also defines a population in terms of experienced temporal sequences, which conveys to later generations the historicity of their own experiences . . . What matters, then, is not the authenticity of the historical record, much less any attempt at 'objective' methods of historicizing, but the poetic, didactic and integrative purposes which that record is felt to disclose. 'History' in this sense must tell a story, it must please and satisfy as narrative, it must be all of a piece, like the Homeric epics and Ossian . . . [7]

The condition of living in history, in the expectation or the angst of knowing that the future will be necessarily different from the present, required a medium by which a common past and a common stock of cultural memories can be defined, and by which a possible route towards that future can be charted without loss of continuity with a founding past. In *Waverley*, or *Great Expectations*, or *Middlemarch*, or *The Last of the Mohicans*, or *War and Peace*, the founding myths of an *ethnie* are framed and shaped so that successive generations of a particular *ethnie* can recognise themselves as the fulfilment of their predecessors. As form, the novel is a force of modernisation, an outcome of the print capitalism which Benedict Anderson has identified as one of the driving forces of modernity;[8] in its content, however, what it does is to render the process of modernisation explicable by turning the welter of events in which humanity is caught up into the orderly trajectory of narrative, a narrative which tames the threat of the future by binding it back as the necessary outcome of the known order of the past, and which renders the past significant by making it the foundation of the values of the present.

The novel re-enacts in imaginary form what Anderson has described as one of the founding experiences of national consciousness, the pilgrimage of functionaries, a pilgrimage of those whose lives are shaped by the career possibilities offered by the post-medieval states of Europe and their empires: 'on his upward-spiralling road he encounters as eager fellow-pilgrims his functionary colleagues, from places and families he has scarcely heard of and surely hopes never to have to see. But in experiencing them as travelling-companions, a consciousness of connectedness ("Why are *we* . . . *here* . . . *together*?") emerges, above all when all share a single language-of-state . . .'[9] Anderson's functionaries are the equivalent of characters in a picaresque novel who leave traces of interconnection that will bind the various regions and geographies of the national space into an apparent unity. The places visited by picaresque heroes are transformed from accidental locations into ones which have developed a representative significance: the individual traveller thus becomes the bearer of a consciousness of the nation as interconnected space, which becomes in turn a sign of the interconnected consciousness of the 'people' of whom he or she is now representative. In a construction which the novel will elaborate with more and more complexity through the nineteenth century, the life of the individual becomes a model in miniature of the life the society, a synecdoche of the national totality that can never be known except in its fragmentary constituents.

Anderson's conception of the nation as an 'imagined' community has been enormously influential on the recent scholarship of national cultures but it has been used by various critics to establish that the very nature of national identity is a 'forgery', one which ought to be overthrown and replaced by some 'real' historical solidarity not bound together by merely fictional ties. The nation as 'imagined community' is subsumed into the concept of the nation as 'fraudulent' or 'mistaken' history,[10] and the 'imagined' of 'imagined community' shifts from being an epistemological truth underlying all communities – as Anderson initially defines it – to being a normative term which can help distinguish 'real' from 'unreal' communities. It may be that all communities are 'imagined' but some are 'fabricated' from imaginary materials and the notion of 'imagined community' comes to distinguish between those whose traditions are invented and others whose traditions are more real – or, at any rate, less fictitious. This shift can be clearly discerned in one of the most influential works about national traditions as imagined pasts, Hobsbawm and Ranger's *The Invention of Tradition* (1983). In the 'Introduction', Eric Hobsbawm lays out a relatively neutral account of what is meant by an 'invented tradition' and presents such inventions of tradition as standard and probably necessary parts of the adjustment of peoples to the unparalleled processes of change provoked by the industrial revolution:

> 'Invented tradition' is taken to mean a set of practices, normally governed by overtly or tacitly accepted rules and of a ritual or symbolic nature, which seek to inculcate certain values and norms of behaviour by repetition, which automatically implies continuity with the past. In fact, where possible, they normally attempt to establish continuity with a suitable historic past.[11]

The analyses of cultural traditions contained in the body of the book, however, do not adopt this neutral tone but develop the further point that Hobsbawm makes in his introduction, namely that 'the peculiarity of "invented" traditions is that the continuity with [the past] is largely factitious'.[12] The essays set out to show how the traditions which people accept as defining their past – and therefore their identity – are fakes, fakes which cast doubt on the substance of their national identities. Imagining an identity is no longer, in this context, the necessary reconstruction through the imagination of a compensatory sense of shared forms of meaning to replace the lost customs of 'traditional' societies: it is the submission to a hoax which distorts and undermines the very basis of the identity which people believe to constitute their nation. The peoples who are most rigorously subjected to this mode of analysis are the Scots and the Welsh; their identities are put in double jeopardy by the fact that they are also participants in the British state's construction of a monarchic national identity, whose traditions are revealed to be equally a tissue of fictions. These two strands come together in Hugh Trevor-Roper's analysis of the visit of the visit of George IV to Scotland in 1822, a visit orchestrated by Sir Walter Scott:

> the guards of honour which Scott and Stewart assigned to the protection of the king, the officers of state, and the regalia of Scotland were drawn from those 'enthusiasts of the philibeg', the members of the Celtic Club, 'dressed in proper costume'. The result was a bizarre travesty of Scottish history, Scottish reality. Imprisoned by his fanatical Celtic friends, carried away by his own romantic Celtic fantasies, Scott was determined to forget historic Scotland, his own Lowland Scotland, altogether. . . Thus was the capital of Scotland 'tartanized' to receive its king, who himself came in the same costume, played his part in the Celtic pageant, and at the climax of the visit solemnly invited the assembled dignitaries to drink a toast not to the actual or historic elite but to 'the chieftains and clans of Scotland'. Even Scott's devoted son-in-law and biographer, J. G. Lockhart, was taken aback by this collective 'hallucination' in which, as he put it, 'the marking and crowning glory' of Scotland was identified with the Celtic tribes which 'always constituted a small and almost always unimportant part of the Scottish population'.[13]

The invented tradition becomes a myth masking real history, and even when it takes on a reality of its own that reality is not accorded the substance of a true 'national imagining', but is presented as a cloak – or perhaps a plaid – for economic interests:

> Lord Macaulay, himself a Highlander by origin, was more outspoken. Writing in the 1850s, he did not doubt the antiquity of the Highland dress, but his historical sense was outraged by the retrospective extension of these 'striped petticoats' to the civilized races of Scotland . . . Macaulay underestimated the strength of an 'hallucination' which is sustained by an economic interest. Scott might regain his balance – he quickly did – but the farce of 1822 had given a new momentum to the tartan industry, and inspired a new fantasy to serve that industry. So we come to the last stage in the creation of the Highland myth: the reconstruction and extension, in ghostly and sartorial form, of that clan system whose reality had been destroyed after 1745.[14]

What we have in Trevor-Roper's account is not a national imagination engaged in the construction of community by forging – in both of its senses – a new relationship between past and future but a fictionalising of the past which leaves the present trapped in a fog of illusion, one that can only make the novelist's engagement with that 'imagined community' doubly false to the real history of the nation.

Trevor-Roper's conception of this fake Scottish imagination is by no means unique. If it is true that the novel is the form *par excellence* of the modern nation state then, in a nation which is not an independent state and is uncertain whether its nationality is British or Scottish, the novel is likely to be the first form to suffer. Flawed novels and fictive national tradition will necessarily collude in a self-destructive cycle of pervasive fraudulence about the nation which can never break through the 'glamour' of this fake invention of tradition to provide a narrative of the modern Scotland of 'real' history. Tom Nairn put it most succinctly in *The Break-up of Britain*:

> They did not ponder mightily and movingly upon the reality of 19th century Scotland – on the great Glasgow bourgeoisie of mid-century and onwards, the new class conflicts, the continuing tragedy of the Highlands. So what was there, instead of those missing Zolas and George Eliots, those absent Thomas Manns and Vergas? What there was increasingly from the 1820s onwards, until it became a vast tide washing into the present day, was the Scots 'Kailyard' tradition.[15]

Kailyard literature, with its inherent sentimentality and its flight from the realities of industrial Scotland, becomes both the symptom of the state of the national imagination – a national imagination without a state – and the sickness to which Scottish writers will continue to fall victim whenever they try to engage with the nature of modern Scotland.

In 1979, in a review of Francis Russell Hart's *The Scottish Novel*, Allan Massie found twentieth-century Scottish novelists still trapped in a nostalgia, whether urban or rural, that meant they had been 'left behind by the modern age'. Of modern novelists, only Kennaway and Spark escaped this trap by locating their fictions outside Scotland, 'where the significant action was'.[16] The failure of the modern Scottish novel, for Massie, derived from two sources. First, there can, in effect, be no such thing as the Scottish novel because there is no continuing nation: with its governance ceded to a British parliament, there can be, in Scotland, no imagining of the nation – the nation with a future rather than simply the nation with a past – that the individual writer can contribute to shaping. The consequence is that Scottish writers necessarily write as isolated individuals; they contribute only to a personal oeuvre rather than a national tradition. Secondly, however, Scottish society is itself a 'second hand society'; as Massie was to point out in his 'Introduction' to the 1982 reprint of Edwin Muir's *Scott and Scotland: The Predicament of the Scottish Writer* (originally published in 1936), it is a nation 'that has become a sham', one that is even less supportive of the novelistic imagination than was Walter Scott's, because,

Scott's Scotland retained a public life; ours has none; or at least none that can invigorate, or prove fertile, to a writer. The writer thus lives in a society which has abandoned responsibility for its own direction, and which, by allowing its "peculiar features" to be smoothed away, finds that whole sectors of it do no more than reflect a way of life that is lived more intensely and more urgently elsewhere.[17]

That Massie should have contributed to the republication of Muir's book in the early 1980s, in the aftermath of the failure to establish a Scottish parliament in the Devolution Referendum in 1979, is a sign both of how pervasive Muir's analysis of Scottish culture had become since the 1930s, and of how much it seemed, still, to address pertinently the 'predicament' of Scottish culture. In the world of blighted political hopes that was the first Thatcher government, Muir's despair of Scottish culture seemed all too accurate – his analysis of Scotland as a place of failed imagination justified by the failure of the nation to turn its imagined parliament into a reality.

Muir's pessimism about Scottish writing in *Scott and Scotland*[18] was founded on the notion that Scottish writers were afflicted by the ineradicable psychological damage of a divided linguistic inheritance, caused by the gradual supplanting of Scots by English after the Union of 1707, and by the consequent fact that 'Scotsmen feel in one language and think in another' (21). For Muir, 'the prerequisite of an autonomous literature is a homogeneous language' (19), and Scotland, whether in Gaelic, Scots or English, had failed to establish such a homogeneous language, 'a common language' which would be 'continuously created and preserved by the highest spiritual energy of a people' (19). A common language, in other words, was the precondition of a national imagination and the consequence of the failure to establish either was that even Scotland's greatest writer, Walter Scott, was incapable of fulfilling his talent because,

> he spent most of his days in a hiatus, in a country, that is to say, which was neither a nation nor a province, and had, instead of a centre, a blank, an Edinburgh, in the middle of it. But this Nothing in which Scott wrote was not merely a spatial one; it was a temporal Nothing as well, dotted with a few disconnected figures arranged at abrupt intervals: Henryson, Dunbar, Allan Ramsay, Burns, with a rude buttress of ballads and folk songs to shore them up and keep them from falling. Scott, in other words, lived in a community which was not a community, and set himself to carry on a tradition which was not a tradition; and the result was that his work was an exact reflection of his predicament. His picture of life had no centre, because the environment in which he lived had no centre. What traditional virtue his work possessed was at second hand, and derived mainly from English literature . . . (11–12)

The failure of the nation, the failure of its traditions, the empty spaces of Scottish culture that are filled with a 'second hand' literature, connect Scott,

Muir and Massie in a problematic that is apparently unresolvable by political or cultural action. Political independence would not re-establish a cultural tradition, since the tradition has already failed; revival of the cultural tradition would only be antiquarianism: each undermines the other's potential in a mutually destructive equation whose outcome is always 'Nothing', an annulment instead of a fulfilment of national imagining.

Muir's view of the Scottish past as constituted by a few isolated writers with a 'rude buttress of ballads and folk songs to shore them up and keep them from falling', echoes T. S. Eliot's *The Waste Land* – 'these fragments I have shored against my ruin' – and points to the sources of Muir's conception of Scotland in the model of 'culture' which linked thinkers from the time of Matthew Arnold in the mid-nineteenth century, through the work of Eliot and F. R. Leavis in the 1920s and 1930s, to the work of critics such as Raymond Williams in the 1950s and 1960s.[19] It is a conception of culture to which 'tradition' is central. Looking back from 1923 on the definition of tradition in his already famous essay of 1919, 'Tradition and the Individual Talent', Eliot commented,

> I was dealing then with the artist; and the sense of tradition which, it seemed to me, the artist should have; but it was generally a problem of order too. I thought of literature then, as I think of it now, of the literature of the world, of the literature of Europe, of the literature of a single country, not as a collection of the writings of individuals, but as 'organic wholes', as systems in relation to which, and only in relation to which, individual works of literary art, and the works of individual artists, have their significance. There is accordingly something outside of the artist to which he owes allegiance, a devotion to which he must surrender and sacrifice himself in order to earn and obtain his unique position. A common inheritance and a common cause unite artists consciously or unconsciously.[20]

For Eliot, works of literature can only have significance insofar as they participate in the 'organic wholes' of a 'common inheritance and a common cause'. By the standards of this notion of tradition, and for exactly the reasons adduced by Muir, Scotland has to be a failed literature, since it can never, with its three languages, be an 'organic' whole. Indeed, Scotland's is fundamentally a dead literature, the literature of a nation which once existed but now has no independent identity, and whose periodic 'renaissances' will simply produce more isolated figures who are incapable of relating to the national past and who will offer no national ground for future writing.

If the elitist view of cultural tradition propounded by Eliot and by Leavis in the 1920s and 1930s came to seem irrelevant in post-Second World War Britain, its successors were to be no less damning when applied to the Scottish condition. 'Tradition' remains central, for instance, to the work of Raymond Williams, whose criticism attempts to reclaim 'tradition' for a democratic and populist culture, and relocates it from the upper class world of 'ceremony, duty and respect'[21] to the lower class world of struggle and resistance, or, at least, to that lower class world witnessed through an educated perspective. Writing about Thomas Hardy in *The Country and the City*, Williams argues,

> That real perception of tradition is available only to the man who has read about it, though what he then sees through it is his native country, to which he is already deeply bound by memory and experience of another kind: a family and a childhood; an intense association of people and places, which has been his own history. To see tradition in both ways is indeed Hardy's special gift: the native place and experience but also the education, the conscious inquiry.[22]

If Eliot's tradition is primarily a tradition of artistic works, or, later, of religious beliefs, Williams's is the combination of working-class recollection with educated understanding. Both, however, are founded on the same sense of an organic unfolding of values: for Williams the iconic figure is Hardy's Jude:

> not the story of the man as he was, distant, limited, picturesque; but slighted in a struggle to grow – to love, to work with meaning, to learn and to teach; enduring in the community of this impulse, which pushes through and beyond particular separations and defeats. It is the continuity not only of a country but of a history and a people.[23]

Jude the Obscure becomes the enactment of a national imagination – 'the continuity not only of a country but of a history and a people' – in its struggle from past towards future. The absence and emptiness of Muir's sense of Scotland is the distorted mirror image of the fullness and completeness of tradition as exemplified by English culture and its literature, which Williams finds to be 'perhaps richer than any other', at least 'in the full range of its themes of country and city'.[24]

The consequences of applying this model to Scottish culture can be seen in the work of a critic such as David Craig – like Williams, a left-Leavisite turned marxist – who cannot see in Scottish culture anything but the slow dissolution of what was once a real and unified culture, in which each apparent achievement – as, for instance, in the culture of the Scottish Enlightenment – is no more than a stepping stone towards the destruction of any authentic Scottish culture. For Craig, Scottish culture is doomed to failure by history, geography, by ideology – all of which conspire to produce a cultural waste land:

> In a culture so thin and so badly placed as the Scottish there were few conflicts in society that did not lead to waste and confusion. Much of the national spirit, often in a rabid form, went into the Low Kirk religion, but

its spirit – utterly uncompromising . . . – was irreconcilable with the cultivated ethos . . . – a man's religious belief was justified by his own consciousness of God-given salvation and inspiration – and the right of the community to apply it for themselves in judging who should be their minister, constituted the main issue over which the religious life of contemporary Scotland was divided: it led directly to the Disruption of 1843. This is another of the deep dis-unities which ran off the energies of 18th century Scotland into dispute and the partisan bitterness, anyway characteristic of the race, which made for a stultifying monotony of idiom, religious, political, poetic – an inhumane extreme of partiality, in which positions defined themselves more by violence of opposition than by their positive natures.[25]

Scotland's culture is a 'waste', a 'confusion': the elements of that culture are irrelevant to modern definitions of culture – they take 'rabid form' – and the ways in which the culture expresses itself in political terms – through the Disruption of the Church of Scotland in 1843, for instance – are presented as the petty irrelevancies of parochial religion rather than, as contemporaries thought, one of the most noble and heroic acts of the modern age.

Instead of continuity, what Scottish culture presents, in this model, is erasure: each stage of development – or degradation – wipes out what went before it and destroys the very possibility of continuity upon which tradition is founded. Thus for Edwin Muir, the ritual world of Scotland's medieval catholicism is presented as having been utterly abolished by the Reformation –

> . . . Knox and Melville clapped their preaching palms
> And bundled all the harvesters away [26]

– and Knoxian Calvinism, rather than an expression of national identity, comes to be the negation of the nation's once authentic culture. Muir's presentation of Knox is the culmination of a long process in which the iconic founder of the nation came to be viewed as its subverter and destroyer. It was a presentation of Knox which had begun to alter in the late nineteenth century, when the hagiographic biography of him by McCrie,[27] much published in the nineteenth century, was challenged first by Andrew Lang[28] and then by almost everyone who wanted to escape from the world of Victorian puritanism, seen as one of logical outcomes of Knox's Reformation. Muir perceived in Knox's own life precisely the blight which he believed to afflict Scottish culture: Knox's biography, for Muir, is almost identical with what happened to Scotland since,

The life of Knox is broken in two. For the first forty years we can vaguely discern a devout Catholic; for the next twenty-seven we see another character, with the same name, the same appearance, and probably the same affections and passions, but with entirely different opinions. This new figure is born at the age of forty, and seems to have no ancestry. For Knox left no record either of his early life or of his conversion: the one is like an absolute event which had existed from eternity, the other is as if it had never been.[29]

Knox becomes the embodiment of a culture of erasure, a man with 'no ancestry', the first half of his life completely negated by the second; Knox becomes the model of a culture incapable of maintaining continuity precisely because it lives in defiance of the imagination. For Muir, the effect of Knox's influence can be seen by comparing the cultural legacy of the hundred years after his death in Scotland and in England:

> Knox, the reformers, and the Covenanters have made Scotland what it is . . . Yet during the same hundred years the nearest living country could show Shakespeare, Spenser, Jonson, Marlowe, Donne, Milton, in poetry and drama; Bacon, Hooker, Browne, Taylor, Clarendon, in prose; the beginnings of modern science; and music, architecture, philosophy, theology, oratory in abundance. Was it the influence of Calvinism which preserved Scotland from that infection? There are reasonable grounds, I think, for believing so. Calvinism, in the first place, was a faith which insisted with exclusive force on certain human interests, and banned all the rest. It lopped off from religion music, painting and sculpture, and pruned architecture to a minimum; it frowned on all prose and poetry which was not sacred. For its imaginative literature it was confined more and more to the Old Testament, and though the Old Testament contains some splendid poetry, it has at all times been over-praised at the expense of greater works. Calvinism, in short, was a narrowly specialized kind of religion, but it was also a peculiar religion – a religion which outraged the imagination, and no doubt helped, therefore to produce that captivity of the imagination in Scotland which was only broken in the eighteenth century.[30]

Scotland is a nation imagined into a new existence by a Calvinism whose very purpose is to repress and distort the imagination. The destructive effects of Knox's denial of ancestry would only be healed, according to Muir, in the eighteenth century, but in that century the most powerful intellectual figures – Hume, Smith – would commit themselves to writing in English, and so, though they might overthrow the effects of a repressive religion, they contributed further to the disintegration of Scottish society. Thereafter, the major figures of Scottish culture will, for Muir, have to struggle ever harder with the disintegrative effects of Knox's legacy, and if 'Hume, Burns, and men like them . . . lifted it from its isolation for a time during the next hundred years', Scotland nonetheless would remain 'an object lesson in savage provincialism', because 'what Knox really did was to rob Scotland of all the benefits of the Renaissance'[31] – in other words, of a continuous and evolving tradition of the imagination's engagement in national life.

   The consequences of Muir's view of Scotland are manifest in much of the writing about Scotland in the second half of the twentieth century; they can be seen, for instance, in the work of the most influential modern historian of Scotland, T. C. Smout. Smout's two studies of Scottish history, *A History of the Scottish People 1560–1830* and *A Century of the Scottish People*, enact between them a paradigmatic version of these erasures of the Scottish past. The first volume rises towards a culmination in 'The Golden Age of Scottish Culture', which recounts the achievements of the Scottish Enlightenment, the take-off of industrialisation and an early entry into the world of potential plenty which it promises, while the second volume tells of the failure of Scotland to benefit from the consequences of that industrialisation, producing the iron age of Victorian poverty and misery to which 'culture' is almost irrelevant. Smout's first volume concludes with the question, 'How can we account for the unprecedented cultural achievements of the Scots in the century after 1740?',[32] as though Scotland's achievement of any kind of cultural success is a miracle incapable of rational explanation; while the second begins,

> The age of great industrial triumphs was an age of appalling deprivation . . . I am astounded by the tolerance, in a country boasting of its high moral standards and basking in the spiritual leadership of a Thomas Chalmers, of unspeakable urban squalor, compounded of drink abuse, bad housing, low wages, long hours and sham education.'[33]

The word 'sham' points to Muir's influence – in 'Scotland 1941' he describes Scott and Burns as the 'sham bards of a sham nation' – and the rhetoric of Smout's presentation is designed to set the two epochs against one another, as though these two 'ages' of Scotland's experience were not joined together across the chronology of mathematical impositions of historical divisions, as though no one had lived from one epoch into the other, as though the second had utterly erased all traces of the first, leaving modern Scotland totally detached from the achievements of its 'golden age'. Scotland's history is opaque, inexplicable: it is a country under erasure whose past offers no relationship with the present.

One of the other leading historians of modern Scotland, Christopher Harvie, in the second edition of his study of *Scotland and Nationalism*, dramatises precisely this dislocation as the condition of modern Scotland: just as Enlightenment Scotland is, for Smout, wiped out by Victorian Scotland, so Harvie images Scotland in terms of his home town of Motherwell, symbol of a country where, in the title of one of his chapters, 'nothing abides', as the Scots journey to 'no sure land', but also, symptomatically, a place of significance to Edwin Muir:

> In 1936 a visit to Motherwell decided Edwin Muir to write his *Scottish Journey*. The sprawling, silent, steel-manufacturing town seemed to him to exemplify, in its total subordination of community to material development, the fatal impact of industrialisation on Scotland. With the slump it had ceased both to work and to exist as a community . . .

Nine years later Motherwell gave the SNP its first election victory, and fifty-seven years later it remains a paradigm of the Scottish predicament. Few of the houses of 1936 still stand. New housing schemes and multi-storey blocks, a new civic centre, a new station have opened. The Clyde valley is now a huge recreation park . . . A town has been created which Muir would hardly recognise, a town which is strange to me, and I was born and brought up in it between 1944 and 1949.[34]

The Scottish 'predicament' – Muir's subtitle echoes into Harvie's prose – is not simply the residue of a harsh industrial world, nor the effort of a people to build a better environment than the one they have inherited: it is the total elision of the evidence of the past and its replacement by a novelty so radical that it is impossible for the individual to relate to it his or her personal memories. And impossible, therefore, for that environment to be 'related' as a coherent narrative.[35] The constant erasure of one Scotland by another makes Scotland unrelatable, un-narratable: past Scotlands are not gathered into the being of modern Scotland; they are abolished. Modern Scotland thus has no past, since no past Scotland can be related to the actually existing Scotland, and no narrative can be constructed to constitute its continuing identity. Unrelated and unrelatable, Scotland becomes invisible:

What is true for Motherwell applies to the other settlements of the Scottish central belt, from the former colliery villages of Ayrshire to the textile towns of Strathmore. A combination of policies to attract work to areas of unemployment and to disperse the congested population of the Glasgow conurbation has created a new Scotland, neither urban nor rural, which straggles westwards from the fringes of the Firth of Forth to the lower Clyde. It is this unknown Scotland, not in the guidebooks, away from the motorway, seen fleetingly from the express, that holds the key to the modern politics of the country.[36]

A 'new' Scotland, an 'unknown' Scotland: not a culture travelling somewhere but one travelled through, by-passed, defining itself neither in terms of a relationship with the past nor a relationship with the future but living in suspended animation, by-passed by those with somewhere to travel to: the warped and distorted outcome of a failed history, a broken tradition, and a second-hand imagination.

The 'predicament' of the imagination in Scotland is that it is neither a real imagination – having been maimed by Calvinism – nor is it effectively national – since Scotland has failed to maintain a continuous identity as a nation of the modern kind. If the novel is indeed the index of national consciousness and the national imagination, then the regularly asserted failure of the Scottish novel (as opposed to the success of individual Scottish novelists) can be seen simply as the reflection of the ongoing failure of

Scottish culture as a whole – or, rather, the failure of Scottish culture to *be* whole.

II

For cultures such as Scotland, the destructive consequences of the application of ideas of 'tradition' makes it tempting to think of abandoning the term altogether and refusing to try to see the achievement of Scottish writers as in any way connected with the maintenance of a tradition. This was in part the route taken by Muir's embittered antagonist of the 1930s, Hugh MacDiarmid, when he demanded 'precedents not traditions' in fulfilment of his battlecry of 'not Burns – Dunbar!'[37] Such a policy, however, amounts to a kind of cultural 'scorched earth' tactic, obliterating everything belonging to the actual, historical development of the culture in order to get back to a pure origin. The best that it can produce is a few major figures who represent possible precedents; what it cannot produce is a sense of an ongoing culture whose development is a relevant part of our present relationship with the past. To foreground precedents rather than traditions subjects the national past no less to the kinds of erasure that follow from Muir's views. However opposed Muir and MacDiarmid were, their conceptions of the actual development of Scottish culture were deeply similar, and equally negative.[38] There may be a certain freedom for the individual writer in this liberation from tradition – and MacDiarmid exploited the freedom he gave himself to reinvent Scotland in his own image – but in the end its consequences for the nation's sense of itself can only be destructive. Radical individualism may represent a morally challenging position but it is also an invitation to radical isolationism, leaving writer and audience confronting each other in mutual denial: the audience will always fail to match the imagination of the writer and the writer's imagination will fail to participate in any process of communal self-imagining. Lines from MacDiarmid's 'A Drunk Man Looks at the Thistle' may speak to such an antagonistic position more truly than MacDiarmid intended:[39]

> The Scottish poet maun assume
> The burden o' his people's doom.

Artist and audience are trapped in a mutually destructive embrace, each doomed by the other's failures.

A very different account of 'tradition' has been given by Alasdair MacIntyre, whose intepretations of the evolution of Scottish philosophy have been among the most important interventions in our sense of Scottish culture in the last quarter of the century. MacIntyre argues in *After Virtue*[40] that there is no such thing as thought unconditioned by 'tradition':

For all reasoning takes place within the context of some traditional mode of
thought, transcending through criticism and invention the limitations of what
had hitherto been reasoned in that tradition: this is as true of modern physics
as of medieval logic. Moreover when a tradition is in good order it is always
partially constituted by an argument about the goods the pursuit of which
gives to that tradition its particular point and purpose. (222)

Far from tradition being a defective mode of understanding, 'tradition' is
the inescapable context without which thought could not proceed at all,
and central both to 'traditions' and to the lives of individuals is the role of
narrative. Narrative, for MacIntyre, represents the fundamental organising
principle of human experience – 'man is in his actions and practice, as well
as in his fictions, essentially a story-telling animal' (216). To make sense
of 'a story-telling animal' one requires not only to know what events have
happened to happen to a particular individual but to have a sense of *telos*, an
end towards which and by which the quest of the individual life is judged:
'There is no present which is not informed by some image of some future
and an image of the future which always presents itself in the form of a
telos – or a variety of ends of goals – towards which we are either moving
or failing to move in the present' (216–17). Such ends, however, are not
merely constructed or asserted on an individual basis; they are formed as
part of a tradition:

For the story of my life is always embedded in the story of those communities
from which I derive my identity. I am born with a past; and to try to cut
myself off from that past, in the individualist mode, is to deform my present
relationships. The possession of an historical identity and the possession of
a social identity coincide. Notice that rebellion against my identity is always
one possible mode of expressing it . . .
    What I am, therefore, is in key part what I inherit, a specific past that is
present to some degree in my present. I find myself part of a history and that
is generally to say, whether I like it or not, whether I recognize it or not, one
of the bearers of a tradition. (221)

For MacIntyre, both individual life and social traditions are narratives of
quest for the fulfilment or discovery of a *telos* which will justify the past
that is embodied in the tradition, because 'a living tradition is an historically extended, socially embodied argument, and an argument precisely in
part about the goods which constitute that tradition' (222). The novel, as
MacIntyre's analysis of Jane Austen (239–43) enforces, has been one of
major modes through which modern societies have shaped the argument
about the 'goods' of their tradition and therefore about the very nature of
the tradition of which they are a part. The novel is an 'embodied argument'
which both carries forward a tradition as an inheritance from the past and
projects a path for tradition by defining or redefining the *telos* towards

which the tradition is directed. What MacIntyre describes in terms of moral traditions we can see as a version of the relationship between novel and national tradition: novels are symbolic enactments of debates about the *telos* which justifies individual life as part of a social, a national narrative.

The paradox of MacIntyre's position, however, is that having established the significance of traditions to our understanding of the national past, he uses that argument to perform exactly the same kind of erasure of Scottish tradition that we have seen in Muir and Smout. MacIntyre views the major moral philosophies not simply as theoretical arguments but as the distillation into theoretical form of the social practices of a particular time and place: the 'rationality' of moral argument is based on its being the coherent development of an evolving tradition within such a set of social practices. MacIntyre's sense of the importance of tradition to all forms of thought is presented by him as a challenge to the whole project of the Enlightenment in its desire to release knowledge and decision-making from the burden of the past. In the case of Hume, the challenge is a double one, because in *Whose Justice? Which Rationality?*[41] MacIntyre views Hume's moral philosophy not only as an Enlightenment theory which has to be challenged in terms of its presuppositions about the ends of humanity, but also as a deliberate subversion of Scottish traditions in philosophy. MacIntyre takes the linguistic argument traditionally levelled at Hume – his concern to avoid Scotticisms in his writing – and turns it into an argument about the social nature of Hume's thought, a social nature which reflects not Scottish *mores* but English ones, and which results in the Scottish tradition abolishing itself from within.

> Hutcheson therefore engendered a new type of conflict within Scottish intellectual life, and it is a mark of his importance that he set the terms of debate for that conflict. Just because he did so, it is easy in retrospect to view that conflict as a continuation of the debates internal to Scottish tradition. The participants after all were all Scotsmen. But it was a conflict in which the continuing existence of the Scottish tradition was put in question. What Hume represented in almost every important respect, what indeed Smith too was to represent, even though he was Hutcheson's most distinguished and well-regarded pupil, was the abandonment of peculiarly Scottish modes of thought in favour of a distinctively English and Anglicizing way of understanding social life and its moral fabric. (280)

Though engaged in a debate within Scottish tradition, Hume is, for MacIntyre, the subverter of Scottish tradition, the denier of past Scottish thought just as much as Knox was for Muir.

In constructing his argument, however, MacIntyre gives a very different sense of the Knoxian inheritance from that provided by Muir: far from being a 'savage provincialism', MacIntyre sees in seventeenth-century Scottish Calvinism a powerful attempt to synthesise the Aristotelian inheritance of

European thought with the Augustinian tradition that was fundamental to the evolution of Christian theology, including Calvinism. The result was a philosophy which addressed the problems of 'the emerging modern state and the growing market economy' (211), but did so by continuing to assert that 'the first principles of the sciences, conceived in a mode that was still in a large measure Aristotelian' were to be 'treated as evident and undeniable in their own right, without dialectical or any other rational support' (225). The characteristic structure of Scottish thought in the seventeenth and early eighteenth centuries was one in which 'it was almost an intellectual commonplace that those first principles, by deduction from which subordinate judgments were rationally justified, had a quality of evidentness that made them recognizable truths by everyone of sound mind who understood the terms in which they were stated and whose understanding had not been subverted by false doctrine' (223). This deductive method of Scottish thought was not simply an intellectual argument but was part of a whole social practice informing those elements of civil society – law, education, religion – which remained, despite the Union, distinctively Scottish: all those social practices were to be founded on the same 'rationality' of tradition, so that 'it was part of the peculiarly Scottish ethos to envisage Scottish principles and institutions as those that could be rationally vindicated within an international community of Protestant civility, within which standards of rational justification were shared' (220).

The great expression of this tradition and the medium by which it will be reinforced in Scottish culture is Stair's *The Institutions of the Law of Scotland* (1681), in which 'no English legal commentator is ever mentioned, nor is any English statute or case' and in which the foundation of law is presented simply as 'the dictate of reason' (227). In the context of such a tradition, the unique position of the professor of moral philosophy was 'that of providing a defense of just those fundamental moral principles, conceived of as antecedent to both all positive law and all particular forms of social organization, which defined peculiarly Scottish instititutions and attitudes', with the result that 'moral philosophy assumed a kind of authority in Scottish culture which it has rarely enjoyed at other times and places' (239). Far from a 'savage provincialism' what the Calvinist tradition produced in Scotland in the late seventeenth and eighteenth centuries was 'that very rare phenomenon, an educated public, in this case a philosophically educated public, with shared standards in rational justification and a shared deference to a teaching authority, that of the professors of philosophy and especially of moral philosophy' (248). And what it also produced was a coherent tradition, one in which 'the established scheme of human knowledge in the Scottish seventeenth and eighteenth centuries was – and to some limited degree this persisted into the nineteenth century – a unitary and more or less integrated scheme, the articulated disciplinary parts of which involved continuous reference to each other' (250).

The key figure in sustaining this tradition into the eighteenth century was, for MacIntyre, Francis Hutcheson, whose 'account of the moral sense supplied for those contemporaries . . . a rationale for their reliance upon the felt evidentness of what were taken to be moral truths', and so provided 'a secular counterpart to the appeal to inward feeling so characteristic of the doctrine of Evangelical conversion' (278). Hutcheson's achievement in maintaining that tradition, however, is entirely undone in MacIntyre's account by Hume, and by a Hume who has a remarkable similarity to Muir's Knox in terms of the division of his life and values into mutually negating aspects. Thus 'his published work presented a series of the profoundest challenges to and ruptures with the fundamental convictions which had been embodied in the dominant Scottish tradition', but 'at any point at which this fact might have had an impact on Hume's personal life, he tried so far as possible to minimize and to disguise the facts of challenge and rupture' (280). Just as, for Muir, Knox's life is 'broken in two' across the divide of his fortieth year so that we suddenly see 'another character, with the same name, the same appearance, and probably the same affections and passions, but with entirely different opinions' (11), so, for MacIntyre, Hume presents parallel private and public selves with quite different identities: in private he 'had no hesitation in avowing his hostility to religion', in public he challenged those who 'denominated me an infidel, on account of ten or twelve pages which seem to him to prove that tendency' (282); like Knox 'the devout Catholic' who is transformed into the radical reformer, Hume, heir of Scotland's independent legal tradition, 'adopted so far as he was capable of doing, the manners of an Englishman' (283) and, travelling in the opposite direction from Knox, declared his *dependence* on English culture with the same insistence that Knox declared the *independence* of his church: 'London is the capital of my own Country' (284). However much MacIntyre may see the Scottish tradition as continuing into the nineteenth century, it is, fundamentally, undermined by its greatest son, and would have suffered eclipse more quickly had Hume's works 'upon publication been read widely and accepted within Scotland', because it would have 'subverted among that country's educated classes some of the central loyalties essential to maintaining a distinctive Scottish cultural identity' (299).

MacIntyre's analysis of 'tradition' is a powerful argument from many points of view. First, it presents a sense of the significance of tradition that challenges all those theories of culture which insist that, after the entry into modernity, traditions can have no value; equally, it challenges all those theories which insist that traditions are simply the retrospective constructions of our contemporary ideologies: the fact that thinking is always, for MacIntyre, conducted in and through traditions gives to cultural history – and to the histories of our cultures – a significance that it does not have in other styles of thought, something of importance in small cultures whose traditions may seem easy to give up for the 'traditionless' thinking of a contemporary internationalism. Secondly, it underlines the significance of Scottish traditions which many have been quick to repudiate, by showing both how Calvinism underpins the great achievements of the Scottish Enlightenment, and how that Enlightenment was not simply the expression of a placeless universalism. MacIntyre's version of Calvinism's development undoes both the arguments of those who would see in Scottish Calvinism only cultural destruction, and, equally, of those who would see the Enlightenment in Scotland as purely the product of traditions alien to Scotland itself. Thirdly, MacIntyre's construction presents 'tradition' as something dynamic: far from resting on a sense of the 'age-old' and invoking 'ceremony, duty and respect', MacIntyre's sense of tradition involves a constant evolution within the terms of the founding propositions of a philosophical perspective, an evolution within a framework of thought which cannot be escaped because it is the very structure through which we see the world.

Nonetheless, MacIntyre's application of his notion of tradition to Hume perpetuates the view of Scottish culture as a process in which a truly 'Scottish' tradition is erased and supplanted by an alien tradition. In MacIntyre's analysis the great figures of Scottish culture necessarily destroy the very Scottishness which produced them. The paradox of MacIntyre's position is that, having provided the tools by which it is possible to identify and valorise the significance of Scottish tradition, he then negates that tradition by denying that its greatest mind has any place within it. If Walter Scott, for Edwin Muir, is maimed by his effort to stand within a Scottish tradition, Hume's achievement, for MacIntyre, rests precisely on his success in doing what Muir had urged on Scottish writers – escaping from the Scottish failure of tradition by identifying with English values.

There are three serious defects in MacIntyre's account, defects which, because of the very power of his argument, reveal typical procedures by which Scottish culture has been undermined by generations of cultural theorists. First, MacIntyre identifies 'Scottish' with one particular strand in cultural life, as though the culture's continuation depended on that aspect of tradition only. He may use the term 'dominant' of that tradition, acknowledging that there were other traditions within the culture, but he does not situate the tradition alongside those others or in contest with those others, so that if that one tradition is abandoned, Scottish tradition itself is seen to come to an end. The apocalyptic consequences of the abandonment of this one tradition of thought come from MacIntyre's residually marxist way of seeing traditions as inscribed in social structures, so that the whole social structure must be in some sense undermined if the philosophical coherence of its tradition is undermined, and vice versa. But a culture is broader than a single tradition of thought and a social structure can find other ways of maintaining the sense of its own integrity: if the deductive principles which informed that unusually educated Scottish public were undermined by the development of philosophical thought, it was perfectly possible that the structures underwritten by them then found alternative modes of validation; the values of a tradition which was based on an underlying logical schema could be transferred to an alternative environment (in the works, for instance, of Burns and Scott) where its pholosophical *consistency* was no longer the fundamental issue. The traditions of a culture survive in many ways: the centre of gravity of a culture shifts from religion to philosophy to literature to the visual arts and in each of these offer different resources through which the culture can find the means for the continued assertion of its traditions and of the values which they embody.

Second, MacIntyre insists that Hume's philosophy represents an acceptance of English values when, in terms of his own account, what it clearly registers is a set of *class* values. Those class values may be most evident among the English upper classes and Hume may, in his younger days, have wished to attach himself to that class, but the relationship of class values to national traditions is, quite simply, not debated by MacIntyre. This is the more problematic in the case of class values in Britain because, of course, it is part of the project of Scottish culture in the eighteenth century, as Linda Colley has demonstrated,[42] to exploit the benefits of the British Empire through the creation of the multi-national culture of 'Britishness'. 'Scottish', 'English' and 'British' form a set of relations which mean that it is impossible simply to set Scottish and English as antitheses of one another in this or in any period since 1707. That 'London is the capital of my own Country' for Hume is not a simple statement of commitment to English culture: it is a commitment to the construction of a new British culture which works through the language of class as the common bond for its diverse national groups. The property values of the upper classes which, if MacIntyre is right, are at the centre of Hume's moral philosophy are thus the expression not of Hume's commitment to English culture but of his commitment to the new British culture which, at this early stage in its formation, was only beginning to develop a language in which to express itself – as, for instance, in the writing of 'Rule Britannia' by that other Scot bound up in the creation of the new British culture, James Thomson.

Thirdly, 'anglicizing' is taken by MacIntyre to be identical with becoming part of English culture. Not only is this clearly not the case in the formation of a new British culture, but 'anglicizing' is something which can only happen within a culture that is not – or not yet – English culture. If it were to be fully achieved there would be no difference between Scottish culture and English culture, in which case it would become irrelevant: the effect of 'anglicizing' in cultural terms is one which can only occur as part of a process between two cultures which are not, and do not become, identical. 'Anglicizing' is a tendency *within* Scottish culture whose relevance lies precisely in the impossibility of its succeeding without its becoming irrelevant. That we can still talk of 'anglicizing' tendencies in modern Scottish culture points to the fact that no matter how anglicized Scots become, they do not become English: if they were to do so there would be no need to distinguish 'anglicized' from other Scots. 'Anglicized Scots' may be participants in English culture but that does not prevent them from also being participants in Scottish culture, and it does not mean that their works may have very different meanings in the two cultures, as Conor Cruise O'Brien demonstrated in his analysis of the possible meanings of Burke's *Reflections on the Revolution in France*.[43] O'Brien points out that for Burke, defence of 'tradition' in an English context was, implicitly, an appeal for political inclusion in British life of the group which was most bound by 'tradition' – Irish Catholics. MacIntyre recognises that in Burke, as in Hume, something strange is occurring within English culture, since the definition of English traditions are being constructed not by English writers but by writers who have acquired English culture as though it were a 'classical' tradition. The construction of the Englishness to which Hume and Burke aspired is therefore not, in origin, an aspect of English culture but a projection upon England of Scottish and Irish culture. Of course, they then become part of the on-going definition of English culture, but they can be read equally as the Scotticising or Irishing of English culture rather than anglicization of Scottish or Irish culture.

Within MacIntyre's own text, there is in fact an alternative reading of Hume's works which resists his explicit argument about Hume's subversive role, for MacIntyre notes that 'Hume never succeeded in making the English recognize him as an Englishman' and as a result 'came to reidentify himself as a Scot, and to take pride in the poetry of such inferior Scottish writers as Blacklock and Wilkie' (284); indeed, MacIntyre's argument is so contorted that he has to claim that Hume's life was 'by design to a large degree an English life, even when lived out in France' (284). MacIntyre's argument about the nature of tradition could itself have been better made by arguing the case for Hume as developer of a specifically Scottish tradition, a tradition which was in evolution from the Calvinism of the seventeenth century towards a secular philosophy which would retain Calvinism's double sense of the self as both intensely private – and known only to God or introspection – and, at the same time, committed to the public and social self which has to be developed in conformity with the requirements of our relations with others. Indeed, MacIntyre acknowledges that Hutcheson, whom he takes to be the last of the Scottish tradition had, 'by acceptance of Shaftesbury's rather than Aristotle's account of the role of reason in practical life', already 'moved radically away from what had been a central thesis of the seventeenth-century Scottish tradition' (285). The dynamic sense of evolving tradition which MacIntyre offers us is effectively undone by his insistence on constructing essentialist conceptions of national traditions: 'Scotland had no viable future', he tells us, 'except by integration into and assimilation to the commercial, financial, political, social, and cultural ways of a wider and essentially English world' (295–6). It is pre-cisely the point of a dynamic conception of tradition that there could have been no 'essentially English world' – there was an England which was, as much as Scotland, being reconstituted through the effects of its developing Empire and the internal security allowed by its relationship with Scotland. As England was being transformed by the construction of a new British identity which had significant Scottish components – to which the likes of Hume were prime contributors – so Scotland was being transformed by the English elements of that same British identity, and both were resisting uniformity by discovering new ways of relating to their independent pasts. The idea of 'traditions' as logical arguments which are suddenly aban-doned because irrelevant or refuted may make sense if one is dealing with the past as though it were simply a series of philosophical propositions; it makes no sense when one is dealing with it as a process in which iden-tity is developed not as something 'essential' but as a dialogue between a variety of interacting discourses. Hume's philosophy would not have been the same had he actually been English: his effort to liberate Scotland 'from the Christian superstition' defined a context for his work which shapes its trajectory – even in its desire for anglicization – in ways which would not have been the case had he actually been English.

Far from being an index of the abandonment of Scottish traditions, MacIntyre's Hume, the Scottish philosopher deeply committed to his Scot-tish family and friends, deeply committed to redeeming his nation from the perversions of its religious past, is a reductio ad absurdum of all those readings of the Scottish past which see in each historical development not the evolution of a tradition but the erasure of the Scottish past, not the dialogue of one generation of Scots with an earlier one but the denial by later Scots that they have any connection with their past. As MacIntyre himself notes in a later chapter, though referring only to 'rational traditions', 'Some core of shared belief, constitutive of allegiance to the tradition, has to survive every rupture' (356): this is equally true of the more diffuse traditions within which a national imagination operates.

If we are to engage constructively with the traditions of the nation we need a sense of tradition which is essentialist neither in its historical mode – iden-tifying the 'real' nation with one portion of its past – nor in its denial that the nation exists in a continual series of interchanges with other nations, and with ideas and forms of life which can be traced to an origin outside of the nation itself. The idea of the nation as a single and unified totality is itself an invention required by a specific phase of the development of the system of nation-states in the global development of modernity, one which has continued to exert enormous influence in British culture precisely to the extent that England has been presented as the most effective example of such a unity. The nation-as-unity is the reflex of the idea of the nation as founded on linguistic purity and homogeneity, but as Bakhtin pointed out, such conceptions of a unitary language are in fact the expression of a desire to limit what is fundamental to the nature of language – its diversity and its tendency to fragment into a multiplicity of voices:

> Philosophy of language, linguistics and stylistics . . . have all postulated a simple and unmediated relation of speaker to his unitary and singular 'own' language, and have postulated as well a simple realization of this language in a monologic utterance of the individual. Such disciplines actually know only two poles in the life of language, between which are located all the linguistic and stylistic phenomena they know: on the one hand, the system of a *unitary language*, and on the other the *individual* speaking in this language.[44]

This desire for unity Bakhtin sees as ideologically motivated; it is the imposition of an order – a standardised language – which 'is not something given but is always posited', a positing which can never succeed because it is in denial of the fundamental nature of language, whose dynamics are those of stratification, multiplication and the incorporation of apparently alien elements – what Bakhtin terms 'heteroglossia'. 'Tradition' is a term which has been used as an insistence on inner unity, but like the proponents of standardised languages such unity is in fundamental conflict with the very nature of the processes of tradition-making and tradition-receiving: traditions are heteroglossic; every tradition is a combination, like every utterance in Bakhtin's conception of language, in which 'the "unitary language" (in its centripetal forces and tendencies)' is engaged with and against 'the social and the historical heteroglossia (the centrifugal, stratifying forces)'.[45] Nations are not undone because they adopt modes of life or modes of discourse from elsewhere: the nation is a space in which those influences are put into play with the inheritance which is specific to that particular place. The nature of a national imagination, like a language, is an unending series of interactions between different strands of tradition, between influences from within and without, between the impact of new experiences and the reinterpretation of past experiences: the nation is a series of ongoing debates, founded in institutions and patterns of life, whose elements are continually changing but which constitute, by the nature of the issues which they foreground, and by their reiteration of elements of the past, a dialogue which is unique to that particular place. The national imagination is not some transcendental identity which either survives or is erased: it is a space in which a dialogue is in process between the various pressures and inheritances that constitute the particularity of human experience in a territory whose boundaries might have been otherwise, but whose borders define the limits within which certain voices, both past and present, with all their centripetal and centrifugal implications, are listened for, and others resisted, no matter how loud they may be.

Nations *imagine*: not in the sense that they fictionally construct themselves but in the sense that a group of people living in a particular place live within a set of circumstances which has inheritances, limitations, possibilities. It is the nation which imagines not because there is some transcendental subject which 'thinks' separately from all the people who happen to live in the nation, but because the nation is the medium in which institutions have their being and which turns individual thinking into communal action. To act, in a national context, requires operating through (or in opposition to) those institutions – from the ritualised structures of everyday life to the vast organisations of modern bureaucracy – which are the carriers of the nation's 'embodied argument'. Those institutions provide the language(s) available in that place and time; they provide the medium through which the symbolic enactment of the possibilities of the future turns into the realities we have to live through and which, having become the past, constitute in turn the givenness from which our imagination of the future has again to begin. The nation and its institutions, as 'embodied arguments', are bound together as the carriers and enactors of the values which those arguments propose, the *telos* to which they are directed. Institutions are the *text*ure of national life and they have to be constantly reread and re-expressed – re-imagined – as they are re-written and re-inscribed by the events which govern national decision-making.

The nation 'imagines' because it is the nation through which the agency of human groups is primarily exerted in the modern world: the nation acts upon the individual – by the educational opportunities it provides and the economic potentialities it makes available, by the wars in which it engages and the laws that define the limits of individual action – and individuals act through the nation, by extending the effectiveness of their own will power into the will of the institutions which shape national life. The imagination of a nation is both the nation's imagining of its future – something we are all constantly engaged in since the nation shapes our individual futures – and it is the process of reconstituting the nation's past by retelling to ourselves the values which the nation embodies and by which those futures ought to be governed. National imaginings have such power precisely because they are the means by which power is governed, both in terms of how it is enacted and, even more importantly for most nations, in terms of how it is possible to resist others' power. Within a national imagination traditions are not simply the construction of the past according to the dictates of the present: they are the elements of the dialogue which underwrite the institutions of the nation. Neither are traditions simply inherited responses to the problems encountered by human beings in coping with particular environments: traditions emerge through debate and dialogue and constitute the site of ongoing debates which have certain premises and certain limits. They can be negated only by establishing new premises and new limits, and the very act of negation becomes itself a part of the tradition to which later participants in the debate have to accede as one of the elements of their own condition. Traditions are not the unitary voice of an organic whole but the dialectical engagement between opposing value systems which define each other precisely by their intertwined oppositions.

The tradition of the modern Scottish novel which this book seeks to explore is not an 'expression' of a national 'geist', nor a singular founding principle to which any work must conform to be 'Scottish': the tradition is a space of debate, a dialogue between the interacting possibilities of a medium shaped by the conditions of those living in Scotland – its languages and its economic and social circumstances – and within the institutions which give shape to its national imagining. It is an attempt to identify a national tradition of the novel in Scotland, not as an essence which will exclude or include various writers as the 'truly Scottish', but as a dialogue between the variety of discourses which, in debating with each other, constitute the space that is the imagining of Scotland and Scotland's imagination. That there is a tradition of the Scottish novel is also, however, an index of the continuity of the nation and the national imagining to which it contributes.

III

In a now famous passage in Alasdair Gray's *Lanark*,[46] Duncan Thaw explains to his friend McAlpin the problem of Glasgow:

> "Glasgow is a magnificent city," said McAlpin. "Why do we hardly ever notice that?" "Because nobody imagines living here," said Thaw. McAlpin lit a cigarette and said, "If you want to explain that I'll certainly listen."
> "Then think of Florence, Paris, London, New York. Nobody visiting them for the first time is a stranger because he's already visited them in paintings, novels, history books and films. But if a city hasn't been used by an artist not even the inhabitants live there imaginatively. What is Glasgow to most of us? A house, the place we work, a football park or golf course, some pubs and connecting streets. That's all. No, I'm wrong, there's also the cinema and library. And when our imagination needs exercise we use these to visit London, Paris, Rome under the Caesars, the American West at the turn of the century, anywhere but here and now. Imaginatively Glasgow exists as a music-hall song and a few bad novels. That's all we've given to the world outside. It's all we've given to ourselves." (243)

Thaw is the inheritor of Scottish culture as erasure: the culture which has actually existed in Glasgow, the paintings of the Glasgow Boys and the Glasgow Girls, the work of designers and architects like Rennie MacIntosh, the novels of Catherine Carswell or George Friel, the theatre of James Bridie, have disappeared in an all-encompassing cultural amnesia. Thaw is a child of the Second World War, a War in which the construction of a British identity had sought to obliterate the cultural specificities of Britain's constituent cultures except as those few music-hall songs. Thaw's imagination encounters Glasgow as an unimagined place, an unrecognised place: "Glasgow never got into the history books, except as a statistic, and if it vanished tomorrow our output of ships and carpets and lavatory pans would be replaced in months by grateful men working overtime in England, Germany and Japan" (244). What the novel will demonstrate, however, is that it is not Glasgow which is is unimagined but Thaw's imagination which is so alienated from its environment that it recognises no other imagination than its own. Thaw concludes:

> Of course, our industries still keep nearly half of Scotland living round here. They let us exist. But who, nowadays is glad just to exist?"
> "I am. At the moment," said McAlpin, watching the sunlight move among the rooftops.
> "So am I," said Thaw, wondering what had happened to his argument. (244)

Thaw's argument is undone by McAlpin insistence on looking directly at the 'magnificence' by which they are surrounded, but it is an argument which has regularly been made about Scottish culture in the twentieth century, an argument based on a profound amnesia about the real nature of Scottish culture and the actual history of the arts in Scotland.

By the 1950s, when the young Duncan Thaw was struggling to come to terms with his environment, all that remained visible of past Scottish culture was a 'few bad novels', the products of the much-berated 'Kailyard'.[47] But 'Kailyard' writing was only one aspect of Scotland's significant contribution to the development of the new generic forms of a mass popular culture, which included Conan Doyle's development of the detective novel (a form continued by contemporary writers such as William McIlvanney and Ian Rankin)[49] and John Buchan's espionage thrillers (which were to spawn the works of Ian Fleming and Alistair MacLean). With its long tradition of a literate working-class, Scotland's literary tradition fed powerfully into the literature being consumed in Britain and North American by the newly literate lower-class readers, as well as into the films being produced for that mass public. The very success of Scottish writing in this mass market defined Scottish culture as 'populist', as the antithesis of everything demanded by the elitist arts of 'modernism', represented in Scotland itself by Hugh MacDiarmid. That focus, however, obscured the fact that in the last quarter of the nineteenth century – from Alexander Graham Bell's invention of the telephone to Clerk Maxwell's theories of electromagnetism, from MacIntosh's *art mouveau* to J. G. Frazer's *The Golden Bough* – the 'Second Scottish Enlightenment' had provided some of the key elements in the transformation of Western culture which we now identify as 'modernity', and which gave birth to 'modernism' in the arts. By identifying Scotland with its popular literary successes, from J. M. Barrie and Annie S. Swan to A. J. Cronin and Comptom MacKenzie, and ignoring its contributions to the development of modern consciousness through its contributions to such emergent disciplines as psychology and social anthroplogy, Scottish culture as a whole has been represented as retarded and parochial, trapped in the form that Tom Nairn famously described in *The Break-up of Britain* as 'the tartan monster', 'this insanely sturdy sub-culture' (165). Dividing Scotland into its 'insane' subculture and its failed high culture produces exactly the neurotic inability to relate to the national imagination that Gray analyses in Duncan Thaw's self-enclosed and self-destructive imaginative amnesia: recovery from that condition has required not the much-demanded escape from the Scottish past, but a much more complex understanding of the nature of past Scottish culture and its imaginative products.[50]

This then is a study of the Scottish novel in the period described by literary history as that of 'modernism' and 'postmodernism', from the late nineteenth to the late twentieth centuries. It is not a history of the modern Scottish novel: it is an attempt to situate the Scottish novel within an intellectual environment, to define some of the distinctive elements that constitute a tradition, and to define some of the traditions that have gone into the maintenance of a specifically national imagination. I have made no effort to be all-inclusive in terms of the novelists I have used and have concentrated on what might be regarded as 'canonical' texts – partly because they are readily available and partly because I want to focus on the underlying features which constitute the distinctiveness of a Scottish tradition and to do so must revisit a limited number of works in several different chapters. There are writers who get very little attention – like Eric Linklater and James Kennaway – not because they are not important in themselves but because they are not as consistently relevant to my purpose. This book should be regarded as being in the manner of a prologue to another one which will look at the work of a wider range of individual novelists in terms of their particularity, rather than using novelists as examples of underlying thematic or formal issues central to the Scottish tradition.

If there is a stress in my argument on the Calvinist inheritance of Scottish culture, that is not to ignore the significance of other religious and intellectual traditions in Scotland, but rather it is recognition of the powerful role that Calvinism has played in shaping the institutions which have, in many ways, defined and maintained the nation in the absence of a national government. It is also a deliberate challenge to those readings of the nation which have seen in Calvinism nothing but a negation of the imagination and of the creative potentialities of the nation.

Any version of a tradition is, of course, in part a retrospective construction, an organisation of the past from the point of view of the present. But in the terms deriving from MacIntyre's definition of a tradition it is also an embodied argument handed on from the past to the present, an internal dialogue between the values inherent in a set of institutional contexts, the readings they and others generate of the nation's past, and the imaginings, both present and past, of its possible futures. The narrative forms which writers have found to express or dramatise these dialogues become themselves parts of the dialogue with which later writers have to engage. This then is an attempt to define some of the key elements which constitute a specifically Scottish tradition of the novel and some of the ways in which that tradition has imagined the nation which it addresses. It is written in the context of Scotland's newly regained political status and has been shaped by the explosion of creativity that has characterised Scottish culture since the 1970s – an explosion in part stimulated by the political idealisms, both socialist and nationalist, which have resisted the incorporation of Scotland into the prevailing orthodoxies of British politics since the late 1960s. In terms of the novel, no period in Scottish culture has, perhaps, been as rich as the period between the 1960s and 1990s: precisely because of its richness, and because so many of its major writers have been accepted as the voices of an 'international culture', the argument of this book is designed to establish some of the underlying continuities – both in terms of the issues of Scottish society and in terms of the formal development of the novel – that link Alasdair Gray, James Kelman, Janice Galloway, A. L. Kennedy – and even Irvine Welsh – in the 1980s and 1990s to the founding moments of the modern Scottish novel in the work of Stevenson, Brown, Barrie and Buchan a century before. Through works such as theirs Scotland went on imagining itself as a nation and went on constituting itself as a national imagination in defiance of its attempted or apparent incorporation into a unitary British culture, a defiance which has had profound political consequences in the last decade of the twentieth century.

CHAPTER 1

FEARFUL SELVES:

CHARACTER, COMMUNITY,
AND THE SCOTTISH IMAGINATION

At the conclusion of his *Traditions of the Covenanters*, the Rev. Robert Simpson tells how he has tried to authenticate his tales by searching out the 'hiding places of these saintly wanderers of the Covenant among the bushy ravines, and in the deep glens in the bosom of the lonely hills', and how he has 'visited spots where the martyrs fell in the bleak and solitary wilds', and 'contemplated the ruined huts that erst were the abodes of God-fearing families, who bore witness to the truth in those dreary times, when the best blood of land flowed warm on the purple heath'.[1] 'God-fearing': there is no more powerful term of approbation in the language of Scottish presbyterianism; suffering and death are as nothing to maintaining the virtue of being 'God-fearing'; fear inflicted by one's fellow-creature is irrelevant if it asks the believer to forego fear of God. Fear of God is the ground of a human fearlessness that can outface the worst that humanity can do; the fear of God is the ground of a strength that is fearful to the world. Though three hundred years has passed from the shadow of the 'killing time', and the nation has long-since passed from the grip of the religion that it tempered to a necessary severity, the potency of fear remains central to Scottish culture – both the fear-stricken submission to a greater power and the fearful – because fear-inspiring – denial of the ordinary limits of human suffering.

Calvinism was the foundation of the key institutions – religion, education – through which Scottish identity was shaped, and through which it maintained its distinctness during Scotland's participation in the British Empire: whether for or against Calvinism's conception of human destiny, no Scot could avoid involvement in the imaginative world that Calvinism projected. In *The Scottish Novel*, Francis Russell Hart suggested that 'a noteworthy feature of Scottish fiction is the moral primacy of community', and that 'from Galt to Duncan, it is implied that true community matures genuine individuality'.[2] Calvinism, as Hart notes, certainly underwrote that strong sense of a communal commitment, but the notions of community that it bequeathed to the Scottish imagination were less harmonious than Hart suggests: the Scottish community, and the Scottish imagination, was ruled in large measure by fear, and, equally, by a fearlessness which refused to submit to the fears of those who did not dare challenge the powers that ruled their universe. The fierce communal ethic of the repressive forms of Calvinism – forms which have attracted so many strictures and so much satire from Scottish pens – creates its own antagonist in a form which is equally Calvinist, for the only individual capable of surviving a repressive society of this kind is one who accepts a terrible – a fearful – isolation, one who engages in a terrifying extension of the self, an aggrandisement of the ego, until the individual is transformed from a God-fearing into a fear-inspiring creature – a diabolically 'fearful' presence to all who live within the boundaries of our ordinary and fear-haunted society.

The republication in 1947, of James Hogg's *Private Memoirs and Confessions of a Justified Sinner*, with an introduction by André Gide,[3] makes that remarkable work a part, almost, of twentieth-century rather than nineteenth-century Scottish writing; and that Hogg's novel of Calvinist obsession should have become so significant in the second half of the twentieth century suggests the extent to which the issues raised by a Calvinist ethic remain crucial to the Scottish context – and, equally, the ways in which that Scottish experience, despite the regular claims about the 'parochialism' of Scotland's religious past, can reflect upon the terrors of a European century as fearful as any in its history. Hogg's novel dramatises precisely the dialectic of the fearful self: Robert Wringhim, repressed by a terrifying religion of almost inevitable damnation, transforms himself from victim of a fearful God into the fear-inspiring companion of the devil and terroriser of his own family and friends. Robert's sudden translation from certain damnation to unchallengeable justification allows him to transcend the fears by which his early life is claustrophobically imprisoned and to become a creature set apart from ordinary humanity, awe-inspiring in his denial of the limits set for fallen humanity. The real significance of this conflict has, however, often been obscured in readings of the novel that see it simply as a satire upon Calvinist notions of the elect:[4] the power of Hogg's narrative lies not simply in the fact that Robert comes to be more and more under the control of destructive external forces – or of the externalisation of internal forces – in the form of the satanic Gil Martin, but in the ways in which Robert is unable to know how his own beliefs and values will be read by the future, including his own future self. Robert's self looks back fearfully upon the actions which it may itself, in its fearful refusal of ordinary humanity, have committed, as the actions of another: the self is divided between the submissively frightened social creature, desirous of social acceptability, and the terrifying mediator of God's will, capable of committing murder in the belief that it acts on behalf of, and for fulfilment of the Word of, the God of fear.

Wringhim's tale is not simply an account of the false assumption of election: it is realisation that what, at one moment in life, may seem an undeniable truth, justifying a certain course of action, will come in retrospect, to have an entirely different significance, subject to revision both by ourselves and by the processes of history – dramatised in the later and misconstruing narrative of Hogg's 'Editor' – that will make our beliefs incomprehensible to the future. Far from being a rehearsal of contradictions within the inheritance of a Calvinist theology, *The Confessions* spoke out of the particularities of Calvinist experience to all those who, in the world of post-war Europe, discovered that they had spent the decade before the War supporting the unjustifiable monstrosities of political beliefs by which they believed their every action could be justified, no matter how horrific. The anguish of Hogg's tale spoke directly to André Gide, and spoke increasingly powerfully, not only because of his own Calvinist background but because it dramatised what so many who had committed themselves to fascism or to communism in the 1930s had experienced when they saw their beliefs scrutinised in relation to outcomes that they had never personally willed. The power of Hogg's tale is able to connect the foundations of Scottish Calvinism, with its desperate resistance to external repression in the conflicts of the seventeenth century, to those twentieth-century forms of belief in predestined justification that were to wreak havoc across Europe. Calvinism becomes a prescient metaphor for commitment to any absolutism based on the assertion of the individual ego, however rational its apparent justifi- cations: all those modern philosophies and ideologies that claim a special insight into the nature of truth repeat, in secular form, the same traumas that Wringhim suffers – a transcendence of fear achieved by a pact with the devil that will produce an even more fearful outcome.

The continuing centrality of Hogg's novel to late-twentieth century Scottish fiction – it forms the intertextual structure of many recent works, including Muriel Spark's *The Comforters* (1957) and *Symposium* (1990), Emma Tennant's *The Bad Sister* (1978), Frederic Lindsay's *Brond* (1983), Robin Jenkins's *Just Duffy* (1988), William Boyd's *The New Confessions* (1987), Alasdair Gray's *Poor Things* (1992) – is testimony not simply to the ways in which Hogg's novel can be read as prescient of many modern concerns: it is testimony to the enduring legacy of Calvinism itself in the Scottish imagination, and to the fact that even when the Calvinist God is overthrown what is left is a world still in thrall to fear but denied the tradi- tional religious resolutions of that fear. The confrontation between the two poles of fear – the fearful and the fear-inspiring – that Wringhim embodies within one character was to be repeated by Robert Louis Stevenson in that other most influential text of nineteenth-century Scotland, *Dr Jekyll and Mr Hyde*,[5] where 'fear' is the context of Henry Jekyll's experiments with his own nature, both the fear that he inspires in those around him – the servants are 'all afraid' (33) or in 'terror' (32), his friends suffer 'the dead- liest terror' (47) – and the fear which is the outcome of his experiments: 'I have been made to learn that the doom and burthen of our life is bound for ever on man's shoulders; and when the attempt is made to cast it off, it returns upon us with more unfamiliar and more awful pressure' (49).

In the end, Jekyll, become Hyde, will consist of nothing but fear: 'He, I say – I cannot say, I. That child of Hell had nothing human; nothing lived in him but fear and hatred'. Fearful in both senses, Hyde terrorises others – 'the waiter visibly quailed before his eye' – by the very intensity of his own fear, 'he walked fast, hunted by his fears' (59), and will end in 'the most strained and fear-struck ecstasy' (62). *Dr Jekyll and Mr Hyde*, however, was only a mythic instantiation in one personality of a conflict that obsessed Stevenson's imagination. In *The Master of Ballantrae*,[6] the narrator, Mackellar is plagued with 'an extreme of fear' which can become, on occasion, the source of 'a brutal kind of courage' (124), but not the courage for confronting a figure like James, the Master, for 'a man more insusceptible of fear is not conceivable.' (55). At the same time, Mackellar's 'horror of solitude' (104) requires him always to have a companion, even one he is terrified by, so that it is as if his own need calls up James, the very figure before whom he stands fearful. The duel which James and his brother Henry fight is sparked off by Henry's accusation that James is a 'coward' (90), and Mackellar, who acknowledges himself 'a coward' that 'is a slave at the best' (91), must suffer through the fight in a condition in which his head 'was gone with cold and fear and horror' (92). The cowardly Mackellar, however, like Henry, whom he serves, is doomed to suffer the continual return of the very force which terrifies him, the force represented by the figure who has mastered fear and who, capable of living outside the limits of the ordinary human community, takes on in both their eyes a satanic immutability: 'nothing can kill that man. He is not mortal' (116).

The fearful are haunted by the fearless; the fearless drawn inevitably to confront those whose fear is their only justification in the world. It is the conflict at the heart of Stevenson's final, unfinished novel, *Weir of Hermiston*, in which Archie Weir finds himself trapped between the demands of a charitable Christianity, as represented by his mother, and the terrifying power of his father, which seems to derive from some more ancient source than the God of Christianity:

> The character and position of his father had long been a stumbling-block to Archie . . . The man was mostly silent; when he spoke at all, it was to speak of things of the world, always in a worldly spirit, often in language that the child had been schooled to think coarse, and sometimes with words that he knew to be sins in themselves. Tenderness was the first duty, and my lord was inevitably harsh. God was love; the name of my lord was fear. (8)

It is a fear that dominates the lives of mother and child and against which their 'tender' religion is no consolation. Archie's mother dies with fear on her lips:

> "Godsake, what's the maitter wi' ye, mem?" cried the housekeeper, starting from the rug.

"I do not ken," answered her mistress, shaking her head. "But he is not speeritually minded, my dear."

"Here, sit down with ye! Godsake what ails the wife?" cried Kirstie, and helped and forced her into the lord's own chair by the cheek of the hearth.

"Keep me, what's this?" she gasped.

"Kirstie, what's this? I'm frich'ened."

They were her last words. (11)

Her life is lived and ends in fear, a fear which she has bred into her son. Archie's public act of defiance of his father's performance as a judge when he yells out at a hanging that "I denounce this God-defying murder" (21), reveals the extent to which he can challenge the values of his community, 'as if he were marked at birth to be the perpetrator of some signal action' (21) – as if he were cut out to inspire rather than to suffer fear. But 'bred up in unbroken fear himself', he finds that the courage he had briefly been able to raise deserts him: he becomes 'shrinkingly sensitive' under the awareness that 'the providence of God alone might foresee the manner in which it would be resented by Lord Hermiston' (24), as though Hermiston and the deity sit side by side, equals in their implacable judgment of human weaknesses. The fearful judge and the fearful son confront each other in a dialectic from which there is no escape, for the son's more humane values are themselves built upon the very foundations of the father's power, just as the God of love is founded upon the God of fear and of vengeance.

Father and son in *Weir of Hermiston* enact between them not only a version of the relation between Jekyll and Hyde – 'Jekyll has more than a father's interest; Hyde had more than a son's indifference' (55) – but a conflict which was fundamental to Scottish religious and intellectual life in the late nineteenth century, and which was, even as Stevenson was writing, being enacted in the relations between two of the most influential Scots of the time – William Robertson Smith and J. G. Frazer. Frazer was inspired in the explorations of the 'savage' mind that were to be recorded at such length in *The Golden Bough* by the work of Smith, whose *Religion of the Semites* (1889) offered a groundbreaking approach to the understanding of the origins of Christianity.[7] Smith had been expelled from the Free Church of Scotland for his views but remained nonetheless a firm believer both in Christianity and in the Free Church, whereas Frazer, a true follower of David Hume, saw his own work as an implicit undermining of the uniqueness of the Christian message. When Frazer came to summarise the difference between himself and his intellectual 'father' in 1911 it was on the issue of fear that he focused:

. . . it had long seemed to me that Smith, influenced probably by his deeply religious nature, under-estimated the influence of fear, and over-estimated the influence of the benevolent emotions (love, confidence, and gratitude), in moulding early religion. Hence his view of sacrifice as mainly a form of communion with the deity instead of a mode of propitiating him and averting his anger. The latter is the ordinary view of sacrifice, and I believe it on the whole to be substantially correct.[8]

As Robert Ackerman notes, 'Frazer enrolls under the banner of those who regarded ancient and primitive people as motivated primarily by fear of their surroundings, and religion as a response to their fear'.[9] In a reversal of the relationship between Archie Weir and his father, in this case the intellectual 'son' (Frazer) comes to reinscribe the ancient ethic of fear in defiance of the more humane principles of his 'father' (Robertson Smith). Intellectual progress will, in effect, force the recognition of the continuing power of the primitive role of fear in human society against the ameliorating notions of a progressive liberalism. As Robert Ackerman puts it, Frazer's

> assumption throughout is that the vast engine of funereal superstition is pow-
> ered only and entirely by fear of the dead and of ghosts. Nowhere does he
> intimate that the natives might be motivated by affection or reverence for the
> departed or that they might even be indifferent to those gone before . . . the
> question was whether religion was rooted in fear or love of the gods. Frazer,
> that last best son of the Enlightenment, comes down unquestionably on the
> side of fear.[10]

In Frazer, the liberal theology of the nineteenth century that remodelled the God of vengeance into the God of love did not displace the ethic of fear, but simply relocated it as the origin of all religion. Beneath the surface of modern society, the whole history of humanity is the history of its fundamental fearfulness, and its refusal to move beyond the boundaries of that fear-ruled world: 'superstitions survive', Frazer wrote, 'because, while they shock the views of enlightened members of the community, they are still in harmony with the thoughts and feelings of others who, though they are drilled by their betters into an appearance of civilization, remain barbarians and savages at heart'.[11] Fear continues to rule the human imagination and every journey into that imagination is a journey back into the terrors of the primitive past.

It is exactly such a journey which the young John Buchan was to describe in his earliest novel, *John Burnet of Barns* (1898),[12] written only a few years after the first publication of *The Golden Bough*. *John Burnet of Barns* is set in the turbulence of the religious civil wars of the seventeenth century but it is a 'romance' rather than a historical novel, full of dream-like sequences in which the hero, Burnet, has again and again to overcome his own fearfulness – 'My first thought . . . when I felt my steel meet the steel of my foes, was one of arrant and tumultuous fear' (122) – in order to save his lover from the threat of his cousin Gilbert, a fear-inspiring döppelganger: 'I feared my cousin as I feared no other on earth' (161). In a world terrorised by government forces, Burnet joins with outlaw gypsies who, in order to revenge themselves on the people of Biggar for an insult to one of their people, construct a fantastic assault upon the town dressed in strange crimson clothes:

> The three of us dressed in the crimson suits, and monstrously fine we looked . . . We trotted out over the green borders of the bog to the town, where the riot and hilarity were audible. The sight of the three to any chance spectator must have been fearsome beyond the common. William Baillie, not to speak of his great height and strange dress, had long black hair which hung far below his shoulders, and his scarlet hat and plume made him look like the devil in person . . . And yet we touched no one, but kept on our way to the foot of the street, with our drawn swords held stark upright in our hands. Then we turned and came back; and lo! the great fair was empty, and wild, fearful faces looked at us from window and lane. (244–5)

The outlaws, supposedly fearful of organised society, become the inspirers of fear and, in a diabolic reversal that calls the primitive back into the midst of civlisation, force the god-fearing into fearing them. The scene is like the enactment of some ancient ritual, like the eruption into the ordinary world of one of the myths in *The Golden Bough*. Behind the fear-demanding world of Calvinism lies the primal world of fear, the world of totems and taboos described by Frazer.

Buchan's novel is a series of journeys which take the hero from the civilized world of rational philosophy (he is a student of Plato and a follower of Descartes), through the political and religious conflicts of the seventeenth century, into a world of surreal power whose sources are in the unconscious, in the 'heathen Egypt' to which the gypsies are still connected (246). That journey through the layers of civilisation to an ultimate fear parallels the narrative of Frazer's account, which seeks the sources of primitive fear in order to lay them to rest, but succeeds only in revitalising them in the imaginations of his contemporaries and revealing that the very science he uses to analyse them is itself subject to a similar terror:

> Brighter stars will rise on some voyager of the future – some great Ulysses of the realms of thought – than shine on us. The dreams of magic may one day be the waking realities of science. But a dark shadow lies athwart the far end of this fair prospect. For however vast the increase of knowledge and of power which the future may have in store for man, he can scarcely hope to stay the sweep of those great forces which seem to be making silently but relentlessly for the destruction of all this starry universe in which our earth swims as a speck or mote. In the ages to come man may be able to predict, perhaps even to control, the wayward courses of the winds and clouds, but hardly will his puny hands have strength to speed afresh our slackening planet in its orbit or rekindle the dying fire of the sun.[13]

The fearful impotence which was the very origin of science in magic returns as its outcome: science's power to ward off the terrors of the universe ends up being less effective than the power of the religion which it has super-seded. The God of fear has been displaced only for a universal terror for which their is no assuage.

The same reversal of history was to be enacted in Buchan's later his-torical novel set in the same epoch, *Witch Wood*.[14] The plot involves the conflict between a minister, David Semple, who is surrounded by a terri-fied community and stalked by primitive fear – 'that he, a grown man and a minister of God, should be in such a pit of terror' (83) – and one of the elders of his Church, Chasehope, a 'fearless' justified sinner. Their conflict is symbolic of the debate between theologies in seventeenth-century Scot-land; Chasehope, however, not only represents the antinomian version of Calvinism but does so because he is also a reiteration of ancient, primitive fears, fears celebrated in rituals in the woods around the town: 'It is the Wood, and the blackest kind of witchcraft. Some old devilry of the heathen has lingered in that place, and the soul of my miserable parish is thirled to it' (113). In those woods David discovers fear – 'Terror entered into David's soul, and his chief terror was that he had not been afraid before' (128) – and discovers also the re-enactment of the fear-stricken religions of the past: 'The hound-faced leader stood above them with something in his hand. The mysterious light seemed to burn redly, and he saw that the thing was a bird — a cock which was as scarlet as blood. The altar top was bare, and something bright spurted into the hollow of the stone. From the watchers came a cry which chilled David's marrow and he saw that they were on their knees' (128). Modern fear is revealed simply as the mask of some more ancient terror, and as context for the re-enactment of ancient forms of propitiation of a terrifying universe: 'He looked at her as she lay, mindless, racked, dying perhaps, and an awful conviction entered his mind. She was a human sacrifice made by the Coven to their master' (210).

Buchan's role as one of inventors of the 'thriller' genre is perhaps the result of the fear which is fundamental to his perception of the world, with his fearless heroes in continual flight across a world riddled with fear.[15] But it is Frazer's terror of a displacement of the God of fear that will leave humanity staring only at a more fearful kind of universe that most haunts Buchan's imagination. In *The Gap in the Curtain* (1932),[16] Sir Edward Leithen, protagonist of many of Buchan's novels that straddle the popular and the serious, is participant in a mind experiment conducted by Professor Moe, who claims to be able (in the fashion of T. W. Dunne's popular *An Experiment with Time*)[17] to draw 'aside the curtain' to the future. Moe 'had a lot to say about the old astrologers and magic-makers who worked with physical charms and geometrical figures, and he was clear that they had had a knowledge of mysteries on which the door had long been locked' (37–38). The effect of such knowledge turns out to be destructive, and particularly so for Leithen's acquaintance Robert Goodeve, in whose house Leithen sees a painting which summarises Goodeve's own perception of the world:

On the floor some ten couples were dancing, an ordered dance in which there was no gaiety, and the dancers' faces were all set and white. Other people were sitting round the walls, rigidly composed as if they were curbing some strong passion. At the great doors at the far end men at arms stood on guard, so that none should pass. On every face, in every movement was fear – fear, and an awful expectation of something which was outside in the night. You felt that at any moment the composure might crack, that the faces would become contorted with terror and the air filled with shrieks.

The picture was lettered "La Peste", but I did not need the words to tell me the subject . . .

"My God, what a thing!" I said. "The man who painted that was a devil!"

"He understood the meaning of fear," was the answer. (159–60)

The experiment with the future, like the occult knowledge of the past, is simply a gateway to the primal emotion underlying human life, that which existed before the 'eve' of 'good' and will return again after 'good' reaches its 'eve'. Goodeve himself will die not from the recorded physical cause of his death – 'heart failure' – but from a more primitive cause – 'the slow relentless sapping of fear' (187) that his vision of the future had given him.

The same fear is what has maddened the French-Canadian whom Leithen is in search of in Buchan's final, posthumously published novel, *Sick Heart River* (1941):

Galliard was speaking again. It was a torrent of *habitant* French and his voice rose to a pitch which was almost a scream. The man was under such terror and he held out imploring hands which Johnny grasped. The latter could follow the babble better than Leithen, but there was no need of an interpreter, for the pain and fear in the voice told their own tale. Then the fit passed, the eyes closed, and Galliard seemed to be asleep again.

Johnny shook his head. "Haywire," he said. "Daft – and I reckon I know the kind of daftness. He's mortal scared of them woods." (142)

Galliard has 'gone back into a very old world, the world of his childhood and his ancestors, and though it might terrify him, it was for the moment his only world' (146); he is 'suffering from an ancient fear and there could be no escape except by facing that fear and beating it' (258).[18] Leithen, himself dying, has to travel into that world of fear in order to master it, a journey which will take him to 'a part of the globe which had no care for human life, which was not built to man's scale, a remnant of that Ice Age which long ago had withered the earth' (241). Just as Frazer had concluded by fearfully imagining a future universe to which human life and its hard-won knowledge may be irrelevant, so Leithen journeys to the North as the image on earth of the vast impersonality of the universe:

The universe seemed to spread itself before him in immense distances lit and dominated by a divine spark which was man. An inconsiderable planet, a speck in the infinite stellar spaces; most of it salt water; the bulk of the land rock and desert and austral and boreal ice; interspersed mud, the detritus of aeons, with a thin coverlet of grass and trees – that vegetable world on which every living thing was in the last resort a parasite. Man, precariously perched on this rotating scrap-heap, yet so much master of it that he would mould it to his transient uses, and, while struggling to live, could entertain thoughts and dreams beyond the bounds of time and space. (294–5)

Leithen journeys back to that which is the ultimate denial of human life, a place where 'the hand of God had blotted out life for millions of miles and made a great tract of the inconsiderable ball which was the earth, like the infinite interstellar spaces which had never heard of man' (174). That landscape is a version of the personal extinction that he is facing, a place where 'There was no space for lesser fears when the most ancient terror was close to him, no room for other mysteries when he was nearing the ultimate one' (242). Leithen's salvation will lie in achieving the fearlessness of 'a man who had succeeded in putting all fear behind him' (311). It might be seen as a recovery of precisely the Free Church theology in which the young Buchan, like Frazer himself, had grown up and which was bent upon translating the fearful God of an older calvinism into the God of love by casting out fear: 'Brought up under the Calvinistic shadow, he had accepted a simple evangel which, as he grew older, had mellowed and broadened' (172). But those who achieve fearlessness do so only by journeying into the ultimate fears: there is no other way through. Though *Sick Heart River* allows Galliard to return to ordinary life carrying Leithen's lesson with him, it is clear that the world of fear is never defeated: it is the one enduring reality of human life.

Its insistence can be seen in the fact that it continues to haunt the late twentieth-century Scottish imagination with the same chthonic power: in A. L. Kennedy's novel of 1993, *Looking for the Possible Dance*,[19] a character whose name, we discover later, is Webster (weaver, in this case, of plots) announces to the protagonist, Margaret, in a dentist's surgery, that 'You have to control your own life' even if, 'for example, I kill someone' (47). He then confirms that he has killed someone but that, 'the fact of the killing can't be denied. I mean the moral fact. Whoever is punished, for whatever reasons, by whatever powers, I myself must be punished because I am a murderer.' Knowing the fact of his own guilt but refusing to submit to any outside authority, Webster declares himself the only person justified in judging and passing sentence on his own crime:

'I consider the true nature of my crime. The degree of pain and pleasure I created. My pleasure, his pain, although that need not always be the case. I note the current opinions on crime and punishment, the expressions of public disgust and I decide upon a sentence of eight years. Without remission, effective from the date of malefaction.

'Hard to do. Hard to arrange. I can't lock myself up. I must earn a living, eat, conduct my affairs, but somehow, I must also be imprisoned. It takes thought, but is quite simple in the end.

'I remove my pleasure. Fearless and thorough, I take it all away.' (48)

'Fearless' in his self-condemnation he is fear-inspiring in his denial of society's values: his completion of his self-imposed sentence allows him to experience an absolute freedom that goes beyond the ordinary freedoms of human life: 'I passed beyond my release, everything changed. I was free. Free in capital letters. Effaredoubleee. FREE. Nobody will ever understand that'. It is a freedom that is terrifying to possessor and to the people whom he threatens by it: 'I sat on one of the benches and I cried. Because of the joy. And the fear, too; at first it can scare you, to know how alive you are' (49). The fearful freedom of Webster's self-control is the foundation of the fear that he spreads through the community; the fear that he is generating in Margaret in this scene in the quiet of a dentist's waiting room; the fear with which he will later terrorise Margaret's boyfriend Colin:

You are an example, Colin. People will hear about you and will not admire what you did. They will not wish to repeat it. This is our own small Terror, Colin. You can gather it every day from everywhere; post offices and court rooms, your evening paper, your evening streets. We just make our own use of it. This is the way we live, do you see; we cannot exist outside society and so we do our best to use it. To offer it reflections of itself. (230)

Webster is both modern criminal and the medium of Frazer's mythic fear: his method of controlling his world is to submit Colin to a primitive ritual of sacrifice, a crucifixion whose meaning is not the announcement of the arrival of the God of love but the permanency of the primitive terror which humanity must repeatedly endure: 'Colin was frightening for Margaret when she took delivery of him' (240). For Colin the fear will be endless: nailed to the floor he 'was aware, sometimes, of being alone and afraid of rats. He had a great fear of turning in his sleep' (232). That fear will not dissipate but will be etched forever into his consciousness like the recollections etched in the consciousness of all humanity in Frazer's anthropological studies:

. . . Colin was still listening to Webster, playing him over and over again inside his head.

'Do every tiny thing you want to do.'

Those words.

'We might have to do it all again: waste everyone's time. Be alive, Colin, don't forget.' (233)

Fear is the unforgettable ground behind the crucifixion, the inescapable reality upon which the illusions of freedom and choice and redemption are founded.

II

The Scottish imagination's return to a pre-Christian world, dominated by fear, is underlined by the structure of the novel which, because of its date of publication – 1901 – and its self-conscious challenge to the traditions of Kailyard writing, is often taken to be the foundation of modern Scottish fiction, George Douglas Brown's *The House with the Green Shutters*.[20] In Douglas Brown's novel, fearful selves enact a precise imitation of a Greek tragedy, not as the imagination's acknowledgement of the highest forms of classical literature but in acknowledgement that we have been returned to a world to which the Christian message has proved irrelevant and which is ruled by a far more primitive and vengeful ethic. Douglas Brown's world of small-town Scotland is dominated by the word 'fear', a fear from which only the protagonist, Gourlay, is immune:

> 'Ye mind what an awful day it was; the thunder roared as if the heavens were tumbling on the world, and the lichtnin' sent the trees daudin' on the roads, and folk hid below their beds and prayed – they thocht it was the Judgment! But Gourlay rammed his black stepper in the shafts and drave like the devil o' hell to Skeighan Drone, where there was a young doctor. The lad was feared to come, but Gourlay swore by God that he should, and he garred him . . . I saw them gallop up Main Street; lichtnin' struck the ground before them; the young doctor covered his face wi' his hands, and the horse nichered wi' fear . . .' Coe had told his story with an enjoying gusto, and had told it well – for Johnny, though constantly snubbed by his fellows, was in many ways the ablest of them all . . . They knew, besides, he was telling what himself had seen. For they knew he was lying prostrate with fear in the open smiddyshed. (42)

The fear in which the community lies prostrate before a hostile environment is not an isolated moment in its existence but the very essence of the whole pattern of its life. Gourlay's fearlessness is not only a challenge to the elements, but to the community, for it generates an awe-inspiring 'fearfulness' in him that makes him, in their eyes, like a force of nature rather than a member of their human world. In a society where women – except for Gourlay's wife – are the dominant figures in the households, the men – the 'bodies' – who gather at the village cross are cast down by the vision of Gourlay that Coe has presented: 'They were silent for a while, impressed, in spite of themselves, by the vivid presentment of Gourlay's manhood on the day that had scared them all' (42). 'Manhood' is an elemental force which they have denied in themselves: its existence within the community is a defiance of their communal values, their shared participation in self-denigration and self-denial.

The morality by which the community operates is a morality of mutual fear and mistrust – 'When the Deacon was not afraid of a man he stabbed him straight. When he was afraid of him he stabbed him on the sly' (9) – which holds them together only by reinforcing how much more fearful is the world outside of their little enclave. Gourlay's only positive quality is to appear to the 'bodies' to act without fear. Douglas Brown is careful to endow his tragic hero with no redeeming characteristics: he is neither wise nor moral nor generous nor forgiving; he is not a good husband or father – he is not even, except by accident, a good businessman. But in the context of the destructive fearfulness that rules the town of Barbie his fearlessness comes to seem like a challenge to the very nature of the universe – as Gourlay suggests in describing himself to his son: '"The world was feared, but he wasnae feared," he roared in Titanic pride, "he wasnae feared; no, by God, for he never met what scared him"' (215). Such self-assertion is based on no moral foundation: it is nothing but an inflation of the ego till it refuses to recognise human boundaries. And yet, precisely because it has no values to assert, that ego needs the fearful in order to know itself. It is tied to the community of the scared because it is only in their cowering subjection that it can know its own superiority. It cannot escape the community whose ethic it seems to challenge because only in the fear in others' eyes, in its awareness of their awe-struck deference or their servility, can it prove its own overwhelming power:

> 'What are 'ee laughing at?' he said, with a mastering quietness . . . He was crouching for the grip, his hands out like a gorilla's. The quiet voice, from the yawing mouth, beneath the steady flaming eyes, was deadly. There was something inhuman in a rage so still.
> 'Eh?' he said slowly, and the moan seemed to come from the midst of a vast intensity rather than a human being. It was a question that must grind an answer. Wilson was wishing to all his gods that he had not insulted this awful man. (202)

But though power seems to lie with the 'awful' Gourlay, he has set himself outside the values of his community and the community will take its revenge. The fearful whom he despises will patiently work for his downfall, using his own need to stay above and beyond them, using his secret fear of falling back among them as the lever with which to destroy him. His downfall is inevitable because his separation from them conceals his inner dependence on them: the more they reject him, the more is his superiority confirmed, but the more he needs to return to them in order to have it validated.

That bond of denial and dependence is personalised within his own house through his relationship with his son. Living in Gourlay's shadow, cringing from his elemental presence, young John – like Archie in *Weir of Hermiston* – has developed a habitual and fearful recoil from the world around him:

> 'Tuts, man, dinna be afraid,' [the baker] said, 'You're John Gourlay's son, ye know. You ought to be a hardy man.'
> 'Aye, but I'm no,' chattered John, the truth coming out in his fear. 'I just let on to be . . . I'm no feared of folk,' he went on with a faint return to his swagger. 'But things get in on me. A body seems wee compared with that – ' he nodded to the warring heavens. (113–14)

His father's lack of imagination and of sensitivity – when we first meet him he is 'dead to the fairness of the scene' on a bright summer morning (2) – makes him fearless; John's sensitivity projects outward upon the world a fearfulness that is as extreme in relation to the community's normal code of fear as is the awe-inspiring self-containment of his father. It is from the incompatible extremes of these two responses that the tragedy of the Gourlay family is constructed. Young John's brief and tantalising success at the university, which will make his later failure all the more galling in his father's eyes, is achieved when he is given the opportunity to express that pent-up fearfulness in an essay. His professor's summary of the human condition is his starting point:

> 'The mind, indeed, in its first blank outlook on life is terrified by the demonic force of nature and the swarming misery of man; by the vast totality of things, the cold remoteness of the starry heavens and the threat of the devouring seas. It is puny in their midst.'
> Gourlay woke up, and sweat broke out on him. Great Heaven, had Tam been through it, too! 'At that stage,' quoth the wise man, 'the mind is dispersed in a thousand perceptions and a thousand fears; there is no central greatness in the soul. It is assailed by terrors which men sunk in the material never seem to feel . . . ' (145)

Transformed in a mind which, as his village dominie put it, suffered from 'a sensory perceptiveness in gross excess of his intellectuality' (126), those thousand fears become a vision of a world, like the world Leithen journeys to in *Sick Heart River*, where,

> ice groaned round him in the night; bergs ground on each other and were rent in pain; he heard the splash of great fragments tumbled in the deep, and felt the wave of their distant falling lift the vessel beneath him in the darkness . . . An unknown sea beat upon an unknown shore, and the ship drifted on the pathless waters, a white dead man at the helm. (148)

That image reflects the nature of young Gourlay's mind and reveals his utter isolation from the human community and the desolate inhumanity of the world he has to confront. There is nothing there to give him courage to face the barbs of his community when he returns as a failure; when drink fails to maintain his swaggering pose, and taunted by his father for making him a mockery in the eyes of the fearful, John discovers a 'sudden firmness in his voice. There was no fear in it, no quivering. He was beyond caring what happened to the world or to him' (226). Beyond fear, young Gourlay's act of parricide is not a release from the terrifying presence of his father; rather it strips his personality down to its essential core:

'Mother,' he panted, 'there's something in my room.'
'What is it, John?' said his mother in surprise and fear.
'I thocht it was himsell! Oh mother, I'm feared, I'm feared! Oh mother, I'm feared.' He sang the words in a hysterical chant. (229)

The death of the Gourlays, father and son, is the expulsion from the community of the timid of those who have dared – the one by virtue of his elemental strength and fearlessness, the other by the 'brutal kind of courage' which, like Mackellar's in *The Master of Ballantrae*, comes in the 'extreme of fear' – to challenge its timid ethic. But those deaths only confirm the opposition in which the community has been caught, for when the news is broken to the 'bodies' that 'they have a' killed themselves', 'their loins were loosed beneath them . . . they gazed with blanched faces at the House with the Green Shutters, sitting dark there and terrible, beneath the radiant arch of the dawn' (252). Even in death, the house of Gourlay keeps its fearful dominance over the chorus of the fearing and allows no exit from a dialectic in which the fearful and fearless continually define and destroy each other.

In the modern Scottish novel, fearful selves proliferate, whether in the form of the absolute coward – like the eponymous hero of Eric Linklater's *Private Angelo* (1947), who becomes the moral centre from which to judge a terrifyingly absurd war – or the extravagant and terrifying egotist – like the hero of James Kennaway's *Tunes of Glory* (1956), who attempts to impose a fear-inspiring superiority on the world around him. The dialectic is imaged in a moment from Alasdair Gray's *Lanark*[21] when the young Thaw, 'confident and resolute, for he had been reading a book called *The Young Naturalist*' goes exploring rock pools by the seaside. He discovers a tendency in the winkles he is examining 'for the pale ones to be at the edges of the pool and the dark ones in the middle' and writes in his notebook, in code 'for he wished to hide his discoveries',

SELKNIW ELPRUP NI ECIDRAWOC (137)

'Cowardice in purple winkles' projects Thaw's own characteristics upon the world he is exploring and prefigures his own death by drowning as he tries to escape a world ruled by a fearful God whom he believes in only 'from my cowardice, not from your glory' (298). Thaw oscillates between stricken fear – whose physical consequences are his bodily illnesses and asthma attacks – and the desire to achieve a God-like perspective in which he is released from all human commitments and fears: as a child he 'wanted to seem mysterious to these boys, someone ageless with strange powers' (132); he is inspired to write by the godlike perspective it gives him, like history as presented in Hardy's *Dynasts* with its 'views of Europe down through the clouds, looking like a sick man with the Alps for his backbone' (153). The relationship is pointed up in his first major painting of the gates of the Monkland canal, which starts with a canvas of 'Sunday afternoon activity: children fishing for minnows with jam-jars, a woman clipping a hedge' but which he turns into an apocalypse with crowds who cannot escape: 'they fled along towpaths, over bridges, and collected on heights, yet there was no brutality in their fearful rush' (279). The artist who achieves a God-like fearlessness is bound to the creation a people who suffer the very fearfulness from which he has released himself.

This mutual dependence of the fearful and fearless is the recurring moral problem posed by the modern Scottish novel, and their mutual destruc-tion gestures both to those primitive fears that Frazer saw as everywhere underlying the thin crust of civilization and to the antagonistic internal divisions within the Scottish Church, resulting from the Disruption of 1843, when a large portion of the ministers of the Established Church had left to form the Free Church of Scotland in support of what they regarded as the authentic traditional values of the national church. Whether those who had broken from the established national church to form the Free Church were fearful defenders of the truth or fearless hypocrites is a con-flict that Robin Jenkins was to dramatise in his novel *The Awakening of George Darroch* (1985):[22] Darroch is fearful – 'He was considered timorous, by his sons, by his brother-in-law, by his brother Henry the sea-captain, by most men in his congregation' (9) – and fearless, combined in a single personality. His example, as he walks from the Church in the moment of the Disruption, 'gave courage to his colleagues' (265). He is presented by Jenkins as both ruthless self-seeker and submissive self-denier, exemplary Christian and bourgeois hypocrite. Rather than the fearless conviction of a supporter of the true faith what his son sees in him is a man who, 'given the best opportunity of his life to show off . . . had not been able to resist it. For the sake of a minute's vanity he had sentenced his family to years of hardship' (266).

The intellectual and social energy of the Disruption produced in the children of Free Church parents, and particularly in the children of Free Church ministers, an intense, if secularised, evangelicism and an equally intense resistance to traditional God-fearing calvinism. It is no accident that so many of the major figures of Scottish literature in the late nineteenth and early twentieth centuries were the children of first generation members of the Free Church. They lived in a world defined by fundamental spiritual choices, choices in continual renewal and debate because of the gradual wooing of the Free Church back in to the Established Church. That it was John Buchan, son of a free Church manse and author of a pamphlet on the significance of the reunification of the two churches in 1929, who was the Queen's representative at the General Assembly in 1933 is symptomatic of the role played in Scottish intellectual life in this period by the children of those who first established the Free Church. And that his mother regarded this as the crowning moment of her son's career testifies to the significance both of the division, and the desire for reunification, which dominated Scottish presbyterianism at that time.[23]

If the Free Church was founded as an act of fearless challenge to existing society, it was also a step into a fearful future guided by a return to a fearful God who continued to brood over the Scottish imagination and accorded fearlessness only to those who were elected to His grace. In Willa Muir's *Imagined Corners* (1935),[24] for instance, one of the central characters is William Murray, minister of the burgh of Calderwick, who believes that 'absolute forgiveness was merely a second-best, a concession to ordinary flesh and blood which was too imperfect to enter at once into the full peace of God' (16), the latter being a condition of 'fearless trust in the love of God, a fearless acceptance of the universe, acceptance without criticism, without fear of criticism'. William believes his purpose in life is 'to cast out people's fear of each other, as a step on the way to boundless trust in God' (17). William's facile fearlessness is, however, balanced by the condition of his younger brother, Ned, who suffers from an excessive sensitivity that means 'he filled the world with the shapes of his fear . . . His fears were so monstrous that mere persuasion could not dispel them' (17); William believes Ned to suffer from 'a fear of the evil in the human heart' (205). Fearless and fearful brothers, William and Ned are bound together, the pivot of the novel's plot and opposite ends of the spectrum of the debate between those in the Scottish church who believed in the necessity of original sin and damnation and those who sought to present God as benign and tolerant of humanity: Ned, who is 'twisted with fear' (140) 'saw nothing but evil around him' while William 'had seen nothing but good' (141). As a student, Ned had been so fear-stricken as to attract victimisation from those around him: 'He scuttled round corners . . . And so they ragged him. He had a chest of drawers and a table piled against his door; he was as frightened as that . . . And they pulled him out. He screamed until they had to gag him . . . They shaved half his head and nearly drowned him in a fountain . . .' (192). The ring-leader of this savage ritual, however, is Hector Shand – later husband of Elizabeth, the central figure of the novel – and a man who 'had no consequences of fear: whatever he said or did would be wiped out by the simple act of departure' (164). Elizabeth, on the other hand, after her marriage undergoes the 'anguished feeling that she was lost and no longer knew who she was', a condition that leaves 'the world stretched out on all sides into dark impersonal nothingness' in which she herself 'was a terrifying anonymity'. The dissolution of her own identity forces her into a resistance to him that leaves her 'terrified at herself', 'she felt such a cold ferocity in herself that she was frightened' (94).

The characters are trapped in mutually destructive patterns of fear and fearlessness until their relationships are disrupted by the return of Hector's elder sister, Elise, who has been living abroad after escaping from Calderwick as a young woman – 'She had been running away from things all her life' (235) – an escape she now sees not as courageous but as fearful, and as determining her later life as a series of evasions because 'she had feared for what she called her independence' (235). Returning as a widow she experiences an 'aversion from her past cowardice' (235). There can, however, be no resolution of these conflicts within Calderwick: William drowns – literally – as a consequence of being unable to resolve how he could 'know if it were God or the devil that prompted him' (271); Hector flees his responsibilities with a common woman from the town; Ned is locked in an asylum and Elizabeth and Elise escape together back to Europe. For Willa Muir, as for many Scottish novelists, the conflict of the fearful and the fearless is unresolvable in the social – and male-dominated – world of Scotland.

A world defined between the poles of the fearful and the fearless can have no narrative outcome except mutual destruction or flight from Scotland: the fearful will always call into being the fearless which terrifies them; the fearless will impose fear as the only justification of their power. In Gordon Williams's *From Scenes Like These* (1968),[25] for instance, the hero turns his back on the usual Scottish road out of the working classes – education – because of his fear that it will isolate him from the community in which he grew up; that choice, however, is one which, for Dunky Logan, involves a deliberate self-violation, a reduction of all his potentialities to the fearlessness of a debased version of Gourlay's 'manhood':

> They made a song and dance about sending you to school and then they laughed their heads off because you learned words like appertaining! His mother should think of that next time she complained about him working at the farm. They wanted you to be as thick and dim as they were, so he'd show them he could win the Scottish cup for ignorance. He'd grow up into a real moronic working-man and balls to them. What did Uncle Charlie know about anything, a bloody clerk, that's all he was. (222)

In Logan, Gourlay's strength declines from an elemental source of selfhood into the lowest form in which it can prove itself to be without fear – a sheer physical brutality that knows its own value only through its ability to threaten others, to spread the fear that it thereby reveals itself to have transcended. The persistence of this self-mutilating ethic can be seen in its centrality to some of the most successful and some of the most innovative writing of the

1980s and 1990s. It underlies, for instance, the narrative of Irvine Welsh's *Trainspotting* (1993)[26] in which the protagonist, Renton, inhabits a world which is defined not simply by the effects of drug-dependence, but by the dependence of the fearful and the fearless.

> *Myth: Begbie's mates like him.*
> *Reality: They fear him.*
> *Myth: Begbie would never waste any ay his mates.*
> *Reality: His mates are generally too cagey tae test oot this proposition . . .*
> *Myth: Begbie backs up his mates.*
> *Reality: Begbie smashes fuck oot ay innocent wee daft cunts whae accidentally spill your pint or bump intae ye. Psychopaths who terrorise Begbie's mates usually dae so wi impunity, as they tend tae be closer mates ay Begbie's than the punters he hings aboot wi. (82–3)*

Fearful and fearless are tied together in a fatality from which there is no escape: Begbie thrives on a sense of injustice that is entirely fictional, but which provides 'him with the spurious moral ammunition he needed tae justify one ay his periodic drink and angst fuelled wars against the local populace' (82). Renton, the failed intellectual who is able to expatiate on Kierkegaardian notions of freedom in court – 'when such societal wisdom is negated, the basis for social control over the individual becomes weakened' (166) – but is fearful of law-abiding conformists – 'Such people really scared the fuck out of Renton. They looked to him as if they hadn't done anything illegal in their lives' (149) – is incapable of any freedom in his relation with Begbie, the terrorising 'hard man' of their group:

> Tae get ma attention, Begbie smashes an elbow into ma ribs with such ferocity that it would be construed as an assault, were it not between two companions. He then starts telling us about some gratuitously violent video he's been watching. Beggar insists on acting the whole fuckin thing oot, demonstrating karate blows, throttlings, stabbings, etc., on me. (77)

Renton has been tied to Begbie since childhood, as mutually dependent as a drug addict and his pusher: 'Begbie is like junk, a habit. Ma first day at primary school, the teacher sais tae us: – You will sit beside Francis Begbie' (83). Even when Renton goes to university he 'half expected tae see Beggars at the freshers ball, beating tae a pulp some four-eyed, middle-class wanker he imagined wis starin at um' (83–4). In the end, Renton's escape from Edinburgh's drugs scene is entirely posited on both his and others' fear of Begbie:

> Ironically, it was Begbie who was the key. Ripping off your mates was the highest offence in his book, and he would demand the severest penalty. Renton had used Begbie, used him to burn his boats completely and utterly. It was

Begbie who ensured that he could never return. He had done what he wanted
to do. He could now never go back to Leith, to Edinburgh, even to Scotland,
ever again. There, he could not be anything other than he was. Now, free
from them all, for good, he could be anything he wanted to be. (344)

Renton's freedom, however, is based on leaving the dialectic of the fearful and the fearless in place in Scotland; his freedom is founded on the
very fact that that dialectic will continue; fear, both others' and his own,
underwrites his freedom, remains its very foundation. Renton has escaped
the mutually destructive embrace of the fearful and the fearless only by
ensuring its continued existence in the place to which he can never return.
In that socially mutilating personal freedom, Welsh constructs a narrative
which is not simply a response to the problems of the 'chemical generation'
but is the recapitulation of the confrontations of the fearful that have been
a defining characteristic of the modern Scottish imagination.

The most insistent analysis of a world trapped between the fearful and
the fearless can be found in the novels of Robin Jenkins. Jenkins's plots
revolve around characters driven by a desperate desire for absolute values
on which to base ther moral decisions, but whose search for certainty is
continuously undermined by the fearful egotism to which such absolutes
necessarily commit anyone who aspires to them. Jenkins's characters – like
the minister in *A Love of Innocence* (1963)[27] who was 'confident of undoing
what this bearded, fierce-eyed predecessor had so capably done; which was
to stiffen and darken the islanders' respect for God with fear' (195) – overthrow fear only to enter into a fearlessness that is terrifying to others and, in
the end, to themselves, since it turns them from believers in absolute virtue
into absolute egotists, fulfilling the egoistic desires of the self in the pretence
of submitting to a higher set of values. In *A Very Scotch Affair* (1968),[28]
for instance, Mungo Niven dares to walk out on his wife and family and
their squalid life in a Glasgow tenement; he dares to set himself free of
the what he sees as an ugly, limited life to which the inhabitants of the
'ghetto' have become so accustomed as to make its acceptance their primary
moral imperative. The dual perspective of the fearless and the fearful is
encapsulated in the book's opening exchanges:

> "I'll never believe you cheated, Mungo." Again he did not notice the
> irony . . . He was too intent on staring back at the lonely anxious child he
> had been.
> "Not often. Not as often as the others. I was too scared."
> "Scared? Never. Too honourable, you mean."
> He nodded: yes, he had always been too honourable to cheat, bully, lie,
> deceive . . . Bess's friend regarded him as a monster of selfishness. (9)

The 'honourable' morality is based either on fear or on an independence of
the community that is monstrous in the eyes of others. Thus in *A Would-*

be Saint (1978),[29] Gavin Hamilton becomes a conscientious objector during the Second World War, and by that decision discovers that 'He was set apart, like a leper in the Middle Ages. His isolation was not physical but moral. He could touch them, even shake hands with them, but he could not share in their joy at victory or their sorrow at defeat' (118). Set apart by his commitment to values which allow for no negotiation with ordinary life – 'I would like to be in a position where I would be able to say that whatever evil things are done in this war I am not responsible' (145) – Hamilton believes himself to stand above the conflicts in which the rest of humanity is trapped, and in that pride he becomes 'a monster of spiritual arrogance whose contempt would be preferable to his pity' (194). Jenkins's ambiguous protagonists who challenge the timid ethics of their community become monstrous, 'monsters of egoism' both in their own and others' eyes.

The ambiguities of Gavin Hamilton's pacifism is reversed in Jenkins's *Just Duffy* (1988),[30] in which Duffy believes he is able to set aside his own absolute standards, including his commitments against violence, precisely because they are not accepted by his community: if the community condones violence, then it will accept his acts of violence even though they violate his own high-minded principles: 'Governed by his own standards he could not kill anyone; but those standards would be dismissed by most people as too extreme and idealistic. He was entitled to judge himself by the standards of civilised society' (150). Duffy, having justified himself in committing murder, discovers himself split between his absolute and his contingent identities, between the fearful and the fearless selves which now inhabit him:

> Duffy watched with horror all this being done. He knew intimately this cool, active, thorough, and resolute person in the black jerkin spotted with blood, but seemed to have no influence over him.
> Together they ran home, Duffy panting and fearful, the other alert and silent. (156)

Duffy, waiting for the police to close in on him, experiences a terrifying sense of repetition as he '. . . imagined the scene in Florence nearly five hundred years ago when Savonarola, who had wanted to make people better than they wanted to be, had been burnt at the stake, having first been strangled as an act of mercy. Duffy felt the tightness at his own throat, smelled smoke, and heard exultant cries' (243). The fearless imagination operates only by returning insistently to the site of its own fearful destruction.

The intense, inescapable structure of the conflict of the fearful and the fearless in the Scottish novel negates any notion of progressive history: humanity lives under the curse of the unending repetition of the same inescapable dialectic. If *The House with the Green Shutters* is the foundation of the modern Scottish novel it is perhaps so because in its form, by its use of Greek tragedy in an alien context, it gestures to the inevitable reiterations that govern human exprience. So powerful was this model that Brown's novel was itself to be imitated in its turn by MacDougall Hay's *Gillespie*[31] in 1914 and by A. J. Cronin's *Hatter's Castle*[32] in 1931, as though repetition was indeed the inescapable burden of the Scottish condition.

III

The House with the Green Shutters was written in defiance of the sentimentality of the Kailyard, but an ethics of fear shapes Kailyard no less than anti-Kailyard writing. J. M. Barrie's *Auld Licht Idylls* (1888),[33] the book which began the rise to dominance of the Kailyard style in the 1880s, is a series of brief 'stories' or sketches, but they are framed in opening and closing chapters which offer a self-conscious commentary on the nature of Barrie's own art and its relationship with its subject matter. The opening section sets its narrator, the village schoolteacher, in an environment as hostile as that imagined by the young Gourlay in his prize-winning essay. The schoolteacher's house is several miles from the town, measuring the distance that his education places between him and the people whose life and whose beliefs he once shared; and in harsh weather he is trapped in a forbidding isolation:

> My feet encased in stout 'tackety' boots, I had waded down to Waster Lumny's fields to the glen burn: in summer the never failing larder from which, with wriggling worm or garish fly, I can any morning whip a savoury breakfast; in winter-time the only thing in the valley that defies the ice-king's chloroform. I watched the water twisting black and solemn through the snow, the ragged ice on its edge proof of the toughness of the struggle with the frost, from which it has, after all, crept only half-victorious. A bare wild rose-bush on the farther bank was violently agitated, and then there ran from its root a black-headed rat with wings. Such was the general effect. I was not less interested when my startled eyes divided this phenomenon into its component parts, and recognised in the disturbance on the opposite bank only another fierce struggle among the animals for existence; they need no professor to teach them the doctrine of the survival of the fittest. A weasel had gripped a water-hen (whit-rit and belties they are called in these parts) cowering at the root of the rose-bush, and was being dragged down the bank by the terrified bird, which made for the water as its only chance of escape. (4–5)

The conflict in nature in the midst of this harsh landscape is an introduction to stories about the struggle of handloom weavers against the extinction of their craft, and the religion which makes it bearable. To both this natural struggle and to the human struggle, the narrator is a 'not altogether passive spectator' (4); to the natural struggle he remains largely an 'unobserved spectator' (6) until the moment when he decides to intervene to save the beltie: similarly, his storytelling is an attempt to save the Auld Licht communities from obliteration by retaining their memory within the current of his narrative which, like the stream, winds through an amnesiac landscape.

The relationship between victim and saviour, however, is complicated by the narrator's own desperate isolation: having saved the bird he comments that 'except for her draggled tail, she already looks wonderfully composed, and so long as the frost holds I shall have little difficulty keeping her with me' (6–7), and thus reveals the extent to which he is as much in need of her companionship as she is of his protection. He is another sufferer from Mackellar's 'horror of isolation'. It is only the hostility of the environment that can maintain this unusual relationship, and, translated to the narrator's relationship with the Auld Lichts, what we see is his clinging to their community and its values because it is his only possible buttress against the horrifying individualism of the 'survival of the fittest'. The narrator is a man with no faith in the beliefs of the Auld Licht religion, but he cannot utterly alienate himself from it, even in memory, because it is his only buttress against an inhumane world: if its religious ideals and its ethics are now absurd, they maintained the possibility of a community, and that community is what he, signally, in his superior knowledge, lacks. It is nostalgia for community that drives his writing, drives him even to envy the labourers in their bothies, for 'life in bothies', hard though it was, 'is not, I should say, so lonely as life at the schoolhouse, for the hands have at least each other's company' (50). The schoolmaster, in search of spiritual sustenance, is afraid that he will be discovered to be the beltie, cowering at the foot of the wild rose bush.

This strange ambivalence between the narrator and his subject matter accounts for much of the tone of Barrie's writing, for the narrator, as superior, educated, worldly commentator, submits the community to our scrutiny as an object of mockery for its narrow-minded parochialism, for its strange rituals and its unrelieved backwardness; at the same time, however, in reaction against the harshness of the immediate environment – more spiritual now than economic, since we are told that 'there are few Auld Licht communities in Scotland nowadays – perhaps because people are so well off' (11) – the narrator becomes the voice of a lingering nostalgia for a lost sense of community based on religious commitments that have ceased to have any validity to Barrie's audience. The world he presents is one dominated by fear – fear of poverty, fear of the workhouse; fears controlled only by imagining an even more potent fear to cast them into insignificance, the fear of God: 'Old wives grumbled by their hearths when (the minister) did not look in to despair of their salvation . . . Mr. Dishart had scarcely any hope for the Auld Lichts; he had none for any other denomination.' (68, 69). To step beyond such a community ought to be an escape from fear, but it is a step into that hostile environment figured in the winter landscape, a world given over to a fearful struggle for survival.

What is true of the narrator of *Auld Licht Idylls* is true likewise of their
creator: Barrie too clings in memory to the community that he himself has
left behind. Barrie may have escaped its narrowness by taking the highroad
to London but in his inability to commit himself to any alternative values
he resurrects that past community as the image of a human fulfilment no
longer available to the modern world. However much the narrator may have
discarded the actual values of the Auld Lichts he is terror-struck with the
possibility of having no community to enclose him from that harsh world
beyond, and his writing turns back from his isolation, therefore, to recall
a world whose values are only valid in the context of his own terrible lack
of alternatives. It is this double movement of separation and identification
which accounts for the characteristic stance of Barrie's narration, a stance
which involves mocking the actualities of Auld Licht beliefs and practices
but then turning that mockery back upon the reader as a condemnation of
his or her lack of feeling. When for instance, he satirises the Auld Lichts'
religious conservatism in the person of Tibbie McQuhatty – who 'protested
against' a change in the service, 'as meeting the devil half-way, but the
minister carried his point, and ever after that she rushed ostentatiously from
the church the moment the psalm was given out, and remained behind the
door until the singing was finished' (59) – he then turns upon the responses
his own mockery has induced, claiming it as a violation of values we cannot
match: 'You may smile at Tibbie, but ah! I know what she was at a sick
bedside. I have seen her when the hard look had gone from her eyes, and
it would ill become me to smile too' (60). Our laughter is evoked only to
be turned back on us as a guilty ignorance of a more profound humanity
than we have shown ourselves capable of: we are guilty of having failed to
acknowledge the community's essential humanity, as if our lack of knowledge of that humanity were not the narrator's responsibility. Beltie becomes
whit-rit, outsider insider. One minute Barrie's narrator is siding with the
readers' condescension towards the characters, the next he is in league with
the community and demanding compensation from us in sympathy and
understanding.

It is by this continual oscillation in perspective, using the narrator now
to conceal, now to reveal, that Barrie is able to evade or to gloss over so
many of the issues that his works raise. He will put poverty starkly before
us, and tell us it does not matter because of the weaver's faith; he will tell
us that their faith was absurd but it does not matter because he remembers
their acts of kindness; he will tell us they died in suffering but it does not
matter because the whole community is long since gone and consigned to
his memory. The fundamental contradiction of this recipe arises from the
fact that Barrie will not locate within the community any of the values
which he himself would hold by, or any of the values which were developing
within that community to oppose the conditions that they suffered. And
he cannot acknowledge any powerful oppositional or constructive values

within the society because they would undermine his own position as the only fearless self: he has dared to leave the community, even though, in imagination, he remains as tied to it as John Gourlay was to Barbie. On the one hand Barrie pays homage to the Auld Lichts' value as community, but on the other he demonstrates that no one within that community has the complexity of consciousness or the human value equal to his own. He cannot oppose any fearless self to the fearful community because that would be to undermine the ultimate denial of fear that is his own removal from the community into authorship. Values which go along with the act of writing or the potentialities of the imagination upon which writing draws can have no existence in Barrie's Thrums because they have all been drawn off into the personality of an author who would not be and cannot be contained – even in embryo – within the community he writes about.

Thus in the final tale of *Auld Licht Idylls*, 'A Literary Club', Barrie provides us with a failed version of his own escape from the communal ethos in Tammas Haggart, who is almost seduced from religion by English literature, until saved by the minister, Mr. Dishart, in whose name we may find a punning reference to his role in this escapade:

> It was from Sandersey that Tammas Haggart bought his copy of Shakespeare, whom Mr. Dishart could never abide. Tammas kept what he had done from his wife, but Chirsty saw the deterioration setting in and told the minister of her suspicions. Mr. Dishart was newly placed at the time and very vigorous, and the way he shook the truth out of Tammas was grand. The minister pulled Tammas the one way and Gavin pulled him the other, but Mr. Dishart was not the man to be beaten, and he landed Tammas in the Auld Licht Kirk before the year was out. Chirsty buried Shakespeare in the yard. (237)

The community's symbolic refusal of literature and the narrator's apparent pleasure in Tammas's discomfiture are set in ironic counterpoint to our knowledge that Barrie has himself taken the opposite course and joined the literature of Shakespeare, and that it is only through his stories, stories we have just finished reading, that (some of) the community's values will be saved. But precisely because that escape into literature is the only value Barrie has to offer, his art clings to the very environment he escaped, but clings to a version of it that has been evacuated of the very qualities which made his escape possible.

It is here that Douglas Brown's anti-Kailyard and Barrie's Kailyard, despite all their differences in vision, share the same dynamic: each imagines Scotland as a place exiled to the imagination, incapable of envisaging a future for itself. The author, as source and fulfilment of the imagination, who has found himself a location in another culture, cannot allow the possibility of any alternative imagination within the community he has left: it must be stranded, suspended between the fearful and the fearless in a mutually destructive and interminable dialectic. Thus at the conclusion of *The House with the Green Shutters* the characters of the novel are left looking at 'The House with the Green Shutters' – at Brown's novel as well as Gourlay's home – and the work of fiction itself becomes the terrifying apparition before which the community will bow down, unable, in its limited timidities, to comprehend the powers that the author has encompassed. The novel itself lives in the same dialectical tension with the fearful as its protagonists, for it needs their stricken, awe-struck gaze as homage to its fearless creation.

What makes Douglas Brown's novel so bleak as a projection of the national imagination is that there is no character within the community who is capable of representing, let alone sustaining, the author's values. Those values can only enter the novel through the voice of the narrator, so that the distinction that is being drawn is not between characters *in* the community (one of whom carries the burden of the author's commitment), but *between* the author and his characters as the totality of the community; between values which only the author is capable of achieving and a value system, belonging to the characters, which could never become a location for that authorial potential. The powers of the imagination, those which can 'consecrate the world to a man' (67), have no place in Scotland; beyond the timid ethics of a commercial visualising in which 'imagination and caution were equally developed' (68) there is only the fearlessness born of a complete lack of imagination, and the terror born of too much insight with too little intellect – the Gourlays, old and young. Young Gourlay suffers from having just a modicum of imagination of the wrong kind in a world to which it is entirely alien:

> In his crude clay there was a vein of poetry; he could be alone in the country and not lonely; had he lived in a green quiet place, he might have learned the solace of nature for the wounded when eve sheds her spiritual dews. But the mean pleasures to be found at the Cross satisfied his nature, and stopped him midway to that soothing beauty of the woods and streams, which might have brought healing and a wise quiescence. (160)

Imagination might have saved him but his imaginings cannot escape into a real imaginative perception: it is corruptible because it was never more than false currency. In young Gourlay's killing of his father George Douglas Brown dramatises the imagination's inability to sustain itself in such a place: the imaginative, in its fearful weakness, must destroy the only power that can defy the community because there is nothing in the community to sustain the value of imagination. Even young Gourlay's escape to Edinburgh and to the university can only drive him back to the half-hearted imitation of his father's manly defiance of the 'bodies', because, 'at Barbie his life, though equally devoid of mental interest, was solaced by surroundings which he loved. In Edinburgh his surroundings were appalling to his timid mind' (126).

The community presented in Barbie is irredeemable, but the values by which it is judged so are values which have – and can have – no existence in the community itself: they have to be continually brought in from outside, from literature and the literary ('when eve sheds her spiritual dews' reeks of a debased romantic nature poetry), and, therefore, from the England which has been 'consecrated' to the imagination by literature. When the characters travel beyond their bleak streets they carry their bare, gaunt, consciousnesses into the midst of the ripeness of nature which ought to provide their imaginations with solace but they can take no benefit from it:

> The brake swung on through merry cornfields where reapers were at work, past happy brooks flashing to the sun, through the solemn hush of ancient and mysterious woods, beneath the great white-moving clouds and blue spaces of the sky. And amid the suave enveloping greatness of the world, the human pismires stung each other and were cruel, and full of hate and malice and petty rage. (117)

Or such natural ripeness, as in young Gourlay's whisky-inspired brain, turns monstrous in their perception:

> From an inland hollow he saw a great dawn flooding up from the sea . . . Then an autumn wood rose on his vision. He was gazing down a vista of yellow leaves; a long, deep slanting cleft, framed in lit foliage. Leaves, leaves; everywhere yellow leaves, luminous, burning. He saw them filling the lucid air. The scene was as vivid as fire to his brain, though of magic stillness. Then the foliage turned suddenly to great serpents twined about the boughs. Their colours were of monstrous beauty. They glistened as they moved. (179)

The imagination warps ripeness into threat in this sterile environment; nature has no succour to offer because its potential goes unnoticed – unnoticed by the characters, but not by the author. The narrative voice continually establishes patterns of comparison which will assure us that this is not the world; only in a community so alienated from the imagination could the author fail to find a location for the values which he recognises in other communities. Gourlay's fearful selfhood is the only vehicle for internal opposition to the community ethic: but that opposition is the vehicle for a deeper opposition – the author's own – which can only survive because it has found sustenance elsewhere, has found a soil in which can grow more than the 'crude vein of poetry' that leads to a disabling fearfulness within Barbie itself.

The House with the Green Shutters constructs for us the model of a society in which the creative imagination and the community which it has to express are utterly sundered from one another: this is why fear has become an immovable obstacle, locking the society into an eternal moral stasis, no matter what changes are thrust upon it from without. In one sense, one might say, these novels represent the true condition of Scottish society, since its creativity – like much of its power – was being drawn off to London and incorporated into English values; but the novels do not present that situation – they present a situation in which no one within their Scottish communities has the capacity for insight which the novel itself claims, and in which, therefore, the Scottish community's inability to escape the dialectic of fearful and fearless is the inevitable outcome of its own innate characteristics. It is not, for Douglas Brown, that the imagination has been repressed or exiled from Scottish society, but that the Scottish imagination is – by virtue of Scottishness – incapable of reaching those qualities which are fulfilled in English culture. The dead-end conflict of the fearful and the fearless, tied together in communal terror and individual aggrandisement, is thus presented as the inevitable outcome of Scottish society's own innate characteristics rather than a function of the dialectic between Scottish values and English values. Those sons who are too weak – and too weakly imaginative – to oppose the father are the scapegoats for the sons who had the courage or the ability to go into exile: the imagination projects itself back into Scottish society as a cripple, while the breeding of the imagination of the author himself is wiped from the map of the Scottish experience which the novelist claims to be charting. The author's commitment to the imagination becomes a commitment to English culture, where alone it can grow and mature: all the potentialities of the imagination are transferred out of the Scottish environment, leaving Scottish culture denuded of the only power which could release it from its fearful condition.

IV

Lewis Grassic Gibbon, while writing the novels – *Sunset Song* (1932), *Cloud Howe* (1933) and *Grey Granite* (1934) – that became *A Scots Quair*,[34] was in precisely the position of the imaginative exile that Barrie had dramatised, recreating the world of his childhood with every likelihood of evacuating it of imaginative value exactly as both his kailyard and anti-kailyard predecessors had done. A series of asides in *A Scots Quair*, carefully placing the 'real' author as the butt of the community's mockery, reveals a shift in strategy which asserts the continued vitality of the literary imagination in Scotland. What Gibbon does is to include himself, or his surrogates, within the text as comic failures known to the community that he is describing, so that the author's own situation does not haunt the community as a vampirous shadow. Thus the Reverend Gibbon, in *Sunset Song*, an assertive preacher and luster after the flesh of country girls, carries the author's pseudonym as an ironic image of the outsider who tries to enter the community and bend it, hypocritically, to his own theology and his own desires. Grassic Gibbon mocks the genealogy of both himself and the Rev. Gibbon when he thinks of Kinraddie as 'the Scots countryside itself, fathered between a kailyard and a bonny brier bush in the lee of the house with the green shutters' (24). The way in which such a community has been perceived through literary conventions is thus self-consciously articulated within a work which knows the dangers of its own generic genealogy, but it can be articulated precisely because, in *Sunset Song*, Grassic Gibbon has invented a radical narrative strategy which displaces the third person, omniscient – and anglocentric – author in favour of a narration organised through the voices and the gossip of the folk themselves. In *A Scots Quair* the author's alienation is the basis not for a disenchanted and literary framing of the community's life, but for a narrative structure in which the community, through its gossip and its reminiscence, becomes the organiser of the narration, inserting into the body of Grassic Gibbon's fiction the fictions with which it embroiders its own life and through which it expresses its own imaginative vitality:

> Some said that that was all a damned lie, the minister had nothing to do with the quean, she'd left the Manse of her own free will. The Reverend Mr. Robert Colquhoun wouldn't bed with an angel never mind a red-faced maid in his house, he was over decent and fond of his wife. But you shook your head when you heard that, faith! it clean took the guts from a fine bit tale. (*Cloud Howe*, 121)

The validity of the tale is in its 'fictional' rather than its factual strength, and the validity of the telling is in the integration and power of the 'folk voice' through which the tale is told. Indeed, the whole structure of the trilogy is based on an exploration of the changes in the 'folk voice' and the changes in the nature of its gossip and its inner imaginative vitality as it undergoes the transition from an agrarian to an urban form of communality: the 'voice' of *Sunset Song* is a healthy and vigorous one in comparison with the vicious, self-deceiving voice of *Cloud Howe*, and in *Grey Granite* the folk voice has to struggle against the mechanised class propaganda and self-conscious fictionalising of the newspaper. But the voice of the community remains, even when it has been corrupted and debased, the medium of Grassic Gibbon's narration, because it is only through the acceptance of the priority of that voice that the author's own retreat from the community will cease to determine his perception of it. In a narrative which is uttered not by a distanced and educated voice, trained in another culture, but in the inner dialogue of the community with itself, it is the distant author who is mocked and whose values are parodied. In *Cloud Howe* the Gibbons disappear, but the Leslie Mitchell who lurks behind the pseudonym of Lewis Grassic Gibbon sneaks in as Old Leslie, whose natter is a parodic version, within the community of the young Leslie who is engaged in writing reminiscent novels of Scotland from Welwyn Garden City:

> Old Leslie heard the story in the smiddy and he said the thing was Infernal, just. Now, he minded when he was a loon up in Garvock – And the

sweat dripped off him, pointing the coulter, and he habbered from nine
until lossening-time, near, some story about some minister he'd known; but
wherever that was and why it had been, and what the hell had happened if
anything ever had, you couldn't make head nor tail if you listened; and you
only did that if you couldn't get away. Old Leslie was maybe a fair good
smith: he was sure the biggest old claik in Segget. (37-8)

The writer, like old Leslie, performs for those who 'couldn't get away',
but it is the community which mocks him, not he who mocks the community; his heroine Chris forgets him, though he cannot forget her:

And when they had finished with drinking their milk and eating their cakes
Chris offered to pay. But the farmer's wife shook her head, she'd not have it,
she'd heard of Chris from her son, she said, he lived in London and wrote
horrible books: but he and Chris were at college together. Chris couldn't
mind much of the son at all, she supposed they'd met sometime or another,
but she didn't say that . . . (172-3)

Chris Guthrie is not measured, therefore, against the author's values, but
against the community's, and is measured against them in a context in
which she has specifically refused the author's own escape route into English
culture:

So that was the Chris of her reading and schooling, two Chrisses there were
that fought for her heart and tormented her. You hated the land and the
coarse speak of the folk and learning was brave and fine one day; and the
next you'd waken with the peewits crying across the hills, deep and deep,
crying in the heart of you and the smell of the earth in your face, almost
you'd cry for that, the beauty of it and the sweetness of the Scottish land
and skies. You saw their faces in the firelight, father's and mother's and the
neighbours', before the lamps lit up, tired and kind, faces dear and close to
you, you wanted the words they'd known and used, forgotten in the far-off
youngness of their lives . . . (*Sunset Song*, 32)

Of the 'two Chrisses' that struggle for dominance in her it is the 'English
Chris', the Chris of education and books, that loses. Unlike her creator – because of the advantage, or disadvantage, of being a woman – she
remains in her community, while her brother emigrates to South America
and the men around her are gradually called away to the War. Her choice
allows her a perspective upon the community that can chart its failings
without transferring to an entirely different cultural environment all her
potentiality for growth and development.

When Chris confronts the fearful community, therefore, it is not as one
pole of a dialectic which is self-consuming and self-defeating; when Chris,
like Gourlay, defies nature's violence in despite of the fearful community
around her, it is not the gateway to a *hubris* brought about by stepping

beyond the community's boundaries: it is a fulfilment of one set of values which the community has helped to breed in her; through her, as a result, the community itself will be enlarged and made more significant. At the moment when Chris has to defy the conformist ethics of her aunt and uncle who, after her father's death, think she should not try to work the farm herself, she and they have to test themselves against the elements which Gourlay had defied:

> It was then, in a lull of the swishing, she heard the great crack of thun-der that opened the worst storm that had struck the Howe in years . . . The thunder clamoured again, and then she suddenly sat shivering, remembering something – Clyde and old Bob and Bess, all three of them were out in the ley field there, they weren't taken in till late in the year. Round the ley field was barbed wire, almost new, that father had put up in the Spring, folk said it was awful for drawing the lightning, maybe it had drawn it already.
>   She was out of the bed in the next flash, it was a ground flash, it hung and it seemed to wait, sizzling, outside the window as she pulled on stockings and vest and knickers and ran to the door and cried up *Uncle Tam, Uncle Tam, we must take in the horses!* He didn't hear, she waited, and the house shook and dirled in another great flash, then Auntie was crying something, Chris stood as if she couldn't believe her own ears. Uncle Tam was feared at the lightning, he wouldn't go out . . . (29-30)

The fearful cower in their houses; for them their 'folk voice' in the com-munity's gossip is only an attempt to ring the individual with a barbed wire of communal disavowal of any assertion of individuality. But Chris can transcend such narrow-mindedness without destroying in herself the continuities and the values she has learned from that folk voice, because her own strength is the strength of the community at its best. After her father's death her 'fearlessness', her lack of emotion, is appalling to the community – 'It was fair a speak in Kinraddie, her coolness, she knew that well but she didn't care, she was free at last' (90) – but the strength with which she opposes the community is itself given to her by her father, and by her recollection not of the tyrannical and lustful John Guthrie who had ruined his own family, but of 'the fleetness of him and his justice, and the fight unwearying he'd fought with the land and its masters to have them all clad and fed and respectable, he'd never rested working and chaving for them, only God had beaten him in the end' (95). Fearless defiance of the timid communal ethic goes side by side with the need to test that defiance against the store of memory and of humanity which the community makes available.

The dialectic of the fearful and the fearless is no less intense in Grassic Gibbon's work than in Douglas Brown's, but it is a dialectic which is no longer seen as self-destructive because it is no longer set against superior values – embodied in the author – to which the community and the protag-onist do not have access. Chris Guthrie will be able to judge her father's fears and fearlessness – 'And he glanced with a louring eye at the Standing Stones and then Chris thought a foolish thing, that he kind of shivered, as though he were feared, him that was feared at nothing dead or alive, gentry or common' (43) – as she will have to live with her first husband's execution 'as a coward and deserter' (237) in the knowledge that he had left the trenches because he wanted to get back home, knowing 'that he'd be a coward if he didn't try though all hope was past' (238). Equally, she will recognise how her second husband lives with 'the Fear that had haunted his life since the War, Fear that he'd be left with no cloud to follow, Fear he'd be left in the day alone, and stand and look at his naked self' (*Cloud Howe*, 172). But against all these she will assert her own fearlessness not as something imposed on them, but as something surviving them and realised by suffering with them.

Such fearlessness is not achieved without separation from the community, without defiance of its timidity and its fear-inducing gossip, but it is a fearlessness which is the apex of the community's own potential self-knowledge rather than an indictment of the impossibility of its ever achieving self-knowledge. As Chris meditates by the Standing Stones she is at the centre of a pattern which includes rather than excludes the community of the fearful below her: the stones represent an essence of the community which history may obscure and cross and deflect but which endures nonetheless and will find its embodiment in those fearless individuals, like Chris and like her son Ewan, who appear to others of a stony hardness in their selfhood. In those cases, however, the fearless self will challenge the community and will separate itself in isolation only in order to fulfil the community's own suppressed potentialities. Thus young Ewan, become communist leader, will have to deny the integration into the community offered by marriage, and will have to leave Chris behind as a he sets off for London, because he is driven by the desire to liberate others from the conditions which, out of fear, they are crippled. In a place which to her seemed 'the most desolate place that God ever made', he casts off his fearful fiancée, Ellen, who is forced to recognise his identity with the terrifying inhumanity of the landscape: 'his face was a stone, a stone-mason's face, carved in a sliver of cold grey granite' that 'suddenly frightened' her (*Grey Granite*, 194). But Ewan has only been able to achieve that fearless isolation because he is the son of a woman who has herself learned to live outside of fear, who has learned to accept herself as defined by something beyond the timid ethics of the fearful community:

> She'd finished with men or the need for them . . . That dreadful storm she'd once visioned stripping her bare was all about her, and she feared it no longer, eager to be naked, alone and unfriended, facing the last realities with a cool, clear wonder, an unhasting desire. Barriers still, but they fell one by one – (189)

Such fearless selfhood, either as a withdrawal into the elemental or as an imposition of a granite logic upon history, is not a denial of community: in a world where community has been violated and distorted by war and injustice and madness, Ewan and Chris are standing stones, gesturing towards what is permanent in human experience, gesturing towards a community from which fear will have been banished, and, in the present, fearful to others only because the community has forgotten what the Standing Stones represent, and is unable to recognise that its own warmth and vitality are centred on and revolve around their granite implacability. The landscape and its bleak harshness is no longer, as for Barrie's narrator, a justification for clinging fearfully to the community even when history has made it redundant: the landscape becomes the bearer of an ultimate truth that has to be confronted if the fearful community is to be released from its fear:

> And that was the best deliverance of all, as she saw it now, sitting here quiet – that that Change who ruled the earth and the sky and the waters underneath the earth, Change whose face she'd once feared to see, whose right hand was Death and whose left hand Life, might be stayed by none of the dreams of men, love, hate, compassion, anger or pity, gods or devils or wild crying to the sky. He passed and repassed in the ways of the wind, Deliverer, Destroyer and Friend in one. (4)

The repetition which is terrifying in *The House with the Green Shutters*, because it is the condition of a society evacuated of imagination, is transformed into an ultimate truth in *A Scots Quair* – an ultimate truth not of an enclosed and self-mutilating community but of a universe of which the self need no longer be afraid.

The transcendence of fear that Chris achieves in *A Scots Quair* is the goal of the all the novelists of the Scottish Renaissance movement in the 1920s and 1930s – the discovery of a self that is immune to fear, of an escape from the confrontation of the fearful and the fearless into a world defined by a denial of fear, a denial that is not simply the imposition of the fearful self upon the rest of the community but the discovery of values that lie beyond the boundaries of the ethics of fear. In Willa Muir's *Imagined Corners*, Elise, having challenged and overcome the fearful community of Calderwick, 'found her central, dispassionate, impregnable self' (289), a 'central' self' (274) which refuses to submit, like her friend Mabel, to the demands of fear: 'I'm – I'm frightened,' she sobbed . . . 'I hate anybody I know to die. It makes me so frightened' (274). The 'she' is significant, because in many ways it is the women writers of the 1920s who lead the way in denying the dialectic in which the male novelists and male protagonists are trapped. In Catherine Carswell's *Open The Door* (1920)[35] Joanna steps beyond the boundaries of her community to marry Mario, an Italian art teacher in Glasgow:

> 'Afraid, but thrilled through and through, his bride watched him. That man in the grey suit was her husband. He was a stranger to her: at this moment

he appeared a complete stranger. Yet she had left her mother, her home, all
that was familiar, to come away with him.

 This then was life at last! But it seemed less real, more dream-like than
anything that had gone before. She was going to a strange land, was going
among strangers, was going alone with that passionate stranger in the grey
suit. The train of experience was light. Greatly she feared it. But not for
anything would she have escaped. (107-8)

Fear is no longer the defining determinant of Joanna's existence and, in
the novel's final scenes she will, while learning to milk a cow, discover
that 'one must go on tugging firmly and with a fearless rhythm' (421), a
fearlessness that is prologue to her return to the community from which she
had been exiled. In Nan Shepherd's *The Quarry Wood* (1928),[36] Martha,
having survived the loss of her lover and the pain of her Aunt's long illness,
discovers

> . . . the shattering of her selfhood not evil, but the condition of growth. She
> had given love and had received only adoration: and love is so much bigger
> a thing than adoration – more complex and terrible. At its absolute moments
> it holds resolved within itself all impulses and inconsistencies, the lust of the
> flesh, the lust of the eyes, the pride of life, the spirit's agonizing. Martha
> seemed to herself that morning to touch one of its absolute moments. She
> had no more fear of what love might do to her. (199)

The transcendence of fear is the aim of the narrative: not the transfer
from the position of the fearful to that of the fearless but the denial of
the dialectic of fear. The same is true of Shepherd's *The Weatherhouse*.[37]
The protagonist, Garry Forbes, insists to his fiancée Lindsay that Kate, a
character apparently so insignificant as not to merit an entry in the list of
'Main Characters' with which the book opens, should,

> ' . . . see my aunt. She is not fearsome,' he added, smiling.
> 'But I fear her.'
> 'Why?' he asked, smiling protectively down upon her.
> . . . The image of Miss Barbara loomed above her, as she had appeared in
> the winter night, elemental, a mass of the very earth, earthy smelling, with
> her goat's beard, her rough hairy tweed like the pelt of an animal . . . Has
> no mythology deified a bearded woman as its god of earth? Lindsay [was]
> unable to find words to explain her terror, which could not be explained by
> anything within her experience. (70–1)

Lindsay's 'terror' at another woman – 'You think I am a child, to be
afraid' – will be overcome in the novel's conclusion when Ellen, Lindsay's
aunt, is able to acknowledge, 'I've been frightened all my life' and to assert
that 'There's nothing to fear in all the world but deceit. Nothing at all' (189).
Overcoming fear, the protagonists of these novels do not reach towards

a terrifying fearlessness: they strive for a reintegration into a community itself redeemed from fear and to a self-recognition that is not a denial of community.

The novelist of the Renaissance movement most fully committed to exploring and overcoming the structures of fear which have permeated the Scottish imagination was Neil Gunn. One of his earliest novels, *Morning Tide* (1930),[38] sets the pattern for his later work, for it is riddled with the lexicon of fear:

> Grace stole a look at her mother's face. She understood the delicate opposition in the attitudes of her parents. It was elemental, like the wash of the sea – from which her mother recoiled, on which her father adventured. The fear of the woman; the quick pride of the seaman. (55)

> Their voices had the high sad quickening of fear. A sense of mortal loss came upon him. The cry he had heard was a drowning cry. (62)

> He also knew that he could not have gone to the door. Terror had in one moment paralysed him. (65)

> "Yes," said Kirsty; "we'll be going, Mother. You needn't be frightened for us." In her fear for others she was fearless. (66)

> "I can't see," she cried, terrified by the swinging of the bridge, whipped by the spindrift. (70)

> "No!" and Hugh twisted his head seaward in a monstrous half-fearful humour. (71)

The religious sources of the intertwining fears of the relentless natural environment against which Gunn's fisherfolk have to struggle are made explicit towards the end of the novel when Hugh watches a sunset; in its 'piercing shafts of light that turned its darkness to a luminous core', it recalls for him 'a picture of the Crucifixion' (231):

> The eyes might be afraid of the apocalyptic light, but they were sceptical of it, too; in a final surge would dare it and not care. Even if the light had the power, the final power – of death . . . .
> The hand of God the Father, sinking slow and inexorable, of God the Terrible.
> The fear of God.
> The fear of God, to which men cried, praying desperately for salvation. (231–2)

Gunn's novels are a quest beyond that fear, to find an alternative way of relating the imagination to the world. Each character in Gunn's major novels is driven out from the community of the fearful into a terrible and terrifying isolation. So Tom, in *The Serpent* (1943),[39] having challenged his father's Old Testament version of Christianity becomes,

> The outcast moving apart from his own people, wandering in desolate ways through the horror of silence. The communal warmth in life and death. Cast

out, bitterness in his soul, not giving in, cast out. And this he comprehended not in thought but in visual picture, seeing faces and eyes and the massed movement of bodies going away, seeing them with his own eyes – and seeing himself going from them, cut adrift like a criminal, white-faced upon his own empty road. (174–5)

The consequence is an extreme of terror in which the self is threatened with dissolution or destruction, and Tom

began to be afraid lest the ultimate centre in him, that which had been Tom as child, as boy, as young man in Glasgow, that continuing essence, that known cry, would itself get broken and be no more.
    Lost now in an immensity so vast that it transcended terror's utmost bound, an immensity that could not be inhabited, that could not be borne, from which one turned to escape, running in madness, while the immensity swelled behind, and above, and slowly but surely reached over to engulf. (190)

The corrosive consequences of a fear which is destructive within the community and yet annihilating if one steps outside it forms the underlying structure of Gunn's most sophisticated novel, *Highland River* (1937);[40] as so often, it is in the relationship of brothers – Kenn, the central character, and Angus – through which the oppositions of fear are constructed. The book begins with a moment of primitive fear, when the child Kenn encounters a huge salmon by the river where he has gone to collect water, but a fear which is complicated by the social fear induced by a repressive society:

Out of that noiseless world in the grey of the morning all his ancestors came at him. They tapped his breast until the bird inside it fluttered madly; they drew a hand along his hair until the scalp crinkled; they made the blood within him tingle to a dance that had him leaping from bolder to bolder before he rightly knew to what desperate venture he was committed.
    For it was all in a way a sort of madness. The fear was fear of the fish itself, of its monstrous reality, primal fear; but it was also infinitely complicated by fear of gamekeepers, of the horror and violence of law courts, of our modern social fear. (2)

'Fear of the keeper' (112) is the barrier which prevents the Scottish peasant enjoying the fish in his own rivers but it is also the symbolic barrier to the discovery of the wisdom that the salmon represents in Celtic legend. The repressive social fear is then vastly extended by Kenn and Angus's experiences in the First World War – 'He went into action with fear in his throat, the old panic fear he had felt as a lad when the salmon had moved from the well, but thickened with the consciousness of death' (35) – but for Angus there is no transcendence of this fear; just as, when poaching, and almost trapped by the keeper, Kenn sees Angus's face lose 'all the dark proud life' and sees 'doom in the nervous lips' as he gives in to fear, so, in the war, Angus is incapable of escaping the corrosive effects of fear, losing in the immediacy of his terror any sense of connection with his past self: 'There was no reality outside the world in which he was. And the wariness and cuteness served merely to emphasize how inevitable and unending was its maze, with the trapped mind doomed to dodge about forever' (157). Angus is one of the 'fear-held folk' (184) of the modern world, his death in the war symbolic of a people who have lost contact with a folk imagination which is beyond the destructive effects of modern social fear.

Kenn's own journey, however, is precisely a journey beyond fear – 'A strange thing happened to him that night, when he returned at midnight to fetch home the salmon. For the first time in all his experience, he found that he no longer had any fear of the dark' (201) – a journey towards a deeper consciousness that, as his name implies, holds an ancient knowledge that is uncorrupted by the primal or the social fears of a fallen humanity. It is towards this knowledge that Kenn will travel, as his holiday walk to the source of the river beside which he had grown up as a boy becomes a parable of the mind's search for those sources which are uncorrupted by history and by the deformations of religion, for that state in which 'his body was purged of the passions of evil and fear and hate' and was 'reintegrated and made whole' (235). For Gunn, reaching this condition requires not the 'reintegration' of the mind but the recognition of its fundamental doubleness, a doubleness in which an ancient, archetypal consciousness underlies a modern consciousness. Escape from the world of the fearful can only be achieved by discovering a route back to that more primitive mind, as when Kenn and his friends Beel creep into an ancient broch and 'were vaguely disturbed as if the little door telescoped backward into a remoteness that at any moment might come up at their elbow' (119). That ancient world, however, the world of the dark, is not one which ought to be feared: accosted by a cleansed mind 'their aged secrecies were no longer fearsome' (204), for the primitive mind that is the source after which Kenn searches is not the fear-dominated mind of the savage as described in Frazer's *The Golden Bough* but the mind as yet undefiled by the fear that is produced by the beginnings of civilisation: 'The scent of the heath fire has in it something quite definitely primordial. Involuntarily it evokes immense perspectives in human time; tribes hunting and trekking through lands beyond the horizons of history. Indeed by its aid he can see more clearly how man lived before civilisation came upon him than for long periods after it did . . . heath smoke is an affair of time; of family or communal life through immense stretches of time. Its colour is the bloom of mountains on a far horizon – particularly in that evening light which is so akin to the still light of inner vision' (109–110). Back in that primitive world what Kenn discovers is not fear but laughter, 'a wide pagan laughter', one that takes the serpent of Christianity and turns it into a joke: 'it was perhaps the old serpent myth that his folk had forgotten how to interpret. The serpent that stuck its tail in its mouth to suppress its laughter!' (218). The fearful self is dissolved in a laughter more ancient than the gods of fear.

The form of Gunn's novel is designed to enact this journey beyond fear: the movement of time and history which takes us away from the source is reversed by its multiple time-shifts to produce a suspension of the temporal in which the story can hold its end in its beginning like the serpent with its tail in its mouth, Celtic symbol of wisdom. At the end of *The Serpent*, Tom, who has been seen by his own community as the source of evil, dies when bitten by a serpent: the shepherd who finds his body witnesses 'a serpent of monstrous length' issuing 'as it seemed, out of the left arm, out of the very hand, and for a moment so intense was the shepherd's shock of infernal horror that he went muscle-bound' (291). The Christian symbol of the diabolic kills the man whose denial of Christianity has been seen as the work of the devil; the shepherd, symbol of that religion, flees in panic, but, having overcome his 'primal fear' (292), returns to discover that Tom has not died in terror but in a 'timeless calm'. The man who has gone beyond the world of the fearful and fearless dies peacefully, redeemed by the snake whose wisdom, like the wisdom of the Celtic legends in which it is inscribed, goes back beyond the world of fearful selves.

V

In 1979, before the Devolution Referendum held in March of that year, William McIlvanney wrote in a newspaper column that 'what lies behind our hesitancy as March approaches is something else. Not to put too fine a point on it: I think the lot of us are feart.'[41] After the Scottish people had failed to vote decisively for the establishment of their own parliament, he wrote a poem entitled 'The Cowardly Lion' which summed up many people's sense of what had happened: 'the lion had turned to its cage and slunk away/And lives still among stinking straw today'.[42] The Scottish people were too afraid to take control of their own destiny: fear-stricken when confronted by a choice which might allow them to stop being afraid. In the following two decades narratives of mutually destructive fearful selves burgeoned in Scottish writing. In 1997 the Scottish people voted finally and determinedly for their own parliament – perhaps in part because the Scottish novel had plumbed the depths of their fears.

CHAPTER 2
DIALECT AND DIALECTICS

'Open your mouth!' came the snarl – 'wider, *damn ye! wider!*'
'Im-phm!' said Gourlay, with a critical drawl, pulling John's chin about to
see into him the deeper. 'Im-phm! God, it's like a furnace! What's the Latin
for throat?'
'Guttur,' said John.
'Gutter!' said his father. 'A verra appropriate name! Yours stinks like a cess-
pool! What have you been doing till't? I'm afraid ye aren't in very good health,
after a-all . . . Eh?' (217)

John Gourlay's investigation of his son's throat in *The House with the Green
Shutters* stands on the threshold of the new century as an emblem of one
of the fundamental issues that has driven the development of the Scottish
novel and made its productions so distinctive in the English-speaking,
English-writing, world: the issue of the nation's throat, the language it should
utter and the language it should be defined by.

To describe accurately the nature of Scottish experience, and to describe
experience which is distinctively Scottish, the novelist cannot help but
engage with that 'throat': by 1900 the language of education, of politics and
journalism, of the professions, of business and commercial life was irretrievably English, and Scotland was an integral part of the new empire of the
English language which was being forged between British and American
interests worldwide. But precisely to the extent that English succeeded in
this international environment it failed to embody, in Scotland, the 'national'
language. In Ireland, English had rapidly displaced Irish and become the
'common' language of the nation, so much so that Irish writers like Yeats
and Joyce were to assume the right to use the whole tradition of English
literature as though it had lost it roots in English culture, and could be
transplanted into the 'native' speech of Ireland. In Scotland a similar situation might have developed had Gaelic been the only alternative to English,
but in Scotland English confronted not one but two contenders as the
authentic 'voice of the people', and in Scots was a speech which was not
simply in common usage among the lower classes, but was the distinctive
component of the work of Scotland's greatest writers of the previous two
hundred years, the ones who had become identified with the very spirit
of the nation – Burns and Scott. The language – or dialect – spoken by
lower class Scots in the Lowland regions of the country – Scots – could
claim to be an authentic vernacular, as Dante's Italian was in relation to
Latin, and could claim to be an equal and alternative growth from the
same roots as English. Its past success, in literary terms, meant that the

national language of high art and the language of the working masses were bound together, an alternative 'language of the tribe' which could be the foundation of an alternative imagining of the nation – an alternative that was to be mobilised by Hugh MacDiarmid in his 'synthetic Scots' of the 1920s.

Old Gourlay, the dialect speaker, looks into his son's throat and what he sees is a furnace, the melting pot in which the industrial nation is fusing its languages in the speech of the lower classes.[1] From the perspective of English speakers and of English culture, Scots is a language of leftovers, the detritus of proper speech and good writing, a supplement poisonous to the health of the real language of its society, 'thi/ lanwij a/ thi guhtr' as Tom Leonard transliterates it.[2] Burns and Scott are not only the 'sham bards of a sham nation' but bards of a sham language. Nonetheless, Scots displaces English into being the supplementary language because it remains the origin of the nation's literary culture, though it can do so only by allowing Gaelic in turn to assert its founding claim upon the nation's 'throat'. This constant displacement of the source of Scottish identity requires a process of unending translation that makes it impossible for the father to understand his son, or for the child to know its mother tongue. Gourlay's ambition was to have his son educated out of his local language, to cleanse his throat through the acquisition of a non-vernacular speech. Instead, by his verbal violence, he reduces his son to a speechlessness from which young Gourlay can recover only by fleeing from his father's voice; when his own returns it comes as 'A tag of some forgotten poem he had read [which] came back to his mind, and, "Come kindly night and cover me," he muttered' (219). Not self-expression but citation from another language gives him back speech; his choice is between self-obliteration in that 'kindly' otherness, or destruction by the father-language which waits for him within, a father whose 'hands were like outstretched claws, and shivered with each shiver of the voice that moaned, through set teeth, "What do you think I mean to do wi' ye now?" ' (219). Young John's 'meaning' is always someone else's voice *in* his throat, someone else's language *at* his throat. When he escapes his father's threats he ends in a pub fight in which he is struck in the mouth and 'his swollen lip smarted at first, but he drank till it was a mere dead lump to his tongue' (223). 'The dead lump' in his mouth acknowledges the gradual paralysis of all the physical instruments of speech, of all the possibilities of communication, that will lead him to stand over his father's body in 'an eternity of silence' (226), a silence which is, for Brown, the only possible outcome of the irresolvable and destructive confrontation between dialects in which he, as much as his characters, is trapped.

Seventy years later, the same descent into the gutter to discover the mouth of the nation is made by Conn, the protagonist of William McIlvanney's *Docherty*,[3] as he confronts his school teacher:

'. . .what's wrong with your face, Docherty?'

'Skint ma nose, sur.'

'How?'

'Ah fell an' bumped me heid in the sheuch, sur.'

'I beg your pardon?'

In the pause Conn understands the nature of the choice, tremblingly, compulsively, makes it.

'Ah fell and bumped ma heid in the sheuch, sur.'

The blow is instant. His ear seems to enlarge, is muffed in numbness . . .

'That, Docherty, is impertinence. You will translate, please, into the mother-tongue.' . . .

'I bumped my head, sir.'

'Where? Where did you bump it, Docherty?'

'In the gutter, sir.'

'Not an inappropriate setting for you, if I may say so.' (109)

The ear 'muffed in numbness' enacts the destruction of the oral culture from which Conn, like his author, derives the specificity of his identity. Conn draws up a list of equivalents between Scots and English but what he discovers is that the 'mother tongue' is not the tongue of his mother but a language into which her feelings cannot be translated:

> When something sad happened and his mother was meaning that there wasn't anything you could do about it, she would say 'ye maun dree yer weird'. When she was busy, she had said she was 'saund-papered tae a whuppet.' . . .
>
> Conn despaired of English. Suddenly, with the desperation of a man trying to amputate his own infected arm, he savagely scored out all the English equivalents. (113)

English, for Conn, is the supplement, the infection of his healthy language: to attempt to remain within his own community and its fundamentally oral culture he has to envisage the cutting off of his writing hand – the very hand by which his author has inscribed him into a narrative in a highly literary English.

In such narrative patterns and metaphoric structures, the Scottish novelist dramatises the dilemma in which the narrative voice of the novel addresses a fundamentally English-reading (and usually English-speaking) audience across the heads of characters who are given voice only to the extent that they are encased in and, in the end, mutilated or silenced by, an alien linguistic environment. Speaking about William Alexander's *Johnnie Gibb of Gushetneuk* (1869), a novel 'where you have a transcription of dialect in the dialogue, and it's done in a phonetic style, and the narrative is done in ordinary standard English', James Kelman suggested that

> a wee game [is] going on between writer and reader and the wee game is 'Reader and writer are the same' and they speak in the same voice as the narrative

and they're unlike these fucking natives who do the dialogue in phonetics. English Literature is based on that relationship between writer and reader and the person in the middle is the character. For instance, in the average novel written about a working class character, the assumption is that the character doesn't know as much as the writer and the reader, and often you'll get all those wee things such as dialect, for instance, in phonetics. In other words, the person who speaks is not as good, or rather not as intellectually aware as the writer or reader.[4]

The problem, as Kelman poses it, is that in any novel written in standard or 'literary' English, a linguistic hierarchy is established in which, no matter the intent of the author, the dialect-speaking character is always the inhabitant of a linguistically less significant world than that shared by author and reader: the dialect-speaking character is seen as being either in declension from, or in aspiration towards, the moral and intellectual standards – the full humanity – of standard English and its literary traditions. It is conflict about which Douglas Brown is quite specific in *The House with the Green Shutters*:

> That the Scot is largely endowed with the commercial imagination his foes will be ready to acknowledge. Imagination may consecrate the world to a man, or it may merely be a visualising faculty which sees that, as already perfect, which is still lying in the raw material. The Scot has the lower faculty in full degree; he has the forecasting leap of the mind which sees what to make of things – more, sees them made and in vivid operation. To him there is a railway through the desert where no railway exists, and mills along the quiet stream. And his *perfervidum ingenium* is quick to attempt the realizing of his dreams. That is why he makes the best of colonists . . . (72)

The highest powers of the imagination, those which can 'consecrate the world to a man' have no place in Scotland: the Scots are successful precisely to the extent that they are able to go direct from imagination to actions, from dreams to things, by-passing language. Young Gourlay suffers not from weakness and indecision but from a potentiality for *poetry* – 'In his crude clay there was a vein of poetry' (168) – which takes him half-way back towards the world of imagination without giving him a language for it. *The House with the Green Shutters* presents Scotland as a world in which dialect may be vigorous but to which literary language is alien. The language of the novel may 'contain' dialect, but a modern literary language must be imported from the place – England – which has already been 'consecrated' to the imagination by literature. Scots is not at home in the novel; English is not at home in Scotland. Equally, the scenes in which the novel is set cannot be described in their own particularity but must be contrasted with images from an English world in which the language of the novel *would* be at home. There is, for instance, the curious description of the main street of the village of Barbie at the point when Wilson, Gourlay's business antagonist, moves in to set up his shop:

> Rab Jamieson's barn was a curious building to be stranded in the midst of Barbie. In quaint villages and little towns of England you sometimes see a mellow redtiled barn, with its rich yard, close upon the street; it seems to have been hemmed in by the houses round, while dozing, so that it could not escape with the fields fleeing from the town. There it remains and gives ripeness to the place, matching fitly with the great horsechestnut yellowing before the door, and the old inn further down, mantled in its bloodred creepers. But that autumnal warmth and cosiness is rarely seen in the barer streets of the north. How Rab Jamieson's barn came to be stuck in Barbie nobody could tell. It was a gaunt grey building with never a window, but a bole high in one corner for the sheaves, and a door low in another corner for auld Rab Jamieson. (68)

The 'mellow redtiled barn' has no existence within the geography of *The House with the Green Shutters*: it is invoked there by the narrator's language, gesturing towards an alternative environment in which there is the possibility not only of a natural 'ripeness' to the countryside, but also of a continuity between country and the town. There are no equivalents in the Scottish context, no sense of tradition. And the fact that this is fundamentally to do with language is advertised in the name of man who owned this 'gaunt grey building' – Robert Jamieson, a name shared with the compiler of *Jamieson's Scottish Dictionary* which Douglas Brown probably used, in 1895, when he was preparing the glossary for the republication of the novels of his fellow Ayrshire novelist John Galt.[5] Jamieson's barn is like the Scots language of Brown's characters: a gaunt and empty centre around which they circulate as though in search of that other barn that can only exist in the language of their author, a centre which will come to life only as a business – J(ames) Wilson's – whose vitality will erase all trace of old Rab Jamieson, just as, perhaps, the Scots tradition of the eighteenth and early nineteenth century gave way to the fake vitality of the parodic Scots of 'Christopher North', pseudonym of J(ohn) Wilson. Of Jamieson's linguistic barn Douglas Brown might have felt as John Gourlay does while he hides from his father – "'It's the only hame I have," he sobbed angrily to the darkness: "I have no other place to gang back till!"' (220) – but Douglas Brown goes back only in the expectation of participating in the final destruction of that 'hame'.

The irony of Douglas Brown's novel, of course, is that the very vigour and vitality of his characters' Scots speech maintains the potential for Scots to represent an alternative linguistic authority in defiance of the grave to which he consigns them. Brown's novel will inspire others with the possibility of using Scots at the very moment that he despairs of it; his novel resurrects the literary tradition which it comes to bury. As a result, later writers can continue to call on the moral and linguistic authority of the literary tradition of Scots to make their dialect speakers the representatives of a 'higher' rather than a 'lower' morality, representatives of a tradition of national freedom and resistance to oppression going back through Burns to Henryson. In James Barke's *Land of the Leal* (1939),[6] for instance, the central character, David Ramsay, though only a simple labourer on a farm, is presented as an 'instinctive rebel – part of his inheritance from Burns – and naturally he was the type who preferred the Burns of *Holy Willie's Prayer* and *A Man's a Man* to the Burns of *The Cotter's Saturday Night*' (261). As a consequence, David can be made to articulate the author's own proletarian politics as part of the tradition of Burns's vernacular radicalism:

> . . . my father had some of the courage that I admire. He didna fight wi' a woman nor take it out o' her bits o' naked bairns wi' a whip. His was a different courage – the courage of the mind and the spirit – the kind o' courage that Rabbie Burns had – only he hadna Rabbie gifts – and that's what hurts; when you have the vision but havena the gifts – when you know a thing should be, but just canna do it. I know . . . I've had my visions. I've had my dreams and my ambitions . . . and I've some o' the gifts maybe . . . but I havena the courage . . . and my nose has been too sair held to the grindstone. But I know the day'll come . . . Rabbie saw it coming and I think I see it coming myself. Men will no' always be content to see their bits o' bairns starved and thrown out of work . . . (228-9)

Through the power of a poetic tradition that ennobles the language of the working man and makes him the equal of the high-born – 'A man's a man for a' that' – the peasant who has been 'sair held to the grindstone' is allowed to become the equal of his author in his statement of political idealism. Far from being the language of the gutter, Scots, in this context, is the language of an ultimate ideal of solidarity, the medium of a higher morality which is the more powerfully articulated precisely because it enacts equality between 'high' and 'low', the literary and the oral, through the very history of its development as a language and a dialect.

Such equality in discourse can also be achieved by writers working in the context of a Gaelic-speaking community because the language of the characters has to be translated into the English of the narrative voice, and rather than English establishing a norm against which the characters' linguistic achievement is to measured, English has to try to match itself to a subtlety or a complexity which is presented as being alien to, perhaps ultimately beyond, its own nature. Thus early in Neil Gunn's *Butcher's Broom* (1934),[7] the Gaelic-speaking community whose ultimate destruction in the Clearances the novel will trace, is seen at the moment of its highest self-consciousness in the presence of Angus, transmitter of the poetry of 'the Aged Bard' who 'lived in the days before St. Columba . . . maybe before the Saviour Himself was born' (54). In conveying the effect of the ancient poetry upon his characters, Gunn engages in a deliberate performance of a translation, a translation for which the English

language is insufficiently rich except to give an indistinct *impression* of the
original:

> As Angus went on with that ancient poem, his listeners came under its
> enchantment . . . his expression held a gravity softened by memory, as though
> the streams and the sun, the primrose and the green bank, had been enjoyed
> by him in that land that could be seen back in time – as any man can see his own
> childhood. It was the land of the Aged Bard, who was a man like Angus. And
> this Aged Bard was not a simple or uninstructed man, but on the contrary
> was a man grey with years of experience of life, rich in knowledge, who had
> faced all things and exhausted all passions, but who in the end had prayed
> to be placed by the little streams. All his dealings with gods and men had
> winnowed to that. And there came from his words to all their nostrils the
> fragrance of the primrose with its grateful hue. And this fragrance affected
> them like love. (55-6)

Gunn's English acquires a deliberate simplicity in order to emphasise not
the lack of complexity of the original speech which it is conveying, but
a complexity of an entirely different order from any available in English.
Unlike the language in which the novelist has to render their speech, the
characters' language was capable of revealing the world's 'myriad peculiarities and giving each a name'. Rather than a language which lacks words
for the complexities of modernity it is a language more rich in humanity,
being

> full of such names, not only for things but for men; particularly, indeed, for
> men, so that the name evokes each kind of man with an astonishing, almost
> laughable, magic. Naturally with this go diminutives that are the finger-tips
> of fun, phrases that snare the heart with a hair. For love-making, it is a subtle
> tongue. (14)

But the irony of Gunn's novel is the image-in-reverse of the irony of Douglas
Brown's use of Scots: Douglas Brown preserved and made available the very
language which his own literary language supplants; Gunn recaptures and
re-presents the world of a Gaelic-speaking community in the very language
which has displaced and destroyed that community and its language. The
novel is locked into a tragic conflict in which the novelist himself is the
representative of the forces that will silence his characters, while at the same
time trying to preserve a record of those characters' lives and culture, and
to allow them to speak in and through the very medium of their destruction. Whether from the negative or the positive side of the debate about
the value of the 'native' language, the Scottish novelist is caught in a guilty
dialogue in which the characters can only speak for themselves at epiphanic
moments that are but the prologue to their being rendered mute, capable
of being represented only by translation into the very language which has
oppressed and silenced them.

Thus when James Barke wants to present his Scots-speaking protagonist's silent reflections, a free indirect discourse takes over which translates David the dialect speaker into a thinker in standard English:

> He was worried about his sons – what they might do when they grew up. Andrew wanted to be, of all things, an engineer. To David that meant work and the city – Glasgow probably. Tom said he would like to be a carter: he took that to be mere childish dreaming. Especially since Tom showed little inclination for any kind of farm work. (405)

'Mere childish dreaming', 'little inclination': the meeting place between authorial voice and character's thought is one in which the vernacular stands in mute deference, erased by English. And when McIlvanney presents his characters' thought processes in *Docherty* it is in a language so extravagantly erudite and literary that they can only be read, like Neil Gunn's, as a *translation* from one language system into another, a translation designed to elevate the characters not by giving dignity to the actualities of their speech but by insisting on the complexity and integrity of their *feelings*, no matter the apparent limitations of the language in which they might be expressed. Thus Jenny, the wife of Tam Docherty, is shown coming to terms with the fact of her husband's declining ability to outface the world in language which is closer to Henry James than to Robert Burns:

> What Jenny was to gather in the years ahead, to hoard in herself like mementoes of some important person, would be small perceptions, observed perhaps by others but rendered worthless by their ignorance or thrown aside by their indifference or crushed like archaic pottery to powder by the clumsiness of their unearthing. For they would be very fragile things, the truths about a man, for long ignored, buried like refuse under what *was* refuse, secreted like ancient gold under layers of error and misunderstanding. She alone would have the faith to find them, the skill to keep them intact, the love to understand their meaning. (218)

The 'archaic pottery' crushed 'to powder by the clumsiness of their unearthing' might here be a symbol of the novelist's own relationship to his characters. The intensity of the passage turns Jenny into a mirror image of the writer, himself desperately trying to recover those 'fragile things, the truths about a man, for long ignored, buried like refuse' – the 'refuse' that is all that is recognisable in a working-class community and its language. The syntax of the authorial voice may be a paean to the emotional complexity of the characters, but that complexity is almost itself crushed under the effort of its unearthing: the novel manages to have the faith to find the 'ancient gold' and 'the love to understand their meaning', but it does so in the knowledge that it can only save shards from an inevitable 'defeat' and that they will be indistinguishable to anyone else from the simple 'refuse' of time. Tam's defeat, for both Jenny and the author, is measured in terms of his voice:

> In this way she was soon to notice how impossible Tam's promises became, how his certainties went no deeper than his voice. Hearing his desperate convictions brag themselves alive and die of their own intensity, like fireworks leaving the darkness blacker than before, seeing the emptiness that welled out of his eyes in some moments of calm, she knew that they measured not just the defeat of what he was becoming, but the almost unbelievable victory of what he had for so long been. (218)

Tam's 'certainties' can go 'no deeper than his voice' and the narrator's voice can assert *its* certainties only against the silence that his characters have left behind:

> 'He wis only five foot fower. But when yer hert goes frae yer heid tae yer taes, that's a lot o' hert.'
> One of them rubbed his hands together against the cold. Their silence was agreement, a vision achieved. They had found his epitaph. (324)

The 'agreement' which seals the novel is the epitaph of the language the novel sets out to celebrate – a dialect fulfilled in literature, in the end, only by being removed from the dialogue.

At the end of *The House with the Green Shutters* the men of the community stare at Gourlay's house: 'The scrape of their feet on the road, as they turned to stare, sounded monstrous in the silence. No man dared to speak' (247). The dialectic of English-writing narrator and the Scots-speaking characters can only conclude in the monstrous silence of the oral community, the 'blanched' whiteness over which the written text is inscribed; a community of 'bodies' in the Scots sense – 'In every little Scotch community there is a distinct type known as "the bodie"'(59) – who stare at a double incarnation of the House with the Green Shutters: one is Gourlay's house 'sitting dark there and terrible', containing the (dead) bodies of its protagonists; the other the novel itself, containing the last remains of the old Scots tongue but reducing the 'bodies' to silence 'beneath the radiant arch of the dawn' of its literary English.

II

The mutilating dialectic of English-writing author and Scots-speaking character represents a fundamental version of the dialectic of fearful selves explored in the previous chapter, but it is a problematic whose attempted resolutions have also generated many of the Scottish novel's characteristic modes of narrative and stylistic experiment. In 1928 Nan Shepherd published *The Quarry Wood*, a novel whose structure – girl of peasant family succeeds in going to university – replicates in female form the experience of young John Gourlay in *The House with the Green Shutters*, itself an ironic version of one of the paradigmatic emplotments of Scottish experience in the late nineteenth century, that of 'the lad o' pairts'. And just as young Gourlay will return home a failure, so, for very different reasons, despite academic success, will Martha. Thus Shepherd's plot potentially enacts the destruction of Scots speech (Martha is brought up in Aberdeenshire dialect) by educated English and of a continuing disjunction between them when Martha returns home. But Shepherd's narrative is far from pessimistic in its emplotment and even less so in its style, for it presents Scots and English not as antithetically opposed to one another but as alternative potentialities of a continuum within which there are no radical divisions.

> Later a powdery sunlight filled the room, irradiating the feathery caddis from the blankets that had drifted into corners. The steer of life floated in from the road. Hens cackled, dogs barked, women scolded, crying on their bairns in sharp resonant voices that carried far through the empty winter air. Peter Mennie stamped along the road with the postbag, his greeting still in the air when already his voice clanged up from Drocherty. The littlins bickered past from school, chasing cats and hens, flinging stones, calling names after an occasional stranger or carrying on for his benefit a loud and important conversation mainly fictitious. And the bigger loons, with stolen spunks that had all but burned holes in their pooches through the day, fired the whins along the roadside. Prometheus with a vulture indeed! – They tortured the wrong side of his body, those undiscriminating gods. A good old-fashioned skelping would have served the nickum better. What had he to do with anything as sophisticated as a liver? (203)

The narrative voice incorporates words from the vernacular, because they are the *mot juste* (caddis, steer) of this specific locale; adopts vernacular usages that are appropriate to her characters' perceptions (pooches, nickum); glances allusively to classical culture (Prometheus, undiscriminating gods) in a gesture which underlines the syntactic precision of cultivated English while incorporating typical vernacular locutions ('crying on'). The ironic disjunction between the values of the community she is describing (skelping as retribution) and the values which are brought to it from outside (Promethean retribution) are not presented as mutually destructive but juxtaposed in an irony which effectively 'places' and limits the scope and relevance of each. Far from seeking to separate itself from the colloquialism of the characters' speech, Shepherd's narrative voice incorporates their vocabulary and speech patterns as an essential and integral element in her own – just as her central characters will be equally at home in vernacular speech or 'standard' English. Dialect is an apparent extension of the authorial language but the authorial language has been itself founded on dialect.

Shepherd's style directly challenges what Edwin Muir had argued about the relationship of the Scots language to modern Scottish writing, and challenges too the assumptions that Muir makes about the virtues of the writers of the Irish Renaissance, whose achievements Muir wanted Scottish writers to imitate. In *Scott and Scotland* Muir wrote:

> The difference between contemporary Irish and contemporary Scottish literature is that the first is central and homogenous, and that the second is parochial and conglomerate; and this is because it does not possess an organ for the expression of a whole and unambiguous nationality. Scots dialect poetry represents Scotland in bits and patches, and in doing that it is in no doubt a faithful enough image of the present divided state of Scotland. But while we cling to it we shall never be able to express the central reality of Scotland . . . The real issue in contemporary Scottish literature is between centrality and provincialism; dialect poetry is one of the chief supports of the second of these two forces; the first can hardly be said to exist at all. (178–9)

Muir's view of the development of Scottish writing in terms of an absolute opposition between poetry written in dialect and poetry written in English deeply misconstrues the real strengths of Scottish writing from the eighteenth-century onward. The need to understand and be able to write correct English – with all that that implied for the development of rhetoric and the discipline we now, as Robert Crawford has pointed out,[8] think of as English literature – goes hand in hand during the Scottish Enlightenment with the assertion of the significance of dialect and the development of means by which it can be rendered accurately in written texts. It is often those who are most engaged in the improvement of standards of English who are most conscious of the virtues of dialect – and *vice versa*. After meeting Burns, Dugald Stewart commented that, 'Nothing perhaps was more remarkable among his various attainments, than the fluency, and precision, and originality of his language, when he spoke in company; more particularly as he aimed at purity in his turn of expression, and avoided more successfully than most Scotchmen, the peculiarities of Scottish phraseology.'[9] As Tom Crawford notes, the Ayrshire peasantry 'were hardly strangers to abstract English diction . . . For generations, farmers and labourers had been familiar with the Authorised Version of the Bible, English theological works, and interminable sermons full of words like "effectual calling"',[10] so that the interaction *between* Scots and English is not necessarily, as Muir believed, Burns's greatest weakness – 'where poetry is written in a variety of dialects with no central language as a point of reference, it is impossible to evolve a criterion of style (there is no standard of Scots poetic style)' – but rather one of his greatest strengths. In Burns's poetry, as in Shepherd's novels, dialect provides a speech whose localness and provincialism does not prevent it incorporating, with due humility, but also with pride and a sense of equality, the word of God, whether the God of the Authorized Version or the gods of classical literature:

> The Sire turns o'er, with patriarchal grace,
>   The big *ha' Bible*, ance his *Father's* pride;
> His bonnet rev'rently is laid aside,
>   His *lyart haffets* wearing thin and bare;
> Those strains that once did sweet in ZION glide,
>   He wales a portion with judicious care;
> *'And let us worship* GOD*!'* he says with solomn air.

In the language of Burns's 'The Cotter's Saturday Night',[11] 'lyart haffets' and 'solemn air' are no more mutually incompatible than Ayrshire and Zion; the local is simply an incarnation of the universal; they each exist fully only in relation to each other. The same may be said of the way in which English and Scots developed in Scotland from the eighteenth century – each existing *within* the other in a mutually defining – and creatively enriching – relationship:[12] a dialogue that produces more and richer speech rather than the confrontation enacted by Gourlay and his son or by the schoolteacher and Conn Docherty.

If the tragic linguistic destruction enacted by the Gourlays, leading to the imposition of silence on the community, models one way of seeing the relationship between Scotland's languages, the alternative is presented by Martha in *The Quarry Wood* at the moment when she decides to adopt an orphan child who is being fostered by her mother. Martha's experience in the novel is one of a continual translation of herself out of the vernacular language of her family into alternative discourses. At an early point in the narrative she adopts the suppression of her 'voice' in order to fulfil the requirements of entering into a written culture:

> Martha had grown up quite. After all the flaring disquietudes of her child-hood, she had settled into a uniform calmness of demeanour that was rarely broken. Her silences, however, were deceptive. She was not placid, but con-trolled. She had the control that comes from purpose; and her purpose was the getting of knowledge. There was no end to the things that one could know. (26–7)

The 'one' of the final sentence defines the impersonality that she is striving for, a suppression of the individual voice which, in the following scene, is the personal equivalent of her efforts to shut out her family while she does her homework at the kitchen table. Her father, Geordie, has been playing with the younger children while her mother, Emmeline, reads a 'Pansy Novelette' in English – she is an insatiable reader but only of books which 'never . . . depict a ploughman, or a ploughman's wife and family' (43); in his clumsiness Geordie has accidentally dunted Emmeline's chair, jarring her elbow into her chin:

> Geordie was still in his cups, metaphorically speaking, an honest joke suiting him as well as a dram; and Mrs Ironside was grumbling still: 'Garrin' a body bite their tongue . . . I never heard . . . '; when Willie sprang on top of the table and upset the bottle of ink upon Martha's Latin version. She had written half of it in fair copy, in a burst of exasperation at the refusal of the second half to take coherent form. Now she sprang to her feet and watched the black ruin, staring at the meandering of the ink.
>
> 'Ye micht dicht it up,' said Emmeline. (27)

The bitten tongue of the mother in the act of reading English – the suppression of the oral by writing – is juxtaposed with the blotted ink that wipes out the daughter's 'fair copy' – the suppression of writing by the vulgar. The daughter, too, must 'bite her tongue', in the impossibility of complaining about her conditions, but what she is doing is a 'biting of the tongue' in which she has been brought up in order to make herself over into a 'fair copy' of her translation into another culture.

That process of half-fulfilled translation is repeated in her relations with Luke, the student who is married to one of the children – Dussie – whom Martha's mother had fostered; Dussie is almost, therefore, a half-sister to Martha, which encourages her to understand Luke's interest in her as 'fraternal', until she realises,

> . . . that she was for him an earnest of the spiritual world; its ministrant; his Beatrice.
>
> 'I don't worship you. You worship a goddess through flame, don't you? – But I have learned through you to worship flame. The flame of life. Like Beatrice. Making me aware of hierarchies beyond our own. – I'm not making love to you, you know, Marty.'
>
> She said, 'Luke!' with a tongue so astounded that he laughed audibly; and in a moment so did she. The absurdity of the idea was palpable. (76)

She is translated out of herself and into a spirituality which has nothing to do with mere earthly affections, or indeed with her own specific personality, a spirituality which belongs to a different 'tongue'; and because she does not realise she loves him she negates herself and 'became the more fully what he had imagined her' (77) – the irony being, of course, that Dante, in writing about his Beatrice, was creating a new vernacular literature out of a living language, in opposition to the classical Latin tradition, while she is being translated back into a classical realm, displacing her from her own 'tongue' and from her real feelings. After graduation, and the loss of Luke, Martha returns to her home district as a schoolteacher, and discovers that, because of the observation of a midnight meeting with Luke, the local community assume that another of her mother's many foster-children is her own: she is being translated once more, but this time through her mother-tongue into motherhood:

> 'Weel, he's yours, isna he?' Mrs Davie asked it cheerily.
> 'Mine?' said Martha.
> She was astonished.
> 'Is't nae true then?' Mrs Davie asked.
> 'True!' Martha began to laugh. 'I never had a child in my life,' she cried; and instantly thought, 'Of all the ridiculous things to have said!'
> She stopped laughing.
> Her astonishment was turning to dismay.
> 'An' sae it's nae your bairn ava'?' said Mrs Davie. 'Weel, weel, fat'll fowk nae say? They've got a haud o' some story aboot a lad ye used to tryst wi' up in the woodie. "She bides oot a' nicht," Leebie Longmore says to me. "A bonny-like cairry on." An it's nae your bairn?' (174)

The dialect voice speaks of a procreative union where Martha has experienced only a destructive negation of herself, but the dialect voice thereby tells, unwittingly, the truth of her relations with Luke: 'a bonny-like cairry on' to Mrs Davie means an apparently reckless evasion of ordinary morality whereas Luke's immorality has been in seeing in Martha only the 'bonny-*like*'-ness of a beauty beyond her which is more important to him than she is. Martha's response to the community's interpretation of her, however, is, quite literally, to adopt it – by adopting the child *as* her own. She re-translates herself back into the meanings of the oral culture from which she has been transcribed and in doing so allows herself to have the child that the educated world has written out of her life by turning her into a figure from a poem. By adoption she undoes the destructive effects of her adopted languages, but without having to deny any of them:

> 'Ye're mighty concerned wi' him a' at aince,' said her mother.
> 'Am I? Well, yes, I am. And I'm going to be concerned with him. He's going to be mine.'
> 'Weel,' said Emmeline, 'ye micht dae a lot waur nor gie the bairn a shog alang.'
> 'Once I get home again,' Martha answered, 'he'll maybe get two or three shogs along.' (196)

On Martha's tongue language is now like the child she has made hers: a mixture of origins, a mixture of ends; and home is a place where two or three languages 'shog alang' 'a' at aince' by giving each other 'shogs along'.

It is the mixture of languages in dialogue with each other in Scottish writing that has made Bakhtin such a favoured resource for recent Scottish criticism. Bakhtin's conception of 'heteroglossia' can be deployed effectively as a challenge to those who see in the mixed dialects of Scottish writing an unavoidable weakness, since, for Bakhtin, the novel is, by the very nature of its form, committed to such linguistic diversity:[13]

> The novel orchestrates all its themes, the totality of the world of objects and ideas depicted and expressed in it, by means of the social diversity of speech types and by the differing individual voices that flourish under such conditions. Authorial speech, the speeches of narrators, inserted genres, the speech of characters, are merely those fundamental compositional unities with whose help heteroglossia can enter the novel. (263)

Bakhtin's concept of 'hybridization' – 'a mixture of two social languages within the limits of a single utterance, an encounter, within the arena of an utterance, between two different linguistic consciousnesses' (358) – can also be used to explain some of the characteristic effects of the Scottish tradition, with its emphasis on dual linguistic consciousnesses. Indeed, these theories, and others which emphasise the complexity of the relation of speech to writing (as in the work of Derrida and deconstructive criticism) have provided an interpretive context to which many Scottish novels are more responsive than to other forms of criticism.[14] Since 'heteroglossia', however, is an account of the very nature of the novel itself, in all cultures, it may justify the dialogic practice of Scottish novelists but it cannot discriminate the features that constitute a specifically Scottish tradition in the novel. For a local account of the dialogic structure of the Scottish novel, we can look to a concept with a specifically Scottish provenance in John Macmurray's notion of 'heterocentricity', as defined in the second volume of *Persons in Relation* (1957 and 1961), based on the Gifford Lectures given in Glasgow in 1953-54.[15]

Macmurray's work sets out with the radical intention of overturning the whole tradition of Western philosophy from Descartes to Bertrand Russell by challenging the notion that philosophy should begin from the point of view of the philosopher as 'Thinker'; against this, Macmurray sets – in the phrase which is the title of the first volume of his work – *The Self as Agent*,[16] by which he meant that 'the Self has its being only in agency, and that its reflective activities are but negative aspects of this agency' (15). The importance of this shift in Macmurray's view is that,

> ... the thinking Self – the Self as Subject – is the Agent in self-negation. In reflection we isolate ourselves from dynamic relations with the Other; we withdraw into ourselves, adopting the attitude of spectators, not of participants. We are then out of touch with the world, and for touch we must substitute vision; for our real contact with the Other an imagined contact; and for real activity an activity of the imagination. (16)

The Self as Agent, on the other hand, 'exists only in dynamic relation with the other . . . the Self is constituted by its relation to the Other; that it has its being in its relationship; and the relationship is necessarily personal' (17). The Self is neither a monadic thinker nor a pragmatic economic unit: the Self is constituted in, through and by its relationships to others: the failure of the central tradition of modern Western thought is the result of not recognising the extent to which the Self is neither a self-enclosed unity nor a structure determined by external forces. The Other is not an alien world antithetical to Self: Self is the Other in its relations; the Self therefore is a process enacted through relationships which are themselves only possible as a result of the resistance generated by the agency of others and which the Self encounters in trying to act.

Heterocentricity is, for Macmurray, twofold: it is the fundamental onto-logical condition of Self in its construction through Otherness, and, at a moral level, it is the condition in which we recognise and act, on a social and personal level, in full acknowledgement of this fundamental nature of our existence as selves, and therefore in awareness of the demands made on us to maintain the fundamentally communal structure of human life. As *Persons in Relation* describes it, the ideal condition of our personal identity is one in which,

> Each, then, is heterocentric; the centre of interest and attention is in the other, not in himself. The other is the centre of value. For himself he has no value in himself, but only for the other. But this is mutual: the other cares for him disinterestedly in return. Each, that is to say, acts, and therefore thinks and feels for the other, and not for himself. But because the positive motive con-tains and subordinates its negative, their unity is no fusion of selves, neither is it a functional unity of differences – neither an organic nor a mechanical unity – it is a unity of persons. Each remains a distinct individual; the other remains really other. Each realizes himself in and through the other. (158)

For Macmurray, the Other is not simply the necessary antithesis with-out which the Self could not arise, like two mutually antagonistic forces between which is set an unbridgeable gulf; the Self *is* only through the Other; the identity of the Self *is* its relations with otherness rather than its coherence within itself. Development of our fundamentally heterocentric selfhood is what makes us persons rather than isolated egos. The rootedness of Macmurray's conception in the Scottish tradition which I described in Chapter 2 is clear from the fact that 'love and fear' are the fundamental polarities within which human life is constructed : 'Since the "You and I" relation constitutes both the "You" and the "I" persons, the relation to the "You" is necessary for my personal existence. If, through fear of the "You", I reject this relation, I frustrate my own being' (74–5). Persons-in-relation are beings who have overcome fear and a community of persons-in-relation is a community which has liberated itself from fear: 'The ideal of the per-sonal is also the condition of freedom – that is, of a full realization of his capacity to act – for every person. Short of this there is unintegrated, and therefore suppressed, negative motivation: there is unresolved fear; and fear inhibits action and destroys freedom' (159).

This dialogic conception of the self is precisely what is established in Shepherd's *The Quarry Wood*, not because Shepherd would have known the work that Macmurray was beginning to publish when she was writing her novel but because both are working forward from the traditions of Scottish thought that give priority to the communion which is the basis of social existence. What we can see in *The Quarry Wood* is that Shepherd is not simply performing a process of 'grafting' or 'hybridization' in terms of language, but that her use of languages-in-relation is the linguistic equivalent of a narrative that is a powerful enactment of 'persons-in-relation'. Martha, visiting relatives after her time at university, queries their relatedness to her; she 'chafed a little at kinship. Relations . . . but what relation were they to her soul?' (94). What she is to discover, however, is that this isolation of her 'soul' is precisely the destructive denial of heterocentricity in one of the forms of the egocentric which, for Macmurray, always results in a dualistic conception of the world:

> This egocentricity creates a dualism . . . the world divides into two worlds; an actual world which does not answer to our demands, and refuses to satisfy us, and another world, an ideal world which we can imagine, which does. Whether this gives rise to a contemplative or to a pragmatic mode of morality depends upon which of the two worlds is thought as the *real* world, which, that is to say, is taken as being for the sake of the other. Similarly, the self becomes two selves, for each of which one of these two worlds is 'the Other'. There is a spiritual self with a spiritual life and a material self with a bodily life. The positive apperception, through its heterocentricity, escapes this dualism. (123)

These dualisms Martha will discover in the value systems of the two men who court her. Through Luke, she finds herself transformed into her contemplative self, and he can describe his encounter with her in the wood as one in 'she just melted away – if I were a mediaeval chiel I'd honestly be tempted to believe she was an apparition. A false Florimel. An accident of light' (120); in Roy Rory Foubister, on the other hand, she discovers the pragmatist who is unconcerned with her 'relations', particularly her relation to her Aunt Jospehine, whom she is nursing through a long illness:

> Taking life, like Aunt Jospehine, with zest, he could not take it, as she did, for itself; but always for what he might take from it. It was plain he would exact his pound of flesh and see to it that he was not duped with carrion. Martha read it in his impatience at any interruption to his purposed enjoyments, his indifference to her concern over leaving Aunt Jospehine alone: but her judgement remained in the abstract. She had not yet quite learned that the importance of things lies not in themselves but in their relations. (149)

In reaction against the egocentricity of these two men what Martha discovers is a heterocentricity that recognises that 'the importance of things lies not in themselves but in their relations', and that her real self is not to be constituted by negating the peasant community of her relatives in the 'higher' world of education that Luke offers, or in the wider world of imperial adventure that Roy Foubister offers, but in the fulfilment of the community in and through which her self is constituted.

What Shepherd has to do, in *The Quarry Wood*, is to develop a mode of narration that will deny the traditional structure of novelistic narrative as a progression towards the fulfilment of the authentic identity of the protagonist, and the achievement of autonomy – or the tragic failure to achieve autonomy – by the protagonist. In Shepherd's novels the protagonist develops precisely by overcoming the belief that she can 'be (her) own creator' (184), and by the recognition of the self's communitarian basis. For this reason, the novel is a journey away from 'selfhood' and back to the community from which Martha has striven to separate herself, back in fact to the truth that we, as readers, are told in the first paragraph but which we, like she, have forgotten as we follow the development of her story:

> Martha Ironside was nine years old when she kicked her grand-aunt Jospehine. At nineteen she loved the old lady, idly perhaps, in her natural humour, as she loved the sky and space. At twenty-four, when Miss Josephine Leggatt died, aged seventy-nine and reluctant, Martha knew that it was she who had taught her wisdom; thereby proving – she reflected – that man does not learn from books alone; because Martha had kicked Aunt Josephine (at the age of nine) for taking her from her books. (1)

The whole narrative is already complete in the first paragraph: by the end we will have come back to the recognition of the real importance of the relations which, through education, Martha's development into egocentricity – the egocentricity of the written's domination over the oral – will have denied. Martha's development, therefore, is a digression as well as a translation, and Shepherd's novel is built in a digressive mode which continually diverts from the main channel of the action to focus on the host of apparently 'minor' – sometimes, indeed, apparently redundant – characters who will come to be revealed as the structure of relations through which Martha will discover her true – her heterocentric – identity. Shepherd's mode of narration sets out to discomfit our expectations of the novel form by constantly gesturing to the other stories which the very requirement of the novel form would thrust to the margins of the narrative:

> 'I suppose it's impossible that you'd ever come across her,' Martha said when she had told Madge's story.

'Just about it,' said Sally cheerfully. 'Still, there's no knowing. There's queerer things happen than we've the right to expect.' And she began to tell her niece the queer things that happen.

'I've had a venturesome life,' said Sally.

A footnote to her life might have run: For venturesome read betrayed, persecuted, forsaken, hampered and undaunted: but the general public finds footnotes uncomfortable reading and leaves them alone. (181–2)

Shepherd's novels are built out of a whole series of footnotes, footnotes which are a constant revelation of the stories which may seem insignificant and yet without which the supposedly 'central' narrative would be given an entirely false valuation, precisely because it would deny the fact that its protagonist's identity is created not independently but in and through its relations. It will be through the footnote of Sally's example that Martha will discover how to act, and in adopting the child begin to live for others: as a result, of course, she will no longer be Beatrice, caught in the amber of the ideal; nor will she be an pragmatic egotist, living in negation of her origins: she will have discovered, in Macmurray's words, that 'a positive unity of persons is the self-realization of the personal' (158); she will reach the consciousness in which 'she was looking in succession at the events of her life through the eyes of all the different actors in them' (158).

For Shepherd, the novel itself has to be reconstructed as a communal narrative, a communal narrative which can acknowledge life's 'footnotes' in defiance of its own individualistic traditions and root itself back into the communal and oral life of which it seems the negation. In this, Shepherd was setting an agenda, both in terms of language and narrative style, which would form one of the major strands of the Scottish novel in the twentieth century. Dialect becomes the foundation of an alternative conception of the self, a self that has gone beyond fear of the Other precisely by knowing its selfhood exists only in and through dialogue with the Other, in and through the recognition of the dialects which are the expression of otherness. It was an example which was to be followed by Lewis Grassic Gibbon in developing the narrative strategies of *A Scots Quair*. In a scene which replicates Shepherd's presentation of Martha studying in the family kitchen, Chris is at her books, thinking of her friend Marget who has been sent off to school:

So that was your Marget gone, there seemed not a soul in Kinraddie that could take her place, the servant queans of an age with Chris were no more than gowks and gomerils a-screech round the barn of the Mains at night with the ploughmen snickering behind them. And John Guthrie had as little use for them as Marget herself. *Friends? Stick to your lessons and let's see you make a name for yourself, you've no time for friends.*

Mother looked up at that, friendly-like, not feared of him at all, she was never feared. *Take care her head doesn't soften with lessons and dirt, learning in books it was sent the wee red daftie at Cuddiestoun clean skite, they say.* And father poked out his beard at her. *Say? Would you rather see her skite with book-learning or skite with –* and then he stopped, and began to rage at Dod and Alec that were making a noise in the kitchen corner. But Chris, a-pore above her books in the glow of the paraffin lamp, heeding to Caesar's coming in Gaul and the stour the creature raised there, knew right well what father had thought to speak of – *lust* was the word he'd wanted, perhaps. And she turned the page with the weary Caesar man and thought of the wild career the daftie Andy had led one day in the roads of Kinraddie.

Marget had barely gone when the thing came off, it was fair the speak of the place that happening early in April . . . (47)

The language of learning is the language of absence, individualism and the denial of personal relations: dialect is the language of community, but a community which Chris is being separated from, driven by the repressive 'fears' of her father away from the 'fearlessness' of her mother. Addressing herself as 'you' – 'That was your Marget gone' – emphasises her double position, within and without the community and its language.

The narrative mode of the novel, however, is to move from Chris's consciousness and her personal recollection of events to their narration in the voice of the community itself: thus the story of the 'daftie' starts in her mother's dialect speech – 'books it was sent the wee red daftie at Cuddieston clear kite' – passes through Chris's reflective consciousness – 'thought of the wild career the daftie' – and passes into a sentence which could be either Chris's thought or retrospective narration – 'Marget had barely gone when the thing came off' – before turning into the voice of the community telling itself its own stories – 'it was fair the speak of the place', a voice which takes over and continues the narrative as though it was a direct extension of Chris's own consciousness: 'That morning it was that the daftie Andy stole out of Cuddiestoun and started his scandalous rampage through Kinraddie. Long Rob of the Mill was to say . . .' (48). Gibbon constructs a narrative which is told in the voice of a community speaking to itself,[17] a voice in which she is both Self and Other. The narrative voice positions Chris as the addressee, 'you', as well as the third person protagonist of the novel – 'So, hurt and dazed, she turned to the land, close to it and the smell of it, kind and kind it was, it didn't rise up and torment your heart, you could keep at peace with the land if you gave your heart and hands' (230) – and in doing so makes her not only the generalised 'you' of the common consciousness of the community, but the enactment of Macmurray's conception of the person: 'Persons, therefore, exist only as one element in the complex "You and I".' The 'person' that is Chris is 'she' in the narrative, but that 'she' must become an 'I' if it is to address itself as 'you', so that the complex 'You and I' which forms the fundamental relation of our communal identity replaces the 'she' and 'I' which separates us into external objects and individual egos. The 'you' represents both the common experience of the community – addressing itself in the form of the inclusive 'you' – and the personal 'you' that is addressed by an 'I', a continuity of 'I' and 'you' that is the foundation of the heterocentric notion of the person.

At the opening of *Sunset Song*, however, this form of community is on the point of extinction. The madness which the daftie's book-learning has produced (and to which Chris herself is being subjected) is prophetic of the madness of the civilised world which will intrude upon the community to destroy it as it destroys its language. Significantly, the story of Andy is immediately juxtaposed with the coming to the village of the ironically-named Reverend Gibbon, voice of a biblical tradition based on the written text whose sermons lust after the oral as he lusts after the girls of the village: the author's mocking transference on to his Reverend double of his own relationship to the text releases the narrative voice of the novel from the imposition of an external linguistic system into a self-communing narrative, one performed through its own gossip and story-telling as an extension of the self of the central character. But that narrative method cannot be maintained when the relationship between self and community breaks down: Chris, in the second and third volumes of the trilogy, becomes more and more distanced from the community, but there is less and less community for her to be attached to because of the class conflict by which it is riven. *Cloud Howe* and *Grey Granite* will reveal the subjection of the narrative voice by a class-ridden bigotry which turns the 'you' from a communal 'You and I' into an aggressive insistence on otherness:

> Why the hell should you waste your time in a kirk when you were young, you were only young once, there was the cinema down in Dundon, or a dance or so . . . You'd chirk to your horses and give a bit smile as you saw the minister swoop by on his bike, with his coat-tails flying and his wee, flat hat; and at night in the bothy some billy or other would mock the way that he spoke or moved. To hell with ministers and toffs of his kind, they were aye the friends of the farmers, you knew. (14)

Grassic Gibbon's trilogy is a quest for the recovery of the heterocentricity that is enacted in *Sunset Song*'s narrative technique in defiance of the fact that the foundations of that communal ethic are being destroyed by industrialisation and the impact of the First World War. It is at Chris's wedding, moment of the community's celebration of its own fertility, that the characters themselves debate the death of their language: 'what a shame it was that folk should be shamed nowadays to speak Scotch – or they called it Scots if they did, split-tongued sourocks! Every damned little narrow dowped rat that you met put on the English if he thought he'd impress you – as though Scotch wasn't good enough now, it had words in it that the thin but scrachs of the English could never come at. And Rob said *You can tell me, man, what's the English for sotter, or greip, or smore, or pleiter, gloaming or glanching or well-henspeckled? And if you said gloaming was sunset you'd fair be a liar . . . '* (156). A novel whose title is *Sunset Song* asserts that the language of its own title is inadequate to the world that Scots describes: the title suppresses the very dialect that the novel sets out to record. The trilogy as a whole seeks to discover a new dialect voice which will also represent a new potentiality of community. It arrives at the moment, in *Grey Granite*, when the strikers are attacked by the police: the 'you' of Chris's self-communing returns:

> As the dozen bobbies cleared the way for the scabs coming out of the Works, the dark was falling, there came a hell and pelt of a rush, you were all of you in it, young chaps and old, one bobby struck at you with his truncheon, missed, you were past him, slosh in the kisser the scab; and all about you, milling in the dark, the chaps broke in and hell broke out, the bobbies hitting about like mad, tootling on their whistles, scrunch their damned sticks . . .
>   And you looked round and there b'God they were, the calsays clattering under their feet, waving their sticks, Christ, never able to face up to them. Around to the left was the way to take nipping by the timber yard over the brig. All the chaps running helter-skelter you scattered, the bobbies wouldn't spare pickets now except to bash in their brain-caps, maybe, after seeing one of their lot on the ground. B'God, this would be a tale to tell when you got back safe to Kirrieben. (120–1)

The folk voice becomes again a voice living in the expectation of its own telling – 'a tale to tell' – just as the picket is an anticipation of the left-wing politics – 'Around by the left was the way to take' – through which a new form of community will be established to replace the old. The dialect voice requires the dialectics of marxism as its conclusion, just as marxism requires the dialect voice of the worker as the source of its own concrete experience of alienation.

For Gibbon, the dialect voice maintains the possibility of a community and a communality in defiance of the hierarchies of the class system that are embodied in and through the voice of standard English. The folk voice may have only momentary presences in *Grey Granite*, and the text may fragment into many different and isolated discourses, but by refusing standard English the position of narrative control over his text, Gibbon enacts in the narrative form of the novel the resistance to the degradation of humanity by capitalism which the novel records. Equally, the increasingly caricatural representation of character in the final novel mimics the decay of self-hood from the full acknowledgement of the other that is a person into the selfish egotism of an economic individualism. It is a decline into the kind of society that Macmurray describes as 'pragmatic' and that receives its philosophical expression in Hobbes, a society in which 'the persons who compose society are, by nature, isolated units, afraid of one another, and continuously on the defensive . . . each isolated individual uses all his powers to secure his own satisfaction and to preserve his own life; and in consequence the state of Nature is a war of every man against every man' (134). Dialect holds out against this society the ghost of another kind of person, another kind of language of relations and of relations of language.

Sixty years after *A Scots Quair*, Irvine Welsh's *Trainspotting*[18] was to use the same structural devices – a community's self-narration in dialect – precisely to satirise the pragmatic society of Thatcherism, full of 'isolated units, afraid of one another'. What we see, and what we hear, in *Trainspotting* is a community – the community of drug users – who are footnotes to the society of the 1980s, but whose descent from communitarianism into egotism, from community into isolation, is itself the mirror image of the pragmatic and egotistic society of which it is the underclass. Rather than outcasts from society, Welsh's addicts and pushers and users are the mirror image of the free market capitalism which they believe themselves to have refused: rather than its antithesis, they simply perform at its most extreme both the inability to become a Person – 'Ah went tae the Central Library and read Carl Rogers's *On Becoming A Person*. A thought that the book wis shite' (185) – and the lack of responsibility for others that means the one with the drugs is the one with power:

> – Back oot ma fuckin light boys, ah snap, gesturing the cunts away wi backward sweeps ay ma hand. Ah know ah'm playing at being The Man, n part ay us hates masel, because it's horrible when some cunt does it tae you. Naebody though, could ivir be in this position and then deny the proposition thit absolute power corrupts. The gadges move a few steps back and watch in silence as ah cook. The fuckers will huv tae wait. Lesley comes first, eftir me. That goes without saying.

The speechlessness – 'that goes without saying' – of a self-destructive selfishness – 'n part ay us hates masel' – emphasises the extent to which dialect speech is the haunting potentiality of a community of persons-in-relation, all mutually interdependent; what is actually revealed, however, is simply a community of dependency – welfare-dependency, drug-dependency, money-dependency – which is the mirror image of the society of isolated, atomistic individuals of modern capitalism. The multiple nicknames for the characters – Renton is Mark, Rents, Rentboy to different characters in the novel – emphasise the potential personalism of individual relationships but act in the end to isolate everyone from a possible community in which they can discover themselves as persons.

In *Trainspotting* dialect is like the empty shell of Leith Central Station where it is impossible now to spot trains: it gestures to the lost community which dialect had represented in the Scottish tradition and which has now been corrupted into fearful individualism:

> We go fir a pish in the auld Central Station at the Fit ay the Walk, now a barren, desolate hangar, which is soon tae be demolished and replaced by a

supermarket and swimming centre. Somehow, that makes us sad, even though
ah wis eywis too young tae mind ay trains ever being there.
– Some size ay a station this wis. Get a train tae anywhair fae here, at one
time, or so they sais, ah sais, watchin ma steaming pish splash oantae the
cauld stane. (308)

'They sais, ah sais' points to the communal voice and the individual voice
as being potentially in unity, but what then happens dramatises the lack of
human connection that the empty station symbolises:

   An auld drunkard, whom Begbie had been looking at, lurched up tae us,
   wine boatil in his hand. Loads ay them used this place tae bevvy and crash
   in.
   - What yis up tae lads? Trainspottin, eh? He sais, laughing uncontrollably at
   his ain fuckin wit.
   - Aye. That's right, Begbie sais. Then under his breath: – Fuckin auld cunt.
   - Ah well, ah'll leave yis tae it. Keep up the trainspottin mind! He staggered
   oaf, his rasping, drunkard's cackles filling the desolate barn. Ah noticed that
   Begbie seemed strangely subdued and uncomfortable. He wis turned away fae
   us.
   It wis only then ah realised thit the auld wino wis Begbie's faither. (309)

The 'trainspottin mind' is a mind that has lost its connection, one whose
language is spoken to no one ('under his breath') and which is 'turned away
fae us' – away from the 'us' of persons in relation. Begbie takes his anger out
in casual violence 'upon a guy in Duke Street' who happens to be passing:
'The expression that guy had when he looked up at Begbie was mair one
ay resignation than fear. The boy understood everything'. And Renton and
Begbie 'continued our walk in silence' (309). When heterocentricity breaks
down, so does language, because the 'other' has become an object, to be
used and abused, rather than a self and an agent to be engaged with.
   Novels committed to the use of dialect necessarily involve themselves
not only in dialogue – the speech of the demotic – and in the dialogic – in
Bakhtin's sense of multiple voices within a text – but also in dialectic,
because the existence of two or more distinct linguistic contexts within
the text presumes the existence of alternative value systems which those
linguistic contexts express, and therefore of a dialectical process of debate
and argument between those values. Far from being simply the attempted
record of working-class or lower-class life, the dialect novel is one of the
foundations of the philosophical orientation of Scottish fiction. As George
Davie has argued, the distinctiveness of the Scottish intellectual tradition
lies in the key role that philosophy played at the Scottish universities and
in the commitment to general ideas which it inculcated:[19] that commitment
to general ideas could itself be seen as the outcome of the need to resolve,
at an intellectual level, both the conflicting value systems of a culture which

had to operate between alternative linguistic codes and the implications of a religious tradition which laid enormous emphasis on the individual's need to resolve the biblical text for him or herself. The dialectic of dialect's interaction with standard speech – of the oral environment of Scots speakers with the written world of biblical truth – underpins a cultural tradition to which dialectic, as a philosophical method, was central. The novel of dialects becomes, almost inevitably, the novel of dialectics. *Trainspotting* acknowledges this when Renton, in court for stealing a book, outlines the philosophical basis of his position:

> – Mr Renton, you did not intend to sell the books?
> – Naw. Eh, no, your honour. They were for reading.
> – So you read Kierkegaard. Tell us about him, Mr Renton, the patronising cunt sais.
> – I'm interested in his concepts of subjectivity and truth, and particularly his ideas concerning choice; the notion that genuine choice is made out of doubt and uncertainty, and without recourse to the experience or advice of others. It could be argued, with some justification, that it's primarily a bourgeois, existential philosophy and would therefore seek to undermine collective societal wisdom. However, it's also a liberating philosophy, because when such societal wisdom is negated, the basis for social control over the individual becomes weakened and . . . but I'm rabbiting a bit here. Ah cut myself short. They hate a smart cunt. It's easy to talk yourself into a bigger fine, or fuck sake, a higher sentence. (165–6)

Renton's philosophical exposition is 'talk' which can get him a 'higher sentence' – both the higher rhetoric in which he is engaged and the sentence he might get in jail. The 'higher sentence' belongs to a culture which he is now stealing as effectively as he stole the book. He is engaging in precisely the kind of dialectics which the society of which he is a part must suppress in order to maintain its own control, because what he is expressing is the philosophy of individual isolationism which appears to challenge society but is actually a justification of society's economic individualism, its negation of the heterocentricity of which his dialect speech is but the ghost.

III

The style of Welsh's *Trainspotting*, like the style of much new Scottish writing in the early 1990s, owes a substantial debt to the work of James Kelman and to Kelman's radical renewal, with the publication of *The Busconductor Hynes* in 1984,[20] of the potentialities of both working-class fiction and the dialect novel. In an interview with one of those influenced by him, Duncan McLean, Kelman stated that the difficulty for working-class and regional writers is that they are told that 'we can't write about certain subjects because we don't have the right voice! They obviously don't realise that language is culture – if you lose your language you've lost your culture, so if you've lost the way your family talk, the way your friends talk, then you've lost your culture, and you'd be divorced from it'.[21] For Kelman most literature is an evasion of reality, either because it is located in a social environment irrelevant to most people – 'Ninety per cent of the literature in Great Britain concerns people who never have to worry about money at all. We always seem to be watching or reading about emotional crises among folk who live in a world of great fortune both in matters of money and luck' – or because it operates in genres deliberately designed to deny reality: 'if reality had a part to play in genre fiction then it would stop being genre fiction'.[22] Kelman's fiction sets out to resist becoming 'literature' by a fundamental commitment to realism in content and language.

Kelman's novels – unlike McIlvanney's earlier works, for instance – take place not in the traditional sites of the working class struggle for power (the mines and factories: *Docherty*), nor in the traditional sites of working class escape from work and exploitation (home and sport: *The Big Man*[23]), but along the margins of that traditional working class life. They do so because, as in Welsh, that traditional life has been decimated: founded on heavy industry and on a mass society whose masses could be brought into solidarity, it has been wiped out by the destruction of the traditional Scottish industries. Kelman's central characters are the leftovers of the collapse of working class life and of the languages which sustained it: they inhabit a fragmented linguistic community which is mirrored by their own inner fragmentation.

Central to Kelman's realism is authenticity in the presentation of his characters' voices and a refusal to compromise with traditional orthographies by which Scots has been rendered. Kelman transliterates his characters' dialogue by a phonetic orthography that seeks neither to patronise nor to dignify the actuality of Scottish speech, as for instance in this interchange between Patrick Doyle, central character of *A Disaffection*[24] and his parents:

> – I'm no prejudiced at all, you just stick up for them.
> – I don't. I just tell the bloody truth, as I see it.
> – I'm no saying ye dont, but let's face it as well Pat, ye do like to be different.
> – Naw I dont.
> – Your maw's right, said Mr Doyle. The same with bringing back the belt, you've got to be different there too.
> – Tch da.
> – Nay tch da about it – you've aye been against the belt. But at least the weans'll show some damn respect. And you canni deny it. (112–13)

'Ye' and 'you' are mixed in this speech, as are traditional Scottish words – 'weans' – with demotic pronunciation of English: 'canni'. Their language is not rendered in terms of an ideal of the Scottish working class as the 'tradition-bearers' of a distinctive Scots language, but in terms of a pronunciation specific to a geographic location. More importantly, however, what Kelman has done is to allow that language to fuse together with his own narrative voice so that, as in Grassic Gibbon, the distinction between the language of narration and the language of dialogue is dissolved. The lack of grammatical markers for speech means that the text can move in an unbroken flow from speech, to thought, to narrative:

> – Mrs Doyle sniffed slightly: Yous'll end up arguing.
> – Patrick nodded. After a pause he swallowed a mouthful of tea and resumed eating. He took another slice of bread and wiped up the sauce at the rim of his plate. His da was looking at him. Pat glanced at him. They both looked away. It was quite sad because it was hitting old nerves or something and shouldni have been causing such a big kerfuffle. He looked at his da again but there was nothing he could give him. He couldnt. He couldnt give him anything. He didnt deserve to be given anything. So how come he should be given it? People get what they deserve in this life. Even parents. Maws and das. They dont have a special dispensation. Except maybe from the queen or the pope or any other of these multibillionaire capitalist bastards. But no from their equals, they don't get any dispensation from them. So fuck off. (113)

The third person narrative voice that relates facts in the world – 'he swallowed ... Pat glanced ... They both looked' – merges into the reflective third person voice that interprets characters' states of mind – 'He was quite sad' – which then fuses with the character's own thoughts and the language in which he 'speaks' to himself – 'He couldnt give him anything. He didn't deserve to be given anything. So how come he should be given it?' – which in turn becomes direct interior monologue – 'So fuck off'. Kelman's particular use of free indirect discourse not only allows modulation between different perspectives (third person narrator, first person self-reflection) but also allows modulation across different linguistic registers.

The standard written forms of language and the representation of oral pronunciation are so mixed in Kelman's language that there is no distinction between the narrative voice and the character's speech or thoughts: no hierarchy of language is established which orders the value to be put on the characters' language in relation to any other mode of speech or writing within the text. The text is designed visually to resist the moment of arrest in which the reader switches between the narrative voice of the text and the represented speech of a character, and what this does is to create a linguistic equality between speech and narration which allows the narrator to adopt the speech idioms of his characters, or the characters to think or speak in 'standard English', with equal status. Where Grassic Gibbon made the community the narrative voice to which the protagonist was subsidiary, Kelman makes the narrative voice a subsidiary component of his character's consciousness. Thus the self-addressing 'you' within the narrative voice of *Sunset Song* becomes the self-addressing 'you' of *The Busconductor Hines*:

> He had been getting himself into a state; and it is daft getting yourself into a state. You sit there getting worse and worse. What is the unnameable. That which is not to be articulated. Some things are not articulately. A horror of rodents is articulately. But the things that are not unable to be not said. What about them. They are not good. They are not good but must also be good. (100)

The 'he' becomes 'you', but then turns into a series of sentences in which it is indeterminate whether they are implicitly 'he thought', 'you thought' or 'I thought'; the subject to which the sentences are attached is 'not articulately' articulated and the sentences take place in a space between 'he' and 'you' where 'I' might have been if it could have been articulated as an autonomous ego rather than being constituted by a dialogue. The same happens to the 'ye' of *How late it was, how late*, which narrates itself to itself both in the second and the third person:[25]

> The thing is ye see about Sammy's situation, the way he thought about things, who knows, it wasnay something ye could get yer head round. Hard to explain. Then these things as well that draw ye in then push ye away I mean fuck sake great, alright ye think alright, it's good man, it's okay. I mean who's gony fucking moan about it, there's nay moan on, it's just being practical, realistic, ye've just to be realistic, ye approach things in a down-to-earth manner. I mean Sammy was never a moaner. (112)

The final 'I' reveals the third person 'Sammy' to be simply the name of the self-addressing 'ye', Sammy talking about himself in the third person as he narrates his own story. The communal heterocentricity of Gibbon's narration becomes an inner heterocentricity in which Sammy becomes the site of 'I', 'ye' and Sammy, each in dialogue with the other. In Kelman's narrators the 'self as other' has been internalised as an other self, other selves, the other voices which Hines encounters, for instance, in *The Busconductor Hines*:

> This sort of escapade is beyond belief. Was it to be taken seriously. Of course, shouted a voice. Whose fucking voice was it. Funny how voices come along and shout, just as if they were something or other, knowledgeable fucking parties perhaps, that knew what was going on. Because Hines doesn't. He doesn't fucking know. (164)

The self has become the space of voices uncontrolled by the 'I': voices can erupt into the self because it is already the space of the Other: 'This isn't Hines who's talking. It's a voice. This is a voice doing talking which he listens to' (167). It is 'voice' rather than writing which erupts into the space of Kelman's narration because the 'objective' narrative voice takes on the characteristics of a 'subjective' speaking voice, and, since a speaking voice cannot control the dialogue in which it is engaged, because other voices will suddenly reply, the narrative is prone to interruption, to precisely the kind of dialogue which the written, operating in its assumed silence, refuses to accept into its carefully constructed sentences. Equally, the vernacular voices of Kelman's characters suffer interruption by a voice which mimics the structures of the written, as in *A Disaffection*, for instance, when Pat Doyle parks his car near his brother's house:

> He shut fast the door and locked it, glancing up to see if anybody was out on the veranda. The flats all had these verandas which were ideal for parties to dive from. Excellent for the district's twelve-year-olds. He patted the car bonnet en route to the pavement where he proceeded to traverse the flagstones up the stairs and into the closemouth. Traversed the flagstones up the stairs and into the bloody closemouth. Is this fucking Mars! Traversed the fucking bastarn flagstones onto the planet fucking Vulcan for christ sake   (252)

The multiple registers of the language produce entirely conflicting meanings: 'verandas which were ideal for parties' – as intended by architects – become verandas ideal for 'parties' (colloquially, 'persons') to dive from – a dramatic refusal of athletic training (diving) through suicide. And with each variation on 'traversed the flagstones' a demotic voice progressively dismantles the high preciousness of the narrating consciousness which dared to describe having crossed a pavement into a block of flats in those alienating terms. The text is an inner dialogue of competing voices and languages, a heterocentric space in which the self is defined not by its unity but by its multiplicity.

By these techniques, Kelman has found his own very specific means of overcoming the distinction between English (as the medium of narration) and Scots (as the medium of dialogue) that has been the constant dilemma of Scottish writers in relation to their working-class characters: the working-class protagonists of Kelman's novels are the site in which the community's voices happen, and in their happening constitute the 'I' which it is the novel's business to narrate. But in their endless self-narration, Kelman's protagonists are images of a working-class for whom the future, as traditionally envisaged by progressive politics, has been abolished. The Busconductor Hines is a modern Charon whose passengers do not cross to the other side, but simply cross and recross the empty and meaningless spaces of the city. The busconductor is the timekeeper of the world's journeys, but he himself journeys nowhere, travelling out only to come back, travelling forward only to reach a terminus which is no conclusion. The Busconductor is a worker whose existence is dominated by the need for *over*time and who lives in the expectation of his own coming redundancy, when conductors are replaced by the drivers of one-man buses. Out of that social situation, however, what Kelman creates is an emblem of humanity's existential condition:

> The position in which he is to be finding himself is no worse than that of countless others whose efforts are no longer negotiable but that that position, that position might yet have become tranquil that they could have multiplied inasmuch, inasmuch as Hines could eventually, he could have become
> He was wanting that becoming. (98)

Kelman's sentence structure oscillates between alternative readings: 'The position in which he is *to be*' points to a certainty that 'in which he is *to be finding* himself' undermines: Hines's 'being' is what he is unable to 'find', whatever the position he is in. The uncertainty of his social position opens up the abyss of 'being', and his repetitive life negates the 'becoming' that existentialism posits as the fundamental nature of human existence: Hines wants 'that becoming' because he knows he is a being who is nothing – not in the social sense that others apply to him but in Sartre's sense, a being who has no essence, whose nothingness is the foundation of his freedom to act. Not being able to act, his nothingness becomes simply an absence:

> There are parties whose attention to a variety of aspects of existence renders life uneasy. It cannot be said to be the fault of Hines that he is such a party. A little leeway might be allowed him. A fortnight's leave of absence could well work wonders.

'Leave of absence' hovers between its standard meaning – time off work – and its existential implication – escape from nothingness. Or, equally, escape into the 'nothingness' which defines humanity's ability to achieve real 'becoming' rather than the fixed social identity of 'being'.

The inner dialectic of Kelman's self-communing narrators is the basis of a quest to establish the nature of Being and its relationship to humanity's becoming: each narrator is an uncomfortable and discomfiting character because, like Hines, 'when all's said and done he is a negation. Being a negation is peculiar' (202). They come at Being by negating the systems of thought through which we enclose and tame existence: their life is one of continual refusal, and their refusal makes others uncomfortable by making them aware, however briefly, of the problem of Being itself. Doyle, in *A Disaffection*, realises why he has offended the woman he thinks he may be in love with – it is his language that causes the problem, his demotic, his refusal to accept the limitations of socially accepted speech:

> It was the word of course, arse, she didnt like it and hadni been able to cope when he had said it. It was an odd word right enough. Arse. There arent many odder words. Arse. I have an arse. I kicked you on the arse. This is a load of arse. Ares. It was an odd word. (146)

'Arse' is the connection of the 'I', the 'you' and the strangeness of a language which tries to come to terms with that which *is* – with the 'ares' of the world. The purpose of Kelman's protagonists is to kick us into awareness of our Arse, our Ares, our Areness. Dialect leads directly to the confrontation with the ultimates of existence: 'Could this be true. Did he have something they didnt. At an early age he had sucked in the ultimates' (118); dialect is the foundation of a philosophical dialectic in which the social realist novelist is necessarily the existential novelist, the novelist of redundancy among the working classes becomes the novelist of the redundancy of existence that Pat Doyle confronts in *A Disaffection*:

> except that it no longer exists. That poor old nonetity Vulcan, being once thought to exist, and then being discovered not to. Imagine being discovered not to exist! That's even worse than being declared fucking redundant, irrelevant, which was the fate of ether upon the advent of Einstein. Whether it existed or not had become irrelevant to the issue. Fuck sake. Ether. After all these centuries . . . (252)

Redundant 'being' is both the working class person without a job and the humanity whose redundancy in the universe they represent.

In one of the most influential accounts of existentialism, John Macquarrie, himself a graduate of and former lecturer at Glasgow University, explains the fundamental bases of existentialism by reference to the work of John Macmurray:[26] 'Macmurray argues that the adoption of the "I act" rather than the "I think" as the starting-place would circumvent many of the problems that have proved to be most intractable in philosophy' (126). Macquarrie acknowledges that 'this does not mean that he is being annexed to the "existentialists"' but Macmurray's analysis nonetheless, for Macquarrie, focuses precisely the problems that existentialism seeks to address. Macmurray is the constant point of reference for Macquarrie's discussion of existentialism and something akin to Macmurray's heterocentricity is the fundamental demand of schoolteacher Pat Doyle in *A Disaffection* when he addresses the children in his class:

> I'm so much bigger than you, he said, these are my terms. My terms are the ones that enclose yous. Yous are all enclosed. But yous know that already! I can tell that just by looking at your faces, your faces, telling these things to me. It's quite straightforward when you come to think about it. Here you have me. Here you have you. Two sentences. One sentence is needed for you and one sentence is needed for me and you can wrap them all up together if you want to so that what you have in this one sentence is both you and me, us being in it the gether. (26)

The 'I' and 'you' are in two sentences, separated – imprisoned – from one another unless it is possible to create one sentence that is 'both you and

me, us being in it the gether'. In 'the gether' Kelman turns dialect into
dialectic: 'the gether' creates a noun to identify that process by which the
dialogue of self and other as mutually defining and mutually creating – the
relation that Macmurray defines as the heterocentric – is created; 'self' and
'other' are gathered to*gether* in a single and unified 'gether' that encompasses
both. That 'gethering' of 'I and you' is what haunts Kelman's protagonists:
it is the lost possibility of the past – Doyle, in *A Disaffection* is haunted
by the generation of Hegel and Hölderlin, the last generation which could
believe that the imagination could turn beneficently into reality – or a failed
possibility of the future. Instead of the ideal of the Greek city state, the
polis – 'We're responsible for it, the present polity' (149) – the reality of
modern life is a state policed by the *polis*, as they are called in demotic
Scots: 'Funny how come so many officers of the law crop up these days.
Patrick appears to be surrounded by them. Everywhere he looks . . . not all
polismen are bad chaps; not all poliswomen are bad chapesses. Only those
who work for the government in such and such a way and do not perform in this that and the other fashion, know what I mean' (209–10). The
policed state is the opposite of the heterocentric acknowledgement of the
other: it is the state in which the individual, as Macmurray describes it, is
forced to be 'at once the spectator-self and a participant-self. But his real
life – his own private life – is as a spectator' (142). Kelman's protagonists
live in resistance to being arrested by the false polis of the modern world,
in resistance to becoming the 'spectator-self' which treats itself as simply
'other'. Sammy Samuels, in *How late it was, how late* goes blind to defend
himself against becoming that spectator self – 'With one weird wee image
to finish it all off: if this was permanent he wouldnay be able to see himself ever again. Christ that was wild. And he wouldnay see cunts looking
at him.' (12). Sammy's blindness defends the possibility of heterocentricity
that the modern world denies by radically negating the 'spectator self' in
himself and everyone else; it returns the world from the 'eye' of the isolated
'I' to the 'I and You' – the 'I' and 'ye' – of true selfhood.

In Kelman's novels, the realism of working-class life is the basis for an
engagement with the philosophical legacy of existentialism: for Kelman the
issue is to present 'a working class experience that is total. Total in the sense
that the character can be at the same time an intellectual and still be a bona
fide member of the working class'.[27] In this, Kelman places himself firmly
in the tradition that George Davie describes in *The Democratic Intellect*, both
in terms of the democracy of the intellect and in terms of the 'commanding
position' of philosophy in Scottish intellectualism: 'It was apparently just
this predominance of philosophy over the other subjects which made the
education system in Scotland so different from that found in England' (13).
It is, perhaps, proof of Davie's views that the philosophy of existentialism has
had a significant – if generalised – attraction to modern Scottish writers. The
thought of Sartre in particular can be traced in writers as diverse as Alexander

Trocchi (whose *Young Adam*[28] and *Cain's Book*[29] were originally written and published in Paris, and who left Scotland for Paris rather London because he 'found the English attitude towards existentialism . . . unsympathetic after the war'[30]), Alan Sharp (whose aborted trilogy, of which *A Green Tree in Gedde*[31] and *The Wind Shifts*[32] were published, is significantly influenced by Sartre's *Roads to Freedom* trilogy) and Alan Massie (whose novels of postwar Europe engage with existential themes).[33] Existentialism also provides the general philosophical context for the 'intellectual' detectives of William McIlvanney's and Ian Rankin's novels.[34] The concern of Scottish writers with issues posed by existential philosophers may also testify to the parallels between existentialism and Calvinism, for if Calvinism throws into relief the issue of human choice by denying its significance in a world of predestination, existentialism's insistence on human choice throws equally into relief the predetermined patterns of life of those who refuse the challenge of authentic choice.

It is on this connection that Muriel Spark has based some of her most profoundly metaphysical novels, for in Spark's novels characters are insistently trapped between predestinations of a Calvinist sort and the possibilities of authentic free choice of the kind emphasised by existentialism. Spark, however, as a Roman Catholic, uses the novel form to expose what she sees as the emptiness and falsehood of those oppositions: her novels are dialectical because they set in opposition to each other opposing philosophical presuppositions about the nature of human life whose *reductio ad absurdum* will reveal our need for a higher truth. In Spark, dialectics is the method by which the limits of our understanding are revealed, leaving us confronting the need for faith.

In *Symposium*,[35] for instance, the meeting which brings Margaret Murchie into contact with William Damien, soon to be her husband, seems random and accidental – they meet in the fruit section of Marks & Spencer – but has, in fact, been as carefully plotted by Margaret as though she is the author of a novel designing the lives of two of her characters. That emplotment, however, is itself based on Margaret's random choice of a potential husband by the use of a pin on a list of names. The plotted and the random by which Margaret organises her life are in turn based on a sense of predestination, for Margaret's life has been a series of close encounters with death, not natural death but the mysterious deaths and murders of others near to her. For these deaths she is not apparently responsible but they are foreshadowed (and may be have been carried out) by her Uncle Magnus, who is afflicted with a knowledge of the future that is the fulfilment of the Covenanting Calvinism of their Murchie ancestors. The novel constructs a web of alternative versions of how the self is related to the lives of others, and Margaret becomes the (hypocritical) expositor of a French philosophy of *les autres*, which is a 'revival of something old. Very new and very old', but which sounds very much like a perversion of Macmurray when it is defined as meaning that 'we have to centre our thoughts and actions away from ourselves and entirely on to other people' (35). The arbitrariness of the relation of self and other which Margaret suffers from is itself a function of the breakdown of the relations of self and other in the society of which she is a part: it is a world where people and things are so confused that the book starts with a male character declaring 'This is rape!' in reference to a burglary of his home – to which the schoolmistressly narrator responds: 'It was not rape, it was robbery' (7). That confusion of objects with sexuality is both cause and consequence of the breakdown of marital relations into casually sexual or straightforwardly materialistic ones: in this *Symposium* love has none of the transcendent significance that it has in Plato's. Love as both choice and as commitment dissolve in the predeterminations of an ancient Calvinism and the random choices of an atheistic materialism. When Margaret decides to take responsibility for her life by marrying a man with a rich mother and then killing her, fulfilling actively the contiguity with death which has haunted her, the object of her plot, Hilda Damien, is equally conscious of a predeterminism which binds her self to this other:

> Destiny, my destiny, thought Hilda. Is she going to poison me? What is she plotting? She is plotting something. This is a nightmare.
> Hilda was right. Except that in the destiny of the event Margaret could have saved herself the trouble, the plotting. It was the random gang . . . of which Margaret knew nothing, who were to kill Hilda Damien for her Monet. (176)

Margaret is caught between the 'random' of a world of contingency and the 'emplotted' world of predestination: the more she attempts to take control of her life and plot it for herself the more she is undone by the random. In a comic fulfilment of a Calvinist universe, Hilda is doomed not by the choices of Margaret but by a higher power – the emplotting control of the author – and Margaret is saved, despite her evil intent, by grace of the same power.

It is in *The Driver's Seat*,[36] however, that Spark most directly confronts the terms of an existential response to the human condition. Like Margaret, Lise has decided to take control of her life but, in a parody of existentialism's demand that choice be made in the consciousness of death, that control will be exerted by choosing the person who will kill her. Lise fulfils in the most direct fashion what Macquarrie, in *Existentialism*, describes as 'the existent's inward awareness that his being is a being-towards-death' (195): she wants to be in the 'driver's seat' not by choosing what to do with her life – to give it an end – but by choosing how to end it, and by that ending giving significance to herself. The trail of strange events which the novel charts in its opening pages as Lise prepares for her journey to an unnamed city in the South seem unmotivated until we realise that this is a detective novel in reverse, in which Lise is leaving the clues by which her own past will be able to be tracked backwards from the moment of her death: 'and it is almost as if, satisfied that she has successfully registered the fact of her presence at the airport among the July thousands there, she has fulfilled a small item of a greater purpose' (20). The 'greater purpose' is the purpose of her identification after death, as though identification was the same as identity; the lack of a 'greater purpose' that can give significance to her empty life is, however, what drives her. The novel is written in a present tense that insists on the world of becoming – a world without ultimate Being – in which Lise exists and in which she will be able to recognise the man she seeks not because she 'will feel a presence' but rather by 'the lack of an absence' (71). *The Driver's Seat* is a parodic rendition of a world in which people live without being aware of 'the lack of an absence' and in which the self is simply the empty signifier of a trail of incidents that constitute its only identity: 'So she lays the trail, presently to be followed and elaborated upon with due art by the journalists of Europe for the few days it takes for her identity to be established' (51). Lise is a Self without an Other except as its negation, a mutual recognition of the lack of an absence, the lack that *is* an absence. And therefore even the author can only ask, 'Who knows her thoughts? Who can tell?' There is no 'telling' the story of the lack of an absence that nonetheless does not constitute a presence because there is nothing that it can signify. Death is necessary to give Lise's life significance because her life will have no meaning except as something she can leave to be read (her name echoes the French 'lisent', they read) by anonymous others who construct her 'identity' only by *not* having had enough of a relation with her for her to have a 'self'. At the novel's opening Lise is addressed by an anonymous 'salesgirl':

> 'And the material doesn't stain,' the salesgirl says.
> 'Doesn't stain?'
> 'It's the new fabric,' the salesgirl says. 'Specially treated. Won't mark . . .
> The customer, a young woman, is suddenly tearing at the fastener at the neck, pulling the zip of the dress. She is saying, 'Get this thing off me. Off me, at once.' (7)

Lise wants a dress that will stain because it has to be a clue; what she doesn't realise is that as someone who lives in a 'material' world there is no stain – nothing will remain of her because the material of which she is composed is not the stained material of an eternal spirit. At the novel's conclusion the narrator notes how Lise's murderer sees

> the gleaming buttons of the policeman's uniforms, hears the cold and the confiding, the hot and the barking voices, sees already the holsters and epaulets and all those trappings devised to protect them from the indecent exposure of fear and pity, pity and fear. (107)

The justifications of Aristotelian tragedy – 'pity and fear' – are irrelevant in a world where the 'polis' can neither be threatened nor saved by an individual death. Our tragedy is the fact that our world is as incapable of tragedy as it is of salvation. Lise is caught in a dialectic in which her every effort to give her life significance – even by death – simply reveals its fundamental emptiness; when she is dead there will be the lack, even, of an absence. As she is about to die, she shouts, "I don't want any sex . . . You can have it afterwards. Tie my feet and kill, that's all. They will come and sweep it up in the morning"' (106). She is to herself now only an 'it' without relations but, as with all of Spark's plotters, her plot fails: 'he plunges into her, with the knife poised high', and as he does so, '"Kill me", she says, and repeats it in four languages.' Suddenly we realise that just as we do not know where Lise comes from or where she has come to, we do not know what language Lise thinks in: the language of the text could be a mimesis of actual conversations or simply their translation into English. She is a text to be read rather than a voice to be heard: her language has no dialect because there is no one to whom she speaks as self to other: 'As the knife descends to her throat she screams, evidently perceiving how final is finality. She screams and then her throat gurgles while he stabs with a turn of his wrist exactly as she instructed' (106–7). The mode of Lise's death only enacts the death of the voice – the death of dialogue – that had actually occurred before the narrative started.

IV

When, in *The Quarry Wood*, Martha adopts the child the community believes already to be hers, she not only repeats the action of her mother's Aunt Josephine, who had taken Martha away from home at the beginning of the novel, but involves herself in one of the fundamental narrative tropes of the modern Scottish novel – the child uncertain of his or her origins. That uncertain origin dramatises the division of languages and cultures to which every Scot is heir. Many of Robin Jenkins's novels, for instance, start from such acts of 'adoption', and explore the destructive consequences of the efforts to integrate the displaced child into a new environment. Thus in *The Changeling*,[37] Tom Curdie, the boy from one of the worst tenements in an industrial city, is taken on a family holiday by his schoolteacher, Charlie Forbes, and despite the fact that 'the changeling' image predicts that he is 'that creature introduced by the malevolent folk of the other world into a man's home, to pollute the joy and faith of family' (51), Tom finds himself answering the phone as 'Tom Forbes', so certain has he become of his 'adoption' into the family which is, in fact, unable to accept him. *A Love of Innocence*[38] similarly explores the adoption of two Glasgow children, whose father has murdered their mother, by a couple living on island off the west coast of Scotland, and ends with another woman of the island also adopting one of their friends, a girl called Jean, from the 'home' in which they had stayed in Glasgow: as she brings the girl back to her new foster home she thinks of her husband, Neil, and of how 'she would have to take care to give Neil his place as Jean's father' (331). Jenkins's novels present a world not only of displaced children in search of parents but of children adopted to displace or replace their parents. In *Fergus Lamont*,[39] the protagonist grows up as son of a worker living in an urban slum while believing himself to be the bastard child of an aristocrat. The same motif is taken up by Alasdair Gray in *1982 Janine*,[40] in which the pornographically fantasising protagonist Jock cannot believe himself the son of a 'socialist timekeeper' who 'only felt happy with the nation during the late forties and fifties, the austerity years of full employment' (138) and 'adopts' himself as the son of 'mad Hislop', his schoolteacher, 'who was perhaps (his) real father' (71); Jock is also obsessed with whether or not the girl whom he abandoned, Denny, might have had a child which 'was probably adopted' (127). Gray has also given us two of the most radical versions of such displacement from origin: in *Lanark*[41] the eponymous protagonist discovers himself in existence in a railway carriage – 'a thumping sound, then either I opened my eyes or the light went on for I saw I was in the corner of an old railway compartment' (16) – and names himself after a picture on the compartment wall (20); and in *Poor Things*[42] Godwin Baxter succeeds in fulfilling his long-term ambition 'to take a discarded body and a discarded brain from our social midden heap and unite them in a new life' (34), thus producing the novel's heroine, Bella. Bella, however, is truly Baxter's child (or bride) because he too has been 'created' in a similar fashion by his own parents.

The echoes here of Stevenson's *Dr. Jekyll and Mr. Hyde* and of Mary Shelley's *Frankenstein* underlines how the Scottish experience of cultural dislocation finds expression in narrative terms in plots of biological uncertainty or familial displacement. Such conditions are the breeding ground of those schizophrenics, amnesiacs, and hypocrites who have so often been taken to represent the essence of Scottish culture. Robin Jenkins gives us a prime example in *The Awakening of George Darroch*[43] in which Darroch, as he prepares himself to leave the Established Church, discovers the multiplicity of his identity:

> As he went upstairs to his room, and afterwards as he lay in bed, he surveyed the two George Darrochs. That meant of course there must be a third.
> There was the George Darroch who had wiped the blood from Taylor's face, held Mrs Cooper's hand, was grateful to Mrs Barnes for her faithful service, wished to throw in his lot with the poor, loved his children and sought to reward them by asking them to share penury and hardship with him.
> There was the George Darroch who had lusted after Eleanor Jarvie, lied glibly about her letter, was eager to associate with rich and important men, loved his children and wanted to give them comfort and affluence, and brutally had dismissed poor Mrs Barnes.

Both of them, and the third one observing them, would be in St Andrew's Church tomorrow. (245–6)

Darroch's self-division is the image of a culture self-divided: his son sees in his actions only 'the disastrous divisiveness of the Scottish nation, which had kept it materially and spiritually impoverished in the past and was still doing so today' (267).

That negative image of Scotland – all too much in evidence in many critical accounts of its culture – is obviously related to the linguistic divides of the nation: the national imagination is seen as necessarily divided between competing expressions of national traditions rather than fulfilling itself as the unfolding of a single and unified identity. If we follow Macmurray's thought in *Persons in Relation*, however, the notion of 'identity' as singular can be seen to be fundamentally false: identity is necessarily relational and the Self is necessarily constituted by its relations with what it regards as its Other:

> The 'You and I' relation, we must recall, constitutes the personal, and both the 'You' and the 'I' are constituted, as individual persons, by the mutuality of their relation. Consequently, the development of the individual person is the development of his relation to the Other. Personal individuality is not an original given fact. It is achieved through the progressive differentiation of the original unity of the 'You and I' . . . We all distinguish ourselves, as individuals, from the society of which we are members and to which we belong. The paradox is the same: for we at once assert ourselves as constituent members of the society while opposing it to ourselves as the 'other-than-I'. So the child discovers himself as an individual by contrasting himself, and indeed by wilfully opposing himself to the family *to which he belongs*; and this *discovery* of his individuality is at the same time the *realization* of his individuality. We are part of that from which we distinguish ourselves, and to which, as agents, we oppose ourselves. (91)

It is perhaps no accident that it is from a society as historically divided as Scotland's that such a theory of the self could develop but the significant issue is that the 'divided self' is not opposed to the 'unified' self in Macmurray's thought: the 'divided self' is the self which has taken itself *out* of dialogue, *out* of dialectic. The divided self is a self which refuses to acknowledge its dependence on the other, whereas a healthy 'self', a 'person', is always an interaction with the Other: 'The self is constituted by its capacity for self-negation. It must be represented as a positive which necessarily contains its own negative' (66). An inner dialectic is essential to selfhood and it is the refusal of such dialectic, rather than the assertion of it, which destroys the self.

'The divided self' was to become the title of R. D. Laing's study of schizophrenia,[44] a study which was to have a direct influence on such

'schizophrenic' texts as Alasdair Gray's *Lanark*. Laing's study of the workings of the schizophrenic starts, however, from Macmurray's concept of the
self:

> ... we cannot give an adequate account of the existential splits unless we
> can begin from the concept of a unitary whole, and no such concept exists,
> nor can any such concept be expressed within the current language system
> of psychiatry or psycho-analysis.
>
> The words in the current technical vocabulary either refer to man in isolation
> from the other and the world, that is, as an entity not *essentially* 'in relation
> to' the other and in a world, or they refer to falsely substantialized aspects
> of this isolated entity ... Instead of the original bond of *I* and *You*, we take
> a single man in isolation and conceptualize his various aspects into 'the ego',
> 'the superego' and the 'id'. The other becomes either an internal or external
> object or a fusion of both. How can we speak in any way adequately of the
> relationship between me and you in terms of the interaction of one mental
> apparatus with another? (19)

Laing's conception of psychiatry is precisely the conception of the psyche
not as an isolated ego but as a person based on an 'I and You' relationship – and the problem with traditional psychiatry is that it is the discipline
rather than its subjects which is schizophrenic: 'unless we realize that man
does not exist without "his" world nor can his world exist without him, we
are condemned to start our study of schizoid and schizophrenic people with
a verbal and conceptual splitting that matches the split of the totality of
the schizoid being-in-the-world' (20). In other words, the split self analysed
by psychiatry is split because of the conceptual tools of psychiatry and not
because of the nature of the self under investigation: there are many ways of
envisaging the inner dialectics of the self and not all of them require that
the self as constituted by its capacity for 'self-negation' is either an illness
or an evil.

Too often in studies of Scottish culture the apparent lack of unity of the
self is taken to be the symptom of a failed identity, of a self-contradictory
and self-destructive identity,[45] rather than that the healthy self is always
a dialectic operating within and between 'opposing' elements of self and
other: 'the science of persons is the study of human beings that begins
from a relationship with the other as person and proceeds to an account
of the other still as person' (21). Laing's analysis of schizophrenics is also
an analysis of a science that treats people schizophrenically – 'we shall be
concerned specifically with people who experience themselves as automata,
as robots, as bits of machinery, or even as animals. Such persons are rightly
regarded as crazy. Yet why do we not regard a theory that seeks to transmute
persons into automata or animals as equally crazy?' (23). It is a demand
for the implementation of Macmurray's proposal that psychiatry seek 'the
logical form through which the unity of the personal can be coherently

conceived' (23), the 'unity' of the personal being precisely, of course, its dialogic relation with the other.

The model of the person that is provided by Macmurray and used by Laing lies behind much of modern Scottish writing – in part because it derives from the same traditions of thought that are shared by those writers and in part because many of the writers of the past half century have been influenced by one or other of these thinkers, or by other writers who have been so influenced. Thus when Sammy Samuels in *How late it was, how late* retreats into blindness – 'What did it matter but what did it matter; cunts looking at ye. Who gives a fuck. Just sometimes they bore their way in, some of them do anyway, they seem able to give you a look that's more than a look' (12) – what he enacts is what Laing presents as the foundation of our genuine selfhood, a foundation which is shared with common notions of schizophrenia rather than being at odds with it: 'We may remember how, in childhood, adults at first were able to look right through us, and into us, and what an accomplishment it was when we, in fear and trembling, could tell our first lie' (37). The 'person', like the culture, is not the unitary identity of the isolated ego but a continual dialectic with its own otherness; exploration of the 'divided self' is not simply exploration of the sickness of the culture, but exploration of the sickness of the notions of culture by which a culture that recognises its own involvement with the 'other' is assumed to be as sick as the self which has withdrawn from its relationship with the other into a self-enclosed and divisive self-identity.

The emphasis on the 'divided self' in Scottish culture is not, therefore, simply the reflection of a hopelessly divided society: it is the exploration of the limitation of notions of the self which have themselves reduced the self from its true complexity in order to produce a false unity in which the person is simply a spectator and a social function; it is a concern with the limitations of those notions of self and society which are founded on false assumptions about the fulfilment of identity being the achievement of singularity and unity. To explore and to celebrate the multiplicities of the self is to recognise the fact that the self is never self-contained – that the 'divided self' is not to be contrasted with the 'unidivided self' but with the 'self-in-relation': the 'divided self' is precisely the product of the failure of the dialectic of 'self and other' rather than the outcome of the self's failure to maintain its autonomy and singularity. The inner otherness of Scottish culture – Highland and Lowland, Calvinist and Catholic – thus becomes the very model of the complexity of the self rather than examples of its failure: the self-division of the schizophrenic is not an 'other' to a unified normalcy but the failure of the acceptance of the other which constitutes the normal self.

There is a moment in Neil Gunn's *Highland River*[46] when Kenn imagines himself looking down from a bird's eye perspective on the landscape in which he grew up and, in defiance of temporality, comes upon himself as a young boy:

Kenn completes the circle and his vision narrows on the winding strath beneath him . . . and suddenly closing his wings, he stoops upon the moving figure on the river bank.

But the small figure does not hear the singing ecstasy in the wings; has no knowledge of the eyes that presently peer at him, noting with scientific care every breath of expression, each detail of the face, the dark hair cut across the forehead . . .

Kenn watches and follows him, and finds him resting in the shelter of some trees near the Lodge Pool. He is excited now lest he be seen. He has never been so far up the river before. Tentatively he steps out on the smooth green bank to look at the pool. (103)

Kenn watches his earlier self, who is physically going further up the river than ever before, while Kenn is psychologically travelling up the same river further than ever before. In this moment Gunn dramatises what he describes in *The Atom of Delight*[47] – a third person autobiography in which he is simply 'the boy' – as the 'second self':

Then the next thing happened, and happened, so far as I can remember, for the first time. I have tried hard but can find no simpler way of expressing what happened than by saying; *I came upon myself sitting there.*

Within the mood of content, as I have tried to recreate it, was this self and the self was me.

The state of content deepened wonderfully and everything around was embraced in it.

There was no "losing" of the self in the sense that there was a blank from which I awoke or came to. The self may have been thinned away – it did – but so delightfully that it also remained at the centre in a continuous and perfectly natural way. And then within this amplitude the self as it were became aware of seeing itself not as an "I" or an "ego" but rather as a stranger it had come upon and was even a little shy of. (20)

This second self watched by a first undoes the 'look that's more than a look' by which Samuels is terrified because it allows the self to look at itself – a double, a self-division which is not self-destructive but which is, rather, the very basis of a more profound identity-in-relation. The 'second self' is not a failure of the identity of the first self – it is the very fulfilment of that identity.

A Scottish culture which has regularly been described as 'schizophrenic' because of its inner divisions is not necessarily sick: it is engaged in the dialogue with the other, a conversation in different dialects, a dialectic that is the foundation not only of persons but of nations. Theories of the nation are still obsessively engaged with the notion of the fulfilment of national identity as the achievement of unity; we can see it, for instance, in the centrality that Benedict Anderson gives, in *Imagined Communities*[48] to what he calls the experiences of 'unisonance':

... there is a special kind of contemporaneous community which language alone suggests – above all in the form of poetry and song. Take national anthems, for example, sung on national holidays. No matter how banal the words and mediocre the tunes, there is in this singing an experience of simultaneity. At precisely such moments, people wholly unknown to each other utter the same verse to the same melody. The image: unisonance ... How selfless this unisonance feels! If we are aware that others are singing these songs precisely when and as we are, we have no idea who they may be, or even where, out of earshot, they are singing. Nothing connects us but imagined sound. (145)

If, however, we adopt a concept of the nation more like Macmurray's concept of the self, this 'unisonance' of the nation is an illusion – it is the nation's inner and outer dialogues, its dialects with their all-too-forceful (as opposed to 'imagined') sounds which form its real identity. The nation, like the self, is a space of dialogue, a place of dissonant voices, a dialectic of relationships: it consists not of undivided individuals but of persons in relation, and it is constituted not by the autonomous unity of its language or its culture but by its inner debates and by the dialectic of its dialects.

CHAPTER 3
ENDURING HISTORIES:
MYTHIC REGIONS

There is no more problematic legacy from nineteenth-century to twentieth-century Scottish culture than the genre of the historical novel. With *Waverley* in 1814, and the subsequent Waverley novels, Sir Walter Scott provided the model by which nineteenth century writers in Europe and America would come to terms with those new forms of society and new processes of development that had been unleashed, almost simultaneously, by the politics of the American and French Revolutions and by the economic consequences of what we have come to call the Industrial Revolution. The transformation which made the nation state the primary form of political and economic organisation, and nationalism the driving force of political change, was given its fundamental literary expression in the historical novel. Insofar as the nation itself is primarily a narrative that unites the past to the present, Scott's novels provided the generic means by which the nation could be narrated as a product of history and history could be seen as the expression of a national identity.[1]

Those same Scott novels which initiate the engagement with history in the rest of the world have, however, been seen in Scotland as disengaging Scotland from the processes of history, or as symptoms of the disengagement of Scottish history from the modern world. No issue has been more debated in Scotland over the past thirty years, in terms of its political and cultural consequences, than the falsification of Scotland's history initiated by Walter Scott, both through his novelistic presentation of the Scottish past and by the real-life re-enactment of his fictions in the construction of a fabricated Scottish identity to celebrate George IV's visit to Edinburgh in 1822. Scott carries the burden of having invented a Scotland which displaced the real Scotland in favour of his romantic illusions. In *The Ragged Lion*,[2] his fictionalised autobiography of Scott, Allan Massie makes Scott acknowledge the sources of this debate in his youthful commitment to the Jacobites: 'Here I am, in my sixtieth year, a man who has seen much, and achieved enough to have won the respect of his fellows, but when I think of the great adventure of the Rising, I become a lad of fourteen or fifteen again' (222). Scottish history is juvenile: interest in it is informed not by a mature sense of how the present relates to the past but by an escapism which turns the past into a romantic fiction. When, in Chapter Thirty-Three of Alasdair Gray's *Lanark*,

Lanark and Rima escape from the Institute, they leave by a door which announces:

> EMERGENCY EXIT 3124
> DANGER! DANGER! DANGER! DANGER!
> YOU ARE ABOUT TO ENTER
> AN INTERCALENDRICAL
> ZONE

It is a door they keep re-encountering as they circle in the hope of a way out back to the 'real' world. They might be circling in the history of Scotland as left by Scott: an 'intercalendrical zone', a timeless world that is outside the causality of real history. It is a view of the Scottish past that Colin Kidd has seen as shaping the whole course of Scottish historiography in the eighteenth and nineteenth centuries, since Scottish historiography, according to Kidd, was incapable of making the Scottish past a significant precursor of the ideological concerns of a modern society: 'The Scottish past remained vivid and distinct, yet denuded of ideological significance. As the threat of Jacobitism receded, the sub-genre of Marian history lost its partisan role, but survived as part of a sterile historiography of local colour and romance.'[3] Scotland is a place with a past but a place without a history – without a history both in the sense of there being no serious need to write histories about that past, and in the sense that the narrative of its past has no relevance to the condition of its present, to the nature of its contemporary historical experience.

It is precisely this condition of a false history that Robin Jenkins drama-tised in *Fergus Lamont*,[4] a novel published in 1979, the same year in which the Devolution Referendum failed to achieve a reconvening of a Scottish parliament for the first time since 1707. *Fergus Lamont* might have been a prophecy of that failure in its presentation of a protagonist whose whole life is a continual attempt not to challenge the nature of modern Scotland but to evade the realities of it. Born into a working class family in Gantock in the West of Scotland, Fergus is deserted by his mother at an early age, but not before she has left him a kilt which he will wear as the badge of his commit-ment to her and, more importantly, to his belief that he is really the son of the Scottish aristocrat in whose house she worked, rather than the son of the working-class man to whom she was married. Fergus chooses a 'fatherland', and that fatherland is the world of kilted aristocracy which has inherited Scott's fictionalised Scottish identity, and thereby becomes a modern ver-sion of the aristocratic leader whom Scott had presented in the character of the Jacobite Fergus MacIvor in *Waverley* – 'You'd look like a prince, Fergie,' she whispered. 'As you should' (2). Fergus thus unites in himself that Lowland adoption of Highland culture which is attributed to Scott – he is 'Dressed like a Highland chief in a Raeburn painting' (133) – and re-enacts in himself what he sees to have been Sir Walter's ambition: 'he was

a Scotsman who had done with success what it was my ambition to do:
that was, write about common people and assort with nobility' (90). Since
Fergus is a modern author, however, his own writing offers itself as a
parallel with the early work of that other self-fictionalising Scottish writer,
Hugh MacDiarmid, pseudonym for C. M. Grieve, for Fergus's poetry is
written in working-class vernacular – 'My imagination was those dauds of
clay, bringing up, out of my Gantock childhood, poems like 'Gathering
Dung' and 'Stairhead Lavatories' (132) – and claims them to be the best
Scots poetry since Burns (139). Fergus's combination of all the elements
of Scottish cultural history is completed by the fact that from his Calvinist
grandfather he acquires a sense of election and predestination, a special
status confirmed by his survival during the First World War: 'The reason
for my confidence was that I felt I had a greatness in me, too valuable to
be lost. I had no idea what supernatural power was interested in preserving
me, but all the time, whether in safe billet behind the lines or on a night
raid or going over the top, I was sustained by that strong assurance of
deserved immunity'; 'The men in my company called me anointed. They
intended sarcasm and achieved truth' (95, 96). In Fergus, Jenkins presents
a character who has constructed himself as a combination of all the elements of modern Scottish culture viewed as a facade of fraud, a series of
hypocrisies, but claiming to be, nonetheless, the expression of and the salvation of Scotland's modern industrial society: 'When I went back to my
native town therefore it must be, not just as hero, aristocrat, and poet, but
as absolver and redeemer' (117).

   Dressed in the fictional clothes of the Scottish past to deny the real nature
of his early life, Fergus is a character who encounters history but does not
participate in it. Everyone around him suffers in the impossibility of escape
from the effects of twentieth-century history – whether it is his childhood
friend Mary, caught up in the contradictions of being a socialist politician;
his best man, who dies at Cambrai two months before the armistice; or the
people of the slums bombed in the Second World War – but for Fergus
there is always an escape route by which he can evade the pain of those
around him. Fergus can live untouched by history because his identity,
like the Scottish past, is pure romance and therefore, quite literally, imma-
terial to the events in which he participates. That fictionalised identity is
confirmed by his marriage to Betty Shields, a novelist whose works, like
Fergus's life, are a kind of magic, an alchemy which, instead of turning
lead into gold, through romance turns 'shit into sugar' (115). Through
marriage, Fergus will be translated into the simulacrum of a character from
her fiction, whom the working-class women he grew up among will see 'as
a hero of one of her books still to be written' (119). In the context of the
sufferings of working-class poverty and First World War destruction, Betty
and Fergus, as they tour the industrial cities to encourage volunteers for the
army, provide a fake history both for themselves and those they address:

Fergus's kilt becomes the image of a sham Scotland by which he and Betty conceal (or is it 'shield') from people the realities of their own historical experience. Fergus walks through the history of twentieth-century Europe as the image of a Scotland which has made itself so fabulous it is untouched by, and unmoved by, the historical reality that it passes through.

The multiplicity of identities by which Fergus protects himself from reality is founded, however, on just the kind of absolute erasure of each stage of his existence which has characterised twentieth-century historiographic constructions of Scotland: 'The groom wears the full-dress uniform of a Highland office, with medals for valour on his chest. Between him and the small anxious boy who once pushed a barrowful of dung up the brae to his grandfather's cottage, what is the connection? And what have I, an old man with shaky hands, to do with either of them?' (81). Fergus's fictionalised identities are incapable of providing any sense of the continuity upon which a real identity would be founded. But this vacuum at the heart of his existence is compounded by a novelistic structure which leaves us in absolute doubt as to whether there ever was a Fergus Lamont, or whether this is all, simply, the construction of an old man by the name of William McTavish, who lingers with other old men in the public library, and is passing his time in writing a fake autobiography. The novel presents its self-fictionalising hero as possibly no more than the compensatory fiction of an old man who has never left the slums in which he was born and who has imagined himself into the role of hero-poet-redeemer which Fergus has assigned to himself. A fiction walks untouched through the battlefields of Europe and the drawing rooms of the aristocracy; or an old man with no story and no connection to the world imagines a past to fill in the emptiness of his actual existence. Whichever way we read the structure of *Fergus Lamont* its version of Scotland is of a country whose history endures only as fictions untouchable by reality, and a country, therefore, where people endure reality as untransformable by their sense of history.

If Fergus is an image of Scotland, then Scotland exists only as history's denial: its past is fictionalised into romance and its present, despite its industrial cities and the participation of its people in two world wars, is a place in which history, the motive force driving the present from past towards future, seems absent. This corresponds to the actuality of a country which lacks even the facade of conflict in terms of a politics fought out through a parliament; a country where the outcomes of its own political processes turn into history somewhere else, in London, a part of English history. History thus becomes, in the title of Jessie Kesson's novel of the Second World War, something that happens in *Another Time, Another Place*,[5] and, like the young woman of that novel, Scotland experiences history at a distance:

Times like these, the young woman felt imprisoned within the circumference of a field. Trapped by the monotony of work that wearied the body and dulled the mind. Rome had been taken. Allies had landed in Normandy, she'd heard that on the wireless. 'News' that caused great excitement in the bothy, crowded with friends . . . Names falling casually from their tongues, out of books from her school-room days. The Alban Hills. The Tibrus . . . 'O Tibrus. Father Tibrus. To whom the Romans pray . . .' Even in her schooldays, those names had sounded unreal. Outdistanced by centuries, from another time. Another place. (101)

The field of modern Scotland is a 'prison', an unbroken 'monotony'; its drab reality makes real history seem 'unreal', uncontactable. History, whether the history of the country's past or the contemporary history of Europe, is a narrative which no longer connects with the experience of Scotland. The First World War plays regularly, in this construction, the last opportunity for Scotland to be reclaimed by history, but an opportunity which simply exhausts the last resources of the country's historical energy and leaves it trapped in an 'intercalendrical zone' which even a Second World War cannot disrupt. In a scene in Allan Massie's *One Night in Winter*,[6] an old man's speech becomes a statement of the Scottish condition:

I'm an old man at the end of a fool's errand. I can't believe this land can be redeemed. Redemption and sacrifice, these are delusions too. You will know how we went to war in 1914. You will have read of the mood. It was all true. Now God be thanked who has matched us with this hour. I marched in that spirit myself, sang that tune. We had lived well, loved beauty given us without a struggle. And we would pay willingly. Well, that was the last of that. Since then, we have all held on to what we could. Resolutely, sometimes, that was the mood in 1940, but without joy. We would cling on. Nothing more . . . '
His voice stopped. In the middle of his message he drifted into sleep. (113)

The old man's sleep becomes the sleep of history itself in Scotland: 'nothing more' after that final effort of the First World War and the fact that

. . . the world is for the big battalions. Small countries cannot withstand it, especially when they are not protected by the barrier of a different language. Their geographical fate determines their nature. You won't stay in Scotland, Dallas . . . Scotland will grow ever less Scottish and ever less stimulating; we live in a withered culture. Sounds of energy are the sounds of the death-rattle . . . I've seen the inexorable force history exerts on the living. In my youth, Dallas, we were distinct. Now? That's gone. So, my dear boy, get out, go where there is life, let your ancestral barracks tumble . . . (112–3)

The 'ever less Scottish' country is a country ever less realisable as the outcome of its past, and its past becomes ever less presentable as the precondition of its present: both are held in limbo ('the good ship Limbo', as Dallas describes it in *One Night in Winter*) and the 'kingdom of limbo' is 'the never-never land of all those lost girls and boys who had been caught half-way out of their prams' (65). The nation is stranded in a narrative whose beginning has no conclusion and whose end develops from no connecting middle: Scottish history, as a significant narrative prefiguring the society which Scotland has become, has been entirely evacuated; it has left behind only a set of stories no longer able to be excavated as the foundations of the later experience of the society.

The old man to whom Dallas listens is an upper class version of the old man encountered by Alan Sharp's central character, Moseby, in *A Green Tree in Gedde*. Moseby is waiting for his friend Harry Gibbon in a pub in Greenock, when he encounters the old man whose conversation also revolves around the First World War. 'Things weren't the same after the war. . . If you'd seen that you couldn't be the same again.' It is a monologue that concludes with the story,

> of a young man who had been to the war and had gone melancholy and suffocated himself in his old army kit bag. He was telling about this when Gibbon came in. He nodded and sat down. 'He got up on the dresser and got in the kit bag and he had a rope through the holes in the kit bag and then just rolled off and that pulled the neck tight and he just suffocated, couldn't get air, and that's how they found him, hanging from the pulley. . .' Moseby could see it, the kit bag and the little kitchen, swinging slightly, and finding him in his canvas shroud. (70)

For the old man the story symbolises a historical experience so horrific, so overwhelming that it cannot be escaped even in the safety of one's own home: the enclosed, domestic pre-war world evoked by an earlier part of his conversation is an idyll – 'Before the war they were, real summers, before your time' (68) – which has been violated by contact with an external history that is brutally destructive: 'I got gassed and so did everybody in my battery' (69). To Moseby, however, the image has a resonance of a completely different kind: it is the claustrophobic kitchen the melancholy Tommy has tried to escape from; it is the experience of history, however brutal, he desires and from which, at home, he feels shut out. After knowledge, no matter how horrific, of that other realm of the historical, the enclosed domestic world is unacceptable, and in wrapping himself in his kit bag the soldier asserts the significance that has been offered and then withdrawn by history. Fergus in his kilt is the antithetic response to the same situation – strutting about in the dress of war, in the pretence of participation in history, while actually haunted by the kitchen to which he will inevitably have to return.

The conflict between the eventless, domestic environment of Scotland and the lost world of historical significance haunts the modern Scottish novel, providing the counterpoints between which many of its most powerful narratives are constructed. It is the contradiction in which Duncan Thaw and his father are trapped in *Lanark*: Thaw senior, like Fergus Lamont, has survived the First World War, but unlike Fergus, Mr Thaw is driven by the experience to try to reconnect with the forces of history which the War has revealed; recovering from a shrapnel wound in Stobhill hospital, he intensifies his understanding of the process of history by reading Carlyle, Darwin and Marx and thirty years later will insist to his son: 'Duncan, modern history is just beginning. Give us another couple of centuries and we'll build a *real* civilization' (295). The War, for Mr Thaw, is a revelation of the force of history that Scotland needs to rediscover, the narrative which it needs, again, to become a portion of. For Duncan, on the other hand, the historical dynamic unleashed by the War has spent itself and history, by the end of the Second World War, is nothing 'but an infinitely diseased worm without head or tail, beginning or end' (160). The encounter with history that was the First World War only intensifies the sense of history's absence in the aftermath of the Second; the possibilities of a new historical narrative offered by working-class political action modelled on the Bolshevik Revolution is undone by the failure of the heavy industries which created the Scottish working class and gave it its power. In *Lanark* the death of both is imaged in the Monkland Canal, whose gates Thaw wants to draw: the Canal had been built by James Watt in 1771, but

> The canal had closed to traffic before he was born. From a channel carrying trade into the depth of the country it had become a ribbon of wilderness allowing reeds and willows, swans and waterhens into the heart of the city. He was puzzled by the phrase [in the 1875 *Imperial Gazetteer of Scotland*] "splendid edifices were called into existence." The only splendid building he knew east of the city was the canal itself, a ten-mile-long artwork shaped in stone, timber, earth and water. (279)

Scotland's history has constructed no 'splendid edifices'; it has aspired to a narrative leading towards a different future only to lapse back into the cyclic world of nature; in the ruins, there is no history because it has been transformed into the stasis of 'artwork': history has happened only to fail. It is an irony which MacIlvanney's *Docherty* explores by celebrating the expectation of an alternative history in the socialism of a mining community in the period of the First World War. Graithnock, despite its industrial base, is a world as distant from history as Kesson's rural world: 'London and Berlin were two places but one scene', the novel records about 1914, but in Graithnock, on the other hand,

> High Street was less hysterical. As a mere distant province of the truth, it received the news already modified by its having happened, as if the distance it had travelled from the capital had left its regal livery stained a little, as if the things that lay between, the sheep rooted in their hillsides, the factory-towns preoccupied with their smoke, the rivers thin with summer and the farms, had all given it accretions of their disbelief, indifference, dismay. Like

a messenger who has come so far that he forgets exactly what his message is, word of the war limped stammering into High Street, barely audible above the shouts of children . . . (131)

The Scottish mining town is only a 'distant province' of history, whose message falters in trying to reach across the apparently changeless landscape in which it is set. However distant from history their world is, however, miners like Tam Docherty live in expectation of a historical change which will transform the conditions of working people and resituate them within a larger and more significant narrative. The novel, however, charts the failure of such hopes, either by the local industrial action of the miners themselves or by the impact of the First World War, in which Tam's son Mick is wounded: Scots may be involved in the world's history, and in Scotland events may occur, but nothing changes:

'Funny thing. Ah've been in mair strikes than Ah can coont. Ah've argied an' focht wi' pit managers till Ah wis blue in the face. An' Ah think Ah'm worse aff than when Ah stertit.' He blew a jet of air down his nostrils, deprecating himself. 'This is the feenish.' (285)

Tam's imminent death will seal that inconclusive finish. McIlvanney, however, in a narrative gesture which imitates the extent to which the socialism of 'Red Clydeside' became a symbol of the possible recovery of history in Scotland in the 1970s, will allow Tam to die in a gesture of defiance, since from the rubble under which he is buried in the mine, his fist only is visible: 'The hand was clenched' (301). The sign of socialist solidarity in expectation of a new history is asserted by the novel in refusal of the actual events through which the country has lived in the intervening period: character and novel gesture together towards a possible future of historical transformation, but the novel's present, which is the character's future, is as unredeemed by the socialist promise of its past as Tam's was. What the gesture actually reveals is the nostalgia for history which unites the author with his characters, the 1970s with the 1920s. The story of socialism's failure to make history happen – particularly, of course, the failure of the General Strike in 1926 – becomes the memory of history's possibility in the later world where history has been suspended and has no 'beginning or end'.

The modern, industrial Scotland of the Lowlands, the place which reveals the emptiness of the old images of Scotland associated with the Highlands, is thus envisaged as being as distant and as divorced from real history as is that romantic escape-world of the past that was figured in the Highlands. Industrial Scotland is a place which has abolished the history of a past Scotland and yet failed to connect Scotland with the processes of modern history. This is the vision presented in J. F. Hendry's influential Glasgow novel, *Fernie Brae*.[7] For Hendry, Scotland's history is not a fulfilment of the nation's identity but its destruction;

the narrative of the country's 'history' is the story of the loss of its real history:

> By Langside lay the battlefield where Mary Queen of Scots was utterly defeated in 1580 by the followers of Knox. That to Scotland he thought was the greatest defeat ever suffered, greater than Flodden, greater than Culloden. He could see the Queen poised on a white charger, awaiting the outcome of the battle, and her dogged, glib-tongued opponents tearing down her cavalry as at Drumclog, fighting down first all the love for women in their hearts to build a grim prison of Calvinism for their country. The ruin of that image, he felt, was the ruin of the Scottish matriarchy, as Culloden was used to discredit Scottish manhood. (129)

Scotland's historical conflicts do not develop the nation; they abolish it. Rather than being the story of the nation's struggle towards freedom, the national narrative is the story of the destruction of its virtues, whether the feminine virtue of Mary or the masculine virtue discredited at Culloden. What it leaves in place of freedom is a 'grim prison of Calvinism', a prison in which, as the novel's opening implies, there can be no significant narrative:

> High Cartcraigs, built in 1789 as a school for the children of planters and known therefore as "The Black Boys' School", stood out of the neighbouring village of Shaws, on an eminence going by the name of "The Green Knowe". As the River Cart ran near, it was given the name of High Cartcraigs by the villages, before being left to its lonely resources.
>
> The French Revolution came and went. In the long field opposite, the local guard drilled to resist the Napoleonic invasion and set their bonfires. No invasion came.
>
> The village prospered, mainly from customs-dues and the traffic of carriages and coaches entering Glasgow from the South. "The Rocket" held its trials, and a railway was built through the meadows which had hitherto been only a gigantic yellow mirror for the sun. As the Scots, in the gathering wheels of industry, lost historical vision and perspective, High Cartcraigs lay at last in a backwater, between tram lines and railway bridge . . . (7)

This place of historical change – the industrial revolution – is also a place of no-history – 'no invasion came'; it is a place which has moved into industrial development only to discover that it has 'lost historical vision' and has nowhere to go to: it becomes a backwater of historical processes that happen elsewhere, neither a fulfilment of the nation's past nor a prefiguration of the world's future.

This desire, deeply inscribed in the tradition of the modern Scottish novel, for the return of history, for the reintroduction of historical dynamic into the suspended world of modern Scotland, was to be parodied by Alasdair Gray in 1994 in *A History Maker*,[8] a fantasy novel whose title is ambiguous since what it recounts is a few days of the future in which Wat Dryhope tries, and fails, to remake history, tries and fails to make 'history' again the medium of people's experience. By the time in which the novel is set the era of 'history', the era preceding the 'modern' age, has been made redundant by the development of a society which 'made cities, nations, money and industrial power obsolete' (203). This ahistorical society, like the Scotland of the Kailyard, is a matriarchy whose business is to maintain peace by diverting the energies of men away from real conflict into fake violence. Wat, whose narrative is modelled on the best examples of history and historical fiction, since it is in style 'like Julius Caesar describing his Gallic wars' and 'like Walter Scott in his best novels' (xi), challenges the domestic world of the dominant matriarchy by the return of real violence, the violence of real history: 'Wee lads of fourteen have never chosen to die like that before – not since the dawn of television. If history wasnae a thing of the past I would say Ettrick *made it* two days ago' (32). The constant danger of the historical is revealed by the fact that Wat's example starts a worldwide mobilization of men for wargames 'played on a scale of almost historical proportions' (130–1) that recalls the rush to arms in August 1914. The desire of those who participate is to return to a world of significant memory: "He made sure we'll be remembered! The lot of us! Living and Dead!" said Joe with a small firm smile, "The bairns, too, in fact the bairns most of all. 'All my fledglings have turned into eagles,' he said. O he was right . . . "'(32). History is the remaking of the power of memory in defiance of the gentle amnesia of an eventless domestic world. It is an opposition which Chris Guthrie, in Grassic Gibbon's *Sunset Song*, had already experienced in the period of the First World War. Chris's husband, Ewan, leaves the domestic idyll of his marriage to Chris to join the army, and returns transformed, brutalised. Before he leaves for the army, however, he comes upon a plaque in Dunnottar Castle, which prefigures his own destiny, and what the meaning of history will be for him:

> . . . and down below, in the dungeons, were the mouldering clefts where a prisoner's hands were nailed while they put him to torment. There the Covenanting folk had screamed and died while the gentry dined and danced in their lithe warm halls, Chris stared at the places, sick and angry and sad for those folk she could never help now, that hatred of rulers and gentry a flame in her heart, John Guthrie's hate. Her folk and his they had been, those whose names stand graved in tragedy
> > HERE : LYES : IOHN : STOT : IAMES : ATCHI
> > SON : IAMES : RUSSELL : & WILLIAM : BRO
> > UN: AND: ONE: WHOSE : NAME: WEE :
> > HAVE : NOT : GOTTEN :
> . . .
>
> But Ewan whispered, *Oh let's get out of this* . . .   (126)

It is as though Ewan catches a glimpse, in that moment, of his own fate, of his name added to such a list on the War Memorial at the novel's conclusion, and that his desire to get 'out of this' matches his despairing attempt, during the war, to ignore it, and to stay out of the history that can only be, to someone like him, destructive. The alternative, however, is to remain in the peasant world, the world that is entirely unremembering – that has no history. In a parallel moment on a visit to another castle, Chris has a different insight:

> In the garden of the castle they wandered from wall to wall, looking at the pictures crumbling there, balls and roses and rings and callipers, and wild heraldic beasts without number, Ewan said he was glad that they'd all been killed. But Chris didn't laugh at him, she knew right well that such beasts had never been, but she felt fey that day, even out here she grew chill where the long grasses stood in the sun, the dead garden about them with its dead stone beasts of an ill-stomached fancy. Folk rich and brave, and blithe and young as themselves, had once walked and talked and taken their pleasure here, and their play was done and they were gone, they had no name or remembered place, even in the lands of death they were maybe forgotten, for maybe the dead died once again, and again went on. (174)

Where Ewan confronts history as remembrance, but remembrance only of violence and death, Chris confronts life as amnesia, cyclic and without progression; a world where history has no meaning. The War calls up Ewan to his destined place in his community's memory of one of its few 'historical' moments: that acceptance into history is, however, like Wat's a 'dryhope'; Chris is left, like her father who 'died a coarse farmer in a little coarse house, hid in the earth and forgot by men (*Cloud Howe*, 52), to the fertile but unremembering and historyless world beyond, a prefiguration of Dryhope's disappearance, in *A History Maker*, back into the 'folk' and to a burial with his lover in 'unmarked graves' (222).

This world trapped between the false promise of history and the enduring repetition of its narrative stasis is one in which endurance itself is the ultimate virtue, an endurance that Chris Guthrie finds only in the land – 'nothing endured at all, nothing but the land she passed across (119)' – but which McIlvanney, like many Scottish novelists, discovers to be the fundamental resource of his characters:

> Like the adherents of a persecuted faith, they had endured long enough to acquire the sense not just of the unmerited privileges of others but of their essential worthlessness as well. Many of them, like Tam, felt militant in the face of these injustices. But it was difficult to mobilise that just resentment because so many carried deep inside themselves, like a tribal precept, a wordless understanding of the powerlessness of any social structure to defeat them. Their bondage admitted them to the presence of a truth from which their masters hid, because to live with necessity is the only freedom. (243)

The freedom to live in eternal bondage from which there can be no salvation; the freedom to endure; a power of resistance as endless as the world in which they are trapped is purposeless and untransformable. In Robin Jenkins's *The Cone Gatherers*,[9] a gamekeeper whose name – Duror – testifies to his shared faith with McIlavnney's miners, is trapped in the Scottish countryside because he is too old to enlist for the Second World War and is married to a crippled woman who 'by merely enduring, . . . could have achieved a superiority over any earthly visitor' (137). Duror, like Kesson's 'young woman' in *Another Time, Another Place*, experiences the war as an imprisonment, leaving him out of touch with the significant world of historical experience. The local doctor thinks of him as someone who, 'for all his pretence of self-possession and invulnerability had been fighting his own war for years' (27). Duror's war is a war unmentioned in the annals of history and 'in which there could be no victory' (27): 'A large elm tree stood outside his house. Many times, just by staring at it, in winter even, his mind had been soothed, his faith in his ability to endure to the end sustained' (28). To endure 'to the end' is the only faith left in a world that has been exiled equally from eternity and from history. It is a philosophy that is recovered by Tam Docherty's grandson in McIlvanney's *The Kiln* (1996):[10] 'Endure and abstain . . . Know thyself . . . As he mutters into the night, he knows that all he is really doing is rearticulating the contribution of the Scottish working classes to the history of philosophy: "Fuck it"' (179–80). That stoicism, however, survives only to be challenged over and again by the temptation of history, while history only returns to be abolished again by the historyless domestic world. The young Tom Docherty, become a writer meditating on his working-class past, discovers,

> . . . that this was the tradition he came from – a long line of logically instinc-
> tive Socialists who lived by principle above materialism because it was the
> only existentially sane thing to do. His father was right. So was his Uncle
> Josey. Before he passed out in his chair, he drank to his relatives, all his
> relatives. (209)

History is encountered only as a prelude to amnesia; memory recovers the past only to discover that neither has any purchase on the future; people endure only as testimony to history's enduring absence. Tom Curdie, for instance, in *The Changeling*, lives in a slum world of darwinian adaptation which challenges all notions of progressive history: slum dwellers like him are born as aliens to their degraded world but rapidly 'acquire the characteristics which would enable them to survive amidst the dirt and savagery' until they are 'as irretrievably adapted to their environment as the tiger to his' (17). This is a world, however much a part of society, which is ruled by nature rather than history. It is a world where endurance is the first principle of survival: 'Never to whine; to accept what came; to wait for better; to take what you could; to let no one, not even yourself, know how near to giving in you were: these were the principles by which he lived . . .' (18). Tom becomes the object of his teacher's effort to save at least one of his pupils

from the degraded conditions in which they live: Charlie Forbes's effort to
salvage Tom's character, however, is based on his sentimental belief in the
virtues of Scottish history and of himself as the inheritor of those virtues:
as their boat sails to Argyll, Charlie, whose name gestures to the failed
history of Jacobitism (and who is married to Mary, that other lost strand of
Scottish history), believes he should be able to point to the landscape and
declare, 'Here it is . . . our heritage, Tom, yours and mine, because we are
Scottish . . . here is the guarantee of that splendid and courageous manhood
to which every Scots boy is entitled by birth' (51). Charlie's 'kingdom',
the place of his annual pilgrimage on holiday, 'where regret, humiliation,
mercenariness, and failure, did not exist' (58), proves, however, to be no
place of reconnection with historical birthright, but rather an invitation to
escapism from the reality of the present:

> He could not keep his imagination from playing: now, knee-deep in the
> water, with his dripping pail in one hand and the spade in the other, he was
> Crusoe, castaway for twenty years, gazing out over the companionless ocean;
> now, crouched, so that the sea's ripples kissed his bottom, he was an ancient
> Caledonian, watching the coracle from Ireland with the men of God; and,
> now, upright, with the spade levelled like a sword, he prepared to resist the
> landing of Redcoats from an English man-o'-war . . . (64–5)

History's 'another time' in which Charlie's imagination 'plays' on holiday
from reality is accompanied by an invitation to Tom to give up his endurance:
'You must let your heart thaw, Tom' (73), Charlie tells Tom (in an image
which reverberates into the name of the main character in Gray's *Lanark*)
but Tom knows that any such thaw would begin to threaten his 'whole
carefully built-up system of self-sufficiency' (74), the same self-sufficiency
which will destroy Thaw and whose melting will destroy Tom. Endurance
is a self-destructive virtue: it allows survival in a desolate environment but
to those who do not require it, its denial of human contact seems an 'inhu-
man silence and endurance' (178). Tom, offered an alternative and playful
world, will not be able to continue enduring; Charlie, having been instigator
of Tom's destruction, will no longer be able to believe in the beneficence
of his historical kingdom. History endures only long enough to undo the
endurance of those who have had to endure its failure.

Fergus Lamont, having lived with a woman who 'endured so nobly' (243),
will return to his home town in the hope that he 'can help it endure' (273),
because a place locked in suspension, between a past history emptied of
significance and a present with no narrative to carry it towards the future,
can only be endured with the fortitude that comes from a stoical obduracy
that has come to expect nothing from history. The First World War, the
War which was supposed to reconnect this society with history's dynamic,
has itself become simply another empty icon of an already lost history.
Visiting the War Memorial, Fergus's private tribute to fallen comrades is

interrupted by 'some little girls' who 'could have been the daughters of men killed at Flodden' (179):

> There were over a thousand names on the four sides of the plinth. The town's grief must have been very great. Yet I had not been here to help it grieve. . . .
>   With tears in my eyes, I hoped that during all the exchanges of hope and sorrow at all the closemouths in those terrible years, some kindly mention had been made of me.
>   I was standing at salute when I heard a spurt of giggles behind me.
> 'Wheesht, Jeanie.'
> 'Don't punch me, Isa.'
> 'He's talking to himself.'
> 'I think he's greeting.'
> 'Dae you ken whit I think? I think he's a ghost.'
> 'Jees, Mary, you're richt. He's the ghost of a sodger that was killed.'
> Their squeals of terror then were only half feigned. They dashed past me, making for the gate . . . As they ate their teas they would tell their families of the ghost of the soldier they had seen talking to himself at the War Memorial. (180)

In the domestic interior the families who are unchanged by history; outside the ghost of history, committed, like Fergus to continuous change and yet become a counterpoint to a world where those changes make no difference, haunts the monument to its own irrelevance.

Escape from false history, escape into real history, might, at some point in the future, be a beneficent outcome for humanity, but in a society which has plunged into industrialisation and urbanisation, the suspension of history consigns its inhabitants to endure a world which is a living hell. Fergus discovers it when he returns to the tenement where he had been brought up: 'In my recollections the close had never stank so rankly of cats' piss. Nor had the walls been so fearfully defaced, not merely with chalk, but with knives, and, in some places, with hatchets apparently . . . We began the ascent to hell' (193). To young Ewan in *Grey Granite*, it is 'A hell of a thing to be History! – not a student, a historian, a tinkling reformer, but LIVING HISTORY ONESELF, being it, making it' (148), but Mrs Trease, wife of the communist who had first suggested to him that it was 'a hell of a thing to be history' (147), ironically notes that 'revolutionary songs gave her a pain in the stomach, they were nearly as dreich as hymns – the only difference being that they promised you hell on earth instead of in hell' (183). It is hell to be caught in the promises of history; hell to be trapped in a history without promise; modern Scotland became the image of both.

It is in that ahistorical hell that Duncan Thaw lives in the aftermath of the Second World War in Glasgow. 'Can Lanark Lead Him Out of Hell?', the Prologue's running head asks on page 116, responded to by page 117: 'Can He Help Lanark Out of Hell?' One of Duncan's emergency escapes exits is to climb to the top of a mountain, driven on by a vision of a girl standing at the top of the mountain whom he will meet there; near the summit, however, he gets caught in a cleft: 'Thaw pressed his chest against the granite and stood on tiptoes and, reaching up, brought his fingertips within an inch of the top. "Hell, hell, hell, hell, hell," he muttered sadly, gazing at the dark rock where it cut against a white smudge of cloud' (141). Trapped in hell, he will escape not by the intervention of the girl whom he had imagined but of the village minister, Mr McPhedron, whom Thaw's mother thinks has 'too much Hell in his sermons' (143):

> ... The minister gave a slight friendly laugh.
> "I admire your father. His notion of education embraces everything but the purpose of life and the fate of man. Do you believe in the Almighty?"
> Thaw said boldly, "I don't know, but I don't believe in Hell."
> The minister laughed again. "When you have more knowledge of life you will mibby find Hell more believable. You are from Glasgow?"
> "Yes."
> "I was six years a student of divinity in that city. It made Hell very real to me." (143–4)

The industrial city, seen from the perspective of divinity or mountain top, is hell – the very place which, as a part of the modern world of technology and progress, ought to be the image of historical process and change has become, in the Scottish context, the place where history is suspended, a place which exists in denial of connection with the past or with an alternative future.

Charting the hell of Scotland's industrial squalor has been a fundamental requirement of the modern Scottish novel. It is not simply the hell of an impoverished working class living in city slums or in squalid housing estates – however fascinating those depths have been to novelists and publishers, from MacArthur and Long's *No Mean City* (1957),[11] about the slum world of Glasgow, to Irvine Welsh's depictions of drug-addicted Edinburgh in the 1990s – it is the hell of a world of endless repetition, of endless endurance; the hell of a narrative without end, without purpose. The world of urban Scotland is no longer a stage of history, such as might have been envisaged by the Scottish Enlightenment, which will pass away to be replaced by something better: it is a world where history has ceased to operate – 'Nothing has happened between these walls since Adam Smith', as J. F. Hendry puts it in *Fernie Brae* (132) – and in that suspension the Calvinism which may have been supplanted as the dominant ideology of the nation leaves behind the intensity of its awareness of damnation not as something to come beyond death, but as the very condition of the present. In his *Autobiography*,[12] Edwin Muir describes how, on first arriving in Glasgow, he would go to watch football games played on 'scraps of waste ground', where 'teams from the slum quarters of the south side played every Saturday afternoon with great skill and savage ferocity': 'I first saw one of these games shortly after I came to Glasgow; a brown fog covered the ground, and a small, tomato-red sun, like a jellyfish floating in the sky, appeared and disappeared as the air grew thicker or finer . . . there was a grimy fascination in watching the damned kicking a football in a tenth-rate hell' (87). It is a hell which becomes only too evident to the young Duncan Thaw, who comes to the sudden realisation that 'Hell was the one truth and pain the one fact which nullified all others' (160), confirming what Mr McPhedron explains to him: man delivered the world over to the devil and 'since then the world has been the Devil's province, and an annexe of Hell' (183).

The industrial hell of Scotland is a world where the forward trajectory of narrative turns into an eternity of repetition, repetition such as Thaw's friend Coulter describes to him when he has started working:

> . . . this business of being a *man* keeps you happy for mibby a week, then on your second Monday it hits you. To be honest, the thought's been growing on you all through Sunday, but it really hits you on Monday: I've tae go on doing this, getting up at this hour, sitting in this tram in these overalls dragging on this fag, clocking on in this queue at the gate. 'Hullo, here we go again!' 'You're fuckin' right we go!' and back intae the machine shop . . . Mind you, this feeling doesnae last. You stop thinking. Life becomes a habit. You get up, dress, eat, go tae work, clock in etcetera etcetera automatically . . . (215–16)

It is this mechanical world of repetition that comes to be mimicked by Thaw's own body, which refuses to become well and goes 'into a repetitive cycle of improvement and deterioration' (311) as though it cannot allow the possibility of change and must, quite literally, embody the suspended animation of the historyless world it inhabits. Such suspended animation will become a regular image of the changeless and paralysed condition of modern Scotland. In Robin Jenkins's *The Cone Gatherers*, Duror is shackled to his monstrously bloated, bedridden wife, the 'sweetness' of whose youth, 'still haunting amidst the great wobbling masses of pallid flat that composed her face' (30) mirrors the stranded immobility of his own existence; in Iain Banks's *The Bridge*,[13] as in Irvine Welsh's *Marabou Stork Nightmares*,[14] the narrator is immobilised in his hospital bed – 'my memory is practically non-existent, this could have been a few days ago or since the beginning of time itself' (4); in A. L. Kennedy's *Looking for the Possible Dance* Margaret meets a severely disabled boy, James Watt, who 'shares his name with a leading Industrial Revolutionary' (71) and whose stranded condition matches the outcome of the industrial revolution in Scotland; in George Mackay Brown's *Greenvoe*,[15] Mrs McKee, living on the symbolically-named island of Hellya, is trapped in the endlessly repeated interrogation of her actions in 1916. For all of them, as for Thaw, there is no narrative way out, no way of reconnecting their own lives to a larger narrative which will offer them a sense either of the significance of their suffering or the possibility of changing it. The hell of suspended history is inescapable except through death; for Thaw, the words of Vergil prove all too true: 'Going down to hell is easy: the gloomy door is open night and day. Turning around and getting back to sunlight is the task, the hard thing' (283).

Even art is no buttress against this desolating world, since art too is transformed into an analysis of the morbid condition of the world it inhabits: Thaw asks permission to 'sketch in the dissecting room of the university' and when it is granted says, 'Thank you, sir, . . . Some sketching in the vivisection room is really necessary at this stage' (252). His Freudian substitution of 'vivisection' for 'dissection' reveals the real nature of his art: he takes the living world and reduces it to a dead one. Thaw, the artist turned vivisector because of the condition of the city in which he lives, would be at home in the New York of Muriel Spark's *The Hothouse by the East River* (1975),[16] a city which is the 'home of the vivisectors of the mind, and of the mentally vivisected still to be reassembled, of those who live intact, habitually wondering about their states of sanity, and home of those whose minds have been dead, bearing the scars of resurrection' (11). In *The Hothouse by the East River* Spark translates the suspended world of Scotland into a universal condition, for in *The Hothouse* New York – the real, vibrant New York of the historical 1960s – is an afterlife, inhabited by people who are, like Jenkins's Fergus, ghosts of an unrealised past – except that in Spark's case the metaphor is all too real, since the characters are indeed the unquiet spirits of people who have died in the Second World War. As spirits in torment, however, they are sufficiently indistinguishable from the rest of the denizens of that city to reveal that modern reality is nothing more than the ghost of the history that had been promised by the slaughter of war. Spark's novel imagines those who died in the war living on in the New York to which they had hoped to emigrate – 'After the war,' Paul is saying, 'Elsa and I are going to settle in America' (123) – and the fact that they died has made no difference. New York as afterlife and New York as reality are one and the same – a city not of God but of His absence:

'. . . Manhattan the mental clinic, cried his heart, where we analyse and dope the savageries of existence. Come back, it's very centrally heated here, there are shops on the ground floor, you can get anything here that you can get over there and better, money's no object. Why go back all that way where your soul has to fend for itself and you think for yourself in secret while you conform with the others in the open? Come back here to New York the sedative chamber where you don't think at all and you can act as crazily as you like and talk your head off all day, all night' (75–6).

Elsa's shadow, that falls the wrong way, is the only indicator that we are not in the world of 'reality', but a misplaced shadow is of no consequence in a world as lost to ultimate reality as New York: 'The hell with her shadow,' says Annie, a psychiatrist, who then lists the city's problems: 'Haven't we got enough serious problems in this city? We already have the youth problem, the racist problem, the distribution problem, the political problem, the economic problem, the crime problem . . .' (108), and so on for a page. Elsa's comment reveals why this world has become hell: 'She missed out the mortality problem' (110). New York is a culture which ignores the mortality problem – Elsa's psychoanalyst is called 'Garven' in denial of the 'Graven' truth of life – and so tries to live life as though it were an eternal childhood. The defiance of time, however, does not take it back to primordial innocence but anticipates the eternal sufferings of the damned.

The childishness of this world, its suspension out of time and history, marks it as the repetition at the very centre of modern civilisation of Scotland's condition of failed history, a connection underlined by the fact that Paul and Elsa's son Pierre is producing a new version of J. M. Barrie's *Peter Pan*. Spark's witty parallel between a Scot constructing an escape – an 'emergency exit' – from time, and a historical world in denial of temporality, is acknowledged at the beginning of Chapter 7, which opens, '"Scotch," says Paul' (111). The one word statement is poised between the novel's (and author's) self-description and the character's instruction to a waiter: '"On the rocks?" says the waiter. "On the rocks," says Paul' (111). However distant, this world is like the Scotland of suspended history – on the rocks rather than founded on the Rock. Paul is without the Peter on whom the Church is built and so is haunted instead by a Scottish alternative to eternity – the Peter of Barrie's 'Never Land', an endless repetition of childhood whose false denial of time is revealed by the mode of Pierre's production, which has all the parts played by aged actors:

> The scene is the traditional Never-Never Land, the island of Lost Boys. Garven breathes heavily with psychological excitement as Lost Boys of advanced age prance in fugitive capers with the provocative pirates, then hover over the crone Wendy. Enter, Peter Pan. At this point Elsa stands up and starts throwing squelchy tomatoes one after the other at the actors. One soft tomato after the other she brings out of the big crocodile bag. (92)

In *Peter Pan*, the crocodile that has swallowed the clock is the symbol of the time to which adult humanity, in the form of Captain Hook, is condemned, but which the play itself transcends and denies through the eternal spirit of Pan. In *The Hothouse by the East River*, on the other hand, the dead skin of the crocodile, in the form of a handbag, contains overripe tomatoes that Elsa – here representing her author, Muriel – will toss at the stage in order to disrupt the false eternity of the world of art, the false timelessness of New York, and allow herself out of the Never Land and back into a world of real time, real death, and the possibility of real salvation.

In New York, as in Glasgow, the negation of 'heaven' – either as transcendent justification of life or teleological outcome of history – leaves humanity stranded in a world of time that seems timeless, a world that mimicks eternity, but only in its endless repetition of a meaningless past no longer connected to the future. Elsa, a ghost who claims to be the 'mother of the author' (93), says to her daughter, who was not conceived till after her mother's death, 'I never had any money in my life. It's all a myth' (137). When the world of history fails we are left in the region of myth, and the myth is hell: the only distinctions are between the kinds of hell in which we have been trapped:

"This *is* Hell," said Lanark.
"There are worse hells," said Jack. (432)

In the Scotland of suspended history the only choice is of which hell to inhabit.

II

Gray's *A History Maker* celebrates what, to a long line of Scottish novelists, has been the despair of Scottish culture – the sense of having reached an end to history, and does so by returning to an equivalent of the domestic, matriarchal world of the Kailyard as, in effect, the best answer to how humanity can live in happiness. It also parodies, however, the search for a place in which history is still significant that has characterised many modern Scottish novels, whether in the return to Scottish prehistory to document the process of history's birth, as in Mackay Brown's *Vinland*[17] (about the consequences of the discovery of North America by Orcadian voyagers) or Neil Gunn's *Sun Circle*[18] (about the early invasion of the Scottish High-lands by Viking raiders and by Christianity); or in the reconstructions of the history of the ancient world, as in Lewis Grassic Gibbon's *Spartacus*,[19] Naomi Mitchison's *The Corn King and the Spring Queen*[20] and Allan Massie's roman novels.[21] Equally, Scottish novelists have sometimes adopted alternative national environments for the exploration of 'significant' history, as in Eric Linklater's *Private Angelo*,[22] or in Massie's novels of twentieth-century Europe (*The Death of Men, A Question of Loyalties, The Sins of the Father*).[23] All are explorations of what twentieth century Scotland has failed to provide for the modern novelist – a world of significant conflict and a place where history can be witnessed in the making. Thus we might see in Grassic Gibbon's *Spartacus* the enactment of the revolution which Scotland did not deliver for its author in 1926 in the General Strike: by using the same kind of linguistic medium that he had used in *Sunset Song*, Gibbon projects backwards upon the ancient world the traditions of Scottish popu-list culture. Equally, Gunn's *Sun Circle* dramatises the conflict between the different elements of ancient culture on Scottish territory in the centuries before the founding of Scotland as a nation, but in the conflicts between Celts, Vikings and the more ancient peoples whom they are displacing is projected the continuing divisions which disable modern Scotland and prevent it from gaining control over its own historical fate. The failure of history that is Scotland's modern condition inserts itself insistently even in the most distant locations to which the novelist flees from the consequences of that failure, like an inescapable shadow haunting the Scottish imagination.

In this respect, Allan Massie's novels are particularly symptomatic, since their central concern is with what Scotland has lacked in the twentieth century – power, and his search is always for the relationship between the story of an individual life and the structure of the history of which he is a part. It is something which Massie turns into one of the games of his self-conscious narrators, who know that history is a narrative constructed to provide a retrospective significance to events – as the narrator of *A Question of Loyalties* puts it 'History is written from then to now, but understood back to front' (166) – in order that its subject can be seen not just as an isolated individual case but as 'a pale reflection of the . . . century' (178). Massie's use of European history can be seen as a search for precisely the kinds of significance in individual lives, a relation between the individual narrative and the historical narrative, that has been impossible in Scotland. If it is indeed the influence of Walter Scott which disengages the Scottish novel from history, then Scott is perhaps the justification of Massie's use of histories other than Scotland's; at the same time, ironically, it is Scott who exerts the most profound influence on Massie's construction of these non-Scottish histories. Massie's narrators, for instance, are almost always people caught unawares between competing historical forces, just as Scott's protagonists are: the narrators may reflect on the action rather than participating urgently in it, but they replicate Scott's deliberately banal heroes in their passive ability to see both sides of a conflict. In *A Question of Loyalties*, for instance, the issue of France's complicity with Nazism during the Second World War is narrated by Etienne de Balafré, son of one of those who participated in the Vichy government. Etienne stands between the generation of his father, caught up in vast historical events, and the generation of his daughter, student activists who 'believe that words can cause movement' (102). Etienne, however, himself resides in Switzerland – an intellectual neutral in the battles of history, a waverer like Scott's Waverley, who contrasts the 'clear imperatives of the Trojan war' with the 'hesitating morality by which I lived myself' (79). Waverley is caught up in the events of history but believes ultimately in the private world and is destined to live out his life in the domestic environment; Etienne confides to us that,

Reality, I told myself, is private life. Reality is the touch of skin on skin, is a flower unfolding, it is weather and the wonderfully creamy onion tart that Dominique would give us for lunch; reality was the grains of sand on the beach . . . Reality is sensuous and imaginative; rhetoric is its enemy. Politics, I told myself, represented a denial of reality, the preference of the airy abstractions over the primal knowledge of sea, rocks, sand, bones, skin.' (101)

Equally, the events in France of his father's generation are rendered in terms of the classic division within the family by which Scott and Stevenson were to dramatise the conflicts of history as reaching down into and transforming personal life. Thus the Second World War in France is presented as 'a civil war', where 'there is always right on both sides' (45), and the two sides are enacted through the division between two brothers, each good in himself but each committed to the opposite side of the cause – Armand to the Free French and de Gaulle, Lucien to Vichy and Pétain. The parallel structure of Massie's presentation of events in France and Scott's presentation of the events of the 1745 ('under which king') is gestured to by the conversation which follows the revelation of Etienne's relation to Lucien by his friend Jamie, whose name inspires the notion that his action is 'sort of Jacobite' – 'a splendid and useless gesture' (53). The issue which Scott bequeathed to the Scottish novel, of history versus the historyless, is itself given a historical construction in *A Question of Loyalties*: in Provence, in his father's house, Etienne finds that 'Stretched out on the rough ground below the tree, listening to the myriad little sounds, which only deepened the silence that was the background of their music, it was possible to imagine that there was no such thing as History' (68); and the conflict between history and its other is seen not as a matter of national imagination but as a matter of generation: 'We are all placed in History, landed there, involuntarily and unconsulted. Some generations have the apparent good fortune to be able to feel free of History. No great questions disturb the tenor of their life' (299). Equally, it is this issue which drives the narrative of *The Sins of the Father*, since Eli, victim of – but also collaborator with – the Nazis 'refused offers of help from his brother – to make him fully experience the guilt of his own freedom from History, as he had put it once' (14). That 'freedom from history' has its illusory counterpart both in the immediate post-war world in which Eli's wife Nell had searched for him in Germany, a place where there 'were no bombs, but it seemed that the world was held in suspended animation' (39), and in the freedom from history sought by former Nazis in Argentina, where they regard their past 'as something irrelevant, "mere history", separate from a new existence' (102). The problem of History in Massie's novels is precisely the problem that has obsessed Scottish novelists, but seen in reverse: in the world of the destructive processes of history it is the historyless domestic and personal world which is continually threatened: 'That was how the Jews themselves must have felt in pre-war Germany: they hadn't been hired out to be players, but had been conscripted. Perhaps that is the meaning, and the horror, of History:

that it spills off the stage. If only it could be left to those who enjoy the game' (185).

The players of history, however, are caught up in a story whose meaning they cannot know: the power they seek is never achievable, because even when in power they do not understand the forces that are shaping the future significance of their actions. This is the tragedy in which the significant and insignificant figures of history are alike trapped in Massie's novels: whatever values they stand by, good or evil, will be seen to have had, in retrospect, an entirely different meaning from what they assumed. Thus Massie's novels play constantly with double time scales: one in which the characters are narrated forwards towards the as yet unresolved future, the other in which the actions are seen in the retrospect of their unforeseen outcomes. In *A Question of Loyalties* the defence of French values which leads Lucien de Balafré to join the Vichy government will be seen as the betrayal of French values after the defeat of the Germans: Lucien's diary entries, living forward in doubt and hesitation, are juxtaposed with the retrospections of his son, recalling the past in his 'hesitating morality'. Once the sides have been chosen, Lucien and Armand, like the brothers in Stevenson's *Master of Ballantrae*, have to play the game out to its conclusion, even though it has declined from heroic epic to 'monstrous farce' (261). The 'question of loyalties' is also a question of narrative, for the same events can be seen as either epic or farce.

It is this double perspective which shapes Massie's novel *Augustus*, in which Augustus's lack of knowledge and control over events increases the more powerful he becomes, so that we read his own story not as an image of the golden age of order and civility that it has come to represent to later ages but as a chaotic struggle against forces he cannot understand or control. Massie's narrative is split between an early account, which tells of his rise to power, and which emphasises the extent to which everything was accident and yet led to what seemed to be a destined conclusion. The second half, dictated when he is old, tells of his years in power, but what it reveals is his fundamental powerlessness – the fact that he is the prisoner of the very state which he thinks he controls, destroying his own family in the name of maintaining his family power. He may believe, for instance, that 'without Livia [his wife] I could not have survived' (335) but the sentence itself takes on an ambiguous double meaning he does not intend when we consider how much of his life has been shaped by the plottings of his wife, plottings which he has to repress from his own conscious:

> '"You know", Maecenas said to me once, "people say Livia poisoned Marcellus."'
>
> (That entry appears on its own, without comment. How, I asked myself when I read it just now, could I have thought to record it starkly, and have added nothing? Yet now, what can I find to say but that it is patently absurd? You

might as well say . . . oh there is no end of people's willingness to repeat
noxious scandal.) (309)

Augustus's suppression of his own awareness of Livia's plotting (which,
clearly, he had earlier been able to entertain), is, equally, his suppression of
the fact that 'without Livia' he 'could indeed not have survived' in another
sense – that she has allowed him to survive to aid her own power rather
than to support his. Augustus has an authorial control of the narrative we
are reading that matches the supposed control he exerted over the Roman
Empire in later histories of it: what his narrative reveals however, is exactly
how limited and artificial is his power. On the one hand he knows that his
early actions were 'gangsterism' – 'three young men . . . come to claim my
inheritance and ready to impose ourselves on the Republic and seize it by
the throat' (183) – governed by chance and luck; on the other, everything
has to be part of some larger design which is being fulfilled in despite of the
wills of individual human beings: ' . . . listening to Virgil, I knew that we
required to consecrate our restored Republic, the New Order of Rome, by
a ceremony which would join its future to our past . . . The time was ripe.
The Sibyl had announced the coming of the reign of Apollo. Virgil himself, divinely inspired, promised an Age of Gold, established by me' (264).
That 'design' is, however, itself a construction: an artifice of art and of
propaganda. The clear and lucid patterns of life that Augustus searches
for through his narrative continually dissolve into subterranean plottings
beyond his control: the world of Rome, of order and clarity, disappears into
that which seems to be its 'other', the barbarian world of Germany:

> There are in Germany dark and trackless forests. Huge trees join their branches
> to deny the sun to the ground below. The undergrowth is thick, tangled
> and full of briars which lacerate the traveller's legs, and even reach above
> the protective leggings of ox-hide such as Ulysses wore when he drove his
> plough in Ithaca. These forests are numinous, spirit-haunted by the demons
> of delusion. In the absence of paths, the traveller must trace his journey by
> notching the trees with his knife. The forests afflict the nerves; no Roman who
> spends any time there comes out unimpaired . . . He sighs for the lucidity of
> the Mediterranean world, for the stark landscape of rock and sky and water;
> he longs for the certainties of these harsh realities. (92–3)

The certainties of that landscape are precisely what Augustus cannot discover
in his own life, which becomes more and more like the German forests in
which his armies get lost. Etienne de Balafré, in *A Question of Loyalties*,
looks at the same relation of Germany to Rome from the other perspective,
both geographically and historically:

> Standing in a butt, his face frozen by the grey wind which cut across the
> marshy wastelands from the Russian steppes, Lucien sniffed the immensity

of Europe, the cruelty of history, the fragility of all he valued . . . When in
the evening his hosts talked of the lost mission of civilisation which had been
German's historic role in the east, he understood the sense of deprivation
which they experienced. Ancestors, they assured him, had belonged to the
Tuetonic Order of Knights; he could picture them in black armour setting
their faces against that east wind, venturing into a land of dry magic, where
no values of Christian man were known. The thought made him shudder,
He, who had been accustomed to think of Germany itself as something barbaric, who was conscious of everything that was Roman in Europe to which
Germany had stood opposed, now felt that Rome was like a stone hurled
into a deep black pond, which sent ripples, diminishing in size, from the
spot where it had landed. He had believed German was beyond the ripple;
he now saw that he was wrong. The Germans were not only the remotest of
ripples themselves, but the guardians of all that that rippling water signified.
He listened in the evening to Brahms on his wind-up gramophone; there was
forest-music there, but beneath its pagan mystery throbbed the affirmative
note of Rome. (166-7)

Germany, once the antithesis of Rome, has become, for Lucien, its outer
guardian, the limit within which Roman order is contained against the darkness beyond and which justifies his collaboration with Germany, protecting
Europe against the loss of connection with Rome. Lucien, however, is as
self-deceiving as Augustus, giving a romantic lineage to the modern bar-
barism with which he will do business in the name of ancient civilisation,
just as Augustus constructs the image of an orderly civilisation out of the
destructive conflicts of his own *polis*. Both are men trapped in the illusion
of an order of history which dissolves at every turn, and trapped, equally,
in the illusion of a power that flows from that order.

Power, however, does not derive from the 'affirmative note of Rome';
power has another source altogether, and what drives those in power is
not the ideal affirmative note joining 'its future to our past' but something
primitive and barbaric, something ordered not by reason but by magic.
Augustus's success in taking over the Republic is governed not by clear-
sighted policy but by magic, the magic of his name – 'Caesar, Caesar,
Caesar . . . the magic word ran round the camp till Anthony pressed his
fingers in his ears against it' (40) – and his soldiers belief in his magical
destiny. The accidents of events take on the shape of destiny not in response
to his will but by a magical revelation: 'I had all the certainty of the
great artist who finds a long-projected and much brooded-on work slowly
assuming the perfect, hardly-understood, shape before his eyes; a moment
of magic, as Virgil once described it to me . . . ' (49). It is in search of
the source of that magic that the failing poet and his Emperor Augustus,
turning against the 'lucid light of Reason' (260), go to Eleusis, to encounter
'the mystery cults, which are not masculine and reasonable like our Roman
ones, but feminine and emotional. They speak with a strange music to parts

of our nature that we do not, and cannot, know. All Romans fear them in their hearts' (260). The mystery of the feminine is, of course, at the root of Augutus's actual power, but the mysterious source of power can never be brought into the light of Reason, and defeats the cumulative processes of history: 'stranger, wilder, as if it came from a great distance, recalling what we had never known and yet seemed always to have known' (261). It is this magical power which haunts Massie's novels: the supernatural moments when history is revealed as simply the concealment of a deeper, more primitive, purpose.

Massie's Walter Scott experiences the power of that primitive defiance of history when, in a close in Edinburgh, he re-encounters the lower-class boy whom he had fought as a child:

> Then, as if a stage curtain had been drawn, a thin light flooded the close and the music struck up. At the top of the steps the girl appeared, and held out her hand, but not to me. A figure emerged from the shadows, a boy with long hair, a torn shirt and breeches that ended in rags about his knees. He was barefoot, and his hair and cheek were streaked with what I knew to be blood. They held my gaze, and at first I could not recognize him. And then I saw that he was Green-breeks, and called out to him whether he did not know me. He looked as he had in the days of our 'bickers', indeed as if the swordblow which had felled him then had proved mortal. (212)

Scott's encounter with this primitive source of his own creative energy – 'for sometimes it seemed that I had won a great victory and survived a trial, and at others that I had been deprived of what I most desired' (214–5) – leaves him unable to 'believe that I had really held the skeletal hand of Michael Scott, astrologer, philosopher, and tutor to the Emperor Frederick II, known as *stupor mundi*, the wonder of the world', or, equally, to 'believe either that I had not done so': unable to 'know whether I had been threatened with something fearful, or whether a promise of delight had been extended to me' (215).

For Massie's characters, the effort to connect with the sources of power that drive history always end in such uncertain encounters and the effort to understand the rationality of history is but the gate towards an encounter with the supernatural, the mythic. It is this which Virgil explains to Augustus, contrasting the story of Cincinnatus with the story of the priest who guards Diana's temple at Nemi:

> Cincinnatus is legend: he belongs to a young world when everything was straightforward, and right-doing was rewarded by a calm spirit . . . But the priest of Diana who guards the Golden Bough and Temple at Nemi present no legend but myth, which reveals the truth darkly to grown men. The world has gone beyond Cincinnatus, and you cannot lay aside your toga and return to the plough. You are bound for life to prowl with naked unsheathed sword round the temple that is Rome. (132)

History is not journey forward into greater knowledge but the continual dissolution of the present into the repeated mystery of the mythic: 'We cannot fathom the mystery, but we can acknowledge its truth' (132). What Virgil reveals to Augustus is what J. G. Frazer has revealed to Allan Massie in the image of the King at Nemi who can never sleep for fear of the one who will come to slay him – the powers which lie beyond the boundaries of history and which continue to shape it no matter how far from that primitive origin we may feel we have travelled. What endures is not history, but myth: understanding history requires a journey into the regions of myth. In this respect, Massie's novels of the ancient world and of modern Europe build on the fundamental foundation of the Scottish novel in the twentieth century: if the question asked by Scottish philosophers in the eighteenth century was 'how did society develop in history?', the fundamental question asked from the late nineteenth century onwards was, 'what is history founded on? What precedes and shapes the historical?' Massie's fiction may focus on very different historical contexts from those of other Scottish writers, but it shares with them the fact that its fundamental answer to the question of history rests on the mythic and, in particular, on the sense of the development of history that derives from Frazer's *The Golden Bough*.

The most powerful version of this in twentieth-century Scottish fiction, published only a few years after the final, one-volume edition of *The Golden Bough* had appeared in 1922, was John Buchan's *Witch Wood* of 1927.[24] *Witch Wood* is a historical novel in the manner established by Scott, with the protagonist, the Reverend David Sempill, as the man who stands between the two extremes of the parties to the civil war in the 1640s. He is a good presbyterian and yet responsive to the graces of ancient culture – the 'Pagan writers' as one of his kirk elders points out to him (13). David is forced into confrontation with his own presbyterian church as a result of providing refuge to a wounded royalist soldier, and comes into conflict with Chasehope, who is committed to the notion of his election to grace and therefore freedom from moral laws. What David is in confrontation with is not simply the historical contradictions of a particular epoch: what he is confrontation with is a the force of myth, of the survival into his own historical epoch of the 'god of darkness and passion'. Chasehope, like Massie's Augustus, re-enacts the rites of the ancient gods of the woods:

> 'It is the Wood, and the blackest kind of witchcraft. Some old devilry of the heathen has lingered in that place, and the soul of my miserable parish is thirled to it. You will not find in Scotland a doucer bit, for there are no public sins and shortcomings. Man, there's times when Woodilee seems as quiet and dead as the kirkyard. But there's a mad life in its members, and at certain seasons it finds vent. In the deeps of the night and in the heart of the Wood there are things done of which it is shameful even to speak.' (113)

In that wood what David discovers are the innocence of 'the happy riot and the far horizons of childhood' (127) but also the forces that come from the childhood of the human race, 'all the unforgotten things of memory', which reveal themselves as the re-enactment of ancient, pre-christian rituals:

> ... he saw that the figures were indeed human, men and women both – the women half-naked, but the men with strange headpieces like animals. What he had taken for demons from the Pit were masked mortals – one with the snout of a pig, one with a goat's horns, and the piper a gaping black hound .... As they passed, the altar was for a moment uncovered, and he saw that food and drink were wet on it for some infernal sacrament. (84)

Buchan's historical novel confronts precisely the failure of history to have abolished the depths of the past, all the unforgotten things of memory: the 'justification' of the Calvinist elder is not simply a historical fact about a particular period of Scottish history – it is the route to the recovery of an ancient force that has never left the woods. Far from being a historical novel, *Witch Wood* is an anti-historical novel, precisely to the extent that it perceives history to be the product of the continual eruption into the present of forces from the depths of the past in defiance of history's progressive development. In the 'Prologue', the narrator has a vision of the landscape dissolving backwards into its primal form:

> Then one evening from the Hill of Deer I saw with other eyes ... The colliery headgear on the horizon, the trivial moorish hill-tops, the dambrod-pattern fields, could never tame wholly for me that land's romance, and on this evening I seemed to be gazing at a thing antique ... I saw an illusion, which I knew to be such, but which my mind accepted ... It was the Woodilee of three hundred years ago ... My mouth shaped the word 'Melanudrigill', and I knew that I saw Woodilee as no eye had seen it for three centuries, when, as its name tells, it still lay in the shadow of a remnant of the Wood of Caledon, that most ancient forest where once Merlin harped and Arthur mustered his men ... ' (3–4)

It is that return to the past, and return of the past to the present, which the narrative then enacts, with Frazer's account of the workings of the primitive mind as guide: that Buchan's seventeenth century has actually been invaded by the knowledge of the twentieth in the form of Frazer's theories, is only confirmation of the fact that the novel is engaged not with the reconstruction of history, but with history as the prefiguration and postfiguration of an underlying reality known only to modernity. History is governed not by the laws of economic and political progress but by those mythic forces, which, if they sometimes present themselves as beneficent, nonetheless appear to modern humanity more often as diabolic: 'To David it seemed a vision of the lost in Hell' (84). When history fails, myth returns: when history is suspended, humanity is not redeemed but damned to an eternity in hell.

Massie's *The Sins of the Father*, in attempting to come to terms with that 'Hell in which no one believed' (41) that was the Third Reich, presents an account of the development of Rudi, the Nazi whose past will be uncovered and who will be tried for his crimes in Israel, an account designed to explain how he came to commit himself to a cause which will lead directly to committing terrible crimes. In the midst of economic depression, he 'found a job, as a clerk in a factory where they made glue out of bones' (195). The description of the bone factory prefigures the atrocities of Auschwitz:

> The bone factory stood in a dismal eastern suburb of the city. It was a place where the city trickled like dirty water into a countryside that had no grace or charm about it. The factory stood between a canal that needed dredging and a railway line. Trucks bearing bones from various abattoirs halted there. There were fat yellow and white maggots clinging to the bones, to which a few shreds of flesh and sinew were still attached. If you picked up a bone a handful of maggots would fall off. That wasn't the worst of it. Far worse was the stench from the furnaces. It hung over the dismal quarter . . . I was a clerk keeping records, but I would sit at the grimy window overlooking the yard and watch the seagulls that picked at them, always quarrelling. (197)

The psychological effect of this infernal landscape, an image of the hell in which he will live through the Nazi years, emerges when he had been working late,

> and the tram which I took back to the quarter where I now had my lodgings was empty. It was raining, and the few poor lights in that fringe of the city were mere spots, like a bulb shining through a shroud. Then though the tram had not stopped, the carriage was full of people, and they all had the same face, they all wore damp overcoats with the collars turned up, and all gazed at me. They did not speak, but they directed their eyes at me. Only they had no eyes. The rest of the face was normal, pale wet skin stretched over bones, but the eye sockets were empty.' (198)

The two scenes, of the bone factory and the tram, may be presented as the past of Rudi Kestner, German war criminal, but they are scenes are derived from a very different history, that of Edwin Muir, Scottish poet and novelist, and, together with his wife, translator of Kafka. The vision of hell which Rudi Kestner recalls is based on a very Scottish vision of hell – the vision of the West of Scotland that Edwin Muir presents in his *Autobiography* (1954), where he tells of his time in the inappropriately named 'Fairport':

> This was a place where fresh and decaying bones, gathered from all over Scotland, were flung into furnaces and reduced to charcoal. The charcoal was sold to refineries to purify sugar; the grease was filled into drums and dispatched for some purpose which I no longer remember. The bones, decorated with festoons of slowly writhing, fat yellow maggots, lay in the adjoining

railway siding, and were shunted into the factory whenever the furnaces were ready for them. Seagulls, flying up from the estuary, were always about these bones . . . (122)

Muir's life has been absorbed into Massie's fiction, as has the key moment of his awareness of the dehumanisation that he suffers, a moment which, like Rudi's, occurs in a tram:

> I did not believe in the immortality of the soul at that time; I was deep in the study of Nietzsche, and had cast off with a great sense of liberation all belief in any other life than the life we live here and now, as an imputation of the purity of immediate experience, which I had intellectually convinced myself was guiltless and beyond good and evil. I was returning from my work; the tramcar was full and very hot; . . . Opposite me was sitting a man with a face like a pig's, and as I looked at him in the oppressive heat the words came into my mind, 'That is an animal.' I looked round me at the other people in the tramcar; I was conscious that something had fallen from them and from me; and with a sense of desolation I saw that they were all animals . . . The tramcar stopped and went again, carrying its menagerie; my mind saw countless other tramcars where animals got on or off with mechanical dexterity, as if they had been trained in a circus; and I realized that in all Glasgow, in all Scotland, in all the world, there was nothing but millions of such creatures living an animal life and moving towards an animal death as towards a great slaughter-house . . . (42–43)

Muir's Nietzschean release from moral imperative turns into a nightmare of the animal insignificance of human life: Glasgow becomes Hell, a Hell of unbearable mechanical repetition: 'I realized that I could not bear mankind as a swarming race of thinking animals, and that if there was not somewhere, it did not matter where . . . a single living soul, life was a curious, irrelevant desolation' (43). Muir later came to understand his own vision in terms of 'the sacred tradition of human society, which is old, and nature, which is always new, for it has no background' (44): for Muir, man has fallen out of human society and back into nature, has gone from a creature with a history to one with none. Rudi, who undergoes in Massie's novel the same experiences in bone factory and tramcar, will be redeemed not by discovering a single 'living soul' but by Nazism: the Nietzschean imperative that 'Since God is dead all is permitted' (150) leads directly to the creation of a politics designed to accept the Hell in which humanity is now consigned to live: 'For almost two thousand years the Christians set themselves to imagine the geography of Hell. Then when they no longer believed in Hell, or in Heaven, or atonement or redemption, or anything, except good manners and culture, they were able to make Hell real in the Third Reich' (255).

On the wall of the apartment in Argentina where Eli, holocaust survivor, will decide to reveal the identity of the former Nazi who is the father of his daughter's boyfriend is Turner's painting of 'The Golden Bough', from which Frazer's work takes its beginning, and which introduces the story of the priest 'who has won the post by killing the previous priest, and all the time he is on the look-out for the new contender who will kill him' (*The Sins of the Father*, 90). Frazer's presentation of the underlying myths that shape human culture is a revelation of what modern humanity has discovered about the primitive but also about what it has repressed in order to believe in the benign force of history, a repression that is symbolised for Eli by another ancient text, *The Bacchae* of Euripedes:

> 'Pentheus, King of Thebes, and his mother Agave, deny the divinity of Dionysos, the god of darkness and passion, and instead insist on the supremacy of reason, order and light. But it is too much of a strain, this denial. Agave becomes a secret devotee of the god she has tried to deny, and Pentheus is tempted to spy on his mother and the other worshippers in their secret rites. Inflamed by the god, they seize the king and tear him to pieces. (167)

For the powers of reason, descent into the mythic is violence and destruction, but it is a descent made inevitable by reason's rejection of the enduring powers of the mythic.

The historical consciousness which Walter Scott's novels did so much to inculcate can be seen, in the light of his great successor, Frazer, to be in thrall still to those mythic forces which history has believed itself to have abolished.[25] It is a point that Massie makes indirectly by naming the putative editor of the text of *Augustus* Aeneas *Fraser*-Graham, and less indirectly by similarly naming the central character of his novel about Scottish politics, *One Night in Winter*, *Fraser* Donnelly, and making the ideologue of a new Scottish nationalism someone whose power rests on his belief in 'old religions, the Ancient Greek mysteries' (125) and who thinks that 'you have to go back in time to make the next leap' (124). In Massie's novels, as in Buchan's, history is always a journey towards an encounter with the primordial force of myth: Massie may tackle the major historical events of the twentieth century or of the ancient world, but the terms in which he tackles them derive directly from Frazer and from Muir.

Massie's characters hope to find in myth a source of energy and vitality which will transform the dead world of modernity that they inhabit but in doing so they go against the tenor of Frazer's work which regarded the persisting powers of ancient magic as a 'standing menace to civilisation' (56). The modern Scottish novelists with the most sceptical conception of this confrontation between history and myth is Robin Jenkins, whose characters regularly find themselves entrapped in a world shaped according to the demands of ancient myth. When Charlie Forbes takes his family on holiday in Robin Jenkins's *The Changeling*, he takes them not only to the Scottish seaside but into the world of myth: 'Within a couple of minutes he had caught a spoutfish, a beauty, with its shell almost a foot long: it was bait to boast about, whatever fish it caught. Held in his hand it became a wand: the whole scene became one of enchantment; himself alone save for some oyster-catchers, a ship far out on the Firth, and the hills on every horizon save the sea's receding into a blue legendary remoteness' (63). Charlie is the fisher king (the headmaster whom he has to give way to in his school is called Mr Fisher): his 'wand' enchants the landscape back into legend, but the benign transformation is also the return of the ancient and the primitive as something fearful. In this landscape Charlie initially sees Tom Curdie, the slum child he has brought with him, as 'a squire carrying his knight's shield' (63), but increasingly comes to see him as a more maleficent return of the past, 'seeing the boy's admirable reticence as some kind of sinister senile composure, such as was shown by the changeling of Highland legend, that creature introduced by the malevolent folk of the other world into a man's home, to pollute the joy and faith of family' (51). It is a perception which will come to shape Charlie's whole response to Tom – as he says to his wife: 'You're making him out to be a veritable little monster, Mary; even worse than my changeling' (96) – but that sense of something primitive and alien will lead Charlie to believe himself to be 'in the grip of inimical non-human forces, whose instrument was indeed Tom Curdie' (101). In the confusion of moral values that is Charlie's modern mind, and that destroys the 'kingship' for which he goes on holiday, the demands of ancient legends reassert themselves: Charlie is a worshipper of the bull – when he and his wife Mary are out for an evening stroll he always pauses to visit a bull whom she finds 'disgusting and terrifying' (12) – but the bull which is the guardian of the king's powers requires regular sacrifice: Tom will be the sacrificial 'son', destroyed so that the king can be renewed in his kingship. In this modern secular world, however, the mythic sacrifice will bring none of the benefits believed in by the ancients: Tom will die in 'a shepherd's hut', a lamb for the slaughter, but his death will have none of the significance of ancient or of Christian ritual. The events of The Changeling occur in a disenchanted world where mythic patterns return emptied of all their ancient significance but with all their barbarous destructiveness intact.

The same return of the mythic is enacted in the suspended history of The Cone Gatherers: the brothers Callum and Neil, who are collecting cones for regenerating the woods after the war, become the spirits of a sacred grove, or, in the eyes of the gamekeeper, Duror, its defilers, since Callum is hunchbacked and dwarfish:

> This wood had always been his stronghold and sanctuary; there were many places secret to him where he had been able to fortify his sanity and hope. But now the wood was invaded and defiled; its cleansing and reviving virtues were gone. Into it had crept this hunchback, himself one of nature's freaks, whose abject acceptance of nature, like the whining prostrations of a heathen in front of an idol, had made acceptance no longer possible for Duror himself. (18)

Duror, like Frazer's king of the grove of Diana, haunts the wood, its coming death and future resurrection an image of the death and replacement that Frazer's mythic king feared. As Roderick, future inheritor of the estates which contain the wood, journeys towards the hut in which the cone gatherers live, he is travelling back through the world of Christian belief – he sees himself accompanied by Christian from *Pilgrim's Progress* and Sir Galahad – towards the more primitive world that religion, in Frazer's scheme, had replaced: 'Therefore there was magic and terror. The wood was enchanted, full of terrifying presences' (145). In the midst of the wood, Roderick sees Duror, leaning against a tree, and like one come to replace him as the king of the wood, hopes him already dead: 'The idea sprouted. Duror had been strolling through the wood, had felt a pain at his heart, and had clutched at the cypress to keep from falling; there he had died, and the green bony arms were propping him up' (149). When Duror moves, however, it 'was to the stricken boy like a resurrection' as Duror stands forth, 'as if indeed newly come from the dead' (150). Duror is the resurrection of an ancient, mythic force which requires sacrifice in order to sustain itself, symbol of the war beyond the woods which is not like a part of history but the eruption of the primitive back into the modern world, requiring a vast sacrifice of innocents in order to appease it:

> "It may be your heart, you know, Duror," Lady Runcie-Campbell had said, advising him not to cycle but to travel in her car. He had touched his cap, he had murmured gratefully. She had not seen him suddenly grow enormous and loom over her life like a tree falling; she had not heard him shout, in a voice to be heard in the heaven of her faith, that in the wood his wife had changed for an instant into a roe-deer and he had cut her throat to appease his agony in her blood. She had not seen this monster in her so respectful, so self-controlled, so properly subservient gamekeeper. (118)

Duror's heart is the heart of an ancient mystery which is to be re-enacted in the wood in the sacrificial destruction of those who are substitutes for himself, in the hope of bringing life back to himself, the failing king of the wood who can endure no longer. Callum, shot by Duror, will hang on the tree in an inverted crucifixion, his blood raining on the earth like the return of fertility:

> His arms were loose and dangled in macabre gestures of supplication. Though he smiled, he was dead. From his bag dropped a cone, and then another. There might have been more, but other drops, also singly, but faster and faster, distracted her: these were drops of blood. (222)

For Jenkins the return to the region of myth is always ambiguous – poised between the recovery of an authentic truth about human nature and the appalled revelation of the 'solid layer of savagery beneath the surface of society' (56). The empty world of modern history is confronted by the enduring forms of ancient myths which are, however, equally empty, bereft of the magical significance that once justified them.

III

Frazer's vast study of mythologies was conducted in the tenor of sceptical and rational inquiry, one in which civilisation was menaced by the powers of ancient magic: what *The Golden Bough* produced, however, was a compelling sense of a deep continuity between past and present, founded not only on the rituals and legends of a world more ancient and more enduring than anything in the annals of civilisation but on the fact that the modern mind is entirely dependent on the ancient mind for its fundamental operations:

> ... when all is said and done our resemblances to the savage are still far more numerous than our differences from him; and what we have in common with him, and deliberately retain and true and useful, we owe to our savage forefathers who slowly acquired by experience and transmitted to us by inheritance those seemingly fundamental ideas which we are apt to regard as original and intuitive. We are like heirs to a fortune which has been handed down for so many ages that the memory of those who built it up is lost . . . (264)

Frazer's analysis of magic thus made it not the antithesis of but the precursor to science, and made modern science a more developed form of ancient magic – one that was intellectually more justifiable than the religions which had intervened between the two:

> Every great advance in knowledge has extended the sphere of order and correspondingly restricted the sphere of apparent disorder in the world, till now we are ready to anticipate that even regions where chance and confusion appear still to reign, a fuller knowledge would everywhere reduce the seeming chaos to cosmos. Thus the keener minds, still pressing forward to a deeper solution of the mysteries of the universe, come to reject the religious theory of nature as inadequate, and to revert in a measure to the older standpoint of magic by postulating explicitly, what in magic had only been implicitly assumed, to wit, an inflexible regularity in the order of natural events . . . (712)

Science may displace religion, but it does so by a reversion to the underlying logic, if not the actual postulates, of magic, in which case, of course, there may be deep truths contained in primitive magic, truths not necessarily of the phenomenal world but of the mind and its workings, for even science, Frazer urges us to recall, is no more than 'hypotheses devised to explain that ever-shifting phantasmagoria of thought which we dignify with the high-sounding names of the world and the universe. In the last analysis magic, religion, and science are nothing but theories of thought' (712). From that standpoint, the mythic may be a lost science rather than a false one, and still capable of producing order in 'regions where chance and chaos appear still to reign'. It is that possibility that haunts the historyless environment of the Scottish novel: the failure of history, rather than leaving a 'hell' to be endured endlessly, may be the prologue to the recovery of a more profound form of understanding. Against the temporality of its false and failed histories, the Scottish novel asserts the significance of the geography of the region; against the destructive powers of progress it sets a knowledge more ancient than civilisation, one which is inscribed in and maintained by the particular qualities of its landscape.

If the historical novel was the major formal breakthrough of the Scottish novel in the nineteenth century, it was the regional novel which became fundamental to the development of later Scottish writing. Scott's historical novels, involving as they do journeys into far flung areas of the country, exploited regionality intensively but exploited it in more than simply a picturesque fashion. Frank Osbaldistone, for instance, travelling back to Scotland from England, approaches a landscape to which he is native and which cannot be incorporated under general categories, such as the sublime, precisely because it is in possession of 'a character of its own':[26]

> I approached my native north, for such I esteemed it, with that enthusiasm which romantic and wild scenery inspires in the lovers of nature ... The Cheviots rose before me in frowning majesty; not, indeed, with the sublime variety of rock and cliff which characterizes mountains of the primary class, but huge, roundheaded, and clothed with a dark robe of russet, gaining, by their extent and desolate appearance, an influence upon the imagination, as a desert district possessing a character of its own.

The latter phrase points in two directions: the landscape has its own unique characteristics which make it interesting, but it also 'possesses a character' in the sense that people who have grown up in the district have a character which is shaped by that geography. They are in its possession: to understand the landscape is to be aware of it in their minds; to understand their minds one has to know the landscape. Landscape is fully knowable only through the 'return of the native' whose psychology is shaped to the particularities of that environment.

The theories that lay behind such regionalism were those deriving from the eighteenth-century conception of the mind as based on the principle of the association of ideas. From Hume's *Treatise on Human Nature* in 1747 down to Archibald Alison's *Essays on the Principles of Taste* in 1790, and Francis Jeffrey's summary of Alison's conceptions in the 1812 *Encyclopaedia Britannia*'s entry on 'Beauty',[27] the Scottish Enlightenment offered a sustained attempt to develop a psychological account of the nature of knowledge and, within it, of the nature of aesthetics. All human experience, they suggested, is controlled by the association of ideas; on this basis it was possible to explain both the universality of the effects of the beautiful and the sublime, those major categories of aesthetic experience, and the unique individuality of people's responses to the particularity of scenes related to their own past:

> There is no man, who has not some interesting associations with particular scenes, or airs, or books, and who does not feel their beauty or sublimity enhanced to him, by such connections. The view of the house where one was born, of the school where one was educated, and where the gay years of infancy were passed, is indifferent to no man. They recall so many images of past happiness and past affections, they are connected with so many strong or valued emotions, and lead altogether to so long a train of feelings and recollections, that there is hardly any scene which one ever beholds with so much rapture.[28]

One of the mjor shifts which the associationinst theory of the mind made possible in aesthetic theory was the recognition that the local may harbour the most powerful associations for any individual. What is aesthetically interesting is not the actuality of a place but the interaction of the place with a mind fitted to experience it in a particular way, and it is on the basis of this fusion of individual environment with the particularity of the mind 'possessed' by it, through its associations, that regionalism developed: the territory of a particular region is a blank until infused with a memory which brings it to life by being stimulated to the recollection of its past. From Scott to Hardy, the nineteenth-century regional novel in Britain was to be an exploration of the possibilities of this relationship between mind and landscape; from James Mill to William James, British and American empirical psychology was to be the exploration of the consequences of it for our understanding of the workings of the mind.

It was precisely within the terms of these theories of the mind that J. G. Frazer developed the argument of *The Golden Bough*, which is nothing less than a vast compendium of the associational processes of primitive consciousness: 'If we analyse the various cases of sympathetic magic which have passed in review in the preceding pages, and which may be taken as fair samples of the bulk, we shall find . . . that they are all mistaken applications of one or other of two great fundamental laws of thought, namely, the association of ideas by similarity and the association of ideas by contiguity in space or time. A mistaken association of similar ideas produces homoeopathic or imitative magic: a mistaken association of contiguous ideas produces contagious magic' (49). The mind is a vast storehouse of associations, some true (science), some false (magic), but all are equally the data of another science, the science of the mind. In his *Autobiography*, Edwin Muir describes how the Orkney he was 'born into was a place where there was no great distinction between the ordinary and the fabulous' (4), but how, in the modern world, the relation between the story of ordinary life and the fabulous narrative has become more distant, the fabulous no longer around us but buried deep within us:

> In themselves our conscious lives may not be particularly interesting. But what we are not and can never be, our fable, seems to me inconceivably interesting. I should like to write that fable, but I cannot even live it; and all I could do if I related the outward course of my life would be to show how I have deviated from it; though even that is impossible, since I do not know the fable or anybody who knows it. One or two stages in it I can recognize: the age of innocence and the Fall and all the dramatic consequences which issue from the Fall. But these lie behind experience, not on its surface; they are not historical events; they are stages in the fable. (39)

The 'fable' is the set of associations which have been winnowed through long eras of human culture to a particular pattern, one which underlies and gives significance to the events of our surface 'story': the fable goes back into folk memory and back into the personal unconscious, but 'there are times in every man's life when he seems to become for a little while a part of the fable, and to be recapitulating some legendary drama which, as it has recurred a countless number of times, is ageless' (105). The 'reality' of an individual life is not in its story: it is in the conjunction of the story with its 'fable', the discovery of the pattern underlying the story that reveals it as a repetition of some fundamental structure underlying all human experience. 'It is clear', Muir writes, 'that no autobiography can begin with a man's birth, that we extend far beyond any boundary line which we can set for ourselves in the past or the future, and that the life of every man is an endlessly repeated performance of the life of man' (39). That perception provides a benign version of what Frazer's *The Golden Bough* had taught – and had feared – about the whole nature of humanity: 'that the surface of society all over the world is cracked and seamed, sapped and mined with rents and fissures and yawning crevasses', and that what lies beneath is the 'permanence of a belief in magic' (55).

It is that 'solid layer' that Neil Gunn allows his protagonist, Kenn, to articulate in *Highland River*: 'Rock and bird and plant, grasses and mosses and trees, hollows and ridges, were the world through which their river ran. In this concentration on the river itself, they had no time to learn the names of things' (181). This 'solid' world is 'caught by the mind' in 'a magical perception' (182) which is unique to this place: 'it might well appear that this contemplation of the magical is opposed by scientific knowledge' but that would be wrong because, through magic, 'he is grounded in a relationship to his river that is fundamental and that nothing can ever quite destroy'; 'from his river, the relationship is carried over, in whatever degree, to every other environment in life' (182). The organisation of the mind is in its 'magic' relationship to the reality of the particular landscape in which it was formed. The description of this magic unity with the landscape is immediately juxtaposed with Kenn's descent into the 'infernal conditions in some Glasgow slums': a hell of 'nightmare horror', of a world betrayed by history – 'gaunt outlines that curved inward like iron girders of a gutted ruin, with sub-human life in the base of the ruin, scurrying through putrefying smells' (183) – which he can only survive by clinging to that primitive knowledge: 'Kenn kept himself still as a boulder, kept himself whole, endured with primeval cunning' (183). Endurance is not simply the power of resistance to history: it is a power founded on the magical knowledge that comes from deep sources and is imaged in the landscape:

> Man would not endure for ever the horror of that girl trapped in the slums. If not openly, then by secret, violent ways he will destroy the black cage. Kenn, who has never belonged to revolutionary political societies, knows what moves them. Old as the rocks, nameless as the old woman, warm as sunshine, insinuating as the wind, is this river that flows down the straths of time. (184)

The river of history flows in one direction, but the river in its landscape can be followed back to its source: Kenn's knowledge comes from travelling back against history, accepting that 'we extend far beyond any boundary line which we can set for ourselves in the past or the future', and that the knowledge that comes from beyond those boundaries is of a world that, as *Butcher's Broom* tells, 'had no Hell. They had no God of Vengeance to fear in those days' (57).

Gunn's historical novels thus offer a very different version of 'history' from the nineteenth-century traditions of the historical novel. However carefully researched they are in terms of their historical context, they are fundamentally anti-historical novels: their business is to uncover the mythic regions below the surface of history. Thus in *Butcher's Broom* the destruction of Highland society in the Clearances is presented not simply in terms of the economics of sheepfarming or the callousness of the land-owners towards the plight of their clanspeople: it is presented in terms of the loss and recovery of the ancient knowledge, the magical knowledge, which held a people together with their landscape. Dark Mairi, whose death will symbolise the end of that Gaelic culture, 'seemed to have in her an older knowledge than was common to the rest of her ancient kind in these places' (11), and that older knowledge is expressed in a language which noted 'myriad peculiarities and gave each a name. The old language Mairi used was full of such names, not only for things but for men; particularly, indeed, for men, so that the name evokes each kind of man with an astonishing, almost laughable, magic' (14). The Celtic culture which is, in *Fergus Lamont*, the fake projection of Lowland Scotland's desire for identity is, in Gunn, a magical resource, one enriching the events of everyday life from the fabulous resources of myth: 'The firelight enriched the skin on their faces and glistened in their eyes . . . In the centre of this gloom was the fire, and sitting round it, their knees drawn together, their heads stooped, were the old woman, like fate, the young woman, like love, and the small boy with the swallow of life in his hand' (31). No character is a character in itself: each is a recollection of some ancient form to which life has been shaped in this particular place. It is this very knowledge which makes them easy for history to defeat, because their 'actual chief could betray them, sell them for cash, and then sell their land to pay "debts of honour" contracted at the gaming tables or other places of less mild amusement, and still, by the subtle alchemy of the believing mind, retain the outline of one of [the bard's] heroes of legend; nay, more, as a courtier of repute and a business man of sound principle, as one professing ideals of progress and concern for the material advancement of all humanity, he could clear his clansmen off the ground their forefathers had won for him and themselves, burning their houses over their heads and driving them forth to destitution and exile and death, and yet retain in him some of the magical conception of the chief, so deep did their ways of life run and from so ancient a source' (73).

Matthew Arnold's influential view of the Celt[29] as unfitted for practical life is reinterpreted by Gunn: the Celts' ancient knowledge makes exploitation easy not because they are backward and primitive, but because they have already understood and accepted the disintegration of their own society, the necessity of their suffering, and the enduring reality of the knowledge which will survive all historical defeats and continue to explain to them the real meanings of their experiences: 'The thought of the warmth and generosity of Elie's love up there chilled her to a sudden shiver, and her last weeping in Mairi's arms became something dark and mythic, as if Mairi and Elie were figures in an old and terrible legend boding forth destiny for this place and for them all' (151). At the crucial moments of the narrative the characters are allowed a vision of themselves 'so profound that at extreme moments [their] own unimportance almost made it disinterested' (201); they see themselves through their language and its connection with their landscape, impersonally, and when they need to express themselves it is in forms that have no 'personal stress or sentiment':

> . . . she sang in a tongue and a rhythm that were not merely countless centuries old, but had been born out of the earth on which they starved and feasted and against which their feet pressed now, so that all the millions of influences and refinements that had shaped themselves to make the incommunicable understood were from the very first note at her service. (293)

They live in the sense not of this time in history with its individual stories but in the 'feeling of the conjoint story within [them], as of something very ancient and very intimate' (325).

In Gunn's novels the mythic and the quotidian are not harnessed together by the force of an artistic will – as, for instance in Joyce's *Ulysses*. The mythic is a fundamental part of the consciousness of the people, and the novel, in invoking myth, simply follows the fundamental nature of their thought. Myth is not some deep structure to be discovered only by the consciousness of the artist in defiance of the forgetfulness of the masses: myth is the fundamental folk culture which a people, no matter how modern, carry with them. Myth is, however, no retrogressive force precisely because, as Frazer had suggested, it is a particular kind of knowledge, one which is as exact in its way as science. As Kenn explains to his fellow scientist Radzyn:

> The use of this word primitive – I am not so sure. How would you define it? They were primitive only in their lack of machinery and therefore of a complex industrialism. But they were not primitive in their humanism or social recognition of one another. For example, where in English we have only one word, man, and a few adjectives to differentiate all the kinds of men, they had scores of exact words in their language, each one of which at once evoked a different kind of man. In this matter they were much more complex than we are. (215)

For Kenn, as for Frazer, modernity is the product of exactly the same consciousness as ancient myth: the Forth Bridge is, 'like the great cathedrals of the medieval age. Already a sort of nameless communal effort. The work of the folk' (214).

In its formal structures, the modern Scottish novel continually seeks to establish itself as such a 'work of the folk': this may be through a specifically folk voice generated in linguistic terms (as in Shepherd, Gibbon or Kelman), or it be may be shaped through the use of traditional elements of folk narrative (as in Jessie Kesson's *The White Bird Passes*[30] with its many quotations from ballads, or in Muriel Spark's *Symposium*, with its characters drawn from border ballads), or it may replicate the repetitive patterning of folk narrative (as in the novels of George Mackay Brown), but the effort to make the novel, that most bourgeois and urban of literary forms, bend itself to the requirements of folk narrative has driven much of experimentation of Scottish writers in the twentieth century. In Gunn's historical novels, the forward drive of a destructive history is made to shape itself to the recollective force of a culture founded in myth. At the end of *Butcher's Broom*, therefore, the historical shepherds and their sheep who come to take over the people's land are the economic enactors of a deeper expulsion: the destruction by Christianity of a world of myth that had no hell. And when Mairi is savaged to death by the shepherd's dogs, her body is carried home by her grandson and his father: father, son, and holy ghost of a religion more ancient than Christianity defy its intrusion on their lives: 'Do you think you can manage an end?', the father asks his son, referring to the bier he has made for the body: the novel, as an imitation of history, 'manages an end' that combines the end its own narrative with the apparent end of the culture which it is describing. But there is no end in this cyclic world of myth: 'We'll take it in easy stages,' said the man; 'time matters no more'. (429). When time 'matters no more', history has not brought a conclusion to the culture; rather, history has brought conclusion to a stage of itself and left the world of myth which it cannot abolish, and which returns as the resistant meaning that the characters will carry with them into whatever history they then enter. 'And thus the father and son set out with the body of Dark Mairi for the distant shore', Gunn's novel concludes, but its own recollection of the myths of the culture that history seems to have abolished effectively retains them for the future, reinscribing them into the very language which is the medium of the destruction of that Celtic world. The form of the novel, as re-enactment of the structures of ancient myth, defies its own narrative as presentation of the destruction by history of the culture which was the carrier of that myth. In a gesture which was to be repeated by many novelists in the colonised world in the 1950s and 60s, Gunn makes the novel, the fundamental form of the culture of imperialism, the medium by which the colonised resist that domination and recreate, in the language of the oppressor, the forms by which their own culture can be retained and revitalised. The novel, one of the doorways out of that past culture and into modernity, becomes an 'emergency exit' by which one can step out of modernity and back into a culture which is not past simply because it has been defeated in history: it subsists, it endures, ready to shape and be shaped by the experience of the people who are its carriers.

Butcher's Broom is Gunn's descent into the hell of history, the hell of a history whose real purpose is not the one it sets itself but, if measured in terms of outcomes rather than intents, is quite simply the destruction of one of the most ancient cultures of Europe:

> It could hardly be within God's irony that a world which had forgotten their very tongue should be concentrating all its forces of destruction upon them. What could the pride and power of emperors have to do with this little pocket of self-sufficing earth lost in the hills . . .? . . . Amid liberty, equality and fraternity Napoleon takes command and plays his game of mythic ambition on Continental squares, removing a piece here, a piece there, to set his own pieces in their place. From the battle of the Pyramids to Austerlitz and Jena. And then across the whole board to the Kremlin of Moscow. . . . Is it contended that Destiny was creating these titanic forces in order to use them to destroy, with a perfection and finality they nowhere else attained, this hamlet in its glen that Mairi stood looking upon in the October dusk? How fantastic a conception! How ironic the universal waste of divine and tragic energy to achieve so trifling an end! Hardly less fantastic to believe that Mairi had in very truth brought to her people the earth and its seven seas in her basket. Yet Moscow rose from its ashes, the battlefields of Europe were tilled, and even liberty, equality and fraternity continued to linger as the waking memory of a Utopian dream. Only this glen here, that was itself

and the other glens, suffering fire as did the Kremlin, and destruction as did the battlefield, has remained into time dark and desolate and
dead. (21–2)

History's real meaning, driven by Napoleon's 'mythic ambition', is more
absurd than are the myths of the ancient world to the eyes of modernity.
The novel both reveals the absurdity of that historical process and recre-
ates and sustains Mairi's 'earth and its seven seas' against the forgetfulness
to which history would consign it. The novel, the medium of historical
imagining for European culture, becomes the medium of reimagining what
history cannot allow itself to remember – the myths by which it is driven,
which underlie it and which will survive it.

The descent into hell of *Butcher's Broom* is, in Gunn's career, then
matched with his 'return to the light' in *The Silver Darlings*[31] which celebrates the survival of those same people expelled from their ancient homes
by the forces of historical progress, a survival made possible by the myths
and legends which give significance to their lives. In *The Silver Darlings*
the central figure, Finn, whose family have been cleared from the glens
on to the coast and whose father is abducted by the press gang, grows
into an identity which is the re-enactment of the heroic Finn MacCool of
ancient Gaelic legend. His life, and the life of his community, is a series of
overcomings of the destructive effects of history through the recollection,
both implicit and explicit, of the heroic identities of the people's past. In
the entirely new environment of a fishing village, the people build a new
economic community and their power to do so is both based on the strength
of their ancient culture and a proof of its enduring value. Even the arrival
of capitalism, which transforms their lives, is itself transformed into part
of the pattern of the magical world of their myths:

> The land, the quiet land, which for ever endures, threaded by women and
> children, in the bright patterns of their lives. Remote from the sea, from the
> turbulence of oncoming waves, from the quick movement, the excitement,
> from the mind of a man like Special, with his flow of silver herring that
> changed into a flow of silver crowns. There's money in it, men, money,
> money . . . Money, the power, the wizardry of it, set a man walking on his
> own feet. (101)

The 'Special' value of money happens in the enduring world of 'patterns'
and is the outcome of a mythical metamorphosis: herring turning into silver,
men returned to themselves –'walking on their own feet' – by the wizardry
of its magic. In this new environment ancient knowledge has to be accommodated to new experience but it is precisely the power given by ancient
knowledge that makes it possible for people to survive the new experience.
At New Year, for instance, Finn is witness to the re-lighting of the fire,
an act of no economic significance: 'Through the narrow slit where the

curtains did not quite meet, he saw Roddie on his knees before the fire, not smooring it, but putting it out, extinguishing it, slowly, methodically, ember by red ember. Finn could only stare in astonishment, beyond thought, for no fire was ever put out from one year's end to the other. And with good reason, for the only way to light it again would be by first getting a spark from steel and flint to smoulder in burnt cotton . . .' (216–17). This 'destruction' of the fire is like the extinction that history has enacted on their culture, except that instead of the finality of history's events, what is being performed is a ritual where death is only a similitude – 'Roddie, his body getting darker and darker as the fire disappeared, looked like one performing some dreadful, unimaginable rite . . . like one slowly and deliberately murdering fire' (217) – which turns into a rebirth: 'Fire must be put out and created afresh or it, too, grows old and full of trouble and sin' (218–19). Finn, sitting beside the new fire, is himself being reborn into a new world, but one shaped still on the pattern of an ancient one, as much in touch with the past as their community which is built abutting on old ruins called 'The House of Peace': 'The thrill in Finn's heart was a sweet pain. This was the new life, the life of men. His bright eyes rested on the House of Peace. All at once the place was very old inside him, older than peat-smoke, grey and still in the bright morning' (221). Finn's is a journey forward in historical time only to achieve a recovery of a past which knew nothing of history. When he travels to the Western Isles he hears a girl singing, whose 'antique features' make him realise how everyone moves like a 'figure through the mesh of fate in one of Hector's old stories' (549), but as he moves forward into manhood, to encounter the dangers of the sea, he is, in historical terms, at the beginning of a new society in the Highlands, the first stage in the arrival of capitalism, but the forward movement is performed as the recollection and the re-enactment of that older knowledge. An antique pattern shapes and contains the capitalist novelty of history rather than simply being abolished by it: 'A strange world indeed, older than the House of Peace, old as the legendary salmon of knowledge that lay in the pool under the hazel nuts of wisdom, and perhaps older than that, with more mysterious things in it than the mind dreamt of' (221).

It is into that older mind that Gunn's characters journey, even the most active and heroic of them, like Finn. Out of the hell of destruction and fear, out of the religion which imposes fear and hell upon them, out of the history that has distorted their lives, they travel towards the regenerative power of the myths contained in the depths of the past, in the depths of the mind, in the folk memory of their people.[32] Those myths, coming from the world before history, gesture to an alternative significance to history's cessation than the creation of a living hell, for they point towards a 'golden age' when life was not lived in terms of history's teleology; as *Highland River* puts it: 'The scent of the heath fire has in it something quite definitely primordial. Involuntarily it evokes immense perspective in human time:

tribes hunting and trekking through lands beyond the horizons of history'
(109–10). The failure of history which is the condition of modern Scotland
becomes the ground for establishing the existence of a pre-history with the
opposite significance – not the hell of history's suspension but the idyll of
its not yet having started. For Finn, a purely personal memory acts as the
opening upon this generic memory of a world not yet fallen into history:

> The nights they spent in that remote place were never to be forgotten . . . They
> had the influence on his life of a rare memory that would come and go by the
> opening of a small window far back in his mind. Through such an opening a
> man may see a sunny green place with the glisten on it of a bright jewel, or a
> brown interior place and the movement of faces, or a strand in the darkening
> and the crying of a voice, but whatever the sight or the sound of the moment,
> it is at once far back in time and far back in the mind, so that it is difficult
> to tell one from the other. (535)

For Kenn, on the other hand, the depth of this memory's source is explicable
precisely by its apparent defiance of the normal associative patterns:

> The usual associative excuses are not enough. Many scents and smells were
> familiar to Kenn as a boy: peat smoke, for example. In truth, peat smoke was
> far more familiar to him, and had been sniffed daily by himself and forebears
> back into prehistory. But when he returns from the coal fires of the south
> and gets his first whiff of peat, he is not affected in the primordial way. Peat
> smoke has its own intimate associations; but at core they are social and have
> to do with place. Heath smoke is an affair of time; of family or communal
> life through immense stretches of time. Its colour is the bloom of mountains
> on a far horizon – particularly in that evening light which is so akin to the
> still light of inner vision. (110)

There are associations which are 'domestic' and local, which seem to defy
history by being related to place rather than time, and there are associations
which are of time, but which defy history equally by going far back beyond
any historical recollection.

The importance of the 'regional' novel in Scotland is precisely that the
regional – the associations of place – are the location in which it is possible
to glimpse those associations of time that go beyond history, and that can
bring back into history values denied by the very processes of history. The
region is the location of the 'golden age' in the sense of a place where
it is still possible to glimpse a world as yet unmoved by the destructive
forces of history. In the notion of 'the golden age' can be recovered a
sense of the value of being outside of history, a value which transforms the
historyless suspension of modern Scotland from a negative to a potentially
positive condition. The historical disaster of a lowland Scotland which had
entered upon the world of progress and then got stuck is thus turned into

a 'fortunate fall' by realising the potential of its stasis as an emblem of the alternative realm of value which existed 'before' or 'beyond' history, and which can be recaptured in history's denial. The region, that place set aside from the historical development of modern Scotland, whether it is the Highlands, the Islands or the Borders, becomes the place in which the historyless can manifest itself as an alternative to the re-engagement with history that has shaped the narratives of the Scottish novel primarily in terms of the intrusions of an outside history into the Scottish context. 'The grown Kenn knows quite exactly one quality in the scent of the prim-rose for which he has an adjective. The adjective is innocent' (111). The innocence of the prehistoric is what Gunn's characters seek as an escape from the guilty destructiveness of the historical in which they are caught up:

> Thus the relationship between the primrose and the heath fire is not so much the relationship between man and nature, as that relationship at a particular stretch of time on this earth, the stretch which solitary voices through all subsequent ages and races have called 'the golden age'.
> Nor would all that have been worth writing about primrose scent had it not, in one of those chance flashes that the mind is subject to, presented a certain kind of evidence of the existence once upon a time of the golden age.
> For the heirs of brutal savages, the inheritors of brutish instincts, whence this troubling vision of primrose dawns and wood fires, of fleet and running laughter, when the mounting effect of it all to a flame-bright ecstasy? (111–12)

Gunn's response to this rhetorical question is to provide no answer: the brutality of the savage is one of the assumptions of history which can only be challenged by refusing the terms of history's construction of the past, and the only way of refusing it is on the basis of those fleeting associations which make the region of our earliest memories a gateway into a deeper and an older memory, an emergency escape route out of the hell of history and back to the light. And the term 'escape' is one he is not afraid of:

> ...*for fear of the keeper.*
> The italicised words let the secret out. They are Kenn's answer to any challenge about heather and primroses being a 'way of escape'. .

> For to begin with he knows exactly what the adversary means by 'escape'; what schoolmasters and parsons and statesmen and judges and great land-owners mean by it; even what the literary critic looks like when he dismisses 'poetry of escape' – though there is something in that superior expression that touches the spring of involuntary mirth.
> This escape from the human struggle, this evasion of social responsibility, this denial of all the codes.
> How it echoes back through the ages, in how many tongues, in how many faces, towards how many ends! (112–13)

History is what must be escaped – 'Prison for Galileo. Fire for the Maid. Famine and disease for the hordes. Kings and King-Emperors. Statesmen. Captains of Industry. Children of the hordes in foetid mills' (113) – and the only way of escape is through those mythic memories that point beyond its boundaries, the boundaries which history describes as the entry into savagery but which is, for Gunn, the exit from the savagery of historical civilisations. In *Highland River* Kenn's journey towards the source of the river by which he spent his childhood is a journey back to the world history has forgotten, but which remains, a recoverable region of the mind inscribed in the topography of the region, in the faint associations that go far beyond the boundaries of individual memory: 'It's a far cry to the golden age, to the blue smoke of the heath fire and the scent of the primrose! Our river took a wrong turning somewhere! But we haven't forgotten the source. Why blame me for trying to escape to it?' (114).

The loss and recovery of that alternative to history structures much of the narrative of the Scottish imagination in the twentieth century, and precisely because the mythic is beyond history its fulfilment must come in a moment which denies the very narrative resources upon which history, and the novel, are based: *Highland River* hovers between novel, autobiography, meditation; its disruptions of temporality suspend the forward impetus of narrative in order to emphasise the struggle to get beyond the limits of ordinary consciousness, to get out of history. This is the suspension of temporality that Mackay Brown celebrates in many of his novels, as in *Greenvoe* when, at the conclusion of each section of the novel, we are presented with a ritual which enacts the mythic pattern, the fable, which underlies the story of the lives on the island, a fable which cannot be reached through the story but must be gestured to as continuing to exist beyond it, in a drama whose mythic content emphasises the cyclic return that denies the forward trajectory of the furrow of history:

> *The Lord of the Harvest. The Master Horsemen. The novice who has obtained*
> *the degree of Ploughman: he is blindfolded; he carries a horse-shoe.*
> THE LORD OF THE HARVEST: We have come to the station of
> THE SEED. What are you seeking here, Ploughman, among the master
> horsemen?
> THE PLOUGHMAN: A kingdom.
> *The mockery of the Master Horsemen.*
> THE LORD OF THE HARVEST: The man with a new bride, who has
> ploughed a field in March, what does he know of kingdoms?
> THE PLOUGHMAN: Beyond the blood of beasts, further than axe and fire,
> there it lieth well, in the light, a kingdom. (62–3)

Getting back to the light is getting back out of the hell of history: at the end of *Greenvoe* a defence installation has cleared the island of its people but the men return to perform their ritual on the dead island. As they do so they enact the purposes to which much Scottish fiction has been dedicated – the denial of the history which makes the novel itself necessary: 'The Lord of the Harvest raised his hands. "We have brought light and blessing to the kingdom in winter," he said, "however long it endures, that kingdom, a night or a season or a thousand ages. The word has been found"' (149).

IV

When J. G. Frazer first lighted on the theme of *The Golden Bough* in 1885, he recognised that his particular territory, the one that distinguished him from other early anthropologists, was, as Robert Ackerman has pointed out,[33] the 'use he made of his deep and wide knowledge of classical antiquity': 'no one had ever before focused so intensively on the "primitive" elements of the religions of Greece, Rome and the eastern Mediterranean and had juxtaposed these on so large a scale with the religious activities of "savages"' (63). The end points of this investigation were parallel disruptions of the two major traditions of Western culture: on the one hand, Frazer's study would reveal 'the resemblance of many of the savage customs and ideas to the fundamental doctrines of Christianity' (95), undermining the security of revealed religion; on the other, it would 'dethrone the cultures of classical antiquity from the privileged position they had enjoyed since the Renaissance' (63). From one perspective, the privileged elements of Western culture would be seen as simply the evolutionary outcome of general human development; from another, the whole history of Western culture would be undermined, revealing the illusion of the security of its distance from the "savage". Frazer saw himself as the 'practitioner of a historical science' (171), but it was a historical science which dissolved history back into the 'timeless' world of myth, or, as Andrew Lang was to argue fiercely in his denunciation of Frazer's work, *Magic and Religion* (1901), it dissolved history into a series of imaginative conjectures and conjunctions which was no history at all. History, as verifiable narrative, either retreated back into myth or disappeared into the inner consciousness of the narrator. The apparent desperation with which Frazer rethought, revised and rewrote his massive work from its first edition in 1890 till its final *Supplement* in 1936 is testimony to the enormous need to find the real foundations of history, real foundations which he keeps discovering to be beyond the limits of historical investigation, because beyond the limits of history.

As Frazer was working on completing the first edition of *The Golden Bough* in Cambridge in 1889, Robert Louis Stevenson was writing the 'Dedication' to *The Master of Ballantrae*, which might almost have been a description of *The Golden Bough*: 'Here is a tale which extends over many years and travels into many countries' (xiii). Stevenson's novel is to drive its central characters out of the civilised world and into a savage one; it is to gather the people of the far-flung British empire – the two Scottish brothers, the wife, real or desired, of both, their servants, one Scottish, one Indian – into the American wilderness, into the regions of savagery; it is to make the borders of that savage world a repetition of the very conflict between the regions of Scotland that had set the narrative of family division between the brothers in motion in the first place: 'Here, on the borders, he learned that he was come too late . . . His standing with the painted braves may be compared to that of my Lord President Culloden among the chiefs of our own Highlanders at the 'Forty-Five; that is as much to say, he was, to these men, reason's only speaking-trumpet' (207). Beyond the borders of reason, Henry Durrisdeer will not believe in the death and burial of his brother James:

> 'He's not of this world,' whispered my lord, 'neither him nor the black deil that serves him. I have struck my sword throughout his vitals,' he cried; 'I have felt the hilt dirl on his breastbone, and the hot blood spirt in my very face, time and again, time and again!' he repeated with a gesture indescribable.
> 'But he was never dead for that,' said he, and sighed aloud. 'Why should I think he was dead now? (209)

James, like the dark realities of myth, rises continually from the dead to re-enact the same undying conflict with his brother, just as Frazer's myths are discovered at the boundaries of history to be only a prefiguration of all that will be enacted in history. When MacKellar arrives at the Master's grave what he sees might be a grotesque mirror image of Frazer's vast narrative, for the 'savage' devil, Secundra, is digging up the Master's body and as he does so he is an image of Frazer's rewriting ancient myth back into modernity:

> And yet it was not this which struck us into pillars of stone; but the sight (which yet we had been half-expecting) of Secundra ankle-deep in the grave of his maser. He had cast the main part of his raiment by, yet his frail arms and shoulders glistened in the moonlight with a copious sweat; his face was contracted with anxiety and expectation; his blows resounded on the grave, as thick as sobs; and behind him, strangely deformed and ink-black upon the frosty ground, the creature's shadow repeated and parodied his swift gesticulations. (216)

Secundra's shadow 'writes' upon the white ground like Frazer's writing over the buried depths of myth: at one and the same time the writing buries the past in 'history' and revives it in memory; in the very form of its own telling it is a 'secondary' repetition of myth's ritual slaying and revival of the dying god. The Master, a creature of mythic power, whether dying god or devil, will be revived not by Secundra's efforts to dig him up but by Mackellar's writing; that revival, like the myths of Frazer's writing, will become the haunting presence of the lost purpose of the history from which he has been exiled, mastering it again from beyond the grave.

It is a conflict which will drive the narrative imagination and the formal inventions of Scottish novelists throughout the twentieth century. The drive beyond history, whether in terms of a real boundary crossed into the primitive or a psychological boundary into the mythic, will be matched by the desire to have the suspended condition of Scotland returned from its limbo to the narrative of history. Thus in one of the most powerful historical novels of the century, Naomi Mitchison's *The Bull Calves*,[34] the narrative divides the movement beyond the boundaries of history between its principal female and male protagonists. Kirstie, widow of a repressive minister of the Church, in her isolation takes up with lower class women of a mining community, who form a witches' coven. She confesses her past to her second husband William, explaining how 'I would find myself going with them, out beyond the coal bings and up on to the moor. We would strip and dance and the appearances would dance with us and we would be caught in hot gusts and whirled about and up and the feel of a pressing and sweating dance partner against one's belly or a merry hell's riding beast capering between one's thighs' (166). It is an experience of the depths that matches the business of mining the earth, yet an experience of something that Kirstie thinks might have been of good rather than evil: 'Yet times I had a feeling that we were near to understanding in the heart of things that could have been turned to good, yet not the good of a kind that would be recognized by the respectable and the members of the congregation' (166).

Kirstie's is a confession that William is able to understand, both because of his own Highland background, with its awareness of the spirit world, and also because he has spent time in the American wilderness; as Kirstie talks 'he was thinking of rain makers and corn growers and healers, and interpreters of dreams and those that could find the wrongdoer and those that had dealings with the spirits' (166). The knowledge of the savage beyond the boundaries of modern history allows William to understand and forgive Kirstie's knowledge of what underlies civilisation: he himself had seen his American bride and her father first as someone 'who brought magic . . . a man and woman of the Sidhe, of the fairy people' (275). What is encountered in the primitive is the same as what is already known in Scotland's own 'primitive' world of Highland culture: as Stevenson, in *The Master of Ballantrae*, presents the Indians in terms of the 'Forty-five rebellion, so Mitchison presents William's experiences in America as the direct outcome of his familiarity with magic in his own, highland, culture. The region of myth encompasses both the Scottish highlands, the satanic 'other' of calvinist election and the as yet uncontrollable places on the boundaries of empire: as symptoms of that which refuses history each can figure the other. Knowledge of them is what Kirstie and William bring back into the world of historical improvement, a knowledge without which it could not know its own sources and its own underlying principles, and could not begin to enact the forgiveness necessary to overcome the aftermath of the Rebellion. For Mitchison, without this double knowledge of history and its other, the conclusion of Stevenson's narrative is inevitable, and history will conclude in its own negation, imaged in the two brothers who will be buried in a trackless wilderness that symbolises the forces they have not been able to accommodate to the demands of history.

Those journeys outwards and downwards, beyond the limits of history, are regularly re-enacted by Scottish novelists in search of that which endures, or makes history itself unendurable. The formal implications are profound, since the narrative of the modern world has to be dramatised as shadowing a primitive narrative, or has to be constructed around those moments when the primitive narrative erupts through the surface of civilisation or when 'civilisation' interrupts the eventless world of myth. In Grassic Gibbon's *A Scots Quair*, for instance, three different timeschemes are simultaneously enacted by the narrative: the events of the period between the early twentieth century and about 1930 which encompass the life of Chris Guthrie re-enacts in miniature the history of Scotland, as Chris moves from the peasant farming community of *Sunset Song*, symbolic of an early Scotland, through the world of the Reformation, as instantiated in her second husband, Robert, the minister of Segget, to the world of modern industrial society, in *Grey Granite*; the same narrative, however, also re-enacts the history of civilisation, as it moves from a pre-agriculatural world ('the golden age') through the world of agriculture, with its repressive religions and priests, to the 'rational' world of modernity that believes in the process of history. This triple timescheme enacts Frazer's sense of a world moving in different epochs at the same moment: still trapped in the world of magic and myth even while believing itself to have escaped into the world of reason and history.

Such doublings of the world become a typical device of Scottish fiction: in Neil Gunn's *The Green Isle of the Great Deep* (1944),[35] a symbolically named old man called Hector and an equally symbolic young lad called Art, fall into a world parallel to their own, in which the Highlands becomes a place of repressive dictatorship, combining the elements of a calvinist theocracy with the modern totalitarianisms of communism and fascism. The entry into a parallel universe – a 'fable' underlying history's 'story' – links Gunn's novel to Barrie's *Peter Pan*, from the first decade of the century, with its imaginary world of violence and destruction that is, in fact, simply a representation of the real world of imperialism, and to Gray's *Lanark* in 1981, with its overworlds and underworlds as parallel dimensions of the same experiences. Frazer's model of a world and a mind divided between a fragile and perhaps illusory process of rational history and a profound but terrifying cycle of myth, between a progressive history stalled part-way towards its goal and a need for savage sacrifice to return the world to its natural order, has deeply shaped the narrative imagination of modern Scottish novelists – perhaps because Frazer's own narration is itself an expression of nineteenth-century Scotland's severe scepticism of the historical journey on which it had embarked.

The enduring significance of Frazer's work to the Scottish imagination is witnessed by Muriel Spark's *The Takeover*.[36] Published in 1976, Spark's novel responds to the economic threat posed by the 1974 oil crisis, but does so by juxtaposing the local historical crisis with the enduring significance of Frazer's representation of Nemi. The novel, like most of Spark's oeuvre, is a comedy but a comedy which reverses the tragic consequences of Frazer's vision of the priest at Nemi, waiting continually for the person who is going to slay and replace him. In Spark's novel the role of priest is played by Hubert, who rents a house from the modern Diana, Maggie (Frazer's goddess of *mag*ic), a house which has been built in defiance of modern laws but which rests close to the site of the ancient temple of Diana. In the aftermath of the oil crisis, which threatens to undermine all of their material prosperity, Hubert and Maggie are engaged in a struggle for control of the property at Nemi and for the valuables which the house contains. The novel is about the fraudulence of the whole Frazerian conception of the significance of Nemi, but at the same time the characters, while enacting fake rituals designed to take us back to the original worship of Diana in the grove, perform the recollection of what, for Spark, is the true meaning of the ancient rituals as narrated by Frazer – their prefiguration of the coming of the incarnate God. For Frazer, writing the prehistory of Christ's sacrificial death is the undoing of the transcendent meaning of religion; but for Spark the path of the false leads directly to the discovery the true; *The Golden Bough*, which is the text that shows retrospectively that Christianity is nothing but the spiritualised version of ancient, primitive sacrificial rituals, is turned inside out to become the foundation on which an ancient belief system points towards the necessary conclusion of Christianity – however absurd its theological and anthropological roots. The stalled history of Scotland is simply the image of the illusoriness of a history whose only purpose is to take us back to the eternal, the eternal which makes the novel itself, the form of the historical, redundant.

The modern Scottish novel thus rests on a fundamental paradox: the forms of history that it charts in its narratives are what it seeks to negate through its creation of narrative forms which will defy and deny the primacy of the historical as the mode in which we should comprehend the nature of human experience. The narrative of the novel, as an imitation of history's forward trajectory, has to be undone by formal structures which defy the progressive force of history and return narrative to the cyclic world of myth, to a world of eternal truths untouchable by history's passage.

CHAPTER 4

THE TYPOGRAPHIC MUSE

In a note prefaced to a *A Scots Quair*, Lewis Grassic Gibbon offered the following apology for his Scotticising of the English of his narrative:

> If the great Dutch language disappeared from literary usage and a Dutchman wrote in German a story of the Lekside peasants, one may hazard he would ask and receive a certain latitude and forbearance in his usage of German. He might import into his pages some score or so of untranslatable words and idioms – untranslatable except in their context and setting; he might mould in some fashion his German to the rhythms and cadence of the kindred speech that his peasants speak. Beyond that, in fairness to his hosts, he hardly could go – to seek effect by a spray of apostrophes would be both impertinence and mistranslation.
>
> The courtesy that the hypothetical Dutchman might receive from German a Scot may invoke from the great English tongue. (xiii)

The final word is poised over a significant ambiguity: the courtesy that the Scottish *writer* requests for deforming the standard written language of English is asked not of the *written* language but of the *tongue*, a tongue, of course, which itself transforms the written language in every act of pronunciation. The note explains Gibbon's refusal to use typographic representations of variant speech forms – 'a spray of apostrophes' – by appealing precisely to the spoken 'tongue' which has no need, or indeed means, of enacting such representations. It is the 'tongue' – rather than the traditional forms of the representation of non-standard language – which will define Grassic Gibbon's programme of writing a Scottish English; but precisely because it is to the demands of the tongue that he will write, the modes of typographic representation, and particularly the representation of speech, become crucial to the *text*ure of his novel. He has to transform the conventions of novelistic *text* if he is to make his narrative bear the imprint of the spoken. Thus direct speech, in *A Scots Quair*, is not set off by grammatical markers or laid out in the traditional conventions that separate it from the narrative voice: it is simply italicised text in the flow of the narrative:

> She'd never heard him swear as he did then, jumping to his feet with his fists tight-clenched. *That about Mollie – they said that, the orra swine! I'll mash that bloody Galt's head till his own mother won't know it!* But Chris told him that wouldn't help much, folk would just snigger and say that there was something, sure, in the story of Mollie's condition. *Then what am I to do?* Will asked, raging still, and Chris blushed and said *Wait. Do you love her, Will?* But she might have known well enough how he'd take that question, maybe

he blushed himself in the lithe of the dark, he threw down the paper torches he'd saved and muttered *I'm away to Drumlithie*, and was running down the hill before she could stop him. (80)

Narrative, reported speech and actual speech flow into one another: the traditional elements of the representation of spoken language – such as the 'spray of apostrophes' – have invaded the narrative text so that it has acquired the traditional characteristics of speech, with only italicisation to indicate what is actually voiced.

By the time we reach the third volume of the trilogy, *Grey Granite*, we have entered a social world in which the oral is no longer the dominant medium of community consciousness: the oral voice of the narrative has to struggle against the written medium of the newspaper; it is the typography of the newspaper which gives shape to the world, thrusting the oral from face-to-face communication back into solipsistic self-communing:

And next day the *Daily Runner* came out and told of those coarse brutes the Gowans strikers, and the awful things they'd done to the working folk that were coming decent-like from their jobs. And all Craigneuks read the news with horror, every word of it, chasing it from the front page to the lower half of page five, where it was jammed in between an advertisement curing Women with Weakness and another curing superfluous hair; and whenever Craigneuks came on a bit of snot it breathed out *Uhhhhhhhhhhhh!* like a donkey smelling a dung-heap, delighted, fair genteel and so shocked and stirred up it could push down its grapefruit and porridge and eggs and bacon and big salt baps, fine butter new from the creamery, fresh milk and tea that tasted like tea, not like the seep from an ill-kept sump. And it said weren't those Footforthie keelies awful? Something would have to be done about them. (121–2)

The speech of the middle classes comes through the folk voice of the narrative as non-italicised written statement, at one with the newspaper which it consumes in a community of isolated individuals and as simply another portion of its exploitative material culture.

Grassic Gibbon's experiment is only one of many examples of the how the written representation of the oral impels alternative typographic representations: from the appropriate conventions for transcribing particular sounds to those apostrophes that indicate missing elements of 'standard' forms of words, the oral has to be marked off by a specialised set of conventions by which the limited fixities of type attempt to represent the flexible and unique forms of the individual voice. The visual effect of novels in which dialect plays a crucial role – the *text*ure of the page – is very different from those written in standard language: typography ceases to be the neutral medium through which meaning is conveyed and becomes itself one of the key components of meaning, drawing attention to patterns of type as indicators of crucial distinctions in significance. Where most authors have little or no concern with, or influence on, the choice of typeface and typestyle, or the design of the page structure, for the author engaged in representing the interaction of standard written forms of language with the representation of the oral, these matters take on a far greater significance: typography itself becomes the medium of creation rather than simply the frame that holds the outcome of creation in place. Instead of language being a mimesis of the world it becomes an imitation of the forms of language itself, in reflection of and in resistance to the condition of a country and a culture where the written language has been the medium through which the native voice of the people has been repressed.

It is this relationship between word and world, between the written and the oral, and their typographic representation, that is fundamental, for instance, to George Friel's *Mr. Alfred, M.A.* (1972).[1] Mr Alfred, named after the monarchic origin of Anglo-Saxon culture, is a Scottish teacher of English for whom his own nation has become no more than a typographic convention:

> He was unnecessary in the world, superfluous, supernumerary, not wanted. Nobody would miss him. He was an exile in his native land. Not that he had any love for his native land. He rated it as a cipher, of no value until a figure was put before it. But it had no figures. It existed only as terra incognita to the north of England. Hence formerly known simply as N.B. Note well. A footnote. Whereas England was where they spoke the language he taught, the language he once thought he knew. But he had been refused an immigrant's visa there many years ago when nine publishers rejected his thirty-two poems. (59)

The language that they 'speak' in England is confronted by Scotland as a written sign ('N.B.') whose meaning to any English speaker is another written language, Latin, which makes Scotland linguistically 'terra incognita' and thrusts it out of the main text of the page and into a footnote. Within the world of the footnote, however, the written language of English is surrounded by a speech as barbaric to Mr. Alfred's ear as its representation is baffling to the eye used to the English of literary convention: Mr. Alfred is under orders to ' . . . pass on our cultural heritage. The tongue that Shakespeare spoke' (171), but is confronted by a 'tongue' that refuses to submit to any of his rules:

> He grabbed Gerald by the scruff and pushed him to the door.
> 'You come and see the headmaster,' he said.
> 'Take your hauns aff me,' said Gerald.
> His dialect vowels were themselves a form of insolence. Normally a boy spoke to his teacher in standard English. (37)

The degradation and the resistance of the working-class Scottish tongue is satirised through an immigrant cafe owner who declares, 'But I work. I learn by ear. My mother and me, we speak our father's language at home . . . Poor boy makes it good. I speak their language. Can they speak mine? Speak mine? They can't even speak their own fucking language' (84). Equally, it is presented in the confrontation Mr. Alfred witnesses between a coloured busconductor and a drunk:

> . . . The coloured conductor stood over him. Tall, patient, dignified, persistent. A good samaritan across the passage offered the money.
> 'No, no, oh no! That will not do,' said the coloured conductor. 'He must pay his own fare or go off.'
> 'Ach, go to hell,' said the drunk man, but quite pleasant about it. . . 'A belang here,' said the little drunk man. 'Mair than you do, mac. It's me pays your wages. Go and get stuffed.'
> The bus weaved on between tall tenements.
> 'Pay your fare or I stop the bus,' said the coloured conductor.
> 'Ye kin stope it noo,' said the little drunk man. 'This is whaur A get aff.'
> He swayed up as the bus slowed, palmed the coloured conductor out of his way, and slithered downstairs. Smiling. Victorious. Happy and Glorious. (52)

Tam O'Shanter's condition of being 'O'er all the ills of life victorious' in Burns's Scots has become simply an excuse for imperial disdain by one who is the inheritor of others' victories, the inhabitant of an unending anthem to the national superiority of a tongue he does not speak. Mr. Alfred's sympathetic comment to the conductor – 'You meet some types, don't you' (70) – turns the confrontation, however, into one which replicates the conflict between the 'type' in which language is standardised and the anarchic oral speech by which it is surrounded.

> 'Muck of the world,' said the coloured conductor. He was shaking. 'They won't pay. Every night they won't pay their fare. White bastards.'
> 'Compose yourself,' said Mr. Alfred. (53)

Mr. Alfred's injunction combines the need for emotional order with the order – the composition – of language as type, an order which is beginning to decay in his own world, as the written is taken over by anarchic forces of linguistic disorder and transformed from text on a page to 'The Writing on the Wall', as the second part of the novel is subtitled. Mr. Alfred is surrounded by a new kind of textuality:

> There was nothing new in the otiose curves intended to represent the female breasts, waist and hips, in the crude sketches of the male organ, and certainly nothing new in the four letter words whose use in print was sometimes supposed to prove the author had a literary talent never attributed to the boys who wrote them in their schoolbooks. What was new was the sheer quantity of obscene scribbling. And the quantity became quality. It gave Waterholm a peculiar aura, increasing his dislike and fear of it. (122)

And what is particularly striking about this new writing is a new relationship between the oral and the written:

> What was new, and what puzzled him, was the frequent occurrence of the word 'Hox'. He saw it everywhere in Waterholm. In textbooks, in exercise books, cut on the desks, scratched on the twelve-inch rules, pencilled in the corridors. The janitor told him it was in the lavatories too, chalked on the walls scrawled in the cubicles, chiselled on the doors. Sometimes it was 'Yung Hox'. (122)

'Hox' is revealed to be the written form of the local pronunciation of 'Young Hawks', the territorial gang of the region and a prefiguration of the eruption everywhere of a new indecipherable language of the world become text:

> The writing on the wall.
> The writing on the wall.
> Everywhere he went he saw the writing on the wall.
> The writing.
> The writing.
> The writing on the wall.
>   TONGS YA BASS   GOUCHO   PEG OK
>   FLEET YA BASS   YY TOI
>   TOWN OK
>   HOODS YA BASS   CODY YYS
>   SHAMROCK LAND
>   TORCH RULE OK YY HAWKS MONKS YA BASS
> On his right in an all night-urinal COGS YA BASS.
> On his left as he rocked YY FANGS OK.
> Outside again, still no taxies. No buses. No people. Nothing but the writing on the wall. On every phone-box, junction-box, and pillar-box, on every shop-front, bus-shelter and hoarding, on every board and paling, on every bridge and coping-stone there was the writing. Scrawled, scribbled, sprayed, daubed. Yellow, red, green, white, black and blue. Six, eight, ten and twelve inch letters. More writing. (167)

The world ('No buses. No people') has been abolished to be replaced by a language which has its own indecipherable semantic and typographic rules. Language has ceased to be a representation of the world and has become its annihilation, its negation, so much so that when Mr. Alfred is spotted by two policemen (called 'King' and 'Quinn', being policemen of the monarch's English) they think 'he didn't look the type' (205): Mr. Alfred, whose ambition was to be a poet in the English language, has been transposed into a world of type in which his own identity disappears into the writing on the wall: '"It's the first time I've seen anybody right in the act," said King. "I mean seen him write"' (169). Mr. Alfred literally writes himself out of existence as he scrawls 'GLASGOW YA BASS' on the walls of the city in defiance of the 'act' of union whose linguistic 'right' he has always asserted.

In the original publication of the novel by John Calder, the conflict between these various representations of language was intensified by the fact that the novel was printed as a reproduction of a typescript produced on an electric typewriter.[2] The type in which the novel is encased is itself a crude version of standard typography, emphasising the disjunction between the inflated rhetoric of the narrative language – which continually thrusts into the foreground of the text words of a specialised or arcane provenance, such as 'her head sinistral, she borded the kitchensink in a defence of temporary kyphosis' (4) – and the degraded world which the novel is representing. The typographic coarseness of the original text makes it seem as though the whole novel has been dragged down, from its beginning, into the crude world of a less finished form of writing than that implied by proper typography; its high-flown rhetorical strategies are as inappropriate to the 'realism' of its subject matter as they are to its typographic form.

The tension between the *text*ure of the page and the style of writing prepares the way for the novel's sundering of its realistic mode when Mr. Alfred, after being beaten up in the streets, encounters and converses with a fantasy antagonist, Tod, the creator of the poetry of the walls and negater of the values of Mr. Alfred's notion of culture. Through this fantasy section, the novel reveals how limited is realism for explaining the nature of the reality it re-presents: mimesis is a trap which tethers us to a world which it cannot explain any more than Mr. Alfred, unaided, can explain the writing on the walls. The mimetic procedures of the novel are revealed, in turn, to be tied to the traditions of a standardised typography, a typography which cannot encompass the forms of writing which challenge Mr. Alfred's conception of the world any more than it can explicate the conflicts of culture in which he is trapped. Foregrounding the diversity of possible typographies becomes the means of asserting not only alternative ways of understanding the relation between writing and the world, but of insisting on alternative realities, alternative worlds, to those inscribed in and implied by the techniques of realism.

In its concern with the dissolution of language's relation to reality Friel's work, despite its very different social content, was developing elements which had already begun to be explored by Muriel Spark. In Spark's first novel, *The Comforters* (1957),[3] the central character, Caroline, who is writing a book on *Form in the Modern Novel*, but is 'having difficulty with the chapter on realism' (57), comes to believe that she can hear the typewriter which is composing her own thoughts as a character in a novel:

A typewriter and a chorus of voices: What on earth are they up to at this time of night? Caroline wondered. But what worried her were the words they had used, coinciding so exactly with her own thoughts.

Then it began again. Tap-tappity-tap: the typewriter. And again, the voices: Caroline ran out on to the landing, for it seemed quite certain the sound came from that direction. No one was there. The chanting reached her as she returned to her room, with these words exactly:

What on earth are they up to at this time of night? Caroline wondered. But what worried her were the words they had used, coinciding so exactly with her own thoughts.

And then the typewriter again: tap-tap-tap. She was rooted. 'My God!' she cried aloud, 'Am I going mad?' (43–4)

While Friel allows that Mr. Alfred's fantasy encounter, however artificially constructed by the author, can still be interpreted simply as the delusions of Mr. Alfred's consciousness, Spark will not allow that Caroline's awareness that she is being written by a typewriter *is* simply madness: what she expresses is the truth – she is a character in a novel who is ruled over by her God, the author: 'it is as if a writer on another plane of existence was writing a story about us' (63). Caroline, and all the characters who are part of the plot in which she is trapped, are recorded by 'The Typing Ghost' (161) whose voices she tries, but fails, to record on a disk.

There are, however, aspects of reality of which the 'Typing Ghost' has no knowledge: 'The Typing Ghost has not recorded any lively details about this hospital ward. The reason is that the author doesn't know how to describe a hospital ward. This interlude in my life is not part of the book in consequence' (161). Caroline is, quite literally, the product of a typographic machine, and she is aware both of her role within the novel and the process by which she is being created, so that she knows, for instance, that the book 'is nearing the end' (167), despite the fact that she is a character within it whose life, at the level of the plot, is not nearing its end. The typographic machine ascribes identity to characters insofar as it is able to describe their lives: in the confused ontologies of *The Comforters*, this means that characters quite literally cease to exist when not being written about: 'as soon as Mrs Hogg stepped into her room she disappeared, she simply disappeared. She had no private life whatsoever. God knows where she went in her privacy' (156). When the typographic machine ceases to function, the characters disappear. Resistance to the typographic machine is pointless, as Laurence discovers at the novel's conclusion, when he writes a letter to Caroline about the notes for the novel which he had discovered in her flat. The notes appear in a different point size from the rest of the text and assert that the novel she has been planning 'misrepresent[s] all of us' (203). The novel, as mimesis, is false and its falsity is at one with its typographic form: Laurence destroys his own letter – 'He took it out of his pocket and tore it up into small pieces, scattering over the Heath where the wind bore them away (203) – only to discover that 'he did not then foresee his later wonder, with a curious rejoicing, how the letter had got into the book'. The letter which no longer exists within the ontological world of the novel continues to exist within the ontology of the fiction; the time which is unredeemable in reality is redeemed in its re-presentation, even while that re-presentation is declared to be false. The catholic world of free choice and redemption is invaded by the protestant world of God's foreknowledge of all the ends of narratives: 'Laurence and I sent each other a wire with exactly the same words, at the same time. It was horrifying. Like predestination' (62). The textual, in its typographic fixity, becomes an image of the calvinist world of predestination, encasing (in type) the future of the characters and thus negating their sense of having choices which will separate them from their past or make for them a new future. Are we within the novel, a typographic world of predetermined types, or are we in the representation of a real world of undetermined futures, disconnected from the determinations of the past and the structures of type?

The issue was to haunt all of Muriel Spark's fiction: from the obsessive taperecordings of *The Abbess of Crewe*[4] – a taperecording turns the immediacy of speech into a repeatable and reformulable text – to the repetitions of ballad narratives in *Symposium* (1990). But it is in *The Ballad of Peckham Rye* (1960)[5] that Spark most fully engages with the typographic as both the muse of an alternative reality and as an alternative to realism. Dougal Douglas (the first vowels of his name are pronounced differently despite their textual identity) has 'joined the firm of Meadows, Meade & Grindley' (whose name has a similar disjunction between the typographic and the phonetic, as well as an unpronounceable typographic substitution for 'and'), a company who are 'manufacturers of nylon *text*iles', and whose business will connect the 'industrial depths of Peckham' with the *text*ual concerns of a Leavisite view of literature, since, according to Douglas, 'Industry is by now . . . a great tradition' (17). Dougal is surrounded by characters who are obsessively concerned with the nature of language because of its class implications in English culture – 'He hasn't got nothing to be a snob about,' said Dixie. '*Anything,* not *nothing.*' 'Anything,' said Dixie, 'to be a snob about.' (25) – but who miss, thereby, the real meanings in what they say: 'any thing' is better than 'no thing' in the degraded world of industry, but everything becomes nothing in a world committed to merely material values. 'Dixie' is a character devoted etymologically to speech (Latin, dixit, she speaks) but her second name – Morse – points to the fact that all speech is a code that requires to be understood through a set of conventions which are by no means transparent:

> 'My own American dad pays my keep,' Dixie said.
> 'He thinks he do, but it don't go far.'
> 'Does. Doesn't,' Dixie said.

Dixie's obsession with grammatical correctness un*does* meaning, suspending it between alternatives that negate each other and make it impossible for her to act, to do. It is these self-negating structures of language that Dougal parodies – 'Dougal said then to Dixie, "I didn't never have no money of my own at your age"' – turning the *act* of speech into a representation and repetition of speech, into an act to be performed rather than a performative act. Dougal makes clear that all human beings are the actors of a script produced by language and therefore, far from being the 'real' human beings of the realist novel, are like characters from a novel substituted into the texture of life.

Dougal is the point of contact between a world of characters so banalised by the standardised requirements of a modern industrial environment that they are nothing more than repetitions of each other. Such characters replicate the formal procedures of the novel as a 'repetition' of the world in art, since they are already, by their very nature and the nature of their language, as limited in relation to what a 'real' human being ought to be as is a 'realistic' character in a novel – a series of textual conventions rather than a living language. Spark's novel, like Dougal himself, is attempting to redeem the inhumanity of its characters' subjection to mere repetition and must, therefore, refute the the terms of a literary realism which would be in itself simply the acceptance of the limits of their degraded reality. Dougal, engaged on his 'human research' in the factories of the district, is the diabolic alter ego of the author engaged in her 'search' for the truly 'human'. Dougal 'dances' through life, his dances at one and the same time a revelation of the degraded world in which the people of Peckham live – a world of deliberate restriction and repetition – and a revelation of the human potentiality for transcending that world which will be matched by his creator in her refusal of the limits of the real to which realism would confine her. The novel, like its central character, must dream an alternative to the world of industrial automation to which both are subjected:

> 'I have a dream at nights,' Dougal said, pouring the wine, 'of girls in factories doing a dance with only the movements of their breasts, bottoms, and arms as they sort, stack, pack, check, cone-wind, gum, uptwist, assemble, seam and set. I see the Devil in the guise of a chap from Cambridge, who does motion-study, and he's the choreographer. He sings the song that goes, "We study in detail the movements requisite for any given task and we work out the simplest pattern of movement involving the least loss of energy and time." While he sings this song, the girls are waggling and winding, like this – ' and Dougal waggled his body and wove his arms intricately, 'Like Indian dancing, you know,' he said. (50)

Deliberate reduction of the human being to a machine is transformed into an art form in defiance of its own restricted vision of human potentiality. At the dance hall where those workers go for recreation they in fact simply re-create the automated environment of their workplace – 'Most of the men looked as if they had not properly woken from deep sleep, but

glided as if drugged, and with half-closed lids, towards their chosen partner. This approach found favour with the girls. The actual invitation to
dance was mostly delivered by gesture; a scarcely noticeable flick of the
man's head towards the dance floor' (58). The characters act as though
they are incapable of awakening again into a world of real human beings.
Into this environment Dougal introduces the energy of a diabolic mimicry,
demonstrating humanity's ability to challenge the limits and restrictions of
the reality within which they are trapped:

> [Dougal] pressed into the midst of the dancers, bearing before him the lid of
> a dust-bin, which he had obtained from the back premises. Then he placed
> the lid upside down on the floor, sat cross-legged inside it, and was a man in
> a rocking boat rowing for his life. The band stopped, but nobody noticed the
> fact, owing to the many different sounds of mirth, protest, encouragement,
> and rage . . .
> Next, Dougal sat on his haunches and banged a message out on a tom-
> tom. He sprang up and with the lid on his head was a Chinese coolie eating
> melancholy rice. He was an ardent cyclist, crouched over handlebars and
> pedalling uphill with the lid between his knees. He was an old woman with
> an umbrella; he stood on the upturned edges of the lid and speared fish from
> his rocking canoe; he was the man at the wheel of a racing car; he did many
> things with the lid before he finally propped the dust-bin lid up on his high
> shoulder, beating his cymbal rhythmically with his hand while with the other
> hand he limply conducted an invisible band, being, with long blank face,
> the bandleader. (59–60)

Dougal's defiance of the limitedness of the dance floor is at one with the
novel's refusal to be restricted to the terms of a realism which would banalise
an already banal world. Where reality is so degraded, realism can only be
the author's accession to the imprisonment in which her characters are
trapped.

One of Dougal's many jobs (in defiance of the contractual restrictions of
the labour market) is writing an 'autobiography' for an old actress by the
name of Maria Cheeseman, or Cheese for short:

> 'But Doug dear,' she said, 'that bit where you make me say I played with
> Harold Lloyd and Ford Sterling at the Golden Domes in Camberwell, it isn't
> true, dear. I *was* in a show with Fatty Arbuckle but it was South Shields.'
> 'I thought it was a work of art you wanted to write,' Douglas said, 'now was
> that not so? If you only want to write a straight autobiography you should
> have got a straight ghost. I'm crooked.' (76).

Dougal is the Typing Ghost of this novel, except that rather than repeating
the events of the novel in conformity with the principles of a mimetic
art, as in *The Comforters*, he transforms reality into entertaining narrative and translates the real into a code to which only he has the key.

The tension between the mimetic representation of reality and world as coded text is dramatised when Dougal and Merle Coverdale are walking together:

> Dougal pointed to a house on the right. 'There's a baby's ram,' he said, 'stuck out on a balcony which hasn't any railings.'
>   She looked and sure enough there was a pram perched on an open ledge only big enough to hold it, outside a second-floor window. She said, 'They ought to be prosecuted. There's a baby in that pram, too.'
>   'No, it's only a doll,' Dougal said.
>   'How do you know?'
>   'I've seen it before. The house is a baby-carriage works. The pram is only for show.' (32–3)

The real object turns into a symbolic object and interpretation of it as in defiance of the law turns into the appreciation of its artifice, a reading of it as 'code'.

It is this disjunction which *The Ballad of Peckham Rye* plays with at the level of its own novelistic discourses. It enacts with self-conscious rigour the banalities of novelistic mimesis as the limitation of language to the re-presentation of the real:

> At the back of Hollis's Hamburgers at Elephant and Castle was a room furnished with a fitted grey carpet, a real upholstered modern suite comprising a sofa and two cubic armchairs, a television receiver in a light wood stand, a low glass-topped coffee table, a table on which stood an electric portable gramophone and a tape recorder, a light wood bureau desk, a standard lamp, and several ash-trays on stands. Two of the walls were papered with a wide grey stripe . . . (90)

The novel is immersed in an almost self-destructive restriction of language to the mere repetition of reality, reduced to a 'standard' set of terms that is like the grey 'ash' left over from a living world. In this environment sit three characters who are imitations of roles in American movies – 'All smoked American cigarettes. All looked miserable, not as an expression of their feelings, but as if by an instinctive pre-arrangement, to convey a decision on all affairs whatsoever' (90). What they are engaged in is the effort to make sense of another representation, a stolen piece of Dougal's writing, which is given its own distinguishing typographic style within the novel's text:

> 'Listen to this,' Trevor said. 'It's called "Phrases suitable for Cheese"'
> 'Suitable for what?' said Collie.
> 'Cheese, it says. Code word, obvious. Listen to this what you make of it. There's a list.

'I thrilled to his touch.
I was too young at the time to understand why my mother was crying.
. . .
I became the proud owner of a bicycle.
He spoke to me in desiccated tones.
Autumn again. Autumn. The burning of leaves in the park.
. .

'Read us it again, Trev,' Leslie said. 'It sounds like English Dictation . . ' (91)

Dougal's notes for his narrative are transformed, on the page, into a series
of narrative gestures and images like a section from T. S. Eliot's 'The Waste
Land', an art work for which the characters in the room seek to become
the interpretive critics:

Collie blew out his smoke as if it were a slow poison. 'Got to work back from
a clue,' he said in his sick voice. 'Autumn's a clue. Wasn't there something
about autumn?'
'How dumb can you get?' Trevor inquired through his nose. 'It's a code.
Autumn means something else. Everything means something.' (92)

The banal world of the realism in which the characters are trapped is full of
symbolism constructed by the novelist in defiance of the degraded reality she
is describing; Dougal's notes which are intended to be appropriate mimetic
repetition of Cheese's account of her own past become symbolic structures
for which an interpretive key has to be sought. The characters, who are all
reduced to 'types' of one another, need an alternative interpretation to be
seen as capable of being uniquely human. Merle Coverdale, the typist who
is typing up Dougal's fictional autobiography of Cheese, declares to Trevor
that what she types is 'not real cheese', 'Cheese is a person, it isn't the
real name' (133), but what she types is also oral speech because she types
to Dougal's dictation:

"Peckham was fun exclamation mark but the day inevitably dawned when I
realized that I and my beloved pals at the factory were poles apart full stop
The great throbbing heart of London across the river spelt fame comma
success comma glamour to me full stop I was always an incurable romantic
exclamation mark . . . And so we parted for ever full stop New Para I felt a
grim satisfaction as the cab which bore me and my few poor belongings bowled
across Vauxhall Bridge and in the great world – capital G capital W – ahead
full stop Yes comma Peckham had been fun exclamation mark" Now leave a
space, please, and – ' (128)

The text of the novel deforms its own typography to reproduce not what
Merle actually types but what Dougal dictates (no capitals at 'great world',
for instance, despite the instruction which follows), and through the elision
of normal grammatical markers it opens up alternative meanings by which

characters are themselves reduced to typographic elements ('an incurable romantic exclamation mark'). The textual version of reported speech will also point codedly forward to what is in store for Merle Coverdale herself – 'ahead full stop' – since she is shortly to be trapped in an interpretive web that will result in her murder by the factory manager with whom she has been having a sterile and repetitious affair and who believes she is in league with Dougal to spy on him. The only way out of the repetitive world of 'types' is by death. Against that reduction of humanity, Spark allows an old woman who haunts the streets of Peckham to cry out, 'The words of the double-tongued are as if they were harmless, but they reach even to the inner part of the bowels. Praise be to the Lord, who distinguishes our cause and delivers us from the unjust and deceitful man' (132). The novelist is 'double-tongued'; her world of mimetic types is transformed into a world of codes which distinguishes the 'causes' that have reduced humanity itself to a series of types to which the key has been lost. Thus it is that at the end of the novel, Humphrey, newly married to Dixie, and depressed by the fact that she already feels as though she'd been 'married twenty years instead of two hours' saw 'the Rye for an instant looking like a cloud and green and gold, the people seeming to ride upon it, as you might say there was another world than this' (143). Spark's fiction plays with type precisely to defy the limitation of the world to a series of one-dimensional types for whom it is impossible to say there was another world than this. Her novels are designed to invoke and to defeat the limits of novelistic realism by returning to the power of type its ability to invoke another world rather than simply to reproduce this one.

II

The implications of typography were to become a matter of crucial importance in the development of the arts in Scotland in the 1960s and 70s through the work of writers and visual artists such as Edwin Morgan, Ian Hamilton Finlay and Tom Leonard. Morgan's play with typography, both for the representation of sound ('The Loch Ness Monster's Song') and for the simulation of particular forms of printed text ('The Computer's First Code Poem'), were closely related to the problematics of the representation of alternative dialects and languages (see 'The First Men on Mercury' and 'The Computer's First Dialect Poems') and foregrounded the technology of print as itself a historically constructed series of meanings rather than simply a medium for the conveying of meaning.[6] In Hamilton Finlay's work an initial concern with the representation of dialect speech (*Glasgow Beasts, an a Burd*) is the foundation of his lifelong effort to combine print into visual and sculptural art, and to translate the textual into the natural as a correspondence with the ways in which the natural is itself transformed into art in the garden.[7] And in Leonard's poems the typographic representation of the vernacular becomes the basis for the construction of complex interchanges between the oral and the textual, as when, for instance, the vernacular pronunciation of 'think' as 'thingk' releases the implication of a thought process thirled to a world of matter.[8] In all of these writers, typography becomes a palette to be used (or abused) for the superimposition upon one another of patterns of meaning which imply alternatives to the reality offered by realism's epistemological and linguistic standardisation.

This development in the Scottish arts in the thirty years after the Second World War was to be put to powerful effect in the novel in the early 1980s in the work of Alasdair Gray. Gray, himself a painter, brought to his use of text an intensely visual awareness so that *Lanark* is not simply a novel, but a novel with 'allegorical titlepages imitating the best precedents' (title page) and an aggressive typography – as, for instance, in the bold small cap running heads. As well as being typographically assertive, however, it is a novel which becomes increasingly conscious as it proceeds not only of its own textuality but of the textuality of the world in which its characters are bound. So, by Book 4, Lanark is moving through a landscape not so much of places and people as of texts – advertisements in bold type (432–3, e.g.), speeches given radical indentation on the page (450–51, e.g.), announcements presented in alternative typefaces (474–75, e.g.). This mixture of typographies enforce our awareness, in reading a representation of a future world, that the character himself is a purely textual construction, deriving his 'being' neither from some original in the world nor from his typicality with anything in the world, but from the processes of type itself:

> "I will start," said the conjuror, "by explaining the physics of the world you live in. Everything you have experienced and are experiencing, from your first glimpse of the Elite café to the metal of that spoon in your fingers, the taste of the soup in your mouth, is made of one thing."
> "Atoms," said Lanark.
> "No. Print. Some worlds are made of atoms but yours is made of tiny marks marching in neat lines, like armies of insects, across pages and pages of white paper. I say these lines are marching, but that is a metaphor. They are perfectly still. They are lifeless." (484–5)

This 'atomic' world of print, in which there is nothing but typography, supports another world, that of the literary forms and the narrative conventions by which novels are structured. These are incorporated into the novel as a series of sidenotes and footnotes which accompany the character as he converses with his 'author', and which explain the textual precursors on which his character and adventures are based. The sidenotes (provided by 'Sidney Workman') are not run in the margins of the text but embedded into the main body of the text, as though shouldering it aside to let us see what has been concealed within it – behind the facade of the 'original' work of art are revealed the 'block plagiarisms' ('where someone else's work is printed as a distinct typographical unit'), the imbedded plagiarisms ('where stolen words are concealed within the body of the narrative') and 'diffuse plagiarisms' ('where scenery, characters, actions or novel ideas have been stolen without the original words') of which the text is composed (485). The page itself thus becomes a site of competing textualities, each establishing its autonomy, or acknowledging its dependence, by dominating or ceding a portion of the page to the others. Reading the pages of this section of the novel involves a complex interplay between different streams of text, each with its own logic and each represented by a different typographical style, but this typographic shape is no more than the visual representation of the whole structure of the novel. The character's struggle for freedom is a struggle against being reduced simply to the product of type, and the world of type becomes a textual enactment of his reduction to being simply a cipher within a larger system of historical meaning over which he can exert no control.

For a culture whose whole existence since 1707 has been shaped by the medium of a learned written language which displaced its own oral cultures, and whose native languages were never properly standardized within the domain of type, typography becomes the symbol of its own culturally repressed condition: to overthrow the rule of type is synonymous with overthrowing the type of rule under which the culture has struggled for self-expression. At the same time, this is a culture with a deeply ingrained method of reading texts in terms not only of typographic awareness, but in terms of typological significance, because the religious traditions on which the literacy of the country was based were themselves rooted in the procedures of reading which sought to see in the Old Testament 'types' – in the sense of prefugurations – of the characters of the New Testament. To read typologically is to be aware of text as a series of intersections between different narratives which are interpreted as preparations for or recollections of one another, the Old Testament prefiguring the New while the New postfigures the Old. To live typologically is to see all the events of life as re-enactments of Biblical narratives. It is precisely this which *Lanark* performs in the textual relationships of its various sections: it is a 'life in four books' as though they were the four gospels, with their different modes of presenting and interpreting the same narrative, or the books of an Old and a New Testament, incorporating a genesis and an apocalypse, with a resurrection – the transformation of Duncan Thaw into his 'redeemer' Lanark – in the middle of it, and with Mr Thaw senior (as in Duncan's painting, 309), as God the Father, who, like the God of the Judaeo-Christian tradition, leaves his son to suffer in the fallen world in order that it can be redeemed.

Thaw's vast and incompletable painting in the Cowlairs church is an attempt to undo the whole history of Scotland since the Reformation, returning the visual arts to a church which had banned them in the iconophobia of the Reformation, and trying to recreate the sense of the significance of the church building itself as the centre of a culture. The historical irrelevance of this – 'Why didn't you give me a railway station to decorate? It would have been easy painting to the glory of Stevenson, Telford, Brunel and a quarter million Irish navvies. But here I am, illustrating your discredited first chapter through an obsolete art form on a threatened building in a poor province of a collapsing empire' (321) – is matched by the impossibility of the task he has given himself – representing change and process in the static forms of visual art: 'His trouble began in the background where history was acted in the loops and delta of the river on its way to the ocean. The more he worked the more the furious figure of God kept popping in and having to be removed.' (320). Transferring the events of the Word into visual form involves an impossible translation from the temporal to the spatial, but the text within which Lanark is himself embedded is, equally, attempting to return its readers from the reading expectations of the novel to the older methods of understanding narrative derived from scriptural analysis. Reading *Lanark* involves the reader in a secularised version of typological methods of reading the Bible, for we have to read Thaw's life as prefiguring Lanark's and Lanark's as a postfigural fulfilment of Thaw's, while, at the same time, reading the novel with Lanark's life as preceding and prefiguring Thaw's, since Book 3 precedes Books 1 and 2. Thaw and Lanark are thus hypotypes of one another, a hypotype being an empty 'type', one whose significance is unknowable until it is fulfilled and completed by another narrative. Thus the psychosomatic skin ailments with which Thaw is afflicted are re-enacted in the dragonhide in which Lanark is increasingly encased: each has to be understood as a figuration of the other. One of the self-referring footnotes of the 'Epilogue' insists that 'the fact remains that the plots of the Thaw and Lanark sections are independent of each other and cemented by typographic contrivances rather than formal necessity' (493); the writer of this footnote is, however, clearly unaware of the extent to which a whole methodology of reading has been developed simply on the basis of the typographic contrivances by which various books have been cemented together to form the Bible. In a world ruled by a typographic God, the distinction between typographic and formal necessity is irrelevant.

At the same time the acknowledgment of textuality on the part of the author becomes the means by which a solidarity with all other workers who are caught up in the vast meaning-system of capitalism can be asserted. As another of the footnotes to the 'Epilogue' insists, pointing out its own postfigural relation to a prefiguration, the text is a vast accumulation of typing and typographic labour:

As this "Epilogue" has performed the office of an introduction to the work as a whole (the so-called "Prologue" being no prologue at all, but a separate short story), it is saddening to find the "conjuror" omitting the courtesies appropriate to such an addendum. Mrs Florence Allan typed and retyped his manuscripts, and often waited many months without payment and without complaining. Professor Andrew Sykes gave him free access to copying equipment and secretarial help. He received from James Kelman critical advice which enabled him to make smoother prose of the crucial first chapter. Charles Wild, Peter Chiene, Jim Hutcheson, Stephanie Wolf Murray engaged in extensive lexical activity to ensure that the resulting volume had a surface consistency. And what of the compositors employed by Kingsport Press of Kingsport, Tennessee, to typeset this bloody book? Yet these are only a few out of thousands whose help has not been acknowledged and whose names have not been mentioned. (499)

The book is, quite literally, the accumulated labour of many workers in type and many types of worker. The book is not – like Duncan Thaw's painting – the work of an isolated genius but a 'work' of art which has to acknowledge its sources in the labour of others (its 'plagiarisms'), and its dependence on the world of labour (the typesetters at Kingsport). Those labours are inscribed in the form of the novel even while the central character of the novel tries to escape that (de)formation. Acknowledgment of its own precursors is itself only an acknowledgment of the fundamentally social nature of all creation, of the dependence of the individual upon the community. Textuality is, at one and the same time, the necessity of enslavement in systems beyond ourselves and the condition of our freedom, the medium through which we, like Lanark, achieve self-expression and some degree of self-control by challenging the powers that shape our world.

If *Lanark* was a novel which was to transform the landscape of Scottish fiction in 1981, then *1982 Janine* was one which was to puzzle critics when it appeared in 1984, not only because of the discrepancy between the date of title and the date of publication but also because the 'pornographic' materials of Jock McLeish's fantasies, which make up the first quarter of the novel, seemed to undermine the seriousness of the novel's reflections on the nature of Scotland, which in turn seemed to be trapped within the parodic version of Scotsmen as, initially, argumentative and, later, melancholic drunks, damaged by a sexually repressive society. But the novel's entrapment within the 'types' of the Scottish past is precisely its point: as Gray acknowledges in his 'Epilogue', 'The matter of Scotland refracted through alcoholic reverie is taken from MacDiarmid's *A Drunk Man Looks at the Thistle*' (343) and the central character's relationship with his schoolteacher – itself a reference back to the centrality of the role of education in the making, and unmaking, of Scottish identity – is based on a poem by Tom Leonard (344). *1982 Janine* is a novel about types, about characters as types – 'I once met another man of my type' (64); 'at school I envied the sickly types' (177) – and about Jock as someone who constructs – or has constructed for him – his identity as a type – as, for instance, when his father decides he should order 'three jackets and three waistcoats and seven pairs of trousers and two overcoats of the same cloth! Let him change his trousers every day of the week. The fabric will suffer so little strain that with ordinary care it will look continually smart and last him a lifetime' (201). The intention is that Jock should spend his lifetime as a fixed type, one with a 'neat, simple, consistent appearance bordering upon the miraculous' (202). This, of course, is precisely what 'type' does to the multiplicity of sounds in a language, and this awareness of the text as 'type' – Jock exists only in and through the 'neat, simple, consistent appearance' of type within the 'bordering' of the page – erupts constantly into the apparently unstructured flux of Jock's fantasies:

> . . . though [Janine] wants her voice to sound casual it comes out husky when she says, "How long till we get there?"
> "About ten minutes," says the driver, a fat well-dressed man who stop. Stop. I should undress first. (12)

The word 'stop' generates a pause in Jock's fantasy but it also the oral instruction for the full stop which visually marks the end of a sentence which has, in fact, not ended and therefore should not be terminated with a full stop. Foregrounding the conventions of the typographic representation of grammar gives a different meaning to the word 'stop' depending on whether it is a self-addressed instruction to the story-teller or an instruction to someone taking dictation. Jock is both: he is his own secretary, dictating to himself the story of his own type, trying not to bring his narrative to a stop but trying to stop telling the narrative of himself as no more than a type, a type destined to play out its role till it stops: 'If I stop travelling and stay in one place I will become a recognisable, pitiable ("Out of pity for your condition I will take no action") despicable drunkard' (176). Here the grammatical markers of parenthetic speech reduce to type the eruption of another voice into Jock's sentence just as Jock is reduced in someone else's speech from an individual into a 'condition' and then into a type. Equally, Janine, the central character in Jock's fantasies, is the feminine reduced to one of the types required by (typo)pornography:

> Sherry says gleefully in her throaty stagewhisper, "Just see the mess I'm in! When they came for me I freaked right out, I yelled and struggled, they slapped me silly and dragged me here and tied me up like this. I admire how you can take it all so calm. But of course this is your first time so you don't know what's in store. Believe me these brutes will do everything they want to us when they get us to the Cattlemarket."
> Keyword. Shift back to Janine reading it. Janine in cowhide britches in Cadillac driven by Frank to a place called the Cattlemarket realises she is reading about Nina in Cadillac driven by Frank to a place called the Cattlemarket where Nina will at last stand in line beside a woman who is Janine. Vertigo. (331)

The 'vertigo' of Janine's discovery that she is reading a fiction about herself is the discovery that her 'first time' is actually a repetition of something already in print: it is prefaced by a 'keyword' which has, of course, been shaped by the keys of keyboard, its capital first letter and lowercase continuation achieved by applying 'Shift' and then 'back' to unshifted type; Janine and Nina stand together not just in line but in a 'line' of type, the kind embodied in the original 'Linotype' hot metal typesetting systems. Instead of being translated by the reader from type into an imagined reality, the text allows its characters to *real*ise themselves as consisting of nothing more than the characters of type.

Gray's play with typographic conventions begins from the cover of the first edition of the novel, the front of which has the title:

1 9 8 2

JANINE

while the spine has 1982, JANINE: the linear representation of the title as text requires a punctuation mark that the visual representation of the title as pattern can dispense with. Equally, the book opens with a 'Table of Contents', which is not a usual feature of a modern novel but in this case it is more than simply a listing of chapter titles: it is an analytical table of contents which sets out in advance the method of reading the characters of the novel as 'types' of other characters, but a reading which is ambiguous as to whether the (psycho)analysis is of the author (who knows he is writing a book) or the character (who doesn't, but narrates the rest of the book and so may just as easily narrate the table of contents).

CHAPTER 2

A recipe for pornography and political history. A Superb housewife, ripe for pleasure and not atall like my wife Helen, sets out to enjoy herself but has trouble with the police and an unexpected miniskirt.

. . .

CHAPTER 6

Caught in Barbed Wire: an open-air film in which Janine and Helga meet a small nasty boy and a big nasty man who are not atall like me and my father the good socialist timekeeper.

The Table of Contents denies the 'originals' on which the 'types' of the characters are based while at the same time providing an interpretive framework within which the novel can be read precisely as the displacement into fantasy of the original (but in this case, fictional) characters – implying, of course, the parallel displacement from the real world of Alasdair Gray into the fictional world of the novel.

As in *Lanark*, the typographic is, in *1982 Janine*, but one face of the typological: the pornographic fantasy world of Jock McLeish is the (false) New Testament of the modern world, the narrative of fulfilment through which all other narratives are to be given their retrospective significance. In

Jock McLeish's world the repressive power of traditional religion has been replaced by the gratification culture of sexual freedom, a culture which he replicates in his fantasies in order to repress, in turn, his memories of that repressive culture. The Old Testament of the hardworking presbyterian virtues has to be read through the new testament of sexual gratification: the old world of duty through the new world of self-fulfilment. But what is revealed is not the transcendental truth of a hypotype made full through the discovery of its appropriate and complementary narrative but the absolute emptiness of the hypotype, its endless incompletability, and the impossibility, therefore, of ever discovering the fullness of meaning which the double narrative promises. On one of his final walks with his father, Jock discovers some flowers and asks his father for their name:

> I said, "What is this one called?"
> "I don't know," said Dad.
> I said, "That's strange. You used to be keen on botany."
> "Me? Oh no. I like flowers but I don't give a damn for botany."
> I reminded him of the book he kept bringing out when I was a child and we went for walks together. He said, "I bought that book because you kept asking me the names of the flowers you saw and I didn't know them. My father discouraged me from asking questions when I was small, I'm sure it impaired my education."
> So I had made Dad's walks dull by asking him questions, he made mine dull by answering them. (100)

The relation of Jock's fantasies to his real life are like his childhood questions and his father's answers – empty performances of a process of understanding which leaves nothing behind. Far from asking questions of each other and providing answers to each other, Jock's double narratives enact simply an empty repetition of one another; far from being a revelation of meaning the double narrative is its concealment, a typological illusion designed to maintain the status quo, just as the sexual fantasies which, for Jock, have to take place in America, are not the revelation of his concealed private life but the means of public concealment of the real processes of war and domination by which the world is actually ruled. Private sexual fantasy is not an escape from the outside world but a re-enactment of the very terms which dominate and repress ordinary humanity. Britain, according Jock, 'is organized like a bad adolescent fantasy' (139) and the international world order is nothing but a fantasy designed to conceal its real motivations:

> 'Our defence systems run like my fantasies which can only continue by getting much bigger and nastier than were first intended. Nobody can keep control of a process like that for ever. In 1914 and 1939 the big industrial nations, having fucked the rest of the planet (in the vulgar sense of the word) started wanking all over each other. None of them enjoyed it but they could not stop. (151)

The sexual fantasy world of Jock's inner consciousness is not, in fact, a retreat from reality or its explanation in an alternative form: it is simply its replication. Despite the apparent difference in the two narratives, as hypotypes they tell the same thing, adding nothing to one another except to emphasise their mutual emptiness and pointlessness.

This is why the fundamental concealment in Jock's fantasies is that the woman on whom he exercises his imagination is, in fact, himself, translated into adult continuation of his adolescent storytelling:

> ... I had started telling myself stories about a very free attractive greedy woman who, confidant in her powers, begins an exciting adventure and finds she is not free at all but completely at the disposal of others. As I aged that story grew very elaborate. The woman is corrupted into enjoying her bondage and trapping others into it. I did not notice that this was the story of my own life. I avoided doing so by insisting on the *femaleness* of the main character. (193)

Jock's fantasies are not simply the occasion for self-abuse but a fundamental abuse of the self: his fantasies are enacted on himself in disguise; they are encouraged by a world economic system which requires the bondage of the self in order to deny the possibility of resistance to the world that it creates. Jock is symbol of Scotland precisely to the extent that he has translated himself into a feminine that he then subjects to sexual abuse:

> ... if a country is not just a tract of land but a whole people then clearly Scotland has been fucked. I mean that word in the vulgar sense of *misused to give satisfaction or advantage to another*. Scotland has been fucked and I am one of the fuckers who fucked her. (137)

Jock's redemption from fantasy will be achieved by allowing the fantasy character that is a version of himself – Janine – to cease to be dictated by someone else's narrative, to realise her typographical entrapment and therefore bring the story to a stop;

> ... and how much they were going to enjoy her – at which the story must stop, because Janine has now been forced to see she is a character in it. *She realises it is her inescapable fate to be a character in a story by someone who dictates every one of her movements and emotions, someone she will never meet and cannot appeal to.* She is like most people, but not like me. I have been free for nearly ten whole minutes. (332)

Janine, like Caroline in *The Comforters*, is the product of the Typing Ghost, in that she represents humanity not by being a mimesis of the real world but by repeating formally the world's reduction of human freedom to a predetermined script, its reduction of humanity to characters in a fiction.

Politics and history are a script which we fulfil, like characters in a narrative, but which we have to resist, and resist by refusing to subject others to playing roles in our fantasies, to being prisoners of our narratives. The hypotype which, within biblical exegesis, entraps two narratives in a mutually determining relationship is precisely the effect of a world in which there can be no choice, because those who play the part in an earlier narrative cannot know the purpose of their own story until it is completed by a later narrative. And since the earlier narrative must prefigure the later one, its whole shape is determined by something which does not yet exist and can be known only from the point of view of God, or from the point of view of the interpreter who comes at the end of the sequence. That whole method of reading, however, is an encouragement to a fatalism which turns life into a book, the future already held in the fixity of print rather than yet to be brought into being by the choices of the characters: as Jock's father's friend, Old Red, declares: 'Those who think the past could not have been different come to feel the present cannot be changed or the future either' (148). The mutually determining books of the Old and the New Testaments, of whatever religion, are the revelation of a world fixed in type, unchangeable, and to be read in relation only to each other and the meanings which fit their hypotypical requirements. Thus when the crisis of Jock's early life arrives, and he is confronted by Mr. Hume, the father of the girl who claims to be pregnant by him, what he hears in Hume's denunciations is not a set of words but the replication of a book. The variant titles of the book that Jock thinks he is re-enacting reveal his powerlessness before male authority, a powerlessness that is equivalent to being trapped within the determined structures of art:

> Five or six years ago I read a novel in which the main character made a speech so like Mr Hume's that I have never since been able to remember them apart. It was a novel which gave the impression of curt masculine authority by having a single surname for the title. *Gillespie* by Hay? No. *McIlvannie* by Docherty? No. *Docherty* by McIlvannie. (298)

The 'Y' of McIlvanney has been transformed, of course, so that even the real author of the novel to which this title refers has been reshaped into a typographic fiction.

The tension between the oral and the typographic in *1982 Janine* is symbolic both of the fact that the character and his culture have been undermined by the imposed structures of an alien language and value system, and of the suppression of the individual voice which a standardised language is – or, at least, in twentieth century Britain, has been – designed to achieve. This is dramatised in the moment in the novel when Hislop – schoolteacher, reproduction of Friel's Mr. Alfred in his commitment to the values of English culture in a Scottish setting and, also, Jock's putative father – tries to belt one of Jock's schoolfriends because of his lisp:

> "Break my name in two," said Hislop very gently, "say Hiss and then say
> Slop. Say Hiss first, all by itself. Press the tip of your tongue tight against
> the base of your teeth and hiss like a snake."
> After a silent struggle Anderson managed to say, "Hith." (335)

The snake that Anderson cannot voice is the suppression of the variety and
individuality of speech patterns that Hislop has made his life's work in the
classroom:

> "Anderson, I am about to do something beautiful. Something that you will
> one day thank me for. Something that will make my name live for ever in
> the annals of the long town. On my gravestone I will order them to chisel
> the words, 'Here lieth the man who cured Anderson's lisp.' Lisp for me.
> Anderson. Say *lisp*. Distinctly."
> "Lithp, thir."
> "Oh dear. Say *stop*, Anderson."
> "Thtop, thir."
> "Worse and worse. I will not ssstop, Anderson. Until you distinctly tell me
> to ssstop. Hold out your hands and double them." (335-6)

Hislop demands at one and the same time that Anderson 'lisp' – 'lisp for
me' – and that he does not lisp; the contradictory instruction is enforced by
his own use of the 'literary' lisp of 'lieth' for 'lies'. The roots of Hislop's
power in the assertion of the written over the oral are revealed in his desire to
have 'chiselled' words assert the significance of his life – though the words
of course will 'lie'. Anderson cannot bring the issue to a full stop and must
therefore live a double life (like his hands), for one of which he must be
punished. Against this imposition of the written code upon the specificities
of individual orality, the young McLeish reacts by challenging this 'father'
of the written by an assertion of the power of the oral:

> ... Anderson, face contorted and tearwet, sometimes whining, sometimes
> muttering, sometimes yelling, kept on saying it wrong *and kept on holding out
> his hand afterwards*. The rest of us sat petrified in a nightmare from which no
> awakening seemed possible because a teacher had gone mad. He had become
> mechanical. He was a machine whose governor had broken and which could
> only work by going on doing more and more of the same vile thing until I
> could no longer bear it and stood up and said, "He can't help talking like
> that, sir." He gaped at me, did Hislop. He came over to me, the Lochgelly
> swinging by his side ... Having no new ideas I said again, "He can't help
> talking like that, sir", and sat down, and folded my arms, and immediately
> felt a lot safer. . . . Hislop never touched people with his hands, only with
> the belt, and when this occurred to me I felt safe enough to become angry.
> I said, "You shouldnae have done that. You shouldnae have done that. You
> shouldnae have done that." (336)

Hislop, at this moment, is as Jock will be in the day of the novel, a man
whose 'governor had broken'; the source of Jock's own problem is in his

forgetfulness of the assertion which he made that day of the value and significance of the local and of individual speech over the standardisation of type: the initial assertion ('He can't help . . .') is in standard English but its follow-up is the assertion not just of moral condemnation but of linguistic independence: 'You shouldnae have done . . .' The recollection of this moment from his childhood combines, for McLeish, an image of what he has himself become – a version of Hislop, his surrogate father – with the power to resist that father through his utterance of his 'mother' tongue; at the same time, it reveals Hislop as himself a victim of the same power structures which have caused McLeish's breakdown, for in the depth of his despair Hisop himself says, 'in the voice of a tiny weeping boy, "O sir they wullnae lea' me alane, they wullnae lea' me alane"' (337). The enforcer of the power of the written over the oral, of the standardly typographic, is defeated by the power of the oral, just as Jock himself will be redeemed by the discovery of his own voice and by his – and his author's – refusal to be bound by the conventions of the world of type.

Through its own play with typography *1982 Janine* rebels against the repressive world of typographic convention. Typography as intrusion into the narrative, rather than simply its medium, begins from the opening sentence of Gray's novel, which incorporates the chapter number into the sentence and connects the first word of the sentence to the chapter number through their sharing the same point size and bold type, as though the convention of the chapter number had become part of the narrative itself:

1: THIS IS A GOOD ROOM. It could be in Belgium, the U.S.A., Russia perhaps.

The form of the novel, as artifice, thus becomes part of the very texture of Jock's narration, as though he is dictating the chapter numbers as well as the narrative. Typography later becomes a substitute for the novel's characters themselves when all of the women in Jock's fantasies stand 'like an upsidedown capital Y' (116), characters reduced to a single typographic character: their appearance is greeted with the exclamation 'yahooohay' which then becomes the name of the degraded god of this sexually abusive universe – 'You bastard YYYYYYYYYahooay' (117) – whose initial 'Y' replicates the shape of the male figure on the front cover of the book, with his arms raised and pointing outwards. Narrative then gives way to typographic sculpture as the inverted 'Y' of the feminine is replicated across half a page, followed by the upright Y of the male 'yahoo', obliterating all other language in their self-mirroring typographic reduction of the feminine and the masculine to a single character(istic). Type's reduction of the voice to singularity becomes the model for a reduction of all humanity to a set of limited replications of one another. The reduction of all meanings to one repeated letter will be reversed at the moment when Jock's personality disintegrates and he tries to commit suicide: the page becomes a series of competing discourses shaped into intersecting triangular units, abstractly modelling the body while, in terms of readable text, travelling in all directions across the page in defiance of the linear conventions of western typography. On these pages Jock is 'SUFFUFFUFFUFFUFFUCKUCKUCKUCKUCKATING' in the sickness of a life lived in the rigidities of a typographically unilinear culture which cannot accommodate the multiplicities of human expression. The novel's destruction of unilinearity is the prologue to several blank pages (when Jock is unconscious) which will provide the pristine context for Jock's revived self to begin to rewrite itself again as memory and not as fantasy. 'Do not make me remember more . . . Stop me remembering' (163), Jock had cried out just before he took the pills intended to kill him: after the typographic disruption and the blank pages, the novel will be dominated by recollection, as Jock comes to terms with the reality of his past rather than the fantastic evasion of it, and within that recollection Janine will be recognised not as the other, forced into bondage in order to give pleasure, but as the self, as the lost soul – 'O Janine, my silly soul, come to me now' (341) – of a Scottish masculinity that has learned to relate the alienating power of the typographic muse again to the sound of his own voice:

"Eight-fifteen, Mr McLeish. Breakfast is being served till nine."

My voice.
"All right." (341)

Jock's recovery of his 'voice' in a text which proceeds again from left to 'right' is symbolic of his ability to inhabit the medium rather than be destroyed by it: type as the destruction of the living voice has become again a medium for self-expression rather than self-repression.

The personal transformation of McLeish's life is thus enacted through specifically typographic means, but *1982 Janine*'s use of typography goes further than this, for each page of Gray's text not only has a page number offset in the margin, but has beneath each page number a specific subtitle, related directly to the content of that particular page:

74	75
MY LAST	ENJOYING
SIGHT	SUPERB
OF HELEN	DUNGAREES

The margin of the page thus becomes the site of an alternative voice, commenting oracularly on the events within the narrative. More importantly, however, what this means is that the novel can never be typeset in any other form than this one: every page must always appear identically if it is going to be the same novel, since the exact places of the page breaks must be replicated if the marginal commentary is to make sense. The margins of the text, which are normally the business of the designer and publisher, have been invaded and taken over by the author in ways which deny the possibility of a re-presentation of the 'correct words in the correct order' ever changing the author's total control over the structure of the book. By increasing the determinate and unchangeable elements of the text the author effectively asserts his control over the world of the text: the typography becomes part of the author's assertion of his own freedom of expression rather than something he submits to. Gray's protagonist is, quite literally, embedded within the determinate and unchangeable world of type, but discovers his freedom through the realisation of his own voice; the novelist, on the other hand, asserts his freedom and responsibility precisely by taking control over the whole world of type within which his character is held, refusing to cede responsibility for it to anyone else. The character's regaining of control over his own life through the oral is matched by the author's achievement of control over *his* medium through typography: the freedom which the character achieves is redemption from the enforced order of the typographic text, but the form which is absolute determinism for the character is the assertion of an equal freedom for the author. The character walks out of the determined structure of the novel into his own life ('Nobody will guess what I am going to do. I do not know it myself'; 341), asserting the same right to govern himself that his author has asserted by the total control he exerts over the typography of his text. Author and character operate in opposition to each other but to the same end: the recovery of control over the medium of their lives, a recovery which is the symbol of the possible recovery by their nation of its control over its own language, both spoken and written.

III

The example of Gray's work has had a profound influence on the writing of Scottish novels since the early 1980s, both in terms of authors' own relation to their text and in terms of publishers' conceptions of what can be done with the novel. Novels as diverse as Sian Hayton's *Cells of Knowledge*,[9] Robert Alan Jamieson's *A Day at the Office*[10] and Irvine Welsh's *Marabou Stork Nightmares*[11] have all made use of typographic disjunction as part of the texture of their narratives.

The writer who has made most effective use of Gray's example, however, is Janice Galloway, particularly in *The Trick is to Keep Breathing*, published in 1989.[12] In this novel two separate streams of narrative time are defined by the fact that the earlier one – the one which relates the death in a swimming pool of the partner of the central character, Joy Stone, while they are on holiday in Spain – is in substantially indented italic type. The elements of this narrative are scattered through the rest of the novel as Joy's mind continually reruns the loop of events which have deprived her not only of her lover but of all sense of self. The loss of self is reflected typographically by the fact that text begins to spill into the margins, trailing off the edge of the page and leaving the words truncated. In addition, the main text is composed of a series of different typographic styles which mimic the discourses by which Joy is surrounded – from magazine articles to hospital signs, from handwritten letters to fragments of music lyrics – and which both displace and substitute for any assertion of her own identity. Joy, whose body is withering in anorexia and who has ceased to menstruate, has become a tissue of other people's discourses, her own voice barely registered, left outside the body of the text and 'bleeding' into the silence beyond its boundaries. The dislocation of typestyles, the extravagant use of white space, underwrite the nature of Joy's condition as that of one who is trapped by the the textual forms which she inhabits and who is a blank upon which the world writes. Typographic form becomes a mimicry of a character who is being written into a series of roles by the texts by which she is surrounded. When Joy, for instance, has to have conversations with people in authority, for whom she has to play a particular role, the conversation becomes 'speeches', represented not in the conventions of the novel but in the conventions of a playscript: the text performs the performance in which Joy is entrapped. The discourses she adopts and their typographic presentation are both her defence against the world and the cause of her illness, the medium of her survival and the imposition that thrusts any real self-expression out of the body and out of the body-text and into its margins.

At the moment of crisis when Joy attends the funeral of her lover, typography reinforces the negation which she experiences when the minister's 'speech', in assertive small caps, reinscribes the dead man back into his marriage, as though their relationship had never taken place. The sinister voice typographically displaces Joy and ruptures the continuity of her sentence by sentencing her to a life without continuity:

ESPECIALLY OUR LOVE

> a split-second awareness that
> something terrible was about
> to about to

TO HIS WIFE AND FAMILY   happen

Half way into the silence for Norma Fisher, my arms were weightless. The rest came piecemeal as the moral started to compute.
1. The Rev Dogsbody had chosen this service to perform a miracle.
2. He's run time backwards, cleansed, absolved and got rid of the ground-in stain.
3. And the stain was me.
I didn't exist. The miracle had wiped me out. (79)

Joy has been written out of the script; she exists between 'about to' and 'happen', what has actually happened having disappeared from public acknowledgment. Her story is a series of typographic conventions which are simply the empty case of an absent life.

Joy, in effect, comes to experience herself as a character in a novel, composed, like Lanark, of a world of type which simply gestures to the absence of that which it claims to be representing. Joy thus inhabits a world of codes, but codes which have lost their significance. The conventions of the traditional novel have decomposed and the problem which the reader faces in relation to the text is the same problem which Joy faces in relation to the 'coded' world with which she has to engage – how do we read a world to whose codes we have lost the key. How do we read, for instance, the word 'presentim' in the margin of the following passage? Is it 'present time', 'present him', 'represent him', compressed and truncated? Or is it 'present I'm' without grammatical and typographical markers? The arbitrariness which Joy finds in the world she now inhabits has come to characterise the very text by which she is presented:

> I spread the cards and choose, radiate six like sun rays on the carpet then flex my fingers and sigh. As soon as they're chosen they become certainties.
>
> presentim
>
>> The first is the hanged Man, inverted. Caught by his heel to the sky, hair rising to the ground. He lifts and settles in the draught under the door.
>> The Empress. A woman in possession of what is rightfully hers.
>> The Wheel of Fortune, inverse. Six spokes and a twin-pillared frame: an ape, a dog and a dragon clasp the revolving wheel.
>
> I wait a moment before turning the fourth: The Fool.
>
> The floor is littered with messages I can't read.
> There is no armour against the arbitrariness of things. Not suspicion, not fear. There is no way to predict, divine or escape. The only certainty is that there is no certainty. Suspicion is never enough.
>
> I pour another drink and turn up the TV. The wall thumps and my neighbour's little girl screams.
>
> ooo   (77)

The character on the card 'lifts and settles' as though he were independent of his representation; the 'wall thumps' as though walls were capable of initiating action. The world has become a place where meanings ('messages') and their causes have become separated, so that we are all 'The Fool' of arbitrary forms which have nothing to do with the actualities of the world.

It is in this world where 'suspicion is never enough' that the reader is confronted by the divider of triple 'o' which regularly, as at the conclusion of the section quoted above, spaces the text and separates one moment of Joy's consciousness from the next. The 'ooo' begins as a typographic marker of temporal and textual division but it steadily acquires an accretion of alternative possible meanings as the visual sign connects itself to various aspects of the text to which it is juxtaposed. Is it, for instance, the minimal discourse of her own inexpressible pain – 'Oh, Oh, Oh'? Or is it the zero to which everything has been brought by the fact that she has been negated by her partner's death, and by the miracle which erased her from the funeral? Joy Stone, whose name contains two 'o's, has become a third and absent person to herself, a circle containing only white space. The 'ooo', however, is also the visual reiteration of the moment of her realization of her partner's death.

I look down and his mouth is a red O. White water runs through his hair.
His mouth is a red O, eyes wide to the sky.

ooo   (40)

The typographic mark of textual division, representing a gap between moments in time, becomes the compressed recollection of the 'red O', the moment of death and absence, continually interruting the flow of the present narrative with its negation of all discourses. The apparently neutral and repetitive marker of a formal property of the text thus becomes the encoded representation of the trauma from which the narrative begins. Typpography becomes the medium in which the inexpressible anguish of the character finds its representation within the text that dramatises her repression of that very anguish.

As in Gray's novels, the marginal material of the text becomes the site of the author's insistence on the fact that her character is not simply contained within her novel but challenges the boundaries by which she is contained. In *The Trick is to Keep Breathing* the boundaries of the page, which belong to the formal conventions of the printed text of the novel rather than its content, begin to be absorbed by the narrative, so that not only does text start to invade the margins of the page but the elements of the page, such as the page numbers, which ought to be fixed and beyond the control of either author or character, begin to respond sympathetically to the condition of the character's psyche. As Joy's state of mind intensifies, page numbers begin to disappear: the abuse of typographic convention implies that the character's state of mind is spilling over on to the margins of the page, and her own loss of any sense of succession in her life has produced a loss of succession in the form of the novel itself. The novel as formal structure is, quite literally, being swallowed by the character – as a substitute, one might say, for the food which she has refused. By the end of the novel the elision of page numbers becomes symbolic of Joy's refusal of the world in which she is trapped, her negation of the order of reality which would negate her: on what would be page 215, for instance – though several page numbers have gone missing, so that, however briefly, it is difficult to know where we are in the text – she begins the recovery of her own voice, a voice independent of its textual representation, with a negation of typography, consuming the page number into the white space that her voice creates ('I never scream') by turning the written ('I can write it down') into sound:

> Screaming would be good. But I never scream. I can write it down but never do it; never actually. Do it. The fist limply into the yellow wall: soft plaster pressing on the side of my hand then hard, miniature rockfalls scuttling like rats inside. My forehead against the plaster leaves a stain. There is no-one here and the house is full of noise. No-one would know if I were to, if I were just to open my mouth and. Just yell. Lungs working, the singing rising in my throat, the pulse in my temples. The moaning noise I make when I'm on my
>
> only me and
> > *what was his name*
>
> so I scream dammit.
>
> I scream.   (215)

The scream – narrated but not phonetically inscribed – *happens* but does not typographically occur within the text: it consumes the rest of the page in white space, including the page number, and leaves Joy coming back into existence through her absence not *within* the text but *from* the text. Control over the page numbers becomes the signature of the character's refusal of the discourses by which she is controlled; it is also, however, the signature of the author, whose control over her text extends not just to the details of typographic layout but also to the details of the marginalia of the text. Joy is a woman who has lost control of her life but who is narrated by a woman who has taken control of the totality of the medium in which her narrative – and her character's story – is contained: the character struggles towards the condition of the author, towards the control of the medium of life that the author asserts through her refusal of the arbitrary conventions by which novels are bound. The trick, within a typographic medium, is to maintain the breath of the oral and not to submit to the despotism of the textual – the trick is to keep breathing meaningful life into the 'ooo's that give themselves initially only to the perception of a dead visual marker.

   At the end of the novel, however, Joy will undergo an experience parallel to Jock McLeish's, as the textual is replaced by the oral in a recovery of the voice:

I take another mouthful of whisky, slide my finger on the volume control.
Waves rippling through the headphones. And something else.
The human voice. I listen watching the coloured lights, fanning like sea
anemones over the ceiling, till the music stops.
A click and tape whirring into silence at the end of the reel.

The voice is still there.
    I forgive you.
I hear it quite distinctly, my own voice in the empty house.
    I forgive you.

Nobody needs to know I said it. Nobody needs to know.   (235)

The return of 'the voice' is escape from the alienating world of typographic
discourse in which she has been trapped, because what is said, what is heard,
is being recorded in what is written, rather than the already written impos-
ing itself as the record of the self: if, within the ontology of the character's
world, 'nobody needs to know' what has been said we are all nonetheless
typographically informed about it. Absence has been replaced by presence;
the 'nobody' of the self which 'needs to know' and which needs to deny
its knowledge, can know itself again as the 'I' which speaks in *own*ership
of its voice and of its body.

Galloway's novel has, however, more in common with *1982 Janine* than
the play of typography and invasion of the marginal space: McLeish (like
Robin Jenkins's Fergus Lamont) is a man who is doubtful of his parentage:
he believes he may be the son not of his socialist father, the time-keeper
in the pit, but of Mad Hislop, his schoolteacher, who belts him more than
any other child in the class as a sign that he has no favourites:

> I was so full of icy hatred that I probably forgot I had hands. Yet when he
> stopped [the belting] I did not lower them, I glared at him with a rigid grin
> I can feel on my face at this very moment, and I stepped toward him and
> raised my hands till they almost touched his chin and I whispered, "Again!"
> He went soft. He smiled and nodded, slipping the Lochgelly over his shoulder
> under the jacket. He said gently, "Go to your seat son. There's a spark of
> manhood in you."
> And I saw the whole horrible pattern of Mad Hislop's soul. He was not
> essentially cruel, just insane. He really believed that teaching small people to
> take torture from big people, and crushing their natural reaction to it, was a
> way of improving them. If he was my father (which I doubt) he must have
> felt belting me was a sort of loveletter to my mother: "You have borne me
> a child, I am making a man of it" (85).

Young Jock may be 'son' to Hislop but dubious parentage reduces him to
an 'it' ('I am making a man of it') which will be shaped only by a denial
of feeling, a denial of relation. Joy's equivalent situation is the ambiguity
of her relation to her sister, who is old enough to be her mother:

> I've been afraid of Myra ever since I remember. She and my mother/her
> mother were pregnant at the same time. She could have been my mother.
> I think about that if I feel hard done by, making myself grateful for small
> mercies. Myra's baby died. I didn't. Maybe that was why she hit me so much.
> I don't know. Hands like shovels. Myra left marks. None of them show. (59)

Myra, the apparent sister, is the real mother whose physical violence leaves
the marks that erase the marks of both their identities, confronting each
other over the unspeakable abyss of their unacknowledged relation:

> Will I not come again?
> My stomach started looping.
> Do you want me to come again? Do you think –
> but she didn't finish the sentence, just let it hang there broken at the end
> with nothing to come after to fill the void
> . . . she wiped her nose again and the rims of her eyes went shiny.
> I'm your sister.

> I looked at the pavement in case she started crying. The last time I saw
> Myra cry was the time my mother wouldn't let her go out with an Italian
> waiter . . . she hit my mother and went out anyway. I was five. I didn't know
> what to say then either.
> Sister.
> She wasn't going to let it go. (71)

Myra, the real mother, cannot be accepted because she is trapped in a social
displacement which requires her to act under the sign of 'sister': the sign
'sister', accepted by all the conventions of the society of which they are a
part, is a displacement of the sign 'mother' which keeps them apart. The
sister-identity and the mother-identity displace each other in continuous
loop around the void they cannot fill: the absent mother-tongue of the oral
is supplanted in the novel by the patriarchal discourses of typography which
encase the character in a series of forms which negate her real identity,
until that identity, through the power of the author, begins to disrupt the
typographic forms of the novel and therefore allow her real self to begin
to speak again.

Dubious parentages and blood relations are the modern equivalent of the
'doubleness' which characterised much Scottish fiction in the nineteenth century,[13] except that instead of a 'doubled' identity what we get are characters
whose ambiguous position between alternative genealogies and alternative
cultures is experienced as displacement, absence, void. In this they match
precisely the ways in which, from the 1930s till the 1980s, Scottish culture
was regularly characterised as an emptiness, a vacuum – whether in terms
of the 'Nothing' in which Edwin Muir believed Walter Scott to have lived
or the 'void' which Tom Nairn's The Break-up of Britain presented as
Scotland's modern culture (119). The ambiguity of a characters' genealogy

produces an absence of the self that mirrors the absent narrative of the ambiguous nation. Jennifer in A. L. Kennedy's *So I am Glad* (1995)[14] records that 'I can dig down as deep as there is to dig inside me and there truly is nothing there, not a squeak. For no good reason, no reason at all, I am empty' (7); the narrating voice of Frank Kuppner's *A Concussed History of Scotland* (1990)[15] notes 'I have always had the keen suspicion throughout my life that I was the hidden person sleeping on the other side of a locked door' (124); being scanned for possible pregnancy, Joy, in *The Trick is to Keep Breathing*, sees her own insides – 'This green cave was me' – on the screen:

> Much as I thought. Nothing there at all. You can see for yourself. Look. You can see for yourself.
> I looked. I was still there. A black hole among the green stars. I had nothing inside me. The doctor smiled directly at me for the first time.
> Nothing for either of us to worry about then. Nothing at all.
>
> (absent page number, 146)

That 'black hole', that 'nothing at all' is the image not only of a woman negated by a patriarchal society but of a society aware of itself only as an absence, a society living, in the 1980s, in the aftermath of its failure to be reborn. The conflict between the typographic medium and the life which it seeks to record is the dramatisation of a society no longer capable of articulating itself. At the same time, however, it is the demonstration of the author's refusal to submit to the imposed conditions of external authority: these novels transform 'stone' to 'joy' in their extravagant play with typography. The characters survive the emptiness, the black hole, and the novel celebrates their survival by revealing the author's playful control over the medium which has been the culture's domination and self-repression – typography transformed from jailor to the muse of a culture recovering its authentic voices – regaining control over its typographic representation just as much as over its democratic representation.

CHAPTER 5

DOUBTFUL IMAGININGS

'. . . standing in the temple of the Lord, he made a covenant that all the people from the great to the small should walk after the Lord, should observe His law, statutes and testimonies with all their heart and all their soul, and that they should ratify and confirm whatsoever was written in the book of God'.[1] John Knox's 'Appellation' announces the priority of one book over all others, 'whatsoever was written in the book of God'. The consequence is Knox's insistent injunction against 'idolatry': 'He further commanded Hilkiah the high priest and the priests of the inferior order that they should carry forth of the temple of the Lord all the vessels that were made to Baal, which he burnt and did carry their powder to Bethel. He did further destroy all the monuments of idolatry, yea, even those that had remained from the days of Solomon. He did burn them, stamp them to powder . . .'[2] The iconoclasm of the Scottish Reformation, with its destruction of all the 'graven images' by which the people had been diverted from their true covenant with the Word, inscribes into Scottish culture a conception that had always played a powerful role in Judaic tradition, that of the imagination as fundamentally evil.

The Biblical injunction against 'graven images' was not simply a rejection of false gods in favour of the one true God: those 'graven images' were the expressions of a human imagination that sought to displace God's original act of creation. By replicating in forms derived from the human imagination the originals of the divine imagination, they enacted humanity's desire to supplant God's creation with its own and so to displace the authority of the one Word with a multiplicity of competing meanings. In each act of the imagination is a repetition of Satan's original rebellion against the Almighty. As Solomon Schechter has argued, in the Judaic tradition all sin can be traced back to this corrupted and rebellious version of the imagination: 'Sin being generally conceived as rebellion against the majesty of God, we inquire after the source or instigator of this rebellion. In rabbinical literature this influence is termed the *yetser hara*. This is usually translated as "evil imagination".'[3] Richard Kearney describes this 'evil imagination' as one which 'epitomizes the error of history as a monologue of man with himself', while an alternative form of the imagination – the *yetser harov* – 'opens up history to an I-Thou dialogue between man and his creator'.[4]

In Knox's terms, however, the dialogue between man and his creator can only take place in and through 'whatever was written in the book of God', not in and through the constructions of the human imagination. Imagination, when not engaged with the Word of God, acts at the behest of the 'yetser hara', and is necessarily in league with the devil. For generations of Scottish writers the created word has been caught in an inevitable conflict with the Word of creation, and this profound awareness of the necessary evil of the work of art is one of the determining elements of the tradition of the Scottish novel: it is not a matter of whether the writer belongs or does not belong to a Calvinist tradition, but to the fact that the Calvinist distrust of the imagination, building on a powerful interpretive tradition in Judaeo-Christian theology, has become part of the very fabric of the traditions of Scottish writing and Scottish thought.[5]

The Judaeo-Calvinist conception of an evil imagination is the absolute antithesis of those Romantic notions of a redemptive imagination which allows the time-bound creature of the mechanical world entry into a higher and timeless spirituality, notions which have profoundly shaped the understanding of the significance of the literary imagination in the English-speaking world. In a Scottish context, however, that redemptive imagination has always been deeply distrusted as one of the snares by which by humanity is lured from the truth of the Word: rather than providing access to that higher form of the truth that Coleridge envisaged as an 'echo of the divine "I am"',[6] the products of the imagination are revealed as simply another graven image, an idolatrous displacement of God's creation. Far from being God's representative on earth, as the Romantics optimistically prophesied, the artist, in this iconoclastic tradition, is the diabolic antagonist of the Truth, denier and negator of the divine Word through the multiplication of human words. Novelists must therefore write in the consciousness of their own evil, must doubt the very products of the imagination by which they create and must turn back from within the novel to gesture to its own essential falshood.

It is this sense of a powerful and antagonistic tradition that Sandy Stranger uncovers in Muriel Spark's *The Prime of Miss Jean Brodie*.[7] Sandy, despite having no direct contact with Calvinism, discovers that it seeps into her life from the very environment:

Fully to savour her position, Sandy would go and stand outside St Giles Cathedral or the Tolbooth, and contemplate these emblems of a dark and terrible salvation which made the fires of the damned seem very merry to the imagination by contrast, and much preferable. Nobody in her life, at home or at school, had ever spoken of Calvinism except as a joke that had once been taken seriously . . . In its outward forms her fifteen years might have been spent in any suburb of any city in the British Isles; her school, with its alien house system, might have been in Ealing. All she was conscious of now was that some quality of life peculiar to Edinburgh and no where else had been going on unbeknown to her all the time, and however undesirable it might be, she felt deprived of it; however undesirable, she desired to know what it was, and to cease to be protected from it by enlightened people.

> In fact, it was the religion of Calvin of which Sandy felt deprived, or rather
> a specified recognition of it. She desired this birthright; something definite to
> reject. It pervaded the place in proportion as it was unacknowledged. (108)

Sandy's awareness of the unacknowledged pervasiveness of the calvinist ethos
is the outcome of her sustained battle with the 'graven images' that are the
product of Jean Brodie's diabolic imagination. For Miss Brodie, life is to
be shaped by the imposition of her own imagination on everything around
her: the girls in her charge are not individuals to be educated into individuality, or responsibility, but puppets who have to perform the preordained
roles assigned to them by their teacher's master narrative of their existence.
Each is famous for some quality Miss Brodie assigns to them, either as
an expression of her own identity or as compensation for the things she
denies herself. When the girls are painted by Miss Brodie's lover, Teddy
Lloyd, they all turn into versions of their teacher: the challenger of God's
creativity turns the artist, her lover, from an originator of images – 'I am
his Muse' (120) – into a replicator of her own image – a displacement both
of God and of the world He had created:

> Teddy Lloyd's passion for Jean Brodie was greatly in evidence in all the
> portraits he did of the various members of the Brodie set. He did them in a
> group one summer term, wearing their panama hats each in a different way,
> each hat adorning, in a magical transfiguration, a different Jean Brodie under
> the forms of Rose, Sandy, Jenny, Mary, Monica and Eunice. (111)

Teddy Lloyd's paintings of the girls pay homage to the real God of their
universe, the Miss Brodie who has shaped and controlled their identities
so that they are (re)incarnations of herself rather than human beings made
in the image of God. Her imagination has displaced the God of creation,
and the artist's imagination mimics her creation rather than His: it is this
diabolic transfiguration which Sandy finds herself compelled to challenge.

Through Sandy, Muriel Spark dramatises the fact that the imagination
by which she creates her own novels must oppose itself and negate itself
in favour of a higher truth. Just as Miss Brodie's temperament was 'suited
only to the Roman Catholic Church' because 'it could have embraced, even
while it disciplined, her soaring and diving spirit' (85), so Sandy incarcerates
herself in a nunnery, gripping the bars of her cell, in order to contain and
restrain the fact that she, too, is the possessor of an imaginative power whose
evil needs to be acknowledged. From Jean Brodie Sandy has learned the
power described in the title of the book that has made her famous – 'The
Transfiguration of the Commonplace'. It is a power which, for Sandy as
for *her* creator, Muriel Spark, must operate in continual doubt of itself, a
doubt of which Jean Brodie is incapable: 'She was not in any doubt, she
let everyone know she was in no doubt, that God was on her side whatever
her course' (85).

In Jean Brodie Spark has constructed a character who seeks an equivalent status to that of her author, plotting the lives of the human beings around her as though they were simply parts of a fictional world of her own making; in so doing Spark dramatises the potential evil of her own authority as inventor of an imagined alternative to God's creation and dramatises the need for that author–ity to negate itself in favour of the higher reality of God's authorship of both Word and World. In *The Prime of Miss Jean Brodie*, the author's anxiety about the evil of creating an alternative universe to God's is transferred to Jean Brodie who, in acting out the bad faith of the author by turning the lives around her into fictions, takes on the burden of her author's guilt and dies for her sins. Within the plot of the novel, the imagination of Jean Brodie has to be negated by the imagination of Sandy Stranger – 'Truth is stranger than fiction' (124) – in a dialectic which replicates the author's awareness that her own creations must always gesture from within the world of her fiction to reveal their corrupted origins. Imagination must counteract its own creations, just as Sandy must resist Miss Brodie's self-dramatising and self-justifying fictions with alternative fictions of her own:

> Miss Brodie was reciting poetry to the class at quarter to four . . . Rose Stanley was pulling threads from the girdle of her gym tunic. Jenny was enthralled by the poem, her lips were parted, she was never bored. Sandy was never bored, but she had to lead a double life of her own in order never to be bored.
>> Down she came and found a boat
>> Beneath a willow left afloat,
>> And round about the prow she wrote
>>> *The Lady of Shalott.*
> 'By what means did your Ladyship write these words?' Sandy inquired in her mind with her lips tight shut.
> 'There was a pot of white paint and a brush which happened to be standing on the grassy verge,' replied the Lady of Shalott graciously, 'It was left there no doubt by some heedless member of the Unemployed.' (21)

Sandy achieves salvation from the impositions of Miss Brodie's imagination by resorting to a generic alternative to Jean Brodie's imaginative identifications: Sandy's imagination juxtaposes against the historical escapism of Tennyson's poem a contemporary realism that shows how false are the artistic 'truths' which the teacher offers to her pupils; on the other hand, she uses her own imagination to escape the demands of the 'real' world – as in having to talk to Mary MacGregor, the dull-witted victim of the Brodie set – by engaging in conversation with the hero of a fiction: 'Sandy kept pacing ahead, fired on by Alan Breck whose ardour and thankfulness, as Sandy prepared to set off across the heather, had reached touching proportions' (29). Precisely because her own imagination is so like Miss Brodie's she is deeply aware of the evil it contains:

> Miss Brodie's old love story was newly embroidered, under the elm, with
> spurious threads: it appeared that while on leave from the war, her late fiancé
> had frequently taken her out sailing in a fishing boat and that they had spent
> some of their merriest times among the rocks and pebbles of a small seaport.
> 'Sometimes Hugh would sing, he had a rich tenor voice. At other times he
> fell silent and would set up his easel and paint. He was very talented in both
> arts, but I think the painter was the real Hugh.'
>   This was the first time the girls had heard of Hugh's artistic leanings. Sandy
> puzzled over this and took counsel with Jenny, and it came to them both that
> Miss Brodie was making her new love story fit the old. Thereafter the two
> girls listened with double ears, and the rest of the class with single. (71–2)

Through narrative, Jean Brodie's imagination seeps into the real, displacing
it, and as it does so she translates herself from being the victim of history
to a controller of it, from a woman maimed by a reality she cannot control
to a shaper of a reality which will match her own desires, from a character
in a larger plot over which she has no power to the author of the plot which
gives her power over the lives of others. Unable to project her imagination
within the strict boundaries of an artistic form, she adopts the pose of the
artist towards the real lives of her 'set' and transforms them from free and
independent human beings, responsible for their own destiny, into works
of art, symbolic aspects of her own personality and fulfilments of her own
sublimated desires. Jean Brodie's relationship with her 'set' replicates the
relationship of a Calvinist God to humanity and in so doing reveals its
fundamental falsehood: 'She thinks she is Providence, thought Sandy, she
thinks she is the God of Calvin, she sees the beginning and the end' (120).
Because she accepts the precepts of a Calvinist God only to displace Him
with her own self-justifying equivalent, Jean Brodie is the incarnation not
of the Son who comes to share human suffering and so redeem humanity
from original sin, but of the demonic imagination which seeks to displace
God's creativity and redeem itself by recreating the world in its own (graven)
image. For Jean Brodie, the commonplace life of ordinary humanity has
been transfigured into the predetermined plot of a novel of which she is
the sole author and in which she is the sole authority: all authors, insofar
as they do not acknowledge the dubiety of their fictions within the very
forms of their art, are imaged in Jean Brodie – diabolic subverters of the
Word.

   Jean Brodie's lack of doubt is the antithesis of her own author's deeply
doubtful relationship to the imagination. Brodie's calvinist self-election parodies the author's awareness of how the novel, by its very form, replicates
the world as envisaged by Calvin, since it presents reality not as an open
future in which human beings have choices to make but as a fixed plot over
which the author broods like 'the God of Calvin', able to see 'the beginning
and the end'. Calvinism presents the universe as though it were a novel
already written by God: if the novel truly depicts reality, then God can

only be the God of Calvin, imaged in the author who plays with the lives of the characters, giving them an illusion of freedom they do not, in fact, possess. If God is not the God of Calvin then the structure of the novel, with its implication of a predestined conclusion, must always be necessarily false to the nature of reality. The Calvinist context forces the author to question the ontological assumptions of her own creation, since the novel translates free human beings from their 'real' environment into a fictional world in which they become the puppets of an author-God: if the novel is an accurate depiction of reality, Calvinism is true, since the author stands to the created universe as does the God of Calvin; if Calvinism is false, then the novelist's relationship to the created universe of the novel is one which is fundamentally evil, a denial of the very ontological bases on which human life is lived, making it impossible for the novel ever accurately to describe the nature of the human condition. In Jean Brodie Muriel Spark dramatises the fact that those who see life as though it were a novel live as if 'elected . . . to grace' (109); their imaginations are powerful precisely to the extent that they seek to identify themselves with the power of the author rather than the limitations of a mere character. In so doing they replicate at the level of the narrative the imagination by which the novelist displaces the reality of God on her own ontological level. The novel thus enacts in its plot the formal dilemma of its author: the destruction of Jean Brodie, the incarceration of Sandy Stranger, represent the negation and containment of the very imagination from which the novel itself is produced.

The paradox which *The Prime of Miss Jean Brodie* exploits is that Spark's anti-Calvinist novel can only come into existence by acknowledging its own formal complicity with the ontological assumptions of the Calvinist universe. It is from this inner contradiction, in which the form of the novel replicates the very Calvinist universe that the author seeks to challenge, that many of the disruptive narrative strategies of the Scottish novel are derived – the unreliable narrators who stand in place of the author, the multiple narrators who compete for control of the text, the characters who replicate the author's control over the text, the doubles who challenge each other as to which represents the good and which the evil imagination. Whether or not modern Scottish writers inhabit a consciously Calvinist environment, these traditions shape their conception of the imagination as diabolic antagonist, rather than spiritual representative, of the truths of the Word. The imagination can assert itself only in intense doubt about its relationship with the reality that it seeks to re-present, so that there can be no formal stability between the world of representation and the world represented. The Word, as revealed in God's book of the world, must necessarily be betrayed by the word that images the world in the author's book. The imagination does not produce fictions which nonetheless convey the truth: its fictions are lies which must be undermined from within the text itself if the true Word is to be allowed to speak, however indirectly, through it.

The pervasiveness of this metaphysical conception of the imagination in modern Scottish writing can be seen in the work of two very different novelists who approach the issue from absolutely opposite directions. In 1979 Allan Massie produced a critical book on the work of Muriel Spark:[8] in its opening chapter he pointed to two different traditions of the novel which shaped the nature of contemporary writing in Britain: on the one hand is 'naturalism' whose 'ambition seems to be to hold up a mirror to nature' and 'such novelists may indeed be said to be at the mercy of their material' (8); on the other,

> we find novelists like Waugh, Firbank, Henry Green and Ivy Compton-Burnett, whose novels seem first of all to be conceived as objects. We are aware of the author standing at an angle to his work. Their novels convince not by challenging comparison with "real life" but by offering us something which is as clearly a part of real life as a piece of furniture; and may be said to stand in the same relation to it. Something has been created to enhance and quicken our sense of being. (8–9)

It is to the latter class that Massie assigns Spark, but almost as if uncertain of his first mode of defining her work he then quotes Robert Louis Stevenson: 'The novel, which is a work of art, exists not by its resemblances to life, which are forced and material, as a shoe must still consist of leather, but by its immeasurable difference from life, which is designed and significant and is both the method and meaning of the work' (10). Spark inhabits the world of English fiction only on terms articulated from within Scottish writing.

Massie, of course, writes novels which are, by and large, 'historical' novels, and therefore must exist in some sense by their 'resemblances' to life, but his historical novels are constantly hedged around with forms of narration which are designed to insist on the doubtful nature of all such efforts at re-presenting reality. Thus in *The Ragged Lion*, the editor, a very Massie-like character who happens to be called 'Allan Massie', relates how, living in Naples, he encountered a Contessa whose 'enthusiasm' for Walter Scott had been 'fired' by a Miss MacIvor from Inverness, who had been her governess. Miss MacIvor 'believed herself to be descended from Fergus MacIvor, the highland chieftain in *Waverley* itself. It may seem odd to claim descent from a fictional character, but, as Graham Greene has since shown in *Monsignor Quixote* Miss MacIvor's case was not unique' (x). The character's 'descent' from fiction into 'reality' (though, of course, only in the language of a fiction which is claiming to be real) reverses the direction of Massie's own work, which turns the 'reality' of Scott's life, as represented at least in the words of Scott in his *Journal* and of his biographer Lockhart, into fiction. The intercourse between reality and fiction that allows each to engender elements of the other is also a game which Muriel Spark has played on several occasions — in *The Hothouse by the East River*, for instance, in which real children are born to 'imagined' characters; and in *The Takeover*,[9] in which Hubert Mallindaine asserts his descent to be from the goddess Diana, a descent which is, in fact, from the writings of J. G. Frazer: 'Hubert descended, then, from the Emperor, the goddess, and from her woodland priest; in reality this was nothing more than his synthesis of a persistent, yet far more vague, little story fostered by a couple of dotty aunts enamoured of the author-image of Sir James Frazer and misled by one of those quack genealogists who flourished in late Victorian times' (42). Hubert, the fictional character in Spark's novel, is fictionally descended from a goddess whose reality is attested for by the supposedly realistic account of her in Frazer's work – which we know, of course, not only to be the account of a myth but a mythic account. Hubert becomes thus not only a composite of reality and fiction within the fiction, he becomes a mirror image of the reader who, possessed by the 'suspension of disbelief' required by fiction, treats fictional characters as though they were real (rather than 'true'); the reader, like Hubert, is 'secure in this lineage in which he could truly be said to have come to believe', except that the reader believes in the lineage provided by Spark – the childhood in London, the dotty aunts – and accepts that as 'true', thus revealing that, like Hubert, 'his capacity for belief was in any case not much' (69). For Spark, anyone who suspends disbelief in fiction shows themselves incapable of understanding the real nature of belief. Fictions within the fiction are undone in a movement which undermines the status of the fiction itself as a narrative-to-be-believed while we are reading it.

In a similar game of the contrasts between the fictional-within-the-real and the real-within-the-fictional, Massie's 'editor' in *The Ragged Lion* provides a fake genealogy for the characters in his supposedly real account of the origin of the text (Miss MacIvor) in order, by comparison, to underline the historical validity of his invented self-portrait by Walter Scott, based securely as it undoubtedly is on 'real' historical documents: because of its similarity to Scott's own writings and to those 'originals' from which we know Scott's life, Massie admits that it 'could therefore be a fabrication made chiefly from these sources' (xiv). This possibility is entertained, however, only to be dismissed on the basis that 'no attempt appears to have been made to profit from it' – ignoring precisely the fact that Massie himself is 'profiting' from this creation. This truly fake opening to the novel is matched by a conclusion in which Scott's son recounts how he has come into possession of the manuscript and is going to deliver it to Lockhart for the biographer's use in writing his life of Scott. Massie's text which draws on Lockhart's thus claims to be the very basis from which Lockhart's derives.

The intertwining of truth of fiction and the fictionality of truth is also emphasised in a novel like *A Question of Loyalties*, in which the narrator, son of the protagonist, comments on the documentary evidence that he is providing about his father's life: 'We are trapped here, it seems to me, in the lie of biography. Biography pretends to tell the truth about people's lives, but it can deal only with what is revealed, and this is not the most truthful element. Autobiographical revelation is always itself an artistic construction, and therefore unreliable.' This 'doubt' about the revelation of biography extends even to the documents on which it is based – letters, for instance, because from these 'we, the readers, receive the least characteristic of utterances' (282). The narrator then says, 'What I would really like to know is what Lucien and Anne said when they were alone, on the terrace of their apartment' (282–3), a statement which, of course, is undermined by the fact that it is the very business of novels to present what its characters say when they are alone, and that portions of the novel of which he is part do precisely that.

Massie's fiction, far from being the 'traditionalist' writing that it is often taken to be, plays with notions of history just as forcefully as Spark's does with notions of reality: the imagining of the past is riddled with doubt about the very sources – the documentary sources in history and the creative sources of the imagination – by which the past is represented. In *The Ragged Lion*, Scott is made to consider the relations of his own writing to the events of the Napoleonic war and its aftermath:

> Of his genius, his transcendent qualities, I have no doubt; but what is one to make of genius which expresses itself in utter indifference to the sufferings it imposes on mankind? Yet, if I encountered a Napoleon, two hundred years back in time, would I not have been so dazzled by the glamour of his achievements . . . as to be blind to the cost? Is there, I wonder now, any difference between what the Emperor demanded of the French and what Prince Charles Edward called for from his Highlanders; and did not the Prince bring ruin on them as Napoleon did on all Europe?
>
> And have I been guilty by means of my writings, of encouraging men to see the glory of war, and to forget its price? (234)

The artistic imagination is inevitably drawn to identify with those whose dominance of history is equivalent to its own dominance over the world of its fictions.

The individual creative imagination is a power deeply attracted to the powerful individual – at the cost of the rest of humanity. This is precisely what Muriel Spark explores in *The Prime of Miss Jean Brodie*: Jean Brodie's imagination is insistently drawn to the politics of power that are the equivalent of her own desire to impose her imagination on reality: 'I have spent most of my summer holidays in Italy', she tells her class, and has brought back photographs of 'a larger formation of Mussolini's fascisti' who 'are doing splendid things' (44). She takes her model of education from Il Duce and makes herself into the fascist leader of her own little troupe: 'Education means a leading out, from *e*, out and *duco*, I lead' (45). Thus it 'occurred to Sandy, there at the end of the Middle Meadow Walk, that the Brodie set was Miss Brodie's fascisti, not to the naked eye, marching along, but all knit together for her need' (31). In Jean Brodie Muriel Spark presents the temptation of the imagination to identify itself with power at the expense of humanity, and it is that imagination which Sandy has to betray:

> Monica came again. 'Before she died,' she said, 'Miss Brodie thought it was you who had betrayed her.'
> 'It's only possible to betray where loyalty is due,' said Sandy.
> 'Well, wasn't it due to Miss Brodie?'
> 'Only up to a point,' said Sandy.

The artist's loyalty to the imagination, too, can only be up to a point – up to the point where the imagination becomes the instrument of repression. In Spark's novels, as in Massie's, the power of the imagination is no more to be trusted than is the power of those towards whom it is so insistently drawn.

In Iain Crichton Smith's novels, on the other hand, we are presented with a reversal of the artist's or character's imposition of patterns on reality, but one generated by the same Calvinist concerns. In Crichton Smith's fiction the central characters are always on the edge of a crisis where meaning will fail, and they will be forced to descend into a world of absolute contingency, a world where all pattern disappears and leaves only the endless randomness of an inconceivable universe. Calvinism has induced in them a deep need for a fundamental and absolute pattern to life which, when removed, leaves only an endless and accidental world in which they can see no significance. In *An End to Autumn*,[10] the protagonist Tom attempts to explain the poetry of T. S. Eliot to his class by a comparison with the work of Picasso:

> 'Eliot', he heard himself saying, 'can be compared with Picasso for he uses the same techniques. In the same way as in a Picasso painting we can see apparently unrelated images, such as heads of horses, candles, faces with three eyes, so we can find in Eliot as well images which apparently seem set down at random and without order.' But what did they know about Picasso and in order to tell them about Picasso he would have to . . . There was no end to the complexity and interrelatedness of the world – everything in the world must be talked of in terms of everything else. (81)

The inner necessity of art consists of the apparently random brought into an order; to try to explain it leads Tom into a world which is endless in its complexity and for which no pattern can be discovered. For Crichton Smith, the necessary world is always the world of the elite: once it was the elite of the Calvinist elect, now it is the elite of the artists and intellectuals – people who create or discover patterns in reality which are unavailable to the world of the ordinary and the accidental which most people inhabit. So Tom, mouthing about Eliot and Picasso, watches 'what was going on outside the window, [and] saw a big yellow and blue machine with a long neck like that of a dinosaur . . .' This cubist machine is inhabited by a young man,

> And it suddenly occurred to Tom to ask himself what the young man was thinking of, what his thoughts were at that particular moment. With great intensity he tried to put his own mind into that of the young man, and was repulsed again and again by a blinding darkness . . . And it came to him with utter certainty, as he watched the young man and the other one who was holding on to a bouncing pneumatic drill, that he didn't have any idea at all what the lad was thinking of, that he was as distant from the world of the young man as he was from the world of the pupils he was teaching. (81)

Those who know the 'complexity and interrelatedness of the world' can connect with nothing in it; they are divorced from a reality which is subject to the accidental and the contingent by their commitment to the necessity of a higher order of meaning. This is precisely the crisis that afflicts Ralph, protagonist of *In the Middle of the Wood*:[11]

> He had never understood 'ordinary' people. For instance they were very conscious of precedence: no one was more reactionary than an 'ordinary' person. Once on a train travelling to Edinburgh he had met a drunk who said to him, 'I don't like you. You think I'm not good enough for you. But I'll tell you something, I'm far better than you.' The drunk had thrust his face at him like a damp torch and he had finally retreated to another compartment. Ordinary people were like another race: they read the *Sun* and the *Star*. (137)

Sun and *Star* point to traditional symbolic necessities which have become degraded into the contingencies of a throwaway society. The drunk who sozzles in the contingent is mirror-image to the elite artist who torches reality to discover order and necessity.

The protagonists of Crichton Smith's novels are all people who have to be redeemed from the necessary – whether the necessity of calvinism or of art – in order to come into an acceptance of the ordinary; they have to be redeemed by coming into a humble acceptance of the meagre but adequate world of the real. In *The Search*,[12] Trevor, a writer who is visiting Australia, goes in search of his long-lost brother. Australia, the desert world 'down under', is the very opposite of the desert of T. S. Eliot's *The Waste Land*, for instead of a world of underlying symbolic meanings, this desert is a place of random signs:

> On both sides of him was the monotonous, unforgiving landscape which hadn't tasted rain for months . . . His failure irritated him as if it was of the deepest significance. If he didn't have the integrity to search for his own brother what did his lecturing signify. CALL IN AT JANET'S said a sign over a ship. I AM SAILING, said the voice on the cassette. (83)

Whereas, for Eliot, the desert is the symbolic unifier of the disparate, revealing the true significance of the apparently random surfaces of life, this desert is the location of the accidental, in which random signs collide. Trevor has imagined his brother's condition to be that of a desperate alcoholic, a condition for which he feels responsible – since he took his brother's girl-friend, now his wife – and because of which he believes he can redeem his own guilt by now becoming his brother's saviour. This imagined pattern, however, is undone by reality, for when he discovers his brother, what he discovers is the person he always was – Norman, Norm, Normal (173) – an ordinary man who bears no grudges and who has no deep significance to offer to Trevor: 'And Trevor felt such piercing sorrow because of it . . . He didn't understand what was wrong with him' (187). What is wrong with him is the desire for significance, the desire for a profound order to reality, a pattern which is the image of the power of the imagination to impose itself on and to dominate reality. What he has to learn to live with is his real brother, the real world of the Norm.

Crichton Smith's characters are always caught up in plots, false plots or perceived but non-existent plots, whose purpose is to mimic and to undo the real plot in which they are trapped – the plot that their author has con-structed for them. Ralph, in *The Middle of the Wood*, comes in his madness to believe that everything that is happening to him is a plot constructed by his wife to have him incarcerated: 'They were all in the plot . . . Even the questions had been thought out in advance. There was a beautiful symme-try to the whole business' (114). Ralph believes himself to be trapped in a world of absolute necessity, a necessity which – like the God of Calvin or the author of a novel – can account for every accident. His determination to trace every event to this underlying necessity breaks down on something that seems to him absolutely accidental and which is to the reader of the novel also absolutely accidental – a Mexican hat adorning the lamp in his room. 'He wasn't sure it wasn't a nurse's prank. There were too many wrong things, too many coincidences. But what was the inner meaning of leaving a Mexican hat? He was sure it must have some deep inner significance. An allegory, symbolism. But he couldn't work it out' (130). Like the author and reader he is, Ralph must have everything become significant, be part of the plot; Crichton Smith's novel reverses that demand and insists that it must incorporate the absolutely accidental, for it is only by admission of the accidental that we can accept the limited 'truths' within which we ordinarily live rather than the profound necessities which the imagination craves.

Crichton Smith's novels, like Muriel Spark's, are negations of the neces-sity of emplotment and significance demanded by the novel form because it mirrors the deep desire, bred from Calvinism, for a world of absolute certainty, a world which cannot be betrayed since neither will-power nor accident can have any effect on it. Those who are committed to the world of the imagination have to be redeemed by discovering the necessity of accident, by discovering that which is rejected by the very medium of which they are a part. The author of fiction can only avoid the temptation to become the mouthpiece of a powerful imagination that will transfer itself into the world as imagination's collusion with power if s/he constructs a novel which undermines its own formal properties: one which, by the power of imagination, rebuts and refutes the imagination's desire for power:

> 'Then all is well,' said Miss Brodie. 'And after all, Sandy,' she said, 'you are destined to be the great lover, although I would not have thought it. Truth is stranger than fiction. (124)

No truth can break upon the sense of destiny that Jean Brodie harbours, just as no freedom can intrude upon the destined patterns of the novel in which she participates: the truth of a world of freedom and contingency is a stranger to fiction, and one that fiction makes strange in reality.

II

In Archie Hind's *The Dear Green Place*,[13] the protagonist, struggling working-class writer Mat Craig, challenges the value of modern art because of its similarity to the world of nature: 'All this bizarre juxtaposition and construction is like an analogue of nature, for accidents occur in the natural world and have nothing to do with the world of art' (137). The novel itself begins by the assertion that, 'In every city you find these neighbourhoods. They are defined by accident' (11), and Mat, inhabitant of Glasgow – 'A Calvinist, Protestant city' where even Catholic and Jewish immigrants 'in the end became Calvinist', a city of 'acquired art, its literature dumb or in exile' (65) – is haunted by another world, one that he believes to be more appropriate to the form of the novel that he is incapable of writing about the modern, the accidental city:

> Mat remembered a description of Rome which he had read somewhere. It had been described as a kind of half buried history where everything, the houses, streets, monuments, churches were a huge physical agglomeration of the debris of history. Yet all of Rome could not have fascinated Mat half so much as the acts of the solid Scottish burghers which were embodied in this crumbling industrial landscape . . . He imagined these old burghers of the eighteenth century with their great heavy walking sticks, their breeches and embroidered coats, their horn snuff boxes, their freemasonry, their mixture of canniness and daring . . . Mat felt a tremendous nostalgia for these people and their way of life. He loved the heavy solidity of the old burghers; their substantial broad fronts spread with waistcoat and fob, their great mansions, their big leather boots, their conservative art, their good plain substantial mundane safety. (27)

The world of Mat's nostalgia is the world for which the novel was originally made, a world in which the contingency of objects is turned into the necessary order of art and the order of art reflects the profoundly ordered nature of society. Setting up home himself,

> What struck Mat about all this, what struck his imagination in a kind of perverse way, was the provisional nature of all the various accoutrements which they had to buy. When Mat had written of his Burghers . . . he had been obsessed by the role which the ordinary household artefact or working tool has to play in the life of men. Giving men a place in which they could live their lives and shutting out what was alien and inhospitable, or chilling, or brief. As if the warm fires, the workaday routine, the traditional family effects, the Bibles and Diaries, had something in them which fronted against what was contingent or provisional, created that order and definition in the material world which [his] little house lacked . . . (122)

For Mat the novel is precisely the medium through which the world of the ordinary can be *imagined* as safe from contingency and accident, and it needs, therefore, a setting in which such safety from contingency and accident seems the very nature of life. This, of course, makes the novel irremediably unsuited to the nature of working-class experience which, far from being built not on security, is threatened constantly by contingency and accident: challenging the real world of contingency becomes, for Mat, far more important than its false resolution into art: 'he would find in making a home with Helen a resolution to all those tensions which he had sought before in writings, and they would be resolved in actuality and not in the false and insubstantial way of art', since art, according to 'Calvinist beliefs', 'was an excess, an excrescence upon life, a luxuriant and diseased growth' (116). *The Dear Green Place* is a novel about the impossibility of a working-class writer in a Calvinist city writing a novel about the city he lives in: novel and environment are antithetic to one another and the only novel that can be written about it is the novel about the failure to write a novel: 'This is fish that never swam,/This is the bell that never rang' (229), it concludes, quoting a children's song – trapped in self-negation.

The metaphysical implications of the conflict between a calvinist theology and the ontological assumptions of the novel are thus compounded in Scotland by the centrality to the traditions of Scottish writing of working-class culture, the modern continuation of the folk culture upon which so much of Scottish literature is based. Many of the most significant Scottish writers have not only come from working-class backgrounds, but have sought, in their novels, to give expression to a specifically working-class consciousness, a consciousness which is seen as being in profound conflict with the nature of the novel form. It is a tension explored by William McIlvanney in his essay 'A Shield Against the Gorgon', from *Surviving the Shipwreck* (1991),[14] which describes the difficulties of trying to learn the lessons of his precursors in presenting working-class experience in the form of the novel. The achievement of a 'true' image of working-class culture, McIlvanney believes, is possible only by undermining the very cultural values for which the novel stands:

> *Sons and Lovers* is for me mainly a libel on the nature of working-class experience. It is the vision of a man in flight and that is inevitably a distorting perspective . . . Being, like so much that has been written about working-class life, a kind of gospel according to Judas, it is a testament of some value but of a limited value in trying to obtain a just sense of the nature of working-class experience, its richness and its dynamism . . . In trying to arrive at the vision of working-class experience I was hoping to reflect, therefore, I had to begin by knowing what I couldn't use, by discarding what would distort the image I felt to be true. It would not be the familiar story of a boy of abilities and sensitivity winning his way out of an underclass into a more enriching form of life, for this is to presuppose the comparative shallowness of the life he is leaving – an assumption with which, having experienced the old life left and the new life found, I have never been able to agree. There is a simple reason for the consistency with which this erroneous assumption has been maintained: it is that to judge working-class culture, once you have left it, by the standards of the established literary culture you have entered is to judge it by terms which were created to deny it. (225–6)

To write from within working-class culture about working-class culture in the form of the novel is to be trapped in a false gospel: the novel has to negate its own implicit values and its own history if it is to reach towards the truth of working-class experience.

The contradiction with which McIlvanney was struggling led to his abandoning the 'serious' novel for a significant portion of his career, and concentrating on the genre of the detective novel in the hope of connecting with those working-class readers whose communities he wanted to write about. The self-negating nature of this formal strategy is revealed in the allegory that concludes *Strange Loyalties*,[15] his final novel about the Glasgow detective, Jack Laidlaw:

> Four experts had an appointment with an ordinary man. They needed him to ratify their findings or anything they achieved would be meaningless. As they drove to meet him, they knocked down a man on the road. He was dying. If they tried to save him, they might miss their appointment. They decided that their appointment, which concerned all of us, was more important than the life of one man. They drove on to keep their appointment. They did not know that the man they were to meet was the man they had left to die. (360–1)

Like those questers after truth, the Scottish novel constantly finds itself in the situation of having destroyed the very object of its quest by the presuppositions of its form.

The fundamental bases of this conflict can be seen in Lewis Grassic Gibbon's *Grey Granite*, when Chris Guthrie's son Ewan, gradually developing his communist politics, goes into an art gallery in order to escape from a storm and there, in an act of modern iconoclasm, discovers both the falsities of art and, by their inversion, the truths to which he will commit himself:

> Plaster-cast stuff of the Greek antiques, Discobolus, blowsily mammalian Venus, Pallas Athene – rather a dirty lot they had been, the Greeks, though so many clean things survived. Why did they never immortalize in stone a scene from the Athenian justice-courts – a slave being ritually, unnecessarily tortured before he could legally act as a witness? Or a baby exposed to die in a jar? – hundreds every year in the streets of Athens, it went on all day, the little kids wailing and crying and crying as the hot sun rose and they scorched in the jars . . .
> There was a cast of Trajan, good head; Caesar – the Caesar they said wasn't Caesar. Why not a head of Spartacus? Or a plaque of the dripping line of crosses that manned the Appian Way with slaves – dripping and falling to bits through long months, they took days to die, torn by wild beasts . . . (72)

For Ewan, the forms of art are a necessary denial of the realities of the world – and not simply as a matter of ideology but as a matter of the very nature of art itself:

> You looked away and about the room, flat seascapes and landscapes, the deadest stuff, why did people make a fuss of pictures. Or music? You'd never seen anything in either. You went and sat down in the Italian room, on the bench in the middle, and stared at a picture, couldn't be bothered to find out the painter, a group of Renaissance people somewhere: soldiers, a cardinal, an angel or so, and a throng of keelies cheering like hell about nothing at all – in the background, as usual. Why not a more typical Italian scene! – a man being broken on the wheel with a club, mashed and smashed till his chest caved in, till his bones were a blood-clottered powdery mess?— (497)

The 'keelies' are necessarily 'in the background, as usual' because art has no place for the masses: by the very nature of its forms, art's focus is on the unique, the individual, the powerful and it can, therefore, have no identification with those whose very existence is defined by being part of a multitude. For Ewan, the truth can only be achieved by an escape from art, by seeing not the contents of the work of art but the frame which necessarily excludes the truths that art cannot confront. The novel is part of that history which will be made redundant when the workers finally overthrow the false civilisation in which they are trapped. To be on the side of the workers is to be against the art-form in which the narrative of *Grey Granite* is itself framed; to break the frame is to see what the novel exists to conceal, 'picture on picture limned in dried blood, never painted or hung in any gallery – pictures of the poor folk since history began, bedevilled and murdered, trodden underfoot, trodden down in the bree, a human slime, hungered, unfed, with their darkened brains, their silly revenges, their infantile hopes' (73).

The aim of the final novel of Gibbon's trilogy, often misunderstood, is to undo the very form of the novel and reveal it as a part of that bourgeois world whose false gods have to be overthrown in favour of the alternative truths of history, and the truths of an alternative history. Just as Ewan can feel himself to be the incarnation of a suffering humanity – 'as though 'twas yourself that history had tortured, trodden on, spat on, clubbed down in you, as though you were every scream and each wound, flesh of your flesh, blood of your blood . . .' (73) – and yet as an individual be irrelevant to the purposes of history – 'when their great black wave came flooding at last, up and up, swamping the high places with mud and blood. Most likely such leaders of the workers as themselves would be flung aside or trampled under, it didn't matter, nothing to them' (481) – so the art-form in which Gibbon expresses his commitment, having been shaped by the bourgeoisie whom the novel so savagely satirises, is one which will not journey into the new world of the masses. The novel is itself one of the many false discourses – gossip, newspaper stories, hollywood films – by which the narrative texture is fissured. Gibbon refuses to make its protagonist, Ewan, the sympathetic hero of a political novel: the novel, like Ewan, is a bourgeois trying to lead the masses towards a future to which it and he are necessarily false. For both character and novel, fundamental honesty lies in their recognition of how false they are as an embodiment of the ultimate truths they seek.

Distrust of the novelistic imagination, and of the principles it uses in structuring the world it represents, is the haunting undercurrent of much modern Scottish writing. It emerges at the conclusion, for instance, of George Friel's *Grace and Miss Partridge* (1969)[16] when the narrator, conversing with his mother about the story he has just narrated, acknowledges that there is something in the narrative that still puzzles him; his mother then reveals that she has not provided him with all of the diaries on which he has based his narrative, and has kept back the final one:

> "Give me that!" I cried snatching.
> My mother held it behind her back.
> "I gave you the other because Miss Partridge asked to me give you them when she died. She knew you were afraid of her. You often hurt her, you know, the way you behaved to her. She thought you might learn to understand her. But you've made such a dog's breakfast of what you got, you're getting no more. Not from me. When I'm dead you can have it."
> She planked it away in the drawer again . . . (187–8)

The story we have been told is suddenly revealed to rest upon false foundations, foundations which remain as absent to us as they are to the narrator, whose relationship to Grace – he has married her – has also been concealed throughout his narrative. The narrative has been framed by a context whose revelation not only alters the perspective in which we must interpret the events but undermines the very presuppositions on which the narrative has been constructed: everything we have read is now subject to a radical and unresolvable doubt about the imagination which has framed reality in order to control and order it for its own concealed and untrustworthy purposes. The same doubt riddles A. L. Kennedy's *So I Am Glad*, in which an unhappy and self-obsessed woman is visited by the ghost of the seventeenth-century French writer Cyrano de Bergerac in the all-too-physical form of a down-and-out drug addict called Martin, and the novel hovers between a strange but real relationship with the degraded underworld of modern Britain and the meeting place of a reader with a text from the past which comes alive in the mind, a ghost to haunt the present:

> He put his hands to his head. 'Jennifer, I wanted to write this, in preference to being present with these words, but I can no longer write, I cannot set a mark on paper. The language . . . I am defeated . . . and I have the concentration of an angry schoolboy. And I have every right to say so, I have been one before. Then I was learning and now I am unlearning. I am nothing but forgetting. Every night God fills my mind with with worlds to express and I can tell them to no one, record them for no one and be certain only that because they are mine, they are lost the moment they are born . . . But now I would ask you to let me write to you.'
> 'I'm sorry, I don't understand again.'
> 'Which is my fault. I am asking that you allow me to be not here. Simple, simple, only simple, nothing complex. Close your eyes and I shall close mine, not to be away from you but to be nearer. With your indulgence, I will make you my reader and now there can be nothing between us, nothing to check your mind from entering mine. What this is, these words, is for ever. This is our lives speaking directly, having set us aside. (176)

Suspended between the represented world in time and the textual world that is eternal, between a real world that is being recounted and a world that is being invented through language, the novel knows that it is playing with the *diabolus* of the imagination as an alternative to the eternity ruled by God; the work of art, the written, becomes a disruptive doubling of the world that God has created, an alternative eternity with a different gospel. Having visited Paris with Martin/Cyrano, both the real Paris of the 1980s and the textual Paris of the seventeenth century, Jennifer declares,

> To tell the truth and shame the devil, I wish I had all of the pictures here. I never did take any myself and without them I have almost nothing left. You know, you must know, that when I finish writing this there will be so little of him here with me I can't think what to do. For almost a year I've had my own doubled life within the present. (262)

Since we are confronted by a narrator who admits that 'Sometimes the best beginning is a lie' (280), the devil will be far from shamed by her inventions:

the devil of art claims to represent the world but instead consumes and
negates it, tells its truths – if they are truths – only through deceits, forcing
us to acknowledge not what we 'must know' but precisely how little we
know. Like Friel's narrator, Kennedy's protagonist confesses her falsehoods
at the novel's conclusion leaving the narrative founded on that deception,
a deception which, embodied as it is in the permanence of the text, can
never be undone. The authorial confession can never be made real, since
the acknowledgement of lying is itself a fiction founded on the original lie;
equally, the novel which seeks to re-present the world invents an alternative
creation, no matter how hard it tries to replicate the real, and that alternative
creation is invested with a purpose that necessarily, and diabolically, wrests
the represented world from its original meaning.

III

For religious, metaphysical and class reasons, therefore, Scottish fiction
has been deeply resistant to those versions of the imagination that accompanied romantic conceptions of art and assigned to it a role equivalent to,
or indeed alternative to, religious faith or scientific rationality, and deeply
resistant also to the ideology of the artist as the ultimate revealer of truths.
The writer, by the very nature of his or her art, needs to be rescued from
the deceits of the imagination, and the falsehoods of the word, in order
to recover the truths of the ordinary world, truths known and understood
by those ordinary folk whose experience is resistant to incorporation into
the very nature of art. The drive of art towards the extraordinary and the
powerful has to be countermanded by a commitment to the ordinary and
the powerless.

There is a moment towards the end of Nan Shepherd's *The Weatherhouse*
(1930), when Lindsay and her Aunt Theresa converse about the past and
about Louie Morgan's dog:

'. . . She had a dog – Demon wasn't it? Oh, I remember how he could run.
Through the wood. I can see him still.'
'Nonesense!' rapped Miss Theresa. 'Louie never had a dog.'
'But I remember. I can see him. A whippet he was.'
'Nonsense! She hadn't a dog. She wanted one – one of the Knapperley whip-
pets, Miss Barbara's dogs. But old Mrs Morgan wouldn't have a dog about
the place. Louie kicked up a waup over not getting it, I can tell you. And
after a while she used to pretend she had it – made on to be stroking it and
all. A palavering craitur.'
Lindsay looked doubtfully.
'Did she? I know she pretended about a lot of things. But Demon – ? He seems
so real when I look back. Did she only make me think I saw him? He used to go
our walks with us. We called to him – Demon, Demon – loud out, I know that.'

She pondered. The dog, bounding among the pines, had in her memory the compelling insistence of imaginative art. He was a symbol of swiftness, the divine joy of motion. But Lindsay preferred reality to symbol.

'Queer, isn't it?' she said, coming out of her reverie. 'I remembered Demon as a real dog.' (199)

In Nan Shepherd's novels the demon of the imagination continually inserts itself into the world to confuse reality; the 'compelling insistence of imaginative art' disrupts the real, replacing it with symbol. The plots of her novels insist on the deep desire of her characters to find a symbolic centre to their universe, and reveal the destructiveness of that desire to the community of which they are part. At the same time, her novels are insistently symbolic in method, so that the novels become self-interrogating structures, generating symbolic significance only to question the very sources of the desire which drives us to find those symbols in the world. For Shepherd, the imagination operates both by the creation of a unity which is false to the complexity of the real world, and by revealing a transcendent spirituality which can only be sustained through the exclusion of the material reality in which life is grounded. Her novels challenge those processes of the imagination by a devious series of displacements, in which the apparent protagonists are revealed as imaginative violators of the world, and the real heroines are those who are excluded, both by the imaginations of other characters and by the very structure of the novel itself.

It is a theme that *The Quarry Wood* (1928) explores in Martha's relation with Luke, each of whom turns the other into a symbol of a higher reality and in so doing denies the real nature of their personalities and the demands of their physical beings. In the first flush of her love for Luke, Martha is transformed into a goddess incapable of connecting with the merely peasant world in which she lives:

So strong was the life in her as she walked onwards in the tossing April weather, that she could afford to be prodigal of herself even to the extent of throwing a greeting to Andy MacPherson, who was walking, also alone, on the uplands. So might Artemis, of her condescension, have graced a mortal with a word. But Andy knew only one way of talking to a girl, and be sure, given the opportunity so long denied, made use of it: whereupon Artemis, who had amassed a very considerable vocabulary during her researches in history and literature, and in her new-found arrogance of spirit discovered she could use it, chid him with such hot scorn and vehement indignation (after making the first advances too!) that Andy's blandness frothed to bluster and his bluster collapsed like a paper bag at a Sunday school picnic; while Martha marched ahead with her chin a little higher and her shoulders more squarely set. O, cruel! – But these goddesses are notoriously unfeeling, up yonder on their Olympian crags. (112–3)

Martha, through love, history and literature, becomes a goddess separated from the ordinary world which she inhabits, a symbolic visitor to a banal reality which dare not respond to her in its own language. Her self-image is a product of the same symbolic transformation that has made her, in Luke's eyes, not the country girl who wears large working boots, but Beatrice, 'the flame of life', a symbolic annunciation of 'hierarchies of being beyond our own' (76): 'because unwittingly she loved him she became the more fully what he had imagined her' (77). Their transformation from mere human beings into symbols of a higher reality requires a denial of their physical natures in favour of the higher ideals which they have come to represent for each other: 'For a moment he realized that her nature might be other than he had perceived, but speedily forgot it and saw her only in his own conception of her' (75). The consummation of their relationship occurs in a world of northern summer light which transforms the physical world into a spiritual one: 'There the light was stranger still. The wood was bathed in it; a wood from another world; as though someone had enclosed it long ago in a volatile spirit, through which as through a subtly altering medium one saw its boughs and boles' (116). The 'altering medium' of the wood transforms them into creatures of pure imagination, meeting not one another but the images with which they have replaced their real identities: 'There was no passion in the kiss. It was grave, a reluctance, diffident and abashed, as of a worshipper who trembles lest his offering pollute the shrine' (117). This transfiguration – the 'flame that burned within herself was fierce enough to transfigure the kiss' (117) – promises union with a divine spirituality. In Luke's memory the wood is all poetry – 'You felt like – or at least I felt like – a stitch or two of chinese embroidery. You know – as though you were on a panel of silk. Unreal . . . You know that thing – Rossetti's – about going down to the deep wells of light and bathing. it was like that' (119); the things of the world have been replaced by insubstantial symbolic presences, 'like being dissolved in a Shelley ode' (119), and Martha's presence becomes, to him, a ghostly 'apparition, a false Florimel. An accident of light' (120). The real quarry in this sacred wood, however, is not a divine spirituality but an all-too-physical passion – 'Her whole being cried, "Take me, take me." But she stood so still, so poised, that it did not occur to him that she was offering herself' (117). The drive of the imagination towards transcendence releases its own opposite, Martha's unrecognised physical passion, but a passion which can never receive expression because it can have no meaning within the world of symbolic significances generated by their imaginations.

The transfigurations of the imagination are what Martha has to escape in order to come into that awareness of the 'complex social inter-relationships of life' (116) that are the antithesis of the tyrannical unities of the imagination. The conflict between these is what Luke encounters but fails to understand when, 'hypnotised by his own creation', he writes a poem in which the Archangel Gabriel ' . . . grew tired of heaven, because he wanted to know what God was really like to the people on earth' (86) and therefore descended and took a man up to heaven. The man's experience of that ultimate unity of the godhead, however, in a movement of transendence which prefigures Martha's own story, only drives him back into the multiplicity of the worlds he has left:

'But the full certainty of understanding
Was his not ever. He had oft to go
Among the worlds, and knew their fierce demanding,
Sharing their troubled littleness, their woe

'Not little. For only thus could he endure
Divinity upon him, and unfold
Its thousand-fold intensity. (87)

Luke cannot advance his poem of a human being transfigured by divine knowledge, because he has 'got them hung up between earth and heaven just now, and . . . can't get them any forrader' (87): trapped between the spiritually symbolic and the materially real his only resort is, poetically, silence; or, in life, escape, running away from his transfiguration of Martha because he cannot accommodate the 'shining symbol' (122) he has made of her – the 'Beatrice' of his imagination – to the practical realities of his life.

Just as, in *The Prime of Miss Jean Brodie* it takes Sandy's counter-imagination to undo the imagination's power to 'transfigure the common-place', so, in *The Quarry Wood*, it takes Aunt Josephine's imagination to undo the falsities in which Martha has been caught. As she is dying, Aunt Josephine believes that Martha has been abandoned by her second lover, Roy Rory Foubister, in the same way that Josephine herself was abandoned by his uncle. Martha's insistence that she 'wouldn't have married him' (198) is taken by her aunt simply as the effort to suppress her hurt:

Martha sighed a little, and remained where she was on the floor, touching with her strong firm fingers the cold and wrinkled skin of Miss Leggatt's hand. Impossible to disabuse Aunt Josephine. But did she want to disabuse Aunt Josephine? She sat a long time quietly on the floor, leaning against Miss Leggatt, and it seemed to her that the heavens were opened and the spirit of God descended on the old woman. She had taken upon herself what she conceived to be the young girl's sorrow and was carrying it. Martha understood that her mistake altered nothing of the grandeur of her action. The strong serenity of life that dwelt in the old woman seemed to possess and inhabit the girl, purchased for her – was it idle to suppose? – by the love and suffering she had divined.

That night she wept into her pillow noiseless and flooding tears, tears without salt in them, that washed the last bitterness from her heart; and in the morning rose and went about her work marvelling at the redemptive vitality of an old woman's misapprehension. (198)

Martha's imagined hurt in Aunt Jospehine's mind becomes the counterbalance to the real hurt that Martha has suffered through her own imagination: the falsehood of one countermands the falsehood of the other and, as the old woman dies, it is as though she has taken with her all the false power of the imagination and returned Martha to the reality which she had been denied. Imagination has to be defeated by the imagined; 'the shattering of her selfhood' which Martha has suffered no longer 'evil' but the precondition of a return to a world 'more complex and terrible' (199) than the imagination can allow.

What Martha has discovered through her relationship with Luke is what Ellen will discover in Nan Shepherd's second novel, *The Weatherhouse*. Ellen believes, like Luke, in the transcendent unity of the world as revealed by the imagination:

> 'But don't you love birds?'
> 'Oh, yes.' Ellen paused, gazing at the eager girl. 'They are a part of myself,' she wanted to say; but how could one explain that? Where it had to be explained it could not be understood. 'You are a part of me, too,' she thought, with her eyes fixed on Lindsay's where she waited for her answer. Her lips were parted and her eyes shone; and Mrs Falconer longed to tell her of the strange secret of life—how all things were one and there was no estrangement except for those who did not understand. (47)

Instead of an engagement with others as persons-in-relation, Ellen transforms everyone into the transcendent unity of her own ego. Her passive incorporation of the world into her self is matched by Garry Forbes's active desire to incorporate all of the world into a new unity. Returned from the War, Garry 'resented those refinements that suggested privilege. This shy lover of the ideal, this poet who clowned away the suspicion of poetry from himself, burned in his heart with no less a fire than love for all mankind' (52). For Garry, 'imagination has to save the world' (115) but that salvation is not something that he can believe will begin from Fetter-Rothnie, the village he has returned to, for it is a place which 'is dead', and 'all the generations of its history would not make up the tale of the fighting men' (56). Garry seeks nothing less than the 'reconstruction of the universe' but it could hardly ' begin in this dark hole, inhabited by old wives and ploughmen' (56). What Garry will have to come to terms with, however, is what Ellen is, in the end, forced to acknowledge, that 'the God who had constrained her in her flaming ecstasy of devotion, whose direct commands she had obeyed . . . was created from her own imagination: a figment of her own desire' (181).

Like so many of the great modernist works of the 1920s, *The Weatherhouse* is a novel trying to bridge the gulf between the world that died in the War and the world that is trying to come to birth in its aftermath. But rather than 'tragedy, superb and dark' what it presents is a plot apparently too trivial even to count as a footnote to the mythic truths of Frazer's narratives or the historic truths of the War: Louie Morgan claims to have been betrothed to David Grey, who has died of tuberculosis while engaged on engineering work associated with the war effort; Garry, Grey's childhood friend, refuses to believe in the betrothal and, in defiance of the beliefs of Lindsay, whom he intends to marry, sets out to force Louie to admit the lie. In the vast narrative of the First World War, David Grey, Louie Morgan and Garry Forbes are incidental players in a drama whose conclusion and significance do not in any way depend on the truth or falsehood of the woman's claim. The novelistic imagination which foregrounds certain narratives as historically significant is challenged by a narrative in which the ultimate suffering of the war is transferred from those who fought to those bereaved; from those whose 'tale' will have a meaning in history to those who simply lost through the War one of life's possibilities; from those who have endured the horrors of war to those who endure in a countryside 'where time and the individual had ceased to matter' (58). Fetter-Rothnie is a place out of history – 'the dark revealed [its] timeless attributes, reducing the particular to accident and hinting at a sublimer truth than the eye could distinguish' (57) – where life is ruled not by the terms of the isolated imagination of the transcendent self but by the folk imagination in which, from the opening of the novel, Garry's 'name had already become a symbol', but a symbol for the deceits to which the imagination is prey: '*You would need Garry Forbes to you. It is the local way of telling your man he is a liar*' (1).

For Garry, Louie's declaration of a betrothal that did not take place is the insertion of a fiction into the real world, a world whose value he has to re-establish because it is his only buttress against a similar fiction which the War imposed on his own life. Trapped during a bombardment, Garry ends up fevered and unable to distinguish between himself and the dead man with whom he shares a shellhole. Having failed to save the man he tries to bury him:

> Now he had detached the other man's feet; the body canted over, a shapeless rigid mass, and he saw the glaring eyes, the open mouth out of which slime was oozing. He pushed with all his might, thrust the thing under; barricaded himself with branches against its presence. (54)

Having buried him, however, he has to resurrect him because, 'In some queer way he was identified with this other fellow, whom he had never seen before, whose body he had thrust with so little ceremony under the slime' (54). Garry's actions mimic the rituals of the killing of tree spirits (thus the 'barricade of branches') in Frazer: the tree spirit must be killed so that its soul can be passed on to a younger and fitter representative. In Garry's case, however, the mechanisation of death that denies traditional spiritual significance results not in the transference of the god's spirit from the dead to the living but of the spirit of the living to the dead. Garry believes himself not to be the new home of the eternal spirit of the god who has been slain but to be the slain body from which the god has departed. Thus by the time he makes it back to his own lines, he cannot distinguish between himself and the other: to save the other is to save himself and he believes himself to be wounded in exactly the place the other man had been.

> 'Queer business that,' he said later, 'about my wound. I was convinced I had a wound. I saw myself . . . I thrust him in, you see, and I had to haul myself out. Queer, isn't it, about oneself? Losing oneself like that, I mean, and being someone else.' (54–5)

Garry's identification of himself with the dead man, his loss of self, is the model for an imaginative transference from self to other in which all the characters of *The Weatherhouse* will be caught up: it is the mirror image of Louie's desperate need to find a new self by linking herself imaginatively to the dead David Grey. Louie, reduced to insignificance by her failure to find a man to marry and by her irrelevance to the war, makes herself significant by inventing the betrothal that allows her to claim the sympathy of the community: she carries a dead man back to the world of the living just as Garry does; she re-enacts what Frazer describes as the relation between a man and his totem since she becomes the totem in whom David's soul continues its existence in defiance of his death. Unwounded by the war, she thus becomes not only one of those mutilated by the loss of a lover and a potential husband, but the carrier of the soul of one of the significant dead. Her spinsterhood is no longer a personal flaw but a public tragedy. Garry's desire to unmask the falsehood of her imaginative identification of herself as David's undeclared fiancée is the public expression of his own desire to assert and, at the same time, discard, the identification of himself with the dead man in the trench: to destroy Louie's fiction would be to return to himself a world of common reality, redeemed from the intrusions – and the illusions – of an imagination over which he has otherwise no control.

Garry and Louie's struggle is replicated in Ellen, whose life is dominated by imagination:

> Imaginations! It mattered nothing to her what the commentators said, the word for her summed up those sweet excursions into the unreal that had punctuated her life. She thought she had forsworn them, fired as she was by the glimpses that Garry had provided of man's real travail and endeavour. But all she had achieved was a still more presumptuous imagination . . . (133–4)

Ellen comes to believe that Louie's salvation from the imagination will be a prologue to her own:

She came to her deepest understanding of Louie when she saw that she was like herself, and built rashly on a foundation of her own imaginings . . . She dwelt on the resemblance till she could hardly distinguish between herself and Louie. 'And people needn't have known her false pretences if it hadn't been for my false pretences.' She remembered Garry's tale of his delirium in the shell-hole. 'I thrust her in, I am rescuing myself.' 185)

Ellen's obsession with saving Louie turns her into the equivalent of that dead soldier, echoing what Louie had said to Garry about her relationship with David and her right to claim him as a lost fiancee: 'I didn't grab. Oh, you haven't understood at all! That part of him is mine, I created it. No one can touch it but me' (106). Each of the characters projects him or herself on to another and then, by saving the other, attempts to save him or herself, as though in that act of imaginative identification they have captured some portion of divinity, some fragment of a higher significance. Salvation through the imagination, however, is achieved only by the negation – the death – of another's reality, and the displacement of it with one's own self. Instead of salvation, what is being experienced is simply the repetition through another of the imagination's false promises of personal redemption into significance. It is a confession Ellen makes to her sister Tris:

'I've been frightened of you all my life, Tris – I'm not frightened any longer. But I've seen a thing this afternoon that frightened me. There's nothing to fear in all the world but deceit. Nothing at all. And I've seen it, I've seen it. I've seen a deluded woman – and he wakened her up from her idle dreams, as he wakened me – despising truth, feeding herself on error, pouring cups of devil's tea – '
'Where were you at all this afternoon?'
'At the Morgans'.'
'Oh, it's Louie you're meaning. Deluded, you may say. Their woman Eppie'll tell you the things she does.' Theresa prepared to expatiate, but Ellen cried, 'It's myself I mean. It was myself I saw. That's what I saw – myself. I'm inside Louie, and I'm a part of her deceit. God's in her, the God I can't get at – ' (190)

Ellen will challenge Louie about the falsehoods of her construction of the past – 'You are entertaining ghosts, demons, delusions, snares, principalities and powers. You are entertaining your own destruction' (188) – only to be told how deceitful has been her own part in the story. What Ellen has to come to recognise is that 'in her imaginings other people had been what she decreed, their real selves she ignored' (182).

In the end, Garry will be unable to condemn Louie – 'There was a queer twisted truth in what she had said' (164) – and he regrets having 'thrown her to the mob' (164). In trying to make her admit her falsehood: both, like Ellen, are trying to save not the real man but an image of a man created by themselves: 'There was a side to him you didn't know. I developed it.

I created him. My own part of him' (100). The twisted truth of Louie's assertions is that each character in the novel invents those around them, infuses them with values and responds to them not as they are, but as they are imagined to be. Imagination infects and distorts; the narrative of *The Weatherhouse* is a tissue of imaginations, from which the truth has to be redeemed precisely by negating the kind of fictionalising which the characters, in imitation of their author, but in denial of her fundamental values, are only too prone to commit themselves to.

In enacting the falsity of the imagination at the level of its own plot *The Weatherhouse* again reverts to the principle of the 'footnote' as Shepherd explored it in *The Quarry Wood*. Where, in the earlier novel, Martha's Aunt Sally represents the narrative which cannot be foregrounded within the novel and so must appear simply as a footnote,[17] in *The Weatherhouse* the footnote is Ellen's daughter Kate, whose narrative, told as it is in the interstices of the rest of the plot, challenges the bases on which the other characters' lives are presented. Ellen's imagination is focused on Garry because she has already decided that Garry will marry her daughter Kate: the old woman,

> had woven a whole romance around the two and hidden it in her heart, hardly believing it had more foundation than the hundred other romances that she wove. But it had, it had. Foundation and a new miraculous lustre. Kate took on a new dignity in her mother's eyes – perhaps the grandeur of a tragic destiny. But no, that must not be – unless he were slaughtered. (74)

In Ellen's view Kate is transformed from an ordinary woman into a tragic heroine, but the irony of this particular relationship lies in the fact that Kate cannot disabuse her mother without giving away the secret of Lindsay's relationship with Garry, and Kate will not do that: in fact, she allows her mother to go on in her imaginings precisely because it is 'as good a way as any to cover Lindsay' (73). Lindsay, however, is not aware that she is herself to some extent responsible for Ellen's condition; like readers of novels she is not interested in the 'footnotes' that are the story of women not destined to be the protagonist. The real footnote to the story of the Weatherhouse, the tragedy locked within it and yet unexpressed, is the love that Ellen's daughter Kate actually has for Garry, a love which can never be voiced because of Garry's love for Lindsay, but a love which dumbly dominates Kate's life, preventing her ever marrying, confining her to looking after other people's children. It is Kate that Ellen thinks must be the reason for Garry's frequent visits to the Weatherhouse and, ironically, it is to Kate that Lindsay first tells the secret of her love for Garry. Unemotional, unimaginative, undemonstrative, Kate's feelings are 'mastered and undivulged' (38) and Lindsay remains entirely oblivious to the real tragedy of the woman to whom she first voiced her own hopes, and the tragedy of the old woman who falls in love with Garry precisely because she imagined her daughter to love him. The ironies of Lindsay's and Kate's relationship reach their climax when Lindsay is appalled by Theresa's suggestion that Louie is 'setting her cap at Garry' (153); when Kate tries to calm her Lindsay demands:

> 'Do you never feel about anything, Kate? You should fall in love. Then you would understand.'
> She banged the door . . .
> Kate, left alone in the bedroom, pressed her hands upon her breast. Her lips drew together in a line of pain. But in a moment she relaxed and began carefully to make the beds. (154)

To refuse imagination, as Kate does, is no guarantee of happiness, nor even of sympathy. Louie's sufferings, falsified and made deliberately public, may be the apparent driving force of the narrative, but it is Kate's suppressed feelings that are the real inspiration of story – an inspiration which can barely be acknowledged because it is of so little consequence to the narrative imagination. The woman who suppresses all feeling before work and duty and the woman who flaunts her feelings before the community suffer differently, but their stories run in parallel, both denied the resurrection they hoped for from the cruel god of spring. Characters like Kate make no appeal to the literary imagination: they are the untransformable reality which art cannot raise to any 'compelling insistence'. Refusers of the imagination in their own life, they are not susceptible to treatment by the imagination in the novel.

The Weatherhouse sets itself out as an explanation of why Garry Forbes's name 'has already become a symbol' in Fetter-Rothnie; the answer is an exploration of the falsehood of the processes of symbolism by which the novel itself operates, in complicity with the very falsehoods it is challenging. Escaping from the imagination is not easy, for even the escapes that we invent, as Ellen discovers, are themselves a function of the imagination's deceptive imposition of our own wishes and values upon the external world, and, more importantly, on our own past: 'How could it be enough to mean well? One came afterwards to repudiate one's own motives, to see that one was responsible in spite of them. One's true self, which one had not known, had worked. Surely if there was a God it was one's real self that He judged' (185). The imagination which, in a romantic aesthetic, connects one to God is, in *The Weatherhouse*, the very principle which makes it impossible to know one's relationship to God: the God of imagination is the God of self-deception. What Garry has to learn is that there is no truth, one, single and coherent, and no lie, either – only relations of doubt:

> 'I should have thought the difference between truth and a lie was clear enough,' he said as she paused.
> 'Oh, no, it's not – not clear at all. Things are true and right in one relationship, and quite false in another. It's false, as a mere statement of fact, that

I was betrothed to David, but true as an expression of – an expression of – '
She faltered . . . (105)

Truth, like identity, is not something in itself but something in relations and
it is those *relations* of truth rather than the transcendent objects of the imagination that *The Weatherhouse* sets our to demonstrate to us. Truth requires
us to escape from the imagination's desire for identity between ourselves
and the world around us, and, in literary terms, from the imagination's
desire to identify with the protagonist of a novel who is God-the-author's
representative in a world made over into significant symbols. The complex
texture of the novel is constructed to challenge the very basis of the traditions
of the novel as another imposition of the imagination upon the world: it is
not the imagination of the author, replicated in Ellen's imaginings, which
should redeem the world but the world of the folk which should redeem
the author. Nan Shepherd's art is an art against itself, an imaginative study
of characters who transform the world into 'a part of my undying self,
possessed eternally, the kingdom within my soul' (181), but a refusal of that
'transfiguration of the commonplace' because it implies a world without
doubt, an elevation of the artist herself to an ultimate knowledge which she
refuses to trust. The imagination of the isolated artist is dangerous because
its egoistic imposition on the world has not been tempered by the anonymous
generosity of a folk imagination; the individual imagination which seeks to
make its life a part of everything is the antithesis of a folk imagination in
which, like the land and the man who sows it, everything 'was transfigured
by the faith that used it', because 'the dead reached through him to the
future' (173).

IV

When, in *Lanark*, Duncan Thaw discourses to his friend McAlpin on
the fact that Glasgow is a city where 'nobody imagines living' (243), he
situates himself directly in the fictional line of descent from those working-
class artists like Archie Hind's Mat Craig, who saw Glasgow as a social
environment to which the imagination was 'dumb or in exile' (65); when
Lanark confronts his creator he is situated in the line of descent from the
metaphysical doubters of the imagination such as Muriel Spark's Caroline
Rose in *The Comforters*: '"Which proves," said Lanark . . ."that the
world's great stories are mostly a pack of lies"' (490). In its two narratives
Lanark encompasses both the social and the metaphysical doubts about the
value of the imagination which have dominated the Scottish novel. The
continuities of these concerns can be seen in the fact that when Thaw
flees the 'real' world and re-emerges as Lanark in the alternative world of
Unthank, he repeats the flight of Barrie's Peter Pan to the Never Land of

the imagination – an imagination which repeats the real world in fantasy form, both de-forming it and revealing the truths that its realistic surface conceals.

Peter's Never Land is not a simple escape from the real: it is the world of imperialism turned into a children's game, but a game which reveals how the distant and heroic exploits of imperial conquest, as told to children in Victorian novels, is the imagination's concealment of the horrific foundations of modern civilisation. In *Peter Pan* the imagination escapes reality only to reveal the ways in which imagination conceals reality from us:

> Around the brave Tiger Lily were a dozen of her stoutest warriors, and they suddenly saw the perfidious pirates bearing down upon them. Fell from their eyes then the film through which they had looked at victory. No more would they torture at the stake. For them the happy hunting-grounds now. They knew it . . . Even then they had time to gather in a phalanx that would have been hard to break had they risen quickly, but this they were forbidden to do by the traditions of their race. It is written that the noble savage must never express surprise in the presence of the white. Thus terrible as the sudden appearance of the pirates must have been to them, they remained stationary for a moment, not a muscle moving; as if the foe had come by invitation. Then, indeed, the tradition gallantly upheld, they seized their weapons, and the air was torn with the war-cry; but it was now too late. (147)

The Never Land is the place of real death, but death which happens according to the dictates of writing – 'it is written that the noble savage must never express surprise' – and the question, of course, is by whom is the writing done, since the savages are by definition without writing. These savages perform their roles as defined by the writings of their destroyers: they exist only in the world of literature which both reveals the destructiveness of the encounter between the civilized (Hook, leader of the pirates, is from Eton) and the savage, and conceals the horror of that encounter within the conventions of a literary imagination. The ultimate element in that convention, of course, is that we know that Tiger Lily's warriors will be ready to do this all over again next time we read the book: the once-and-only existential death of real history is transformed into the symbolic death of repeatable art. That is why 'it is no part of ours to describe what was a massacre rather than a fight': the reality of death is concealed within the artifice of art. That is why, for Peter, the events of the Never Land can be a game. As a game is a pretence of conflict in relation to the real world, so for Peter the deaths that he witnesses are only a play – a play of which he is a part as an eternal presence, but to which the children are mere temporary visitors: 'Wendy was crying, for it was the first tragedy she had seen. Peter had seen many tragedies, but he had forgotten them all' (112). The sentence is poised between Wendy's seeing a tragedy – a work of art – and her witnessing a tragedy in life: Peter is unresponsive not just because he has seen 'many' tragedies but because, in art, each tragedy can be many in its performances.

Barrie's Never Land is an image of art itself, and Peter an image of artist who gets to live within his own artifice – not simply the creator of an eternal world which is the antithesis of the world of time and history in which the artist lives but a spirit inhabiting the eternity of artifice. Imagination has become the reality in which he lives, mirroring the real world but in a form which, by its repeatability, can gesture to the pain of temporal existence only by transforming it into its opposite, an eternal recurrence to which time and death are irrelevant. Peter reveals the diabolic nature of the imagination of which he is a projection, its negation of the real nature of the world it claims to replicate – except, of course, that by so doing he lets Barrie show us the terrors of reality which art conceals from us. It is this transference of imagination into reality on which the double structure of *Lanark* is built: Thaw is an artist trapped by his imagination in an unacceptable reality; Lanark lives in the world of the imagination made real – the Never Land – but is the opposite of Peter because, released from the demands of the imagination, it is possible for him to become the ordinary human being that Peter refused to grow into and that Thaw could never accept himself as being. *Lanark* is a journey to the Never Land, transfiguring the commonplace, in order to be able to discover the commonplace which was unacceptable because untransfigured.

At the beginning of Book 1 of *Lanark* Duncan Thaw dreams of being able to fly, but being a modern Peter Pan there is nowhere to fly to: his father has revealed to him that there is no sky, so 'he dreamed that night of flying up through empty air till he reached a flat blue sky. He rested against it like a balloon against a ceiling until worried by the thought of what was on the other side; then he broke a hole and rose through more empty air till he grew afraid of floating forever' (122). Unlike the children whom Peter visits, however, Thaw cannot fly: sent in disgrace to his room for not eating meat, he would look out on the other children playing and 'feel so lonely and magnificent that he considered opening the window and jumping out. It was a bitter glee to imagine his corpse thudding to the ground among them' (123). Thaw is the imagination become corpse-like: because there is no 'never land' to escape to it falls through reality to its death rather than flying from life towards eternity. In its attempt to fly from life, however, Duncan's art turns life into death, because only a dead world can be the appropriate subject of an art that is shut out from eternity:

> Not everything died at once for the lowlier plants put on final spurts of abnormal growth. Ivy sprouted up the Scott monument in George Square and reached the lightning conductor on the poet's head; then the leaves fell off and the column was encased in a net of bone-white bone-hard fibre. Moss carpeted the pavements, then crumbled to powder under his feet as he walked alone through the city. He was happy. He looked in the windows of

pornography shops without wondering if anyone saw him, and rode a bicycle through the halls of the art galleries and bumped down the front steps, singing. He set up easels in public places and painted huge canvases of buildings and dead trees. When a painting was completed he left it confronting the reality it depicted. (266–7)

Reality comes to imitate the dead world of his painting rather than the static painting offering a monument to the living world.

The reason that imagination kills the world is because under modern conditions – or under Scottish conditions – the imagination is simply an escape route from an unacceptable reality. In this respect, imagination is simply another version of all the other escape routes that human beings provide for themselves – what Sludden, the power figure in the novel's opening sections, describes as 'moments when a man feels exalted and masterful. We get them from drugs, crime and gambling, but the price is rather high. We can get them from a special interest, like sports, music or religion. . . . And we get them from work and love' (5). For Sludden love, like all the others, is simply a means by which 'a man feels exalted and masterful': since Lanark is incapable of any of these he is told that he should take up Art, 'because Art is the only work open to people who can't get along with others and still want to be special' (6). Sludden offers Lanark precisely the escape route from anonymity that Thaw had chosen. That is why we enter the novel, in Book 3, through the Elite cafe: Lanark, like Thaw, is in search of a route into the elite. His effort to achieve this – the gradual hardening of his emotions against other people in Thaw's case; the gradual encasing of his body in dragonhide in Lanark's – will lead to Art College for Thaw, the Institute for Lanark. In both, the individual is protected from reality, but only by being distanced from it; in both, the individual survives by living off the energy of others. Thaw, on the morning when he is about to start Art School, 'thought with awe of the energy needed to keep up a civilization' (223) but spends his morning drawing a dead lightbulb: art exists on the spent energy of civilization. In the Institute, Lanark watches as a body armoured with dragonhide explodes from its own internal heat, an explosion whose energy is collected to keep the Institute in operation. The elite individual feeds on the energy of others: his freedom is other people's slavery: 'I want to be free, and freedom is freedom from other people!', Lanark says (70), not having learned that persons are their relations and that the freedom he desires is his own negation.

The freedom that Lanark seeks is impossible because he is a character in a fantasy universe created by an author: the freedom that Thaw seeks is impossible because he is a working-class artist whose freedom to create is founded on others' enslavement. The two parts of *Lanark* recount the metaphysical and the social doubts of the value of the imagination, each acting as a metaphor for the other. The social repression from which Thaw

flees into the imagination is undone by metaphysical doubts about the value
of imagination; the metaphysical doubts about the imagination that Lanark
confronts when he meets his creator will only lead him to fail to overcome
the social repressions by which Unthank is being strangled. The failure of
his protagonists is, however, fundamental to Gray's purpose, because in both
books it is the desire to be a part of the elite, to make art a social power
and make social power the end of art, that is the destructive force which
the novel itself has to overcome – to be a product of the imagination that
resists the desire for power and retains its commitment to the ordinary.

Thaw-Lanark's quest is a quest to escape from the imagination as part
of the power of the elite and to recover the value of the commonplace and
the imagination's place within it. The 'transfiguration of the commonplace'
must be a transfiguration that does not negate the commonality of the artist
with the folk. When Lanark and Rima escape from the Institute they discover
they are on a road where one side goes downhill and the other uphill and
that the only way to progress is to link arms, so that the uphill toil of one is
counteracted by the downhill race of the other; 'The new way of walking was
a strain on the linking arm but worked very well' (378). The road that they
are on is thus the 'high road' and the 'low road' of the popular song – 'You
take the high road, / And I'll take the low road, / And I'll be in Scotland
afore ye' – but it has a yellow line running down its middle which links it
also to 'the yellow brick road' which Dorothy followed to meet the wizard
of Oz, a meeting which is parodied in Lanark's meeting with his author-
wizard Nastler. 'Oz' is the world of the fantasy resolution of reality from
which one must escape; it is also the world ruled over by *Oz*enfant, the
head of the department of the Institute in which Lanark finds himself when
he has been 'reborn' by being swallowed by the mouth in the Necropolis
which announces 'I am the way out' (47). The name Ozenfant[18] not only
points to the Oz-world of fantasy's escape from reality but also back to *The
Dear Green Place* in which Mat Craig, visiting a bookshop, gets into conversation with someone who is reading a book by Ozenfant about modern
art: Mat announces that he is 'against art' (135), and in justification cites
Ozenfant's judgement that 'what matters to the writers in question is less
Picasso's *oeuvre* than Picasso the phenomenon' (136). Picasso the artist has
become more important than the works he produces, just as Mat himself
is hamstrung by his belief that an 'artist is recognised by what he is rather
than what he does' (51). What Mat has to learn is 'the irony that what he
was experiencing in himself as a dismissal of art was in fact that very doubt
which is at the centre of the experience of art itself' (117) – what Mat has
to learn is the power of a doubtful imagination that can fulfil itself only
because it is not prepared to trust the implications of its own medium, or
the social power that that medium bestows on its creator. Ozenfant, on the
other hand, 'distrust(s) speech therapy'; for him 'Words are the language
of lies and evasions' – not because he has to live with doubt but because,

like romantic theory in which 'all art aspires to the condition of music', he trusts a meaning beyond language: 'Music cannot lie. Music talks to the heart' (66). The doubtful imagination, on the other hand, knows that the dubious truths of language are the limits of human knowledge.

Lanark is a novel built as a series of escapes out of an unacceptable world into an elite – an Oz-world, part will-power, part fantasy – which seems to offer a more humane existence, until the realities which underlie the Oz-world are revealed – the fact that every such escape is built on exploitation of other people, and is built on the repression of the knowledge of the hell to which it consigns the rest of humanity: 'Hell was the one truth' (160). The world of Oz is not an escape from hell but the very condition that makes hell inevitable. That is why it is easy to go down to hell; that is why it is so difficult to get back to the light, because we must get back without simply thrusting others into the hell from which we are escaping; the escape routes to our own personal little heavenly Oz-worlds are all bought at the expense of everyone else's damnation – whether it is the bohemian elite, or the business elite, or the religious elite; each has secured its ability to walk in the light only because of the darkness they impose on the rest of humanity. The temptation of the artist is to imagine that the imagination itself is unalloyed truth, and that through the imagination one comes directly into the presence of an ultimate reality. But in *Lanark* Gray has turned on its head the myth of the artist as revealer of ultimate truths. Glasgow may demand its imaginative fulfilment in art, but Thaw's art – because it is *his* Oz – is life-negating: it is an imagination sustaining itself by such an effort of concentration, by such an effort of exclusion of the outside world, that it demands the destruction rather than the rebirth of the world that it seeks to save.

The paradox on which *Lanark* is built, therefore, is that its hero, Thaw, must be deprived of the escape route of the imagination, of art, if he is to recover his humanity; he can only be allowed to do this, however, through the medium of the novel's own imaginative construction of an alternative reality – through Gray's construction of a fantasy alternative to the 'real' world that Thaw inhabits. Lanark lives out Thaw's art, as Thaw, after his death, is allowed to live on through Lanark's life. In the world of the imagination, Lanark is deprived of any escape route to the elite and must learn that his salvation lies in being, by the novel's conclusion, 'a slightly worried, ordinary old man'. The ordinary has been made possible only by the medium of an imagination which has revealed its own profound doubts about itself. The journey out of imagination and back to the real, out of the convention of 'realistic' fiction and back to the ordinary, is what *Lanark* dramatises – an imagination which can trust itself only to the extent that it absolutely doubts its own validity. Lanark's – and Thaw's – surrogate creator – Nastler – announces the dominion of the imagination to his creation:

" . . . As for my ending's being banal, wait till you're inside it. I warn you, my whole imagination has a carefully reined-back catastophist tendency; you have no conception of the damage my descriptive powers will wreak when I loose them on a theme like **THE END**."
"What happens to Sandy?" said Lanark coldly.
"Who's Sandy?"
"My son."
The conjuror stared and said, "You have no son."
"I have a son called Alexander who was born in the cathedral." (498)

It is not God the Father who has the son, but his creation: the God-author who manages the world in exactly the same way that Thaw sought to do through his art is displaced by the creature whose freedom is a defiance of the dictatorial art that knows no doubts about its own power. If Thaw the procreative father could offer nothing to ameliorate his son's suffering, God the creative father of Lanark's world can only threaten it with destruction. Lanark, however, defies his creator with all the temerity that Thaw defies *his* father and so enables himself to unite the father and son – Thaw senior and junior, Lanark senior and junior – in defiance of the history that dominates realistic fiction and in defiance of the imagination that dictates fantasy fiction. The imagination, self-doubting, is the basis for an understanding of the world that does not inspire humanity to the desire for a (fictitious) heaven that creates only a (real) hell. When Lanark and his dictatorial leader – Ozenfant, now called Monboddo – meet, what Ozenfant-Monboddo announces is that 'At Last the Common Man confronts the Powerful Lord of this world. Except that you are not very common and I am not very powerful' (550). The powerful is doubted: the commonplace is transfigured: Jean brodie's 'transfiguration of the commonplace' is fulfilled but fulfilled by the negation of the dictatorship of the imagination.

A democratic art fulfils itself in refusal of the dominerring traditions of the artistic imagination which it inherits, and in fulfilment of the national imagination that it continues – in defiance of the apparent destruction of the nation – to assert. 'Perhaps an illusionist's main job' Gray has his alter ego say to Lanark, 'is to exhaust his restless audience by a show of marvellously convincing squabbles until they see the simple things we really depend upon . . . Perhaps the best thing I could do is write a story in which adjectives like *commonplace* and *ordinary* have the significance which glorious and divine carried in earlier comedies' (494). The art of the Scottish novel is its refusal of the temptations of art; its insistence on returning its readers to the commonplace and the ordinary for which the traditions of high art has had neither time nor space. A doubtful imagination is the only appropriate medium for a nation founded in the democracy of the commonplace, founded in the transfiguration of its common place into democracy.

CONCLUSION:
NARRATIVE AND THE SPACE OF THE NATION

In 1876 William Robertson Smith, born in Aberdeen in 1846, was in London, engaged in writing *The Old Testament in the Jewish Church* and *The Prophets of Israel*, books designed to defend the views for which he had been arraigned by the Free Church for 'impugning the purity of Scripture', and which would become, in due course, the foundation of the work of J. G. Frazer, then a student at Cambridge;[1] in January of the same year, John Muir, born in Dunbar in 1838, and later the founder of the American National Parks movement, published his first essay on forest conservation, 'God's First Temples: How Shall We Preserve our Forests?' in the Sacramento *Record-Union*;[2] on 25 June 1876, Alexander Graham Bell, born in Edinburgh in 1847, displayed in Philadelphia, Pennsylvania the first telephone at the International Centennial Exhibition, commemorating the anniversary of the Declaration of Independence.[3] Each of them was the product of an intensely Scottish upbringing: Smith was the son of a Free Church minister; Muir the son of a rigorous Calvinist farmer; Bell the son of an elocution teacher, whose system of phonetic transcription was one of the outcomes of Scotland's long engagement with the problem of standard language and dialect.[4] Each of them would contribute directly to that series of transformations which, by the 1880s, had begun to shape a distinctively modern world, and each of them was characterised by a similar restless desire to explore the limits of known space. Smith, despite frail health, travelled the North African deserts, perfecting his Arabic and analysing the origins of religion; Muir trekked endlessly the American North West in search of 'God's First Temples'; Bell became obsessed with flight and was responsible for the first airplane to fly a kilometre in public on July 4, 1908.[5]

All of these explorations were far from Scotland but all of them carried Scotland with them: Smith would die in London, still committed to the theology of the Free Church of Scotland; Muir would return in the 1890s to discover that he was 'a Scotchman and at home again';[6] Bell would be buried at his Nova Scotia home named in Gaelic 'Beinn Breagh'.[7] The greatest Scottish writer of their generation, Robert Louis Stevenson, who had been in the same physics laboratory as Smith when he was a student at Edinburgh University,[8] would die in Samoa in 1894, after a brief life of restless travel, having commented in a letter of 1893 how he would 'fulfil the Scots destiny throughout, and live a voluntary exile' but with his 'head filled with the blessed beastly place all the time'.[9] For each of them John Muir's commentary on his wilderness journeys might stand as epigraph to their relationship with Scotland: 'I only went out for a walk, and finally concluded to stay out till sundown, for going out, I found, was really going in';[10] for each of them, Scotland was an origin which did not provide the *telos* of their life's narrative, but it provided the purposes by which they were guided. In the Robert Louis Stevenson museum in Monterey, California, a hotel where Stevenson had stayed while waiting to meet Fanny Osbourne, visitors can see the dining room table which once graced Stevenson's father's house in Heriot Row, Edinburgh and the rocking chair in which Fanny Osbourne would sit in their house at Vailima in Samoa. Stevenson's life, like those of Smith, Muir and Bell, is lived in a spatial traversal across cultural differences rather than in singular journey within the evolving history of an individual culture.

Our notions of the nation are fundamentally historical: Renan articulated it in 1882 when he argued that the nation is a combination of two things, 'one is the possession in common of a rich legacy of memories; the other is present-day consent, the desire to live together, the will to perpetuate the value of the heritage that one has received in an undivided form'.[11] Renan, at the height of imperialism, refuses to limit the nation to its territory: its spiritual principle can be everywhere and anywhere, can belong to anyone who chooses *its* ancestors as *their* ancestors. The nature of the nation has been deeply intertwined, in the period of the growth of nationalism, with the fact of Empire, and in Renan's historicist construction the nation refuses to be contained by national space. It is built not upon the bounded territory of its own origin but on the ground of the many territories where its flag is planted, for the imperial nation acknowledges no boundaries to its national significance: its history may derive from a particular plot of ground but that history pours outwards upon the empty and the not-so-empty places of the earth as the nation becomes an extended assertion of its own refusal to be bounded by anything but global space.

The irony of the era of nineteenth-century nationalism was that it was founded on an 'organic' notion of the nation at the very moment when the major European nations negated their own 'organic' development by incorporating within themselves vast tracts of the rest of the world, declaring them too to be the inheritors of the nation's 'rich legacy of memories', requiring their 'present-day consent' to be participants in a history which had refused to acknowledge their territorial boundaries. On the eve of modernity, where were the boundaries of the Scottish nation? – a nation which had committed itself to that worldwide formation whose title – the British Empire – was almost the only place in which it was impossible to substitute to the word English for British? If, as Tom Nairn has argued, Scotland failed to develop an 'organic' nationalism in the nineteenth century,[12] it was not because the Scottish nation had collapsed into being simply the facade of a nation – it was because the nation had expanded to treat vast portions of the world as extensions of its spiritual legacy. Scotland had become an unbounded nation; its capital was in London; its people, by necessity or by choice, were scattered across the world, in Scottish communities in Canada, the United States, Australia, New Zealand, various parts of Africa, or individually as representatives of the British state; the population in its own territory came from many other cultures – immigrants from Ireland and from Eastern Europe. If there is a problem about identifying 'Scottish' culture in the nineteenth century it is because Scotland had become, in Renan's words, 'a soul, a spiritual principle'[13] which was no longer contained within the boundaries of a specific geography. The space of the nation extended tentacularly around the world, and like the ships launched on the Clyde to carry much of the world's trade around the globe, took the ground of Scotland only as a launching place. There can be no coherent narrative of the nation not because the nation lacks narrative development but for precisely the opposite reason: its narrative spills out over many territories; it cannot be accommodated within the continuities demanded by the genre of a national history.

Stevenson's *The Master of Ballantrae* represents Scotland in the 1880s precisely by fleeing from it: as Stevenson noted it is a plot in which the scene constantly changes: 'scene Scotland – the States – Scotland – India – Scotland – and the States again; so it jumps like a flea' (ix).[14] Narrative, which holds together national identity in the historicist mode, is disrupted by the multiple spaces into which the nation has entered, the plethora of other narratives with which it is entwined: an alternative kind of narration is required – one which jumps like the flea from point to point across a variety of territories, mingling their narratives with its own. It is this multiplicity of intersecting narratives that John Buchan was to dramatise in the opening pages of *The Thirty-Nine Steps*. Hannay, returned to London from Bulawayo but unsuccessful in getting work, is thinking of going back to South Africa when he is accosted by Scudder, an American from Kentucky who later appears in disguise as a Ghurka officer, linking in his own person the Western and Eastern limits of Empire. Scudder has learned of a plot to kill Karolides, leader of a Balkan country and main bulwark against the deliberate contrivance of a war between Russia and Germany, organised by a 'subterranean' movement headed by Jews wanting revenge on Russia. The world in which Hannay moves is suddenly revealed as the intersection of multiple international narratives, a space of interacting causalities so complex that they can be reduced to the unitary requirements of a novel only by discovering behind them the single narrative of a vast conspiracy: the thriller genre raises the spectre of the unnarratable spacial complexity of the world only because it can then dissolve it back into the singularity provided by the search for the one, individual plotter of the international conflict, the person who is the malign mirror-image of the lost order of history's narrative progression. Buchan's plot raises the threat of the loss of control of the singular national narrative but balances the terror of that loss by replacing it with a particular, conspiratorial individual who can be contested and defeated: the threat of space as the annihilation of national narrative's orderly construction of history can be turned back into a purposive national narrative: 'Three weeks later, as all the world knows, we went to war' (103). The war that has so often been imaged as bringing back narrative purpose into the suspended narrative of Scotland brings back into Hannay's world an orderly progression of history, a conflict fought out on public territory with a single outcome, rather than a complex interaction of multiple narratives whose chaotic intersections leaves all outcomes in doubt.

In *The Thirty-Nine Steps*, however, Hannay will have to escape from London to Scotland, to 'some wild district' which will give him the chance to use his African 'veldcraft' (18): the threat of space to the national narrative has to be met by retreating to the space within Britain which remains an image of the 'wild' districts of the borders of Empire. The space of Scotland is the space in which the conflicts of the world can be brought into the open, since Scotland's space operates as a synecdoche of the wildness beyond the boundaries of the narrative of Imperial history. Scotland is a place where history is suspended – Hannay simply has to stay on the run for twenty days – and where space is dominant, allowing the conjunctions of those different spacial forces to be revealed. Hannay's story will be a series of spacial encounters – 'a hundred yards on I found another wire cunningly placed on the edge of a small stream' – and evasions – 'I did not stop till I had put half a dozen miles between me and that accursed dwelling' (65): a race across space whose hectic encounters are simply a waiting for history to recommence, an effort to prevent the wrong historical narrative, the one that originates from a different space, from taking place.

Buchan's use of Scotland as the space in which history's imperial progress comes under threat underlines the fact that if internally, the space of Scotland refused easy resolution into a unified national narrative, externally it disseminated into the multiple narratives of the British Empire. The national space whose filiations run to London, Nova Scotia, California and Samoa is also fissured into alternative spaces by its own internal boundaries. It runs transverse to the linearity of narrative. In many Scottish novels the narrative, far from being a passage of history in which the individual life mirrors the larger-scale narrative of historical development, is a passage across competing spaces, each with an alternative origin and *telos*. It is this Scotland which Alasdair Gray encompasses in *Poor Things*, a novel in which the life of Bella Baxter (or, as she will later be known, Victoria McCandless) will take place in two different timescales because she is the product of a medical experiment in which her revived body, after suicide, has had transplanted into it the brain of her own child. She thus lives two lives simultaneously in two different phases of history, but, having been reborn at twenty-five, she has no memory of her own earlier narrative. Like the Glasgow in which she is returns to existence, her accelerated growth is founded not *within* a national space and as a continuation of a national narrative, but in an imperial space that generates a profound amnesia about her past. The novel concludes with a series of documentary images of the newly-built public spaces of nineteenth-century Glasgow juxtaposed with images of Imperial military action in India (293–8), figuring the spaces which Bella's own travels, like Gray's mutually defeating narrators, cannot hold together as part of a single, coherent narrative development.

Gray's historical version of Scotland's imperial space is reversed in Alan Warner's *These Demented Lands*,[15] when Morvern Callar, on an island on the West coast of Scotland comes across a miniature railway, a microcosm of the engine of history, whose name – Kongo Express – and whose stops around the island declare its filiations with the global territory of imperial exploration: '"Aye-aye. Wanting dropped anywhere?" The driver looked at me. "Niagara Falls, Mount Kilimanjaro, Makarikari Salt Pans?" he yelled out a laugh' (18). Morvern travels across the island which is like a manic mirror-image of history-in-reverse, taking her backwards from the industrial revolution – climbing 'bended double like the clans at Culloden stepping into the end' (19) – to an encounter with cattle drovers following a fifteenth-century map – who turn out to be university students 'doing hunting and fishing, trying to do the fifteenth-century thing with Gore-Tex and a video camera thrown in' (27). The disjunctive and disorienting effects which Morvern experiences are the result of traversing alternative narrative trajectories grounded in different spatial environments. Those disjunctive spatial relations are caught in Gray's *Lanark*, when Thaw, in Glasgow, looks out at the Kilpatrick hills 'with the clear distant top of Ben Lomond behind the eastward slope. Thaw thought it queer that a man on that summit, surrounded by the highlands and overlooking deep lochs, might see with a telescope this kitchen window, a speck of light in a low haze to the south' (275). That double perspective, from urban kitchen window and from highland hilltop, is what Thaw's paintings mimic, when they attempt to present 'a landscape seen simultaneously from above and below and containing north, east and south' (287); a double perspective – within history, without history – which is driven by the spatial conjunction, and cultural and historical disjunction, of Lowland and Highland space, of national and imperial narratives.

When Morvern gets above the criss-cross narratives of intersecting histories, she reaches a point when she seems to be beyond the boundaries of history, a point which is the recurrent angle of vision sought for by the Scottish novel:

The whole island seemed to slip down through me like a disc, spread out round, saw otherside from up there, distant mountains lifting up as if explosions of steam, cloud pillars like spring blossom, the mountain range I was named after on the opposite side of the Sound that lay with a wet sun along in dazzling shimmers, up to where the water turned angry black – wide wide ocean that goes forever 'cept maybe for Pincher Martin rock jutted out the teeth of the ocean bed. (49)

To have reached mountain top or ocean depth is to have crossed to the 'otherside' of history's narrative: Morvern journeys between the eternal space of the mountains she was named after and the miniature narratives of an inconsequential history, at the edge of an ocean which gives her 'The Rudder Feeling' – 'it gave me scaredness lying in my bed thinking about those rudders, held there forever, punished above the cold Atlantic seabeds that were always rolling out below them' (50). The Rudder Feeling occurs when the direction of history is undone by the limitless space in which its journey takes place.

The space of Scotland is that 'otherside' to history: where history's grand narratives are reflected in absurd miniature, where history abutts on the eternity which is its negation. It is a conjuncton that Garry, in Nan Shepherd's *The Weatherhouse* experiences when he returns from the War to 'a small land; poor, ill to harvest, its fields ringed about with dykes of stone laboriously gathered from the soil. Never before had Garry felt its vastness' (57). That vastness is the perception that Martha's father Geordie, in Shepherd's *The Quarry Wood*, struggles to articulate as, watching the Aurora Borealis in the Northern sky, he tries to recall a childhood rhyme about the boundaries of Scotland:

> Geordie could get no further with the boundaries of Scotland: but his asser-tion that the northward edge was too obvious at the moment to be doubted. They stood on Scotland and there was nothing north of them but light. It was Dussie who wondered what bounded Scotland when the Aurora was not there. Neither Martha nor Geordie had an answer. (20)

The word Geordie has been unable to recall comes back to him, however, in church:

> 'Yon's the wordie, Matty – fat's the meenister was readin' aboot. Eternity. That's fat wast o' Scotland. I mind it noo.'
> Martha said it over and over to herself: *Scotland is bounded on the south by England, on the east by the rising sun, on the north by the Arory-bory-Alice, and on the west by Eternity.*
> Eternity did not seem to be in any of her maps: but neither was the Aurora. She accepted that negligence of the map-makers . . . (20)

The 'negligence' of history and its mapmakers made of Scotland at once the centre of the world's largest Empire and a mere periphery of Europe, a place at the core of history's technological drive towards the future and, at the same time, a place set apart, a space unbounded by history, an opening upon eternity, 'as you might say there was another world than this'.[16]

The fundamental trajectory of the modern Scottish novel has not been within the narrative of history, but between history and its other, between the mapmaker's map and an 'otherworld' where space has different dimensions. It is summarised in Prentice McHoan's account of his father's stories in Iain Banks's *The Crow Road*:[17]

> We learned about the people who had made Scotland their home: the hunter-gatherers of eight or nine thousand years ago, nomads wandering the single great wood and stalking deer . . . then came the Bronze Age and Iron Age people, the Vikings and Picts, Romans and Celts and Scots and Angles and Saxons who had all found their way to this oceanically marginal little corner of northern Europe . . .
>
> He made up stories, about the secret mountain, and the sand-drowned forest, the flood that turned to wood, the zombie peat, and the stone-beings that drilled for air . . .
>
> Other stories were pure fantasy, the result of a kind of child-like quality in him, I think. If you looked at certain stands of trees from a distance, especially in a glen, and when in full leaf, they did look like great bulging torrents of green water, bursting from the depths of the earth and somehow frozen. There was a sort of visual naiviety at work there that verged on the hallucinogenic, but it did, I'd argue, make a warped sort of visual sense. Magmites – the people who lived in the mantle of the earth, beneath the crust, and who were drilling up for air the way we were drilling down for oil – must just have appealed to that part of him that loved turning things around. Opposites and images fascinated him, excited him; magicked inspired absurdity from him. (322)

Scotland is a space of 'turning things around', so that it is impossible to tell whether history or its opposite is 'magicked inspired absurdity'. The modern Scottish novel, from Stevenson to Gray, from Mitchison to Kennedy, from Buchan to Banks, has been driven by the need to encompass within its narrative structures the alternatives to history which McHoan's father, like the voice of the Scottish tradition, insistently narrates. McHoan, confronted by conjunction of modernity – 'the main road to Oban and the north busy with lights' – and its negation – 'the dark landscape . . . with chambered cairns, cup and ring marked rocks, standing stones, tumuli and ancient forts' – is just at the beginning of the modern Scottish novel's narrative when he concludes: 'I looked into that ancient, cluttered darkness, wondering' (324).

NOTES

Chapter 1: Introduction: Novel, Nation and Tradition

1. Timothy Brennan, 'The National Longing for Form', *Nation and Narration*, ed. Homi K. Bhabha (Routledge: London, 1990), p. 49.
2. Benedict Anderson, *Imagined Communities: Reflections on the Origin and Spread of Nationalism* (London: Verso, 1991), p. 33 ff.
3. See Howard Gaskill (ed.), *Ossian Revisited* (Edinburgh: Edinburgh University Press, 1991), and especially Fiona Stafford, '"Dangerous Success': Ossian, Wordsworth and English Romantic Literature', p. 49.
4. The 'untouchability' of the nation is the implication of Anderson's discussion of 'cenotaphs and tombs of Unknown Soldiers' (*Imagined Communities*, p. 9): the point about the remains in the tomb is that they are as unknown as the nation which they represent is unknowable: the remains exist, yet their anonymity is fundamental to their significance. Like the nation itself, the anonymous remains 'represent' sacrifice precisely to the extent that the specific sacrifice cannot be identified; the nation too can only be known through its representations and never in itself.
5. The model of the 'nation as agent' is one I base on the Scottish philosopher John Macmurray's notion of 'the self as agent'; see Chapter 2.
6. Anthony D. Smith, *The Ethnic Origins of Nations* (Oxford: Basil Blackwell, 1986), p. 15.
7. Ibid., pp. 25–6.
8. Anderson, op. cit., p. 37 ff.
9. Anderson, op. cit., p. 55–6.
10. The notion of the nation as a fiction goes as far back at least as Ernest Renan's analysis, 'What is a Nation', first delivered at the Sorbonne in 1882, in which he asserts that 'a nation's existence is, if you will pardon the metaphor, a daily plebiscite' (in Homi K. Bhabha (ed.), *Nation and Narration*, p. 19), a daily plebiscite which he sees as based fundamentally on 'forgetting' and on 'historical error' (ibid. p. 11).
11. Eric Hobsbawm, 'Introduction: Inventing Traditions', in Eric Hobsbawm and Terence Ranger (eds), *The Invention of Tradition* (Cambridge: Cambridge University Press, 1983), p. 1.
12. Ibid. p. 2.
13. Hugh Trevor-Roper, 'The Highland Tradition of Scotland', *The Invention of Tradition*, pp. 29–30, 31. For other accounts of the context of this event, see Murray Pittock, *The Invention of Scotland: The Stuart Myth and the Scottish Identity, 1638 to the Present* (London: Routledge, 1991), especially pp. 87 ff. For alternative accounts of the history and role of tartan, see Hugh Cheape, *Tartan: the Highland Habit* (Edinburgh: National Museums of Scotland) 1991.
14. Hugh Trevor-Roper, 'The Highland Tradition of Scotland', *The Invention of Tradition*, p. 31.
15. Tom Nairn, *The Break-up of Britain: Crisis and Neo-Nationalism* (London: Verso, 1981), p. 157.
16. Allan Massie, 'Tartan Armies', review of Francis Russell Hart, *The Scottish Novel* (London: John Murray, 1979), *The London Magazine*, October 1979, pp. 92–6 at p. 96. For a view of Massie which situates him in terms of his own analysis of the Scottish situation, see Douglas Dunn, 'Divergent Scottishnesses: William Boyd, Allan Massie, Ronald Frame', in Gavin Wallace and Randall Stevenson, (eds), *The Scottish Novel Since the Seventies* (Edinburgh, Edinburgh University Press, 1993), pp. 149–69.
17. Edwin Muir, *Scott and Scotland: The Predicament of the Scottish Writer* (Edinburgh: Polygon, 1982), p. xxii.
18. Edwin Muir, *Scott and Scotland* (London: Routledge, 1936).

19. See my analysis of Williams's relation to this tradition in 'George Orwell and the English Ideology', *Out of History* (Edinburgh: Polygon, 1996), Chapter 5.
20. T. S. Eliot, *Selected Essays* (London: Faber, 1951), pp. 23–4.
21. Raymond Williams, *Keywords* (London: Fontana, 1976), p. 269; in the first edition Williams gives an extensive account of 'tradition' but none, significantly, of 'identity'.
22. Raymond Williams, *The Country and the City* (London: Hogarth Press, 1993; 1973) p. 206.
23. Ibid., p. 214.
24. Ibid., p. 291.
25. David Craig, 'Burns and Scottish Culture', in Hugh MacDiarmid (ed.), *The Voice of Scotland: A Quarterly Magazine of Scottish Arts and Affairs*, Vol. VII, Nos 3–4, Oct. 1956–Jan. 1957, p. 28.
26. Muir, 'Scotland 1941', *Collected Poems* (London: Faber, 1960), p. 97.
27. Thomas M'Crie, *Life of John Knox, containing illustrations of the history of the reformation in Scotland* (Edinburgh: William Blackwood and Sons; 1839).
28. Andrew Lang, *John Knox and the Reformation* (London: Longmans, Green and Co, 1905).
29. Edwin Muir, *John Knox: Portrait of a Calvinist* (London: Collins, 1930), p. 11.
30. Ibid., pp. 307–8.
31. Ibid., p. 309.
32. T. C. Smout, *A History of the Scottish People 1560–1830* (London: Fontana, 1972), p. 470.
33. T. C. Smout, *A Century of the Scottish People* (London: Collins), p. 2.
34. Christopher Harvie, *Scotland and Nationalism: Scottish Society and Politics 1707–1994* (London: Routledge, 1994), p. 115.
35 The case for seeing Scotland as a nation which is 'out of history' because of the failure of narrative is one that I made in *Out of History: Narratives Paradigms in Scottish and English Culture* (Edinburgh: Polygon, 1996).
36 Harvie, *Scotland and Nationalism*, p. 116.
37 See Hugh MacDiarmid, 'Albyn: or Scotland and the Future', in Alan Riach (ed.), *Albyn: Shorter Books and Monographs* (Manchester: Carcanet, 1996).
38 See my 'Scotland's Failure of Nerve', *Études Écossaises*, Numéro 5, *Une Écosse autonome?*, pp. 9–27.
39. Hugh MacDiarmid, *The Complete Poems of Hugh MacDiarmid*, ed. Grieve and Aitken (London: Martin, Brian & O'Keefe, 1978), Vol. I, p. 165.
40. Alasdair MacIntyre, *After Virtue: a Study in Moral Theory* (London: Duckworth, 1985; 1981). See Craig Beveridge and Ronald Turnbull, *Scotland After Enlightenment* (Edinburgh: Polygon, 1997), Ch. 7, for a discussion of the importance of MacIntyre to modern Scottish thought. For general considerations of MacIntyre's work see Peter McMylor, *Alasdair MacIntyre: Critic of Modernity* (Routledge; London, 1994), and John Horton and Susan Mendus (eds), *After MacIntyre: Critical Perspectives on the Work of Alasdair MacIntyre* (London: Polity Press 1994).
41. Alasdair MacIntyre, *Whose Justice? Which Rationality?* (London: Duckworth, 1988).
42. Linda Colley, *Britons: Forging the Nation* (New Haven: Yale University Press, 1992).
43. Conor Cruise O'Brien, 'Introduction' to Edmund Burke, *Reflections on the Revolution in France* (Harmondsworth: Pelican, 1968).
44. Michael Holquist (ed.), *The Dialogic Imagination: Four Essays by M. M. Bakhtin* (Austin: University of Texas Press, 1981), p. 269.
45. Ibid., p. 272.
46. Alasdair Gray, *Lanark: A Life in Four Books* (Edinburgh: Canongate, 1981).
47. For sympathetic accounts of the Kailyard as a phenomenon see Ian Campbell, *Kailyard* (Edinburgh: Ramsay Head, 1981); Gillian Shepherd, 'The Kailyard' in Douglas Gifford (ed.), *The History of Scottish Literature, Volume 3, Nineteenth Century* (Aberdeen: Aberdeen University Press, 1988), p. 309; Thomas D. Knowles, *Ideology and Commerce: aspects of literary sociology in late Victorian Scottish Kailyard* (Gothenburg: Gothenburg Studies in English, 1983); Beth Dickson, 'Annie S. Swan and O. Douglas: Legacies of the Kailyard', in Douglas Gifford and Dorothy McMillan (eds), *A History of Scottish Women's Writing* (Edinburgh: Edinburgh University Press, 1997), p. 329.

48. William McIlvanney, *Laidlaw* (London: Sceptre, 1992; 1977) *The Papers of Tony Veitch* (London: Sceptre, 1992; 1984) *Strange Loyalties* (London: Sceptre, 1992; 1991). For analyses of MacIlvanney's work see Martin Priestman, *Detective Fiction and Literature: the Figure on the Carpet* (Basingstoke: Macmillan, 1990); Simon Dentith, '"This shitty urban machine humanised': the urban crime novel and the novels of William McIlvanney' in Ian A. Bell and Graham Daldry (eds), *Watching the Detectives* (Basingstoke: Macmillan, 1990); also, Keith Dixon, 'Writing on the borderline: the works of William McIlavnney', in *Studies in Scottish Literature*, Vol. xxiv, 1989, pp. 142–57. Ian Rankin's detective novels include, *Black & Blue* (London: Orion, 1997), *The Black Book* (London: Orion, 1993), *The Hanging Garden* (London: Orion, 1998), *Hide and Seek* (London: Orion, 1990), *Knots and Crosses* (London: Orion, 1987), *Let it Bleed* (London: Orion, 1995), *Mortal Causes* (London: Orion, 1994), *Wolfman* (London: Century, 1992).

49. For an account of Buchan's work, see David Daniell, *The Interpreter's House: A Critical Assessment of John Buchan* (London: Nelson, 1975). For the context of the development of the adventure thriller, see Martin Green, 'Adventurer's stake their claim: the adventure tale's bid for status, 1876–1914' in Karen E. Laurence (ed.), *Decolonizing Tradition: New Views of Twentieth-century 'British' Literary Canons* (Urbana, 1992); Juanita Kruse, *John Buchan and the Ideology of Empire: Popular Literature and Political Ideology* (New York: Mellen Press, 1989).

50. The 1980s saw an enormous expansion of our knowledge of the Scottish past as a result of the publication of major histories of particular artforms in Scotland, as, for instance, Duncan MacMillan, *Scottish Art 1460–1990* (Edinburgh: Mainstream, 1990) and John Purser, *Scotland's Music: a History of the Traditional and Classical Music of Scotland from Eearliest Times to the Present Day* (Edinburgh: Mainstream, 1992). In addition, the work of writers such as Billy Kay, both on radio and in print – e.g. *The Complete Odyssey: Voices from Scotland's Recent Past* (Edinburgh: Polygon, 1996) – has transformed perceptions of Scottish popular culture.

1: Fearful Selves: Character, Community and the National Imagination

1. Rev. Robert Simpson D.D., *Traditions of the Covenanters* (Edinburgh: Gall and Inglis, 1888), p. 467.

2. Francis Hart, *The Scottish Novel* (London: John Murray, 1979), p. 401.

3. James Hogg, *The Private Memoirs and Confessions of a Justified Sinner*, intro André Gide (London: Cresset Press), 1947.

4. For a balanced account, see Thomas Crawford, 'James Hogg: the Play of Region and Nation' in Douglas Gifford (ed.), *The History of Scottish Literature, Volume 3, Nineteenth Century* (Aberdeen: Aberdeen University Press), p. 100ff.

5. Robert Louis Stevenson, *Dr Jekyll and Mr Hyde and Other Tales* (London: Dent, 1925; 1886). For a discussion of Stevenson and the supernatural which emphasises the place of Scottish writing within the genre see Glen Cavaliero, *The Supernatural and English Fiction* (Oxford: Oxford University Press, 1995), which also has sections on Spark, Hogg, MacDonald, and Lindsay.

6. Robert Louis Stevenson, *The Scottish Novels* (Edinburgh: Canongate, 1995; 1889).

7. William Robertson Smith, *The Religion of the Semites* (Edinburgh: A&C Black, 1889); the book was originally delivered as lectures at the University of Aberdeen. See Robert Fraser, *The Makings of The Golden Bough: The Origins and Growth of an Argument* (London: Macmillan, 1990), especially Chapters 6 and 7: Fraser quotes J. G. Frazer's 'Preface' to the first edition of *The Golden Bough*: 'My interest in the early history of mankind was first excited by the works of Dr E. B. Tylor . . . But it is a long step from a lively interest in a subject to a systematic study of it, and that I took this step is due to the influence of my friend W. Robertson Smith. The debt which I owe to the vast stores of his knowledge, the abundance and fertility of his ideas and his unwearying kindness,

can scarcely be overestimated' (Fraser, pp. 84–5). For the general context of Smith's and Frazer's work see George W. Stocking, *After Tylor: British Social Anthropology, 1888–1951* (London: Athlone, 1995); Gillian M. Bediako, *Primal Religion and the Bible: William Robertson Smith and his Heritage* (Sheffield: Sheffield Academic Press, 1997).

8. Quoted in Robert Ackerman, *J. G. Frazer: His Life and Work* (Cambridge: Cambridge University Press, 1987) p. 91.

9. Ibid.

10. Ibid, p. 262–3.

11. Ibid, p. 212.

12. John Buchan, *John Burnet of Barns* (London: John Lane, The Bodley Head, 1924; 1898).

13. J.G. Frazer, *The Golden Bough: A Study in Magic and Religion* (London: Macmillan, 1922), p. 713.

14. John Buchan, *Witch Wood* (Edinburgh: Canongate, 1988; 1927).

15. John Buchan, *The Complete Richard Hannay* (Harmondsworth: Penguin, 1992); *The Thirty-Nine Steps* (1915) begins with Hannay's meeting with a man who had 'sheer naked scare on his face' (11); Hannay himself, on the run as a suspected murderer, feels 'for the first time the terror of the hunted on me' (27).

16. John Buchan, *The Gap in the Curtain* (Edinburgh: B&W, 1992; 1932).

17. T. W. Dunne, *An Experiment in Time* (London: Faber an Faber, 1927).

18. Andrew Lownie notes that Buchan was himself prey to such fears and in his own memoirs 'relates three occasions where he suddenly became inextricably terrified while out in the wilds and felt himself being transported back in time to the same location' (*John Buchan: The Presbyterian Cavalier*, London: Constable, 1985, p. 84)

19. A. L. Kennedy, *Looking for the Possible Dance* (London: Martin Secker and Warburg, 1993); see Eleanor Stewart Bell, 'Scotland and ethics in the work of A. L. Kennedy', *Scotlands*, 5.1, 1998, p. 105–13.

20. George Douglas Brown, *The House with the Green Shutters* (Edinburgh: Canongate, 1996; 1901).

21. Alasdair Gray, *Lanark: A Life in Four Books* (Edinburgh: Canongate, 1981); see Domonique Costa, 'In the Scottish Tradition: Alasdair Gray's *Lanark* and *1982 Janine*', in *Literature of Region and Nation*, Vol. 2, no. 3, Nov 1990, pp. 2–7. See also, the *Review of Contemporary Fiction*, vol. XV, no. 2, Summer 1995, which has several articles on Gray, as well as Bruce Charlton, 'The World must become quite another: politics in the novels of Alasdair Gray', *Cencrastus*, no. 31, Autumn 1988, pp. 39–41.

22. Robin Jenkins, *The Awakening of George Darroch* (Harmondsworth: Penguin, 1987; 1985).

23. Buchan was appointed Lord High Commissioner – the Sovereign's representative – during the annual meeting in May of the General Assembly of the Church of Scotland. Andrew Lownie notes that Buchan 'was the first Lord High Commissioner whose father had been a Free Church of Scotland minister' (Andrew Lownie, *John Buchan, The Presbyterian Cavalier* (London: Constable, 1995) p. 227). Lownie also notes that, 'When the Established and the Free Churches had amalgamated again in 1929 Buchan had been asked to deliver an address during the General Assembly on the subject by the Home Mission Committees of the Church of Scotland and the United Free Church. This was published later that year as the pamphlet 'What the Union of the Churches Means to Scotland'. He followed this up the next year with a rather longer book, giving the historical background, called *The Kirk in Scotland*, which he wrote with the biblical scholar George Adam Smith' (227–8).

24. Willa Muir, *Imagined Corners* (Edinburgh: Canongate, 1987; 1935). See Janet Caird, 'Cakes not turned: Willa Muir's published novels', *Chapman* no. 71, Winter 1992–93, pp. 12–18.

25. Gordon Williams, *From Scenes Like These* (London: Mayflower, 1970; 1968).

26. Irvine Welsh, *Trainspotting* (London: Martin Secker & Warburg, 1993).

27. Robin Jenkins, *A Love of Innocence* (Edinburgh: B&W Publishing, 1994; 1963).

28. Robin Jenkins, *A Very Scotch Affair* (London: Gollancz, 1968).

29. Robin Jenkins, *A Would-be Saint* (Edinburgh: B&W Publishing, 1994; 1978).

30. Robin Jenkins, *Just Duffy* (Edinburgh: Canongate, 1995; 1988).

31. J. MacDougall Hay, *Gillespie* (Edinburgh: Canongate 1979; 1914).
32. A. J. Cronin, *Hatter's Castle* (London; Victor Gollancz, 1931); see Lisa M. Schwerdt, 'A. J. Cronin' in George M. Johnson (ed.), *British Novelists Between the Wars* (Detroit: Gale Research, 1998), pp. 71–6.
33. J. M. Barrie, *Auld Licht Idylls* (London: Hodder and Stoughton, 1888); see R. D. S. Jack, *The Road to the Never Land* (Aberdeen: Aberdeen University Press, 1991); Andrew Nash, '"Trying to be a Man': J. M. Barrie and sentimental masculinity', *Forum for Modern Language Studies*, Vol. xxxv, no. 2, April 1999, pp. 113–25.
34. Louis Grassic Gibbon, *A Scots Quair* (London: Hutchinson, 1946).
35. Catherine Carswell, *Open the Door!* (London: Virago, 1986; 1920); see Alison Smith, 'And Woman Created Woman: Carswell, Shepherd and Muir, and the self-made woman', in Christopher Whyte (ed.), *Gendering the Nation* (Edinburgh: Edinburgh University Press, 1995); also Christopher Small, 'Catherine Carswell: engagement and detachment', *Chapman*, nos 74–75, Autumn/Winter 1993, pp. 131–6.
36. Nan Shepherd, *The Quarry Wood* (Edinburgh: Canongate, 1987; 1928); see Roderick Watson, ' "–to get leave to live': patterns of identity, freedom and defeat in the fiction of Nan Shepherd' in Joachim Schwend and Horst W. Drescher (eds), *Studies in Scottish Fiction: Twentieth Century* (Frankfurt am Main, 1990), pp. 207–18; also, Roderick Watson, '"To know Being"': Substance and Spirit in the Work of Nan Shepherd', in Douglas Gifford and Dorothy McMillan (eds), *A History of Scottish Women's Writing* (Edinburgh: Edinburgh University Press, 1997), p. 416.
37. Nan Shepherd, *The Weatherhouse* (Edinburgh: Canongate, 1988; 1930).
38. Neil Gunn, *Morning Tide* (London: Souvenir, 1975; 1930). Recent criticism of Gunn has included, Alistair McCleery, 'Neil Gunn and the Highland Novel: the anxiety of influence', Joachim Schwend and Horst W. Drescher (eds), *Studies in Scottish Fiction: Twentieth Century* (Frankfurt am Main, 1990), pp. 163–80; Margery McCulloch, 'Neil M. Gunn and the Historical Novel', *Études Écossaises*, no. 1, 1992, pp. 243–51; Roderick Watson, 'Visions of Alba: the construction of Celtic roots in modern Scottish literature', *Étdues Écossaises*, no. 1, 1992, pp. 253–64; Richard Price, 'Whose history, which novel? Neil M. Gunn and the Gaelic Idea', *Scottish Literary Journal*, Vol. 24, no. 2, Nov 1997, pp. 85–102. Useful major studies of Gunn's work include Alexander Scott and Douglas Gifford (eds), *Neil M. Gunn: Man and Writer* (Edinburgh: Blackwood, 1973); Margery McCulloch, *The Novels of Neil Gunn: A Critical Study* (Edinburgh: Scottish Academic Press, 1987); Richard Price, *The Fabulous Matter of Fact: The Poetics of Neil Gunn* (Edinburgh: Edinburgh University Press, 1991).
39. Neil Gunn, *The Serpent* (Edinburgh: Canongate, 1997; 1943).
40. Neil Gunn, *Highland River* (Edinburgh: Canongate, 1991; 1937).
41. William McIlvanney, *Surviving the Shipwreck* (Edinburgh: Mainstream, 1991), p. 22.
42. Ibid., pp. 24–5.

3: Dialect and Dialectics

1. For an analysis of the role of dialect in the Scottish novel in the nineteenth century, culminating with *The House with the Green Shutters*, see Emma Letley, *From Galt to Douglas Brown: Nineteenth Century Fiction and Scots Language* (Edinburgh: Scottish Academic Press, 1988), especially pp. 295ff. See also Alan Freeman, 'Realism Fucking Realism: the word on the street: Kelman, Kennedy and Welsh', *Cencrastus*, 57, Summer 1997, pp. 6–7.
2. Tom Leonard, *Intimate Voice: Selected Work 1965-1983* (Newcastle-upon-Tyne: Galloping Dog Press, 1984), p. 86.
3. William McIlvanney, *Docherty* (London: Sceptre, 1987; 1975).
4. Duncan MacLean, 'James Kelman Interviewed', in Murdo MacDonald, *Nothing is Altogether Trivial: An Anthology of Writing from New Edinburgh Review* (Edinburgh: Edinburgh University Press, 1995), pp. 119–20.

5. Dorothy Porter (ed.), *The House with the Green Shutters* (Harmondsworth: Penguin, 1985), p. 257.

6. James Barke, *Land of the Leal* (Edinburgh: Canongate, 1987; 1939). For critical commentary on Barke's work, see Gustav H. Klaus, 'James Barke: a great-hearted writer, a hater of oppression, a true Scot' in Andy Croft (ed.), *A Weapon in the Struggle: the Cultural History of the Communist Party in Britain* (London, 1998), pp. 7-27; Manfred Malzahn, 'Coming to terms with industrial Scotland: two "proletarian" novels of the 1930s' in Joachim Schwend and Horst W. Drescher (eds), *Studies in Scottish Fiction: Twentieth Century* (Frankfurt am Main, 1990), pp. 193–205; John Mansen, 'Ploughmen and Byremen: novels of Barke, McNeillie and Bryce', *Cencrastus*, no. 52, Summer 1995, pp. 3–5. See also, Valentine Cunningham, 'The age of anxiety and influence; or, tradition and the thirties talents', in Keith Williams and Steven Matthews (eds), *Rewriting the Thirties* (London, 1997), pp. 5–22.

7. Neil Gunn, *Butcher's Broom* (London: Souvenir, 1977; 1934).

8. Robert Crawford, *Devolving English Literature* (Oxford: Clarendon Press, 1992), and Robert Crawford (ed.), *The Scottish Invention of English Literature* (Cambridge: Cambridge University Press, 1998).

9. Quoted by Thomas Crawford, *Burns: A Study of the Poems and Songs* (Edinburgh: Edinburgh University Press, 1965), p. 103.

10. Ibid., p. 3.

11. 'The Cotter's Saturday Night', James Kinsley (ed.), *Burns: Poems and Songs* (Oxford: Oxford University Press, 1968), p. 119.

12 For a discussion of the relationship of Scots to English during the period of the Enlightenment, see Charles Jones (ed.), *The Edinburgh History of the Scots Language* (Edinburgh: EUP, 1997), and Jones's own chapter, 'Phonology', p. 267ff. Jones notes that ' . . . there is some evidence to suggest that what was being advocated by several of the most important pronouncing dictionary-type publications produced by Scottish authors in the eighteenth century was not any wholesale abandonment of Scots language characteristics by the socially aspirant, but rather that such speakers should adopt a type of contemporary "Standard Scots" based perhaps upon the language of the legal, clerical and academic profession in Edinburgh' (273).

13. Michael Holquist (ed.), *The Dialogic Imagination: Four Essays by M. M. Bakhtin* (Austin: University of Texas Press, 1981). For the application of Bakhtin to Scottish writing see Alastair Renfrew, 'Them and us?: representation of speech in contemporary Scottish fiction', in Alastair Renfrew (ed.), *Exploiting Bakhtin* (Glasgow, 1997).

14. See, for instance, the account of the relation between the oral and the written in Penny Fielding, *Writing and Orality: Nationality, Culture, and Nineteenth-Century Scottish Fiction* (Oxford: Clarendon Press, 1996).

15. John Macmurray, *Persons in Relation: Volume II of The Form of the Personal* (London: Faber, 1970; 1961). For accounts of Macmurray's thought, see Jeanne Warren, *Becoming Real: an Introduction to the Thought of John Macmurray* (York: Ebor Press, 1989); Frank G. Kirkpatrick, *Community: a Trinity of Models* (Washington: Georgetown Univ. Press, 1986), and 'The logic of mutual heterocentrism: the self as gift', *Philosophical Theology*, Vol. VI, no. 4, Summer 1992, pp. 353–368; Robert Calder, 'Macmurray: Man and Mind', *Chapman*, no. 73, Summer 1993, pp. 72–80; A. R. C. Duncan, *On the Nature of Persons* (New York: Peter Lang, 1990); Louis Roy, *The Form of the Personal: a Study of the Philosophy of John Macmurray* (Cambridge: Cambridge University Press, 1984).

16. John Macmurray, *The Self as Agent: Volume I of The Form of the Personal* (London: Faber, 1970; 1957))

17. For discussion of the narrative voice of Gibbon's novel, see William Malcolm, *A Blasphemer and Reformer: a study of James Leslie Mitchell/ Lewis Grassic Gibbon* (Aberdeen: Aberdeen University Press, 1984); Isobel Murray and Bob Tait, *Ten Modern Scottish Novels* (Aberdeen: Aberdeen University Press, 1984), and Isobel Murray, 'Action and Narrative Stance in *A Scots Quair*', in David Hewitt and Michael Spiller (eds), *Literature of the North* (Aberdeen: Aberdeen University Press, 1983).

18. Irvine Welsh, *Trainspotting* (London: Martin Secker & Warburg, 1993). For early responses to Welsh's work, see Gill Jamieson, 'Fixing the City: arterial and other spaces in Irvine Welsh's fiction', Neil McMillan, 'Junked Exiles: Irvine Welsh and Alexander Trocchi', in Glenda Norquay and Gerry Smyth (eds), *Space and Place: the Geographies of Literature* (Liverpool, 1998); Karl Miller, 'Irvine Welsh and other festivals', *Scotlands*, 5.1, 1998, pp. 1–9; Joe McAvoy, 'Now the drugs don't work – they just make you worse', *Cencrastus*, no. 60, 1998, pp. 12–14.

19. George Davie, *The Democratic Intellect: Scotland and Her Universities in the Nineteenth Century* (Edinburgh: Edinburgh University Press, 1961): see particularly 'The Vernacular Basis of Scottish Humanism', pp. 203–21.

20. James Kelman, *The Busconductor Hines* (Edinburgh: Polygon, 1984). For discussion of Kelman's writing, see Karl Miller, 'Glasgow hamlet', in *Authors* (Oxford, 1989), pp. 156–62; Drew Milne, 'James Kelman: dialectics of urbanity', in James A. Davies (ed.), *Writing Region and Nation* (Swansea, 1994), pp. 393–407; Roderick Watson, 'The rage of Caliban: the "unacceptable" face and the "unspeakable" voice in contemporary Scottish writing', in Horst W. Drescher and Susanne Hagemann (eds), *Scotland to Slovenia* (Frankfurt am Main, 1996).

21. Duncan MacLean, 'James Kelman Interviewed', in Murdo MacDonald, *Nothing is Altogether Trivial: An Anthology of Writing from New Edinburgh Review* (Edinburgh: Polygon, 1995) p. 112.

22. James Kelman, 'The East End Writers' Anthology, 1988', *Channels of Communcation: papers from the higher education teachers of English conference held at Glasgow University* (Glasgow: HETE 88, 1992), p. 25.

23. William McIlvanney, *The Big Man* (London: Hodder and Stoughton, 1985).

24. James Kelman, *A Disaffection* (London: Picador, 1990; 1989).

25. James Kelman, *How late it was, how late* (London: Martin Secker & Warburg, 1994).

26. John Macquarrie, *Existentialism* (Harmondsworth: Penguin, 1973; 1972).

27. Duncan MacLean, 'James Kelman Interviewed', *Nothing is Altogether Trivial: An Anthology of Writing from New Edinburgh Review*, p. 111.

28. Alexander Trocchi, *Young Adam* (Edinburgh: Rebel Inc., 1996; 1954); see also Andrew Murray Scott (ed.), *Invisible Insurrection of a Million Minds: a Trocchi Reader* (Edinburgh: Polygon, 1991); Allan Campbell and Tim Niel (eds), *A Life in Pieces: Reflections on Alexander Trocchi* (Edinburgh: Rebel Inc., 1997); John de St. Jorre, *Venus Bound: the Erotic Voyage of the Olympia Press and its Writers* (New York: Random House, 1996), and Sue Wiseman, 'Addiction and the avant-garde: heroin addiction and narrative in Alexander Trocchi's *Cain's Book*', in Sue Vice, Matthew Campbell and Tim Armstrong (eds), *Beyond the Pleasure Dome* (Sheffield, 1994), pp. 256–66.

29. Alexander Trocchi, *Cain's Book* (London: Calder, 1992; 1960).

30. Andrew Murray Scott, *Alexander Trocchi: The Making of a Monster* (Edinburgh: Polygon, 1991), Ch. 4.

31. Alan Sharp, *A Green Tree in Gedde* (Edinburgh: Richard Drew, 1985; 1965). See Berthold Schoene, 'Angry young masculinity and the rhetoric of homophobia and misogyny in the Scottish novels of Alan Sharp', in Christopher Whyte (ed.), *Gendering the Nation* (Edinburgh: Edinburgh University press, 1995) pp. 85–106.

32. Alan Sharp, *The Wind Shifts* (London: Joseph, 1969).

33. Massie's *The Death of Men* (London: Bodley Head, 1981) and *A Question of Loyalties* (1989) are particularly concerned with Sartrean issues of freedom.

34. William McIlvanney, see note 48, Chapter 1.

35. Muriel Spark, *Symposium* (Harmondsworth: Penguin, 1991; 1990). For discussions of Spark's work see Joseph Hynes, *The Art of the Real: Muriel Spark's Novels* (London: Associated University Presses, 1988); Joseph Hynes, 'Muriel Spark and the oxymoronic vision' in Robert E. Hosmer (ed.), *Contemporary British Women Writers* (Basingstoke: Macmillan, 1993); Joseph Hynes (ed.), *Critical Essays on Muriel Spark* (New York: Macwell Macmillan, 1992); Ian Rankin, 'The Deliberate Cunning of Muriel Spark' in Gavin Wallace and Randall Stevenson, *The Scottish Novel Since the Seventies*, p. 41; Richard

C. Kane, *Iris Murdoch, Muriel Spark and John Fowles: didactic demons in modern fiction* (London: Associated University Presses, 1988); Norman Page, *Muriel Spark* (Basingstoke: Macmillan, 1990); Judy Little, 'Muriel Spark's Grammars of Assent', in James Acheson (ed.), *The British and Irish Novel since 1960* (Basingstoke: Macmillan, 1991); Jennifer Lynn Randisi, *On Her Way Rejoicing: the fiction of Muriel Spark* (Washington: Catholic University of America Press, 1991); Geraldine Meaney, *(Un)like Subjects: Women, Theory, Fiction* (London: Routledge, 1993); Judy Sproxton, *The Women of Muriel Spark* (London: Constable, 1992).

36. Muriel Spark, *The Driver's Seat* (Hamondsworth: Penguin, 1974; 1970).
37. Robin Jenkins, *The Changeling* (Edinburgh: Canongate, 1989; 1958).
38. Robin Jenkins, *A Love of Innocence* (Edinburgh: B&W Publishing, 1994; 1963).
39. Robin Jenkins, *Fergus Lamont* (Edinburgh: Canongate, 1979).
40. Alasdair Gray, *1982 Janine* (London: Jonathan Cape; 1984).
41. Alasdair Gray, *Lanark* (Edinburgh: Canongate, 1981).
42. Alasdair Gray, *Poor Things* (London: Bloomsbury, 1992).
43. Robin Jenkins, *The Awakening of George Darroch* (Harmondsworth: Penguin, 1987; 1985).
44. R. D. Laing, *The Divided Self* (Harmondsworth: Penguin, 1965; 1960). For recent discussions of Laing's work see, Digby Tantam, 'The anti-psychiatry movement' in German E. Berrios and Hugh Freeman (eds), *150 Years of British Psychiatry* (London, 1991); John Clay, *R. D. Laing: a Divided Self: a Biography* (London: Hodder and Stoughton, 1996); Bob Mullen (ed.), *R. D. Laing: Creative Destroyer* (London: Cassell, 1997); Craig Beveridge and Ronald Turnbull, 'Introduction', R. D. Laing, *Wisdom, Madness and Folly* (Edinburgh: Canongate, 1998).
45. The language of schizophrenia is used, for instance, by Tom Nairn, in *The Break-Up of Britain*: 'We noticed a sort of "split" in Sir Walter Scott's world-view, and how that corresponded to the Scottish bourgeoisie's peculiar position in history. Surely the later history of the intelligentsia can be seen as the continuation, the farther manifestation of that same split? That is, of figurative "schizophrenia" imposed on an intellectual stratum which, although strongly national, was in its material conditions of existence quite unable to be national*ist*' (161).
46. Neil M. Gunn, *Highland River* (Edinburgh: Canongate, 1991; 1937).
47. Neil M. Gunn, *The Atom of Delight* (Edinburgh: Polygon, 1986; 1956).
48. Benedict Anderson, *Imagined Communities* (London: Verso, 1991, rev. ed.)

3: Enduring Histories; Mythic Regions

1. See Katie Trumpener, *Bardic Nationalism: The Romantic Novel and the British Empire* (Princeton: Princeton University Press, 1997), Ch. 3.
2. Allan Massie, *The Ragged Lion* (London: Sceptre, 1995; 1994).
3. Colin Kidd, *Subverting Scotland's Past: Scottish whig historians and the creation of an Anglo-British identity, 1689–c.1830* (Cambridge: Cambridge University Press, 1993), p. 210.
4. Robin Jenkins, *Fergus Lamont* (Edinburgh: Canongate, 1979).
5. Jessie Kesson, *Another Time, Another Place* (Edinburgh: B&W Publishing, 1997; 1983).
6. Allan Massie, *One Night in Winter* (London: Futura, 1985; 1984).
7. J. F. Hendry, *Fernie Brae: A Scottish Childhood* (Edinburgh: Polygon, 1987; 1947).
8. Alasdair Gray, *A History Maker* (Edinburgh: Canongate, 1994).
9. Robin Jenkins, *The Cone Gatherers* (Harmondsworth: Penguin, 1985; 1955).
10. William McIlvanney, *The Kiln* (London: Sceptre, 1996).
11. A. MacArthur and H. Kingsley Long, *No Mean City* (London: Corgi, 1957; 1956).
12. Edwin Muir, *An Autobiography* (Edinburgh: Canongate, 1993; 1954). I have used Muir's critical and theoretical writings extensively in the argument of this book, but I have not used his novels; for a discussion of them, see Raymond N. MacKenzie, 'Edwin Muir', in George M. Johnson (ed.) *British Novelists between the Wars* (London, 1998) pp. 237–46.

13. Iain Banks, *The Bridge* (London: Macmillan, 1986); see Tim Middleton, 'Constructing the contemporary self: the works of Iain Banks', in Tracey Hill and William Hughes (eds), *Contemporary Writing and National Identity* (Bath, 1995), pp. 18–28; Victor Sage, 'The politics of petrifaction: culture, religion, history in the fiction of Iain Banks and John Banville', in Victor Sage and Allan Lloyd (eds), *Modern Gothic* (Manchester: Manchester University Press, 1996), pp. 20–37.
14. Irvine Welsh, *Marabou Stork Nightmares* (London: Jonathan Cape, 1995).
15. George Mackay Brown, *Greenvoe* (Harmondsworth: Penguin, 1976; 1972).
16. Muriel Spark, *The Hothouse by the East River* (Harmondsworth: Penguin, 1975; 1973).
17. George Mackay Brown, *Vinland* (London: Flamingo, 1995; 1992); see Berthold Shoene, '"I imagined nine centuries —': narrative fragmentation and mythical closure in the shorter historical fiction of George Mackay Brown', *Scottish Literary Journal*, Vol. 22, no. 2, Nov. 1995, pp. 41–59.
18. Neil Gunn, *Sun Circle* (Edinburgh: Canongate, 1996; 1933).
19. Lewis Grassic Gibbon, *Spartacus* (London: Hutchinson, 1970; 1933).
20. Naomi Mitchison, *The Corn King and the Spring Queen* (Edinburgh: Canongate, 1990; 1931). See Ruth Hoberman, *Gendering Classicism: the ancient world in twentieth-century women's historical fiction* (Albany, New York, 1997), pp. 25–41; Isobel Murray, 'Human Relations: an outline of some major themes in Naomi Mitchison's adult fiction', Joachim Schwend and Horst W. Drescher (eds), *Studies in Scottish Fiction: Twentieth Century* (Frankfurt am Main, 1990), pp. 243–56; Elizabeth Maslen, 'Naomi Mitchison's Historical Fiction' in Maroula Joannou, *Women Writers of the 1930s* (Edinburgh: Edinburgh University Press, 1999); Jennie Calder, 'More Than Merely Ourselves: Naomi Mitchison', in Douglas Gifford and Dorothy McMillan (eds), *A History of Scottish Women's Writing* (Edinburgh: Edinburgh University Press, 1997), p. 444.
21. Allan Massie, *Augustus: The Memoirs of the Emperor* (London: Sceptre, 1987; 1986); *Tiberius: the Memoirs of the Emperor* (London: Sceptre, 1992), *Caesar* (London: Sceptre, 1994; 1993).
22. Eric Linklater, *Private Angelo* (Edinburgh: Canongate, 1992; 1947).
23. Allan Massie, *The Death of Men* (London: Bodley Head, 1981), *A Question of Loyalties* (London: Sceptre, 1990; 1989), *The Sins of the Father* (London: Sceptre, 1992; 1991).
24. John Buchan, *Witch Wood* (Edinburgh: Canongate, 1988; 1927).
25. On the relation of Scott to Frazer, see Robert Crawford, 'Frazer and Scottish Romanticism: Scott, Stevenson and *The Golden Bough*', in Robert Fraser (ed.), *Sir James Frazer and the Literary Imagination* (Basingstoke: Macmillan, 1990), pp. 18–37; for the role of fantasy as an element of the 'mythic' in Scottish writing, see Colin Manlove, *Scottish Fantasy Literature: A Critical Survey* (Edinburgh: Canongate Academic, 1994).
26. Walter Scott, *Rob Roy* (London: Dent, 1906; 1817), p. 37.
27. David Hume, *Treatise on Human Nature*, ed. L. A. Selby-Bigge (Oxford: Clarendon Press, 1967; 1747); Archibald Alison, *Essays on the Nature and Principles of Taste* (Edinburgh: Bell and Bradfute, 1790); see my account of this tradition in the *Revue de Metaphysique et de Morale* (Paris), No. 1, 1998, 'T. S. Eliot, I. A. Richards and Empiricism's Art of Memory'.
28. Archibald Alison, *Essays on the Nature and Principles of Taste*, p. 15.
29. Matthew Arnold, *The Study of Celtic Literature* (Kennikat Press, Port Washington, NY, 1970; 1905; first published 1867).
30. Jessie Kesson, *The White Bird Passes* (Edinburgh: B&W Publishing, 1996; 1958); see Carol Anderson, 'Listening to the women talk' in Gavin Wallace and Randall Stevenson (eds), *The Scottish Novel since the Seventies* (Edinburgh: Edinburgh University Press, 1993).
31. Neil M. Gunn, *The Silver Darlings* (London: Faber and Faber, 1969; 1941).
32. For a discussion of Neil Gunn's use of myth, see Douglas Gifford, *Neil M. Gunn and Lewis Grassic Gibbon* (Edinburgh: Oliver & Boyd, 1983).
33. Robert Ackerman, *J. G. Frazer: His Life and Work* (Cambridge: Cambridge University Press, 1987).
34. Naomi Mitchison, *The Bull Calves* (Glasgow: Richard Drew, 1985; 1947).

35. Neil M. Gunn, *The Green Isle of the Great Deep* (London: Souvenir, 1975; 1944).
36. Muriel Spark, *The Takeover* (Harmondsworth: Penguin, 1978; 1976).

4: The Typographic Muse

1. George Friel, *Mr. Alfred M.A.* (Edinburgh: Canongate, 1987).
2. George Friel, *Mr Alfred M.A.* (London: Calder and Boyars, 1972).
3. Muriel Spark, *The Comforters* (Harmondsworth: Penguin, 1963; 1957).
4. Muriel Spark, *The Abbess of Crewe* (Harmondsworth: Penguin, 1975; 1974).
5. Muriel Spark, *The Ballad of Peckham Rye* (Harmondsworth: Penguin, 1963; 1960).
6. Edwin Morgan, *Collected Poems* (Manchester: Carcanet, 1990), pp. 248, 277, 267, 276.
7. Ian Hamilton Finlay, *The Dancers Inherit the Party & Glasgow Beasts, an a Burd* (Edinburgh: Polygon, 1996; 1961).
8. Tom Leonard, *Intimate Voices: Selected Work 1965–1983* (Newcastle upon Tyne: Galloping Dog Press, 1984); see, for instance, 'A Summer's Day', p. 41.
9. Sian Hayton, *Cells of Knowledge* (Edinburgh: Polygon, 1989).
10. Robert Alan Jamieson, *A Day at the Office* (Edinburgh: Polygon, 1991).
11. Irvine Welsh, *Marabou Stork Nightmares* (London: Vintage, 1996; 1995).
12. Janice Galloway, *The Trick is to Keep Breathing* (London: Minerva, 1991; 1989).
13. For a discussion of the 'dualism' of Scottish writing see Douglas Gifford, 'Myth, Parody and Dissociation' in Douglas Gifford (ed.), *The History of Scottish Literature, Volume 3, Nineteenth Century* (Aberdeen: Aberdeen University Press, 1988), p. 217ff. See also, Karl Miller, *Doubles* (Oxford: Oxford University Press, 1987).

5: Doubtful Imaginings

1. John Knox, 'The Appellation', Roger Mason (ed.), John Knox, *On Rebellion* (Cambridge: Cambridge University Press, 1994), p. 90.
2. Ibid.
3. Quoted in Richard Kearney, *The Wake of Imagination: Ideas of Creativity in Western Culture* (London: Hutchinson, 1988), p. 44.
4. Ibid., p. 46.
5. See Glenda Norquay, 'Moral Absolutism in the novels of Robert Louis Stevenson', 1985; Unpublished Thesis, University of Edinburgh,
6. Samuel Taylor Coleridge, *Biographia Literaria*, Ch. XIII.
7. Muriel Spark, *The Prime of Miss Jean Brodie* (Harmondsworth: Penguin, 1965; 1961).
8. Allan Massie, *Muriel Spark* (Edinburgh: Ramsay Head Press, 1979).
9. Muriel Spark, *The Takeover* (Harmondsworth: Penguin, 1978; 1976).
10. Iain Crichton Smith, *An End to Autumn* (London: Victor Gollancz, 1978); see Douglas Gifford, 'Bleeding from all that's best: the fiction of Iain Crichton Smith', in Gavin Wallace and Randall Stevenson (eds), *The Scottish Novel since the Seventies* (Edinburgh: Edinburgh University Press, 1993).
11. Iain Crichton Smith, *In the Middle of the Wood* (London: Victor Gollancz, 1987).
12. Iain Crichton Smith, *The Search*, (London: Victor Gollancz, 1983).
13. Archie Hind, *The Dear Green Place* (Edinburgh: Polygon, 1984, 1966); see Andrew Monnickendam, 'Literary Voices and the projection of cultural failure in modern Scottish literature' in Ton Hoenselaars and Marius Buning (eds), *English Literature and Other Languages* (Amsterdam, 1999), pp. 231–42.
14. William McIlvanney, 'A Shield Against the Gorgon', *Surviving the Shipwreck* (Edinburgh: Mainstream, 1991).
15. William McIlvanney, *Strange Loyalties* (London: Sceptre, 1991).
16. George Friel, *Grace and Miss Partridge* (London: Calder and Boyars, 1969).
17. See Chapter 2: 'Dialect and Dialectics', p. 92ff.
18. Amedée Ozenfant, *The Foundations of Modern Art*, trans John Rodker (New York: Dover, 1952; 1928): Ozenfant insists on an art of the elite: 'That sort of person I am not writing for, but for artists who seek to scale the summits, and for such men as seek in art grandeur

and the breath of inspiration. I write for the elect whose ideal it is to be the repository of grandeur, and who, because of the jeers they meet with, hide it as a blemish' (xv).

Conclusion: The Space of the Nation

1. Robert Fraser, *The Making of the Golden Bough: the Origins and Growth of an Argument* (London: Macmillan, 1990), p. 30.
2. Frederick Turner, *John Muir: From Scotland to the Sierra* (Edinburgh: Canongate, 1997; 1985), p. 235.
3. For an account of the events surrounding the Exhibition, see Edwin S. Grosvenor and Morgan Wesson, *Alexander Graham Bell: The Life and Times of the Man who Invented the Telephone* (New York: Harry N. Abrams, 1997), Ch. 4, pp. 69ff.
4. Melville Bell *Visible Speech: The Science of Universal Alphabetics* was published in 1868; it provided the model for Shaw's theories of speech in *Pygmalion*; see Grosvenor and Wesson, *Alexander Graham Bell*, Ch. 1.
5. Ibid., Ch. 10, p. 205ff.
6. Turner, *John Muir: From Scotland to the Sierra*, p. 296.
7. Grosvenor and Wesson, *Alexander Graham Bell*, p. 140.
8. See T. O. Beidelmann, *W. Robertson Smith and the Sociological Study of Religion* (Chicago: University of Chicago Press, 1974), p. 4.
9. Quoted in Alanna Knight (ed.), *R.L.S. in the South Seas: An Intimate Photographic Record* (Edinburgh: Mainstream, 1986), p. 25.
10. Frederick Turner, *John Muir: From Scotland to the Sierra*, p. 350.
11. Ernest Renan, Homi K. Bhabha (ed.), *Nation and Narration*, p. 19.
12. Tom Nairn, *The Break-up of Britain: Crisis and Neo-Nationalism* (London: Verso, 1981), Ch. 3, 'Old and New Scottish Nationalism'.
13. Ernest Renan, op. cit., p. 19.
14. Quoted M. R. Ridley, 'Introduction', *The Master of Ballantrae* (London: Dent, 1925), p. ix.
15. Alan Warner, *These Demented Lands* (London: Vintage, 1998; 1997).
16. Muriel Spark, *The Ballad of Peckham Rye*, p. 143.
17. Iain Banks, *The Crow Road* (London: Abacus, 1993; 1992).

INDEX